Larry Yu, PhD

The International Hospitality Business
Management and Operations

Pre-publication
REVIEW

"**T**he hospitality industry has been undergoing rapid globalization in recent years. The globalization of the industry has created an increasing need for competent and qualified managers of international hospitality operations and hence a growing demand for international components in hospitality training and education programs. Dr. Larry Yu's *The International Hospitality Business: Management and Operations* has arrived just in time to meet the demand.

The text thoroughly examines the social, cultural, political, and economic environment within which international hospitality operations compete for survival and growth. It covers a broad spectrum of policy issues in operating hotels and restaurants in foreign countries, ranging from development strategies to organizational structures. The book iden-tifies and analyzes the managerial functions that a global manager has to be familiar with in international operations, including accounting, finance, tax, law, marketing, technology, and human resources. The author introduces hospitality students to a fast-growing and exciting international arena of the industry where they can find tremendous new challenges and enormous career opportunities. The abundant real-world examples and cases provided in the text enable readers to understand the most up-to-date developments in the international hospitality business. It is not only an excellent textbook for hospitality educators and students, but also a useful handbook for international hospitality managers."

Zheng Gu, PhD
Associate Professor,
College of Hotel Administration,
University of Nevada,
Las Vegas

The International Hospitality Business
Management and Operations

The International Hospitality Business
Management and Operations

Larry Yu, PhD

The Haworth Hospitality Press
An Imprint of The Haworth Press, Inc.
New York • London • Oxford

Published by

The Haworth Hospitality Press, an imprint of The Haworth Press, Inc., 10 Alice Street, Binghamton, NY 13904-1580

Cover design by Marylouise E. Doyle.

Library of Congress Cataloging-in-Publication Data

Yu, Lawrence.
    The international hospitality business : management and operations / Larry Yu.
       p.   cm.
    Includes bibliographical references and index.
    ISBN 0-7890-0559-X (alk. paper)
    1. Hospitality industry—Management. 2. International business enterprises—Management.
I. Title.
TX911.3.M27Y82 1999
647.94'068—dc21
                                             98-49067
                                               CIP

To Sarah and Gordon
for understanding, encouragement, and support

ABOUT THE AUTHOR

Larry Yu, PhD, is Associate Professor at the Department of Tourism and Hospitality Management in the School of Business and Public Management at The George Washington University. He received his master's degree from Boston University in 1984 and his PhD from the University of Oregon in 1988. A native of Hangzhou, China, Dr. Yu has been involved in tourism and hospitality operations and education since 1979. His main research and teaching interests focus on international tourism and hospitality development and management. Over the last nine years, Dr. Yu has taught international hospitality management at both Northern Arizona University and The George Washington University. He served as a lead researcher for the White House Conference on Travel and Tourism in 1995. He has co-edited two books, *A Host of Opportunities: Introduction to Hospitality Management* and *Tourism in China: Geographic, Political, and Economic Perspectives.* In addition, Dr. Yu has published over twenty research articles on international hospitality management and serves as a consultant to international hotel firms, such as Choice Hotels International. Dr. Yu serves on the editorial boards of the *Journal of Vacation Marketing,* the *Journal of Hospitality and Tourism Education,* and the *International Journal of Tourism Research.*

CONTENTS

Preface

The hospitality industry has been increasingly globalized in the last two decades. The brand names of Hilton, Sheraton, Hyatt, Holiday Inn, McDonald's, KFC, and Pizza Hut figure prominently in the landscapes of many countries. At the same time, foreign hospitality companies such as Four Seasons, Nikko, Meridien, Accor, Forte, and Supranational are aggressively developing and expanding their hotel business in the United States. The explosive growth of the global hospitality industry has created a great demand for competent hospitality managers to oversee operations in foreign countries. However, many of the management skills needed for operating hotels and restaurants in a foreign country differ from those required for domestic operations, since the business and cultural environments vary from one country to another. A global hospitality manager must acquire the knowledge and skills necessary to deal effectively with the complexity and difficulty of international operations.

This book is about the complex and difficult issues faced by hospitality managers when they are assigned to work overseas. The text consists of five parts with fourteen chapters. It has four distinctive features that cover (1) a broad transdisciplinary perspective in international hospitality education, (2) both lodging and food service management operations, (3) the most up-to-date analysis of international hospitality developments and management, and (4) a comprehensive treatment of hospitality management topics.

International hospitality management is a transdisciplinary study. Management theories and functions are a very important technical tool for international operations. A broader transdisciplinary perspective, including the study of political, cultural, geographic, and economic disciplines, can better prepare a future manager.

The two main segments of the hospitality industry, lodging and food services, are discussed in depth in this book. But the lodging segment is treated more extensively due to the scope and size of its global development. When the management principles apply to both lodging and food service operations, the general term "hospitality" is used. If the discussion refers to only one segment of such operations, then either lodging or food service will be specified.

The most up-to-date developments in international hospitality are introduced in this text. This is a dynamic industry that changes rapidly from year to year, with frequent new developments, new management concepts, and new corporate mergers and strategic alliances. Great efforts have been made to keep up with these changes and new developments; students are thus kept abreast with the most current information on the global development of the hospitality industry.

This book provides a comprehensive treatment of hospitality management functions in an international context. It identifies and analyzes the management functions that a global manager must be familiar with in overseas operations, including finances, accounting, taxation, law, human resources, marketing, technology, and food service operations. It is designed to provide students with comprehensive knowledge of managing hospitality operations in a foreign country.

These four features of this unique text are combined to present the scope and depth of international hospitality management. The text introduces students to this fast-growing and exciting industry, identifies potential career opportunities, and stimulates interest in pursuing these rewarding opportunities. It helps students lay a solid foundation for their future careers as global hospitality managers. It can also be a reference book for professional managers in international operations.

Acknowledgments

I am indebted to many people for their ideas and assistance. My thanks first go to the students I have taught both at Northern Arizona University and The George Washington University in the past nine years. Their cultural perspectives, questions, and input have challenged me to clarify my thinking about many topics and issues in international hospitality management. I also express my sincere thanks to the reviewers who offered invaluable and constructive feedback for improvement.

I gratefully acknowledge the international hotel executives who have advanced my knowledge of international hospitality management through guest lectures and casual conversations: Nitz Ward, Vice President of International Development, Marriott International; Richard Richards, Vice President of Human Resources, Hyatt International; Bruno Jeny, Senior Vice President of International Division, Choice Hotels International; and Samir Gupte, Director of International Human Resources, Choice Hotels International.

I especially acknowledge the leading hospitality and academic journals for permission to quote and adapt extensively from their publications: *Hotels, Hotel and Motel Management, Lodging, Foodservice and Hospitality, Restaurant USA*, and *Cornell H.R.A. Quarterly*. A special note of thanks is extended to the hospitality corporations for kindly providing photos of their hotels, restaurants, and cruise ship. These photos greatly enhance the presentation of the book.

I want to thank Soena Kim and Ying Hu for their diligent research, typing, and clerical assistance. The understanding, encouragement, and support of my family is acknowledged. Finally, I wish to express my gratitude to The Haworth Press editorial team: K.S. (Kaye) Chon, PhD, Senior Editor; Melissa Devendorf, Administrative Assistant; Peg Marr, Senior Production Editor; Andrew R. Roy, Production Editor; Karen Fisher, Copyeditor; Jessica C. Tracy-Hinton, Copywriter; Donna Biesecker, Typesetter; and Dawn M. Krisko, Production Editor, who so professionally guided this book through the publication process.

PART I:
AN OVERVIEW
OF THE INTERNATIONAL
HOSPITALITY INDUSTRY

Part I has two chapters that offer a general discussion on the international hospitality industry and its geographic distribution in the world. Chapter 1 presents an overview of international business and identifies the international hospitality industry as an integral part of the service import and export business. It analyzes the distinctive characteristics of the hospitality industry as a service export. It offers a systematic discussion of the three major aspects of the international tourism and hospitality industry, and examines the motivations that have driven hospitality corporations to globalize business overseas.

In Chapter 2, students study world geography by examining the spatial development and distribution of the international hospitality industry. World travel patterns, major hotel chains, and food service companies in different regions of the world are described and discussed. This chapter is designed to help students grasp the major world regions and basic concepts of economic geography. These two chapters present the scope and spatial development of the international hospitality industry.

Chapter 1

The Hospitality Industry
As an International Business

Twenty years ago no one talked of the "world economy." The term then was "international trade." The change in term—and everybody now talks of world economy—bespeaks a profound change in economic reality.[1]

Peter F. Drucker

LEARNING OBJECTIVES

In this chapter, you will study:

1. Types of international businesses
2. Global shift toward service
3. Hospitality industry as a service export and its distinctive characteristics
4. Balance of payments in travel accounts
5. Three major components of the international hospitality industry
6. Motivations for global hospitality expansion

INTRODUCTION

The most significant development in the world economy during the past few decades has been the increasing globalization of economic activities. In today's rapidly changing world, the economic activities of individual countries do not occur in isolation, nor are they insulated by geographic distance; their economies and markets have become highly integrated worldwide. The priority of this economic development has shifted toward the service sector in the developed countries. Such development trends require management for change: changes in globalizing products and services for worldwide markets.

Hospitality is a very important component of the service industry in any country's national economy. When a domestic hospitality company decides to expand its operation into a foreign country, its overseas development is recognized as international business and its business revenues generated from overseas operations are described as a service export. In this introductory chapter, the discussions are intended to be broad-ranging. The hospitality industry as a service export in international business is explained, and the characteristics, scope, and diversity of the international hospitality industry are discussed. A historical perspective is provided on the development of each segment of the hospitality industry, and hospitality companies' motivations for expanding operations into foreign countries are identified. This chapter offers a systematic overview of the hospitality industry and reveals its place in the overall international business environment.

INTERNATIONAL BUSINESS

When a domestic hospitality company establishes a new business in a foreign market, this company is said to be engaging in international business. International business is defined as business transactions taking place between two or more companies from different countries. These transactions can be in trade, manufacturing, investment, or services. The types of international businesses, encompassing various economic, financial, and commercial activities conducted by both private enterprises and government entities, can be divided into three major categories: (1) merchandising exports and imports, (2) service exports and imports, and (3) investments.

Merchandise imports and exports comprise most conventional trading activities: the importing (buying) and exporting (selling) of tangible goods between countries, such as airplanes, cars, computers, and garments.

Service exports and imports deal with the selling and buying of a business concept or format and the performance of management and services. The franchise of a quick-service restaurant concept or the management service performed by a hotel's management contract company in a foreign country are examples of service exports. Hotel management services, restaurant franchise operations, transportation services by airlines and railroads, legal services by law firms, financial services by banks and accounting firms, and information management services by consulting firms represent some of the fastest growing service export industries in the world.

Investment refers to the movement of capital between countries. Direct investment is defined as a commitment of resources to a foreign business where the investing company has a controlling interest in the enterprise. The controlling stake varies from country to country. Indirect investment refers to foreign portfolio investment (FPI), in which individual companies or public entities invest in foreign financial instruments, such as foreign government bonds and foreign stocks. However, the investors in foreign portfolios do not have control over their investment.[2]

International businesses therefore encompass a wide variety of financial and commercial activities between different countries. Since the focus of this book is on the hospitality industry, a discussion of the characteristics and economic impact of the service export is essential to an understanding of this fast-growing international business.

SHIFT TOWARD SERVICE INDUSTRY

The importance of the service industry has grown rapidly in both developed and developing countries in the past thirty years. The growth of services in a country's national economy reflects a combination of both demand and supply factors. Some of the major factors are listed here:

1. The growth of per capita output and high income elasticity of demand for some consumer services in industrialized countries
2. The increasing role of producer services in the value-added process
3. The growth of financial, legal, insurance, transport, information, and hospitality services[3]

Economists have classified nations as postindustrial if 50 percent or more of their gross domestic product (GDP) is accounted for by the service sector of the national economy. The service sectors in the developed countries have experienced dramatic increases in the past three decades. Exhibit 1.1 illustrates service employment as a share of total civilian employment in five most-developed countries.

As shown, the national economies of these five developed nations are dominated by the service industry in terms of employment. This demonstrates that these developed nations are more oriented toward the service industry, thus creating opportunities for service businesses. A larger proportion of the workforce in these countries is engaged in providing services in such areas as transportation, tourism and hospitality, banking, insurance, advertising, education, retailing, wholesaling, mass communication, and government.

EXHIBIT 1.1. Service Employment As Percentage of the Total Civilian Workforce in Five Developed Countries

Country	Service Employment			
	1980	1990	1993	1995
Canada	62.54	79.23	73.40	73.10
Japan	56.00	68.39	59.30	61.40
United Kingdom	63.00	75.48	71.60	73.10
United States	72.00	78.99	73.20	79.20
Germany*	53.00	64.00	60.00	54.60

Source: OECD Economic Surveys, compiled from various editions (Paris: Organization for Economic Co-operation and Development, 1996).

* Figures for 1980, 1990, and 1993 are only for West Germany. Figure for 1995 is for the unified Germany.

THE HOSPITALITY INDUSTRY AS A SERVICE EXPORT

Service exports differ in many aspects from those of merchandise. In merchandise exports, tangible goods are shipped from the place of production to the consumer in the market; Japanese cars are shipped from manufacturing plants in Japan to auto dealers in the United States for sale to consumers. The places of production and consumption are physically separated. In service exports, particularly in the hospitality industry, four unique business characteristics are identified: (1) export invisibility, (2) location-boundness, (3) intangible service performance, and (4) labor intensiveness.

The international hospitality industry is often described as an invisible export because it does not normally involve the tangible shipment of goods from the place of production to the place of consumption. On the contrary, tourists travel a distance from their home to the destination to receive these services in person. Since there is no tangible shipment of merchandise, only the movement of people, the hospitality industry is thus described as an invisible export.

Since tourists come to hotels and restaurants at various destinations to receive service and experience hospitality, the hospitality industry is characterized as a location-bound industry.[4] Service is tied to the service production location because its time and space constraints are shared by both the producer and the guests. In other words, the guest receives products and services in the same place and at the same time as the product is made and the service is rendered. This location-boundness creates certain unique challenges for hospitality managers. If guests are not happy with certain products or services, they can complain to the manager and demand an immediate solution. The manager needs to come up with spontaneous and creative solutions to solve problems and make the guests happy.

The hospitality industry offers guests a memorable travel experience with a clean and comfortable room and a delicious meal. When tourists purchase foreign travel, there is no ownership of any tangible asset persisting after the stay at the hotel. In other words, when guests check out of a hotel, they have nothing tangible to show to others to prove that they once stayed at that hotel (which is probably why some guests tend to take some tangible things from the hotel as evidence of their visit, such as toiletry amenities or even towels with the hotel logo on them!). The guest's stay at the hotel has become only a memory of an experience. That is why the hospitality industry is characterized as selling intangible services. Therefore, creating a pleasant and memorable experience for international guests is crucial to the success of hospitality operations.

Labor intensiveness is a unique characteristic associated with the hospitality industry. This industry strives to provide a home away from home to international tourists. To provide effective personalized services, the industry relies on individual employees to perform various hospitality functions and services. Unlike the manufacturing industry, where many production procedures have been automated to reduce labor cost, the hospitality industry offers the human touch of personal service to pamper every guest's needs and wants. Therefore, the hospitality industry employs more workers to perform personal services. Normally, the more upscale and luxurious the hotel or restaurant, the more employees are hired.

This labor intensiveness also influences the movement of the global hospitality industry into developing countries, which provide abundant inexpensive labor resources. This development phenomenon can be explained by the factor endowment theory developed by Swedish economists Eli Heckscher and Bertil Ohlin. This theory states that different nations have different factor endowments in land, labor, and capital, the three primary factors for production. The availability of these factors explains the differences in factor costs. The more abundant a factor, the lower its cost. The more land and people a country has, the cheaper the land and labor.[5] These are often the motivating factors for hospitality companies to move into developing countries, such as South America or Southeast Asia, for inexpensive land and labor.

SERVICE INDUSTRY EARNINGS

Service exports play a significant role in a nation's balance of payments. A nation's balance of payments summarizes all economic transactions between a country and the rest of world during a given period of time. Service companies generate revenues from overseas sales, which are used to offset trade deficits in many developed countries. The United States has a large and intractable trade deficit that is bemoaned periodically by the news media, but it is a deficit in merchandise trade. In fact, the United States has a very large surplus in service exports, amounting to two-thirds of the merchandise trade deficit. Therefore, U.S. trade is more or less in balance. However, the public is not aware of the significant contribution made by service exports to the nation's balance of payments.

The travel and hospitality industry in the United States contributes significantly to the national economy. From the standpoint of balance of travel payments, the United States was traditionally a travel deficit country—U.S. tourists spent more money in foreign countries than foreign tourists did in the United States. This imbalance was corrected in 1989, when the United States for the first time had a travel surplus, meaning that foreign tourists spent more money in the United States than U.S. tourists did in foreign countries (see Exhibit 1.2). This surplus was used to balance the deficit in merchandise trade. Obviously, the travel and hospitality industry has a significant economic impact on the U.S. national economy and helps trim the trade deficit with many foreign countries.

INTERNATIONAL TRAVEL AND HOSPITALITY

Thus far, the term "hospitality industry" is used to encompass all facets of the businesses that cater to travelers' needs when they are away from home. Even though the primary focus of this book is on international hotel and restaurant development and operations, it is necessary to describe briefly many interrelated aspects of the international hospitality industry. Once these mutually dependent segments of the industry are identified and explained, a global manager can better understand its complexity and interrelationship.

The international tourism and hospitality industry is defined as the spatial movement of travelers, and the reception and entertainment of travelers away from their home countries. This broad definition includes various businesses that cater to international visitors' travel needs. This complex and diverse industry can be divided into three distinctive yet mutually inclusive components: (1) originating market, (2) international transportation, and (3) receiving destination.

EXHIBIT 1.2. Balance of Travel Account Payments in the United States 1985-1997

Year	Export (Receipts in millions)	Import (Payments in millions)	Balance (in millions)
1985	$22,173	$31,002	($8,829)
1986	$25,967	$32,418	($6,451)
1987	$30,566	$36,593	($6,027)
1988	$38,409	$39,843	($1,434)
1989	$46,863	$41,666	$5,197
1990	$58,305	$47,879	$10,426
1991	$64,237	$45,334	$18,904
1992	$71,214	$50,815	$20,399
1993	$57,621	$40,564	$17,057
1994	$77,900	$56,300	$21,600
1995	$79,671	$60,168	$19,600
1996	$84,133	$68,976	$15,157
1997	$88,928	$75,032	$13,896

Source: U.S. Department of Commerce, *Statistical Abstract of the United States* 1994 and 1997; *International Travelers and Expenditures with Projections: 1989 to 1997.* Washington, DC: U.S. Dept. of Commerce.

Originating Market

The originating market refers to the countries the international tourists come from. An international tourist is defined by the World Tourism Organization as any person who visits a country other than his or her permanent place of residence for any purpose other than following an occupation remunerated from within the country visited. An international tourist must stay at the foreign country for at least twenty-four hours, but no more than one year.[6] International visitors who stay in a foreign country for less than twenty-four hours are defined as day visitors. These definitions are implemented by the United Nations Statistical Commission in its world tourism report, and have been adopted by many countries for compiling international tourism statistics.

The general international travel patterns have demonstrated that most international tourism originates from the developed countries. This heavy outflow of tourists from developed Western nations can be easily explained by the high living standards the citizens of these countries enjoy.

International travel is normally determined by three major factors: discretionary income, leisure time, and travel motivation. Discretionary income is defined as the portion of personal income left after all taxes and daily necessary expenses are paid. This income is at the individual's disposal for personal interest, hobbies, and enrichment. International travel is thus determined by the amount of discretionary income an individual has: more discretionary income allows more leisure activities, such as international travel.

Because international travel consumes time, people cannot travel very far if they do not have long vacations. Due to the high level of technological development and high productivity in developed nations, their citizens normally enjoy longer holidays and paid vacations each year. This is particularly true in Western Europe, where citizens have four or five weeks of annual vacation (see Exhibit 1.3). This partially explains why many Western European countries are major world tourism originating markets.

International tourists travel for various purposes. Travel motivations can influence the way people travel and the destinations they choose. Pleasure travelers seek cultural and recreational experience. Business and professional travelers conduct international business and attend international conferences in foreign countries. People also travel to a foreign country to visit relatives and friends, to seek medical service, or to participate in artistic and athletic events.

EXHIBIT 1.3. Annual Vacation and Holiday Time Taken in Selected Countries

Country	Vacation Time/Holidays (days)
Australia	30
Belgium	32
Canada	29
Germany	40
France	37.5
Japan	44
United States	25

Source: Adapted from Kirstin D. Grimsley "An Ocean of Difference in Vacation Time," *The Washington Post* (July 5, 1998): E1, E5.

Discretionary income, leisure time, and travel motivations therefore influence international travel. Developed countries presently comprise most originating markets for international travel due to their higher living standards. However, some newly industrialized countries have also emerged as originating countries for international travel and tourism. This change in the world travel pattern deserves close attention so that the hospitality industry can respond quickly to these emerging markets and new consumer demand.

International Transportation

International travel and tourism is a spatial phenomenon. People move from their permanent residence to their destination by various modes of transportation. From horse-drawn chariots in the Roman Empire to mail coaches in England and Wales in the eighteenth century to modern jet airplanes, the development of transportation has made a tremendous impact on the changing landscape of the international hospitality industry.

The coach inns in England in the eighteenth and nineteenth centuries were developed to accommodate both the mail coaches and the travelers riding in them. Providing the horses for the mail coaches was a major business function of the early coach inns.[7] When railroads came into use during the Industrial Revolution, many lodging facilities were located near railway terminals. After World War II, motels and airport hotels were developed in response to the improvement of highways and the rapid increase of air transportation around the world. The development of transportation has shaped the development of lodging facilities.

Speed and accessibility are two very distinct contributions that modern transportation has made to the rise of international travel and tourism. Speed of movement is a very important factor of international travel because of the time constraints that tourists have. With the introduction of jet passenger aircraft, travel speed reached 500 to 700 mph, enabling tourists to visit many destinations in a relatively short time.

The jet passenger aircraft, the automobile, the cruise ship, and the high-speed train have redrawn the map for travel and tourism since World War II. These modes of transportation have greatly improved access to various regions. Accessibility is the other factor in long-haul international leisure travel and for choosing holiday destinations. The nonstop maiden flight of Pan American in 1977 trumpeted the opening of the mysterious and exotic China to the outside world. In Europe, it is possible to drive on modern highways all the way from northern Germany to Sicily. These different forms of transportation put many regions of the world within the reach of tourists, making them an integral part of the international tourism and hospitality industry; they are therefore examined in more detail.

International Airline Industry

Since the first recorded international air travel by the Frenchman Louis Blériot, who crossed the English Channel in a monoplane from Calais in France to a point near the Dover Castle on July 25, 1909, the international commercial airline industry has experienced dramatic growth and change.[8] British Air Transport and Travel Ltd. began the first-ever daily international air service on August 25, 1919.[9] However, it was the introduction of the Boeing 247 into commercial airline service that sparked a revolution in international travel. On July 8, 1939, Pan American launched its North Atlantic passenger service to Southampton and Marseilles at a round trip fare of $675.[10] The jet aircraft reduced flight times across the Atlantic and introduced completely new standards of international travel and passenger safety.

World airline service is now a multibillion dollar industry. The world's airlines carried 1.34 billion passengers in 1996 (including both domestic and international travel), an increase of 4 percent over the previous year. According to airline industry estimates, growth of air travel worldwide during the next fifteen years is expected to average about 3.5 percent per year and the passenger volume will reach about 2.2 billion by 2000. This rapid development in the world's commercial airline industry will also trigger increased demand for airport infrastructure development, aircraft manufacturing, and lodging and food service businesses worldwide.

Many developing countries are making efforts to upgrade their commercial aircrafts and are introducing Western-style management and operations. For instance, Aeroflot, the official airline of Russia and one of the largest domestic airlines in the world, has ordered new aircraft from Western countries and has signed several joint-venture agreements with Western nations for technology transfer and service management expertise. With the introduction of Western-standard technology and service management, the developing countries will make a marked impact on the international air transportation industry.

Regional Railway Services

About half a century after Scottish inventor James Watt invented the steam engine, the world's first public railway was built to accommodate trains in England in 1825. The annus mirabilis of the steam locomotives came on September 15, 1830, when Liverpool and Manchester were connected by a thirty-mile double-track line.[11] Before the introduction of commercial jet air travel, railways played a significant role in regional travel, particularly in the European countries, and was responsible for opening up many holiday destinations. The punctual, comfortable, and affordable Eurorail system enjoys great popularity even in today's modern society and sets an excellent example for other countries to follow in the areas of management efficiency and technological development.

The demand for rail travel has been on the rise in the past decade. The elegance of rail travel and nostalgia for the past attract more and more tourists to travel by rail. High-speed trains (technically defined as 150 mph or higher) can transport travelers quickly and comfortably to their destinations. France first built the 186 mph lines between Paris and Brittany in 1989 and it is extending the service to Spain. The Japanese bullet train is another example of an efficient high-speed train. The special high-speed line between Tokyo and Nagano for the 1998 Winter Olympics reduced the travel time from three hours by regular train to just seventy minutes.

Many regions in the world are developing rail service at a record rate. Italy, Sweden, Switzerland, and Spain are all investing heavily in upgrading the quality of their rail systems. The major rail systems of Europe plan to spend $100 billion in the next ten years to develop more efficient high-speed rail lines. The opening of the tunnel under the English Channel in late 1994 significantly expanded the network of high-speed trains now linking London with other major European cities. The new high-speed train, the Eurostar, will reduce travel time substantially in Western Europe. The Eurostar will bring significant integration of the European Union in transportation and communication.

In many other parts of the world, rail travel is still the primary mode of long-haul transportation. The famous Orient Express links many destinations in Europe, Inner Mongolia, and China. Rail travel in Eastern European countries will expand to accommodate the increased travel demand in the region. In Asia and Latin America, rail travel has always been the dominant mode of travel transportation. Foreign investment as well as technological and managerial assistance are badly needed in these regions to upgrade the rail systems and provide services of international standards.

Cruise Line Service

The cruise line industry is a modern extension of the nineteenth-century ocean voyage. It provides a comfortable mode of transportation for travel. Since the inaugural service of pleasure steamers between London and Margate in 1815, and later ocean liners, they have became a well-known and popular feature of travel life. In 1817, James Watt Jr. steamed the *Caledonia* from the Thames to Rotterdam and then up the Rhine to Coblens.[12] The transatlantic voyage is well documented in transportation history literature. The *British Queen* averaged more than 10 knots on her first trip in April 1839, and reached New York City in fourteen days.[13] Ocean liners played a significant role in international travel before the introduction of commercial jet aircraft in the twentieth century.

Today, air travel has reduced the volume of passenger traffic by sea, but the cruise line industry finds a unique niche in the international hospitality market by offering a luxury, elegant, and exciting way to travel. The giant cruise ships, described as "floating resorts," are often compared to resort hotels on land. Cruise passenger growth averaged about 8.5 percent annually from 1990 to 1995 around the world, with an estimated total spending of $14 billion in 1995. North America, particularly the United States, is the major market for cruise business, about 81 percent of the world market for three-day or longer cruises sailing out of North American ports. The global cruise market is expected to reach about 8 million passengers by the year 2000.[14]

The North American cruise market is dominated by three major cruise companies: Carnival Corporation, Royal Caribbean International, and Princess Cruises. The three companies made more than $1 billion profits from operations in 1996. Carnival Lines, the largest in berth capacity, pioneered the new trend of shorter cruises, introducing its popular three- and four-day cruise packages. Some hospitality companies manage their own cruise operations to develop a synergy between their resorts and cruise operations (see Exhibit 1.4). Club Med has developed two high-tech, luxury cruise liners: *Club Med I* and *Club Med II*. Disney Corporation launched its Disney Cruises in 1998 with two ships, each carrying 1,740 passengers. Disney promotes week-long packages that include a visit to Disney World and a three-day or four-day cruise from a Florida port. Carlson Hospitality Worldwide, a conglomerate of travel agencies, hotel chains, and restaurant chains, operates Radisson Seven Seas with three luxury vessels (see Exhibit 1.5).

Russia also has about thirty cruise ships in international waters. The Russian cruise industry offers very competitive rates compared to Western cruise companies. Cruises in the Pacific Rim area have become popular in the past few years. A 960-passenger luxury Japanese cruise ship, built in 1990 for $200 million, was designed to accommodate wealthy Japanese, European, and North American passengers.

EXHIBIT 1.4. Cruises Operated by Hospitality Companies

Company	Ships
Sunotels	4
Club Méditerranée	2
LTI International SA	8
Carlson/Radisson/SAS	3
Mövenpick Hotels International	2
Holiday Inn Worldwide	2
Oberoi Hotels	2
Sonesta International Hotel	2
Forte Pic	1
Sheraton	4

Source: Adapted from Frances Martin, "Chains Operating Cruise Ships," *Hotels* (July 1995), p. 54. Reprinted by permission of *Hotels* magazine, a publication of Cahners Business Information.

EXHIBIT 1.5. Floating Resort—Radisson *Diamond* Cruise Ship with Twin-Hull Propulsion (Photo courtesy of Radisson Hospitality Worldwide.)

The future of the cruise industry looks promising. The markets have been changing recently, with more younger people taking shorter cruises. The industry is responding to these market demographic changes by providing flexible scheduling. The cruise market is also greatly customized and highly themed. The activities range from fitness, to wine tasting, to sports celebrities, to "A Semester at Sea." This highly segmented cruise market requires strategically developed planning to attract potential passengers.

The international transportation industry is an integral part of the international travel and hospitality industry. Commercial jet aircraft, trains, and cruise liners provide speed and comfort while transporting people to their various destinations.

Receiving Destinations

Receiving destinations are the countries that receive and entertain international tourists. To accommodate tourists' travel needs, receiving destinations provide them with attractions, lodging, food service facilities, and various other travel-related services. Receiving destinations want to make tourists feel at home while visiting foreign countries.

Foreign tourists come to a particular destination to enjoy the natural, cultural, historical, and commercial attractions. Natural attractions are the magnificent places of natural beauty each destination has to offer, such as Yellowstone National Park in the United States, the Alps in Switzerland, the Amazon rain forest in Peru, and the island landscape of Indonesia, just to name a few. Natural wonders have always had drawing power.

Cultural and historical attractions offer international tourists a sense of place and permanence. The cultural and historical landmarks in different countries have recorded these nations' glorious pasts and illustrated their cultural heritage. The Egyptian Great Pyramid and Sphinx, the Chinese Great Wall, the Mexican Aztec ruins, the Polynesian Cultural Center in Hawaii, and the Louvre in Paris are just a sample of the world's famous cultural and historical attractions. Seeking cultural experience and meeting people of different cultures have been the major motivations for many international tourists to visit foreign countries.

In addition to natural, cultural, and historical attractions, many destinations have developed commercial attractions, such as the popular theme amusement parks. The United States has well-developed theme park operations that attract millions of domestic and international visitors every year. Walt Disney Corporation operates Disneyland in Anaheim, California and Disney World in Orlando, Florida. These two theme parks have nearly 25 percent of U.S. theme park attendance. Walt Disney Corporation has also been very aggressive in developing theme park operations in foreign countries. The two Disney parks presently operating outside the United States are Tokyo Disney in Japan and Euro Disney near Paris. Tokyo Disney was developed through a franchise arrangement and Euro Disney was developed through a joint-venture partnership. Through Disney's overseas development, American entertainment and amusements have been introduced to many international tourists.

The receiving destinations also cater to international tourists' basic travel needs: lodging accommodations and food services. Before World War II, the hospitality industry in a receiving destination was primarily operated by domestic companies and local proprietors. As international travel increased rapidly after the war, some large American hotel companies saw potential opportunities for expanding their development and operations into foreign countries to serve the international travel markets. In the late 1940s, Hilton International, Inter-Continental, and Sheraton began to expand their operations in foreign countries to accommodate the upscale travel markets. In the mid-1950s, Inter-Continental Hotel Corporation, a subsidiary of Pan American Airlines at the time, was asked to manage hotels developed by several Caribbean countries. The operation of foreign hotels through management contracts was a popular market entry strategy for American hotel corporations because of low capital involvement in their foreign holdings. The geographic concentration of the development by American corporations was primarily in the Caribbean region and Western Europe.

During the 1960s and 1970s, the global expansion of hotel development responded to the steady growth of world travel (Exhibit 1.6). Dunning and McQueen reported a total of 1,025 hotels with 270,646 rooms controlled by 81 international hotel companies in 1978.[15] Of the 81 hotel companies, 22 were American companies that held 56 percent of the total inventory of international hotel rooms. By this time, many American hotel companies had expanded their operations to the oil-rich Arab countries.[16] European hotel companies also increased their global expansion during this period. French and British hotel firms controlled 13 percent and 12 percent of international hotel room inventory respectively by 1978.[17]

The globalization of the hotel industry has been greatly increased in the 1980s and 1990s. New travel markets emerged in Asia and Latin America, and these emerging markets provided great opportunities for international hotel development. Some Asian hotel companies began to invade the European and North American markets. The purchase of American hotels by Japanese firms was particularly noted in the 1980s.[18]

In food service operations, franchising has been the primary mode of entry in global expansions. The Utica, Michigan-based Tastee-Freez International began franchising its fast-food and ice cream operations in foreign

EXHIBIT 1.6. Hyatt Regency Jerusalem (Photo courtesy of Hyatt Regency Jerusalem.)

countries in 1950. Some other early entrants into foreign countries through franchising included Burger King (1963), Long John Silver's (1975), and Canada's Cultures Fresh Food Restaurants (1978).[19] The entry of Kentucky Fried Chicken into Japan in 1972 was arranged through a joint-venture partnership with Mitsubishi, a trading corporation.

Now, as international tourism continues to grow, the hospitality industry has followed the travel markets and management has been increasingly internationalized. U.S. hotel and food service companies are now seen in many foreign destinations. Meanwhile, European, Latin American, and Asian hospitality companies are aggressively jockeying for market positions in North America.

MOTIVATIONS FOR GLOBAL EXPANSION

When a hospitality company decides to expand its business into a foreign country, it is influenced by various motivations, including (1) sales expansion, (2) geographic diversification, (3) resource and labor acquisition, and

(4) worldwide brand recognition.[20] The following discussion explains how these motivations influence hospitality companies to develop overseas business.

Sales Expansion

As discussed earlier, international tourism has increased significantly in the past forty years. With the removal of barriers to trade and travel by many countries, and the improving world economy, international travel will continue to grow rapidly. Such dramatic international travel growth has created new market opportunities for hospitality companies, particularly when companies face a maturing market at home. For both hotel and food service companies, a hotel or a restaurant in a foreign country can serve its own citizens when they travel to that country. It can also serve the local people in that country as well as international tourists from other countries. The sales generated from foreign destinations can increase the total revenues of the company. Exhibit 1.7 demonstrates the global development of McDonald's and the increase of sales from 1990 to 1996. Obviously, McDonald's had globalized its operations in seventy-nine countries by 1996. Overseas sales made up 43 percent of the systemwide sales in 1996 and the overseas sales showed a bigger increase than those in the United States. Therefore, international revenues helped increase the company's sales despite occasional flat sales at home.

Geographic Diversification

The purpose of geographic diversification is to increase business in countries of economic upturn and hedge against economic downturns in other countries. For example, a hotel company develops three hotels in one country. If this country suffers from internal political unrest, these three hotels will all lose money, since it is dangerous to visit this destination. But, if this company spreads these three hotels in three different countries, the company may lose money only on one property and make money on the other properties, which are situated in countries with stable political systems. The money made from the two successful hotels can thus help out the one that is losing money. Therefore, by distributing operations strategically in different countries, hospitality companies can reduce investment risk.

Resource and Labor Acquisition

Acquiring inexpensive resources and labor has been a motivation for hospitality companies in developed countries to move some of their operations to developing countries. As explained by the factor endowment

Exhibit 1.7. McDonald's Increased Sales Through Global Expansion

	1990	1991	1992	1993	1994	1995	1996
# of countries	53	59	65	70	79	89	101
# of units (overseas)	3,227	3,654	4,134	4,766	5,712	7,012	8,928
U.S. sales (in millions)	$12,252	$12,519	$13,243	$14,186	$14,941	$15,905	$16,370
Overseas sales (in millions)	$6,507	$7,409	$8,642	$9,401	$11,046	$14,009	$15,442
Total sales (in millions)	$18,759	$19,928	$21,885	$23,587	$25,987	$29,914	$31,812

Source: Adapted from *The Annual,* McDonald's Corporation 1996 Annual Report (Oak Brook, IL: McDonald's Corporation, 1997), p. 4.

theory, when a country has abundance in certain factors for production, these factors tend to be inexpensive. In some developing countries, undeveloped land and labor are abundant. These production factors are therefore inexpensive. However, these countries lack capital and technology; these production factors then are expensive for the developing countries to acquire. Since hotel development is a capital-intensive business, many developing countries are unable to build luxury hotels to accommodate tourists from developed Western countries. The governments in many developing countries therefore attract hospitality companies from the developed countries to invest in hotel operations. As incentives, the developing countries normally offer tax breaks and concessions on land sales or leases. Inexpensive land is a main motivation for many hospitality companies to build hotels in developing countries. However, developing countries also have the larger proportion of the world's population; therefore, labor is inexpensive in these countries. For example, the current minimum wage in the United States is $5.15 per hour. Many entry-level employees in the hospitality industry in the United States are paid the minimum wage level or slightly higher, but the same employees working in foreign-owned hotels in Russia or China are paid less than $1 per hour. Hospitality companies can reduce labor cost substantially in operations, which is a major proportion of cost-to-sales in the developed countries.

Worldwide Brand Recognition

Building worldwide brand recognition also motivates hospitality companies to expand operations overseas. Brand recognition and brand loyalty are important marketing strategies practiced in domestic operations. As international travel increases, the competition among brand-name hotels and food service companies is also intensified. When people travel to foreign countries, many prefer the familiar hotel and restaurant signs or logos from their own country because they know the quality of the products and the standards of the service. As the customers demand the same products and services in foreign countries, the hospitality companies respond by expanding operations into foreign countries to serve the needs of the tourists from their own countries.

The development of brand-name hotels and restaurants can make the name and service known to the local people in a foreign country. As the local people travel to other countries, they may want to stay and eat at hotels and restaurants they know. For example, many U.S. brand-name hotels are now in Taiwan to serve both international tourists visiting Taiwan and the local Taiwanese. The Taiwanese now know the standards and quality of Hilton, Hyatt, Ramada, or McDonald's. When the Taiwanese come to visit the United States, they may prefer to stay in the brand-name hotel they know best in Taiwan. The hospitality companies thus increase international tourist business at home. That is why every brand-name hospitality company aggressively positions itself in the strategic international travel markets. They compete head-on with long-time domestic rivals in international markets. No one can afford to be left behind and not be recognized by international tourists.

SUMMARY

- International businesses encompass merchandise export and import, service export and import, and investment. The hospitality industry is an important part of the service export and import of international business.
- The focus of the national economy in many developed countries has shifted to the service industry. As an integral part of this industry, the hospitality industry is characterized by being invisible, intangible, location-bound, and labor intensive.
- The hospitality industry contributes greatly to the national balance of payments. In many developed countries, such as the United States,

the positive balance of travel account can offset the negative balance in merchandise trade.

- The hospitality industry encompasses various mutually supportive businesses that cater to travelers away from their permanent place of residence. The entire hospitality industry is studied in this text by examining the originating markets, international transportation, and receiving destinations.
- Many factors influence a potential tourist's decision for foreign travel, such as discretionary income, leisure time, and motivations. The amount of discretionary income for travel and length of leisure time vary among countries. Many developed countries with higher living standards are the major originating markets for international travel.
- International travel is a spatial phenomenon. The movement of people requires speed, comfort, and accessibility. The historical development of commercial air, rail, and cruise travel demonstrated the technological advancement in transportation development.
- Receiving destinations provide international tourists with hospitality and memorable travel experiences. International tourists enjoy natural, cultural, historic, and commercial attractions, such as theme parks, and lodging and food service facilities in receiving destinations. Lodging and food service establishments in receiving destinations are described as "home away from home" for international tourists.
- The global expansion of hotel operations was begun in the late 1940s by several American hotel firms. By the 1960s and 1970s, more European hotel companies were involved. During the 1980s and 1990s, the globalization of hospitality has intensified. Many Asian hotel firms began to expand in the European and American markets.
- Four major motivations were identified to explain the rapid globalization of the hospitality industry: sales expansion, geographic diversification, resource and labor acquisition, and worldwide brand recognition.

STUDY QUESTIONS

1. What has been the most significant economic development in the world in the past few decades?
2. What are the major components of international business?
3. What is the major difference between merchandise and service imports and exports?

4. Where does the hospitality industry fit in the international business environment?
5. What caused the global shift toward the service industry and how is a country's economy defined as service oriented or not?
6. Explain the four distinctive characteristics of the hospitality industry as service export.
7. Can you use the concept of the balance of payments to explain the travel account of the United States?
8. How is the international tourism and hospitality industry defined?
9. What is the difference between an international tourist and a day visitor?
10. What are the three major factors that influence people's decisions to travel internationally?
11. Can you identify some countries that demonstrate a positive correlation between improved national economy and increased outbound international travel?
12. Discuss the two distinct contributions modern transportation has made to the rise of international travel and tourism.
13. How did Russia attempt to improve its air travel services?
14. What is Eurostar? What impact will the Eurostar system have on the integration of the European Union in the twenty-first century?
15. Where is the major market for international cruise operations?
16. Explain why some hospitality companies develop a synergy between hotel/resort and cruise operations.
17. What types of attractions does a receiving destination offer to international tourists?
18. Can you describe the historical development of global hotel expansion since the late 1940s?
19. What was the major market-entry strategy used by many food service companies for expanding their business into foreign markets in the 1950s and 1960s?
20. Can you identify the motivation factors that have influenced hospitality companies to expand their operations overseas?

CASE STUDY: EURO DISNEY RESORT

Euro Disney was officially opened in Marne-la-Vallée, twenty miles (32 km) outside of Paris, on April 12, 1992. This $4.4 billion project was developed through a joint venture between the French government, private investors, and Walt Disney Corporation. Euro Disney Resort is an integral part of the entire theme park development. Learning from its previous development experience in the United States where Disney Corporation failed to control hotel operations (only 14 percent of the hotel operations at Disney World in Orlando), Euro Disney planned to control exclusively all the hotel operations as part of the entire park operations. The development of the six on-site themed resort hotels demonstrated Euro Disney's great interest in hotel development and management, and Euro Disney's desire not to share its theme park's success with other hotel companies. Therefore, Euro Disney Resort was formed as a subsidiary of Euro Disney to manage the lodging operations.

Like many of Euro Disney theme park's thirty attractions, the six resort hotels were designed to provide international visitors with a taste of American culture and natural wonders. The purpose of developing these themed hotels is to continue the excitement and fantasy when visitors leave the park to return to the hotel.

The centerpiece of the resort is the 500-room Disneyland Hotel, replete with Disney artifacts, which is reminiscent of the grand hotels at the turn of the century. The main lobby and its grand staircase were modeled after the famous scene from the movie *Gone with the Wind*. Hotel New York has 575 rooms and offers 24,000 square feet of meeting and convention space and facilities in the Gramercy Park Wing and Brownstone Wing. The Rockefeller Center has a themed ice rink. The Newport Bay Club, modeled after Disney World's popular Yacht and Beach Club Resort, is the largest property in the resort complex and features a harbor lighthouse, a lakeside, a promenade, and a rocking-chair-lined veranda. The 1,011-room Sequoia Lodge represents a U.S. national park transplanted to Europe. The hotel is surrounded by pines, cedars, and sequoia trees. Hotel Cheyenne reflects the cultural theme of the Wild West. A thousand guest rooms are housed in fourteen wood-frame bunkhouses. Hotel Santa Fe also has 1,000 guest rooms and features American Indian cliff dwellings and pueblos. A desert landscape with rusting automobiles and giant cacti is displayed. In addition to these six themed hotels, there is a family-style wilderness retreat called Camp Davy Crockett with 414 cabins.

Euro Disney Resort employs about 5,700 managerial and service personnel during its normal operational season, 75 percent French and 25 percent of other nationalities. A dormitory was built to accommodate about 3,500 employees at a cost of $6.6 million. There are about 600 managers representing thirty-six different countries: twenty-four different languages are spoken by resort managers and staff. The diversity of culture creates an exciting and challenging work environment for managers.

Like the theme park operations during the initial few years, business at Euro Disney Resort did not achieve projected sales and revenues. Occupancy at the Euro Disney Resort was reported at just 55 percent in 1993. The Newport Bay Club was closed from October 1992 to Easter 1993. The management of Euro Disney at one time even wanted to sell the resort operations to reduce the leverage of the entire operations. It lost $366 million in sales in the 1994 fiscal year (ending in September).

The slow start of Euro Disney Resort could be attributed to several complex economic and sociocultural factors. First, market entry timing coincided with the economic recession in Europe. Many European visitors did not want to spend money on the expensive admission fees and resort accommodations. Second, the long winter season in Paris discouraged many visitors from visiting the park. Attendance decreased substantially in the winter months and the resort had to close part of its operations. Third, the theme park is just thirty-five minutes from the center of Paris. Visitors could find more choices in lodging accommodations and price ranges there. Fourth, the initial development of Euro Disney encountered strong opposition from France's media and many people who criticized the development as a threat to French culture. This caused an image problem for the theme park as the development was negatively perceived by many French people.

It has been a learning experience for Euro Disney management, which has been working very hard to modify its products and operations to meet international visitors' demand. Performance of the Euro Disney Resort was greatly improved in 1995, with total sales of $950.5 million and net income of $23.3 million. With an improved regional economy, the opening of the tunnel under the English Channel, and the development of the high-speed train called Eurostar, more European visitors can travel efficiently to the park and stay at the resort for an extended visit. Effective marketing has improved Euro Disney's image in Europe and increased visitation to the park and the resort.

Case Study Sources

Sally Wolchuk, "Mickey's First Summer in France," *Hotels* (October, 1992), 50-52; "Euro Disney—The Not-So-Magic Kingdom," *The Economist* (September 26, 1992), 87-88; Lisa Gubernick, "Mickey N'est Pas Fini," *Forbes* (February 14, 1994), 42-43; Jolie Solomon, "Mickey's Trip to Trouble," *Newsweek* (February 14, 1994), 34-39.

Case Study Questions

1. Why did Euro Disney want to control all the hotel operations in the theme park?

2. What was the rationale for developing the themed resort hotels at Euro Disney?
3. What challenges can be envisioned for managing such a highly diversified workforce at Euro Disney Resort?
4. What caused the poor performance of Euro Disney Resort in its initial years of operation?
5. What recommendations can you make to increase park attendance and room sales at Euro Disney Resort?

Chapter 2

The Geography of International Hospitality Development

Expansion in global hospitality services will continue to be our focus into the next century. . . . No borders, boundaries or limits restrict this vision.[1]

John Norlander
Former President and CEO
Carlson Hospitality Worldwide

LEARNING OBJECTIVES

In this chapter, you will study:

1. Geographic location and world time
2. Absolute location and relative location
3. World regions by examining travel patterns and hospitality development patterns
4. The most globalized hotel companies
5. The most globalized food service companies
6. Regional hospitality development and competition

INTRODUCTION

This chapter offers a geographic perspective on international hospitality development. This development is a spatial phenomenon—traveling across national boundaries and operating hospitality business in unfamiliar places. Knowledge of the locations and certain geographic concepts can help global managers better understand the physical and cultural characteristics of the country in which they are going to develop and operate hospitality businesses. This chapter describes world geography by examining the spatial development and distribution of the hospitality industry. It analyzes world regional travel patterns, hospitality development, and investment trends, and introduces major international and regional hospitality companies. It is designed to familiarize students with geographic places in the world through learning about global hospitality development and distribution.

GEOGRAPHIC LOCATION AND WORLD TIME

An important aspect of geography that affects tourism directly is the study of measuring and indicating exact locations on the surface of the earth. The grid of lines on a map represents the fundamental tool for locating places. The parallel lines extending east and west measure latitudes above and below the equator. Latitude is an indicator for how far north and south of the equator a given location is situated. Latitude is measured in degrees of arc from the equator at 0 degrees. At either pole the value of latitude reaches 90 degrees. All points north of the equator are in the Northern Hemisphere and are designed as north latitude. All points south of the equator are in the Southern Hemisphere and are designated as south latitude.[2]

These latitudes are intersected by lines extending north and south, which are called meridians. They are not parallel because each line originates and terminates at the poles. They converge toward the poles and are most widely separated at the equator. Meridians measure longitude.

The longitude of the Royal Observatory at Greenwich outside London was established as the base point of reference, called the prime meridian, by the British scientists who developed the first accurate system for measuring longitude. Longitude is therefore a measure of how far eastward or westward a point is with respect to the prime meridian of Greenwich. Since the earth is circular, it has 360 degrees. Measuring east or west of Greenwich, there are 180 degrees of longitude.

Knowledge of this grid of latitude and longitude is essential to an understanding of geographic subdivisions. The world is divided into hemispheres (halves) in two ways: northern-southern and eastern-western. With the equator as the dividing line, all parallels of north latitude are in the Northern Hemisphere, and all parallels of south latitude are in the Southern Hemisphere. With Greenwich as the dividing line, the Eastern Hemisphere includes all meridians of east longitude from 0 to 180 degrees, while the Western Hemisphere includes all meridians of west longitude.[3]

Longitudinal location is also important for understanding world time. The world is divided into twenty-four time zones with the initial or zero zone beginning at the prime meridian at Greenwich. This zero time zone is traditionally known as Greenwich Mean Time (GMT). However, the term GMT was replaced in 1979 by Universal Time Coordinate (UTC) which is now used throughout the world for marine and airline navigation. But GMT is still commonly used in the United Kingdom and the United States.[4]

At the "starting point" of time at Greenwich, a time zone change occurs every time a traveler moves 15 degrees longitude in either direction away from Greenwich. To determine what time it is anywhere else in the world, add one hour to the time in Greenwich for every 15 degrees east (+) or subtract one hour for every 15 degrees west of Greenwich ($-$). The Eastern Standard Time zone in the United States (EST) is 75 degrees west of Greenwich; that means EST is five hours earlier than GMT (75/15 = 5). Therefore, Boston is designated as -5 GMT, which means Boston is five hours earlier than London. When hotel guests start their breakfast at 7 a.m. in Boston, it is time for hotel guests in London to have lunch.

However, some countries do not follow the 15-degree rule to set their time. For example, China has only one time zone, called Beijing Time, for its vast territory. The sun shines at 8 a.m. on the east coast, but it is still pitch dark at 8 a.m. in the western interior mountain regions. India sets its clocks one-half hour off from most of its neighbors, and Nepal decided to be ten minutes off from India. Daylight saving time, when clocks are adjusted by one hour for winter, makes things more complicated, as some countries observe it while others do not.[5]

Exactly halfway around the world (180 degrees) from Greenwich is an imaginary longitudinal line in the Pacific that separates East and West. This line, called the International Date Line, is both twelve hours ahead of and twelve hours behind GMT. The International Date Line marks the change in time from one day to another because of the earth's rotation. If tourists cross the International Date Line while traveling east from Tokyo to San Francisco, they gain a day (but subtract one day when figuring the date); if traveling west from San Francisco to Tokyo, they lose a day (but add one day to figure the date). For instance, traveling from San Francisco to Tokyo takes about twelve hours. When you leave San Francisco at 1 p.m. on Sunday afternoon, you arrive at Tokyo's Narita Airport at 4 p.m. Monday afternoon. You lose a day! When you return from Tokyo to San Francisco, you depart at 5 p.m. on Thursday afternoon and arrive at San Francisco at 9 a.m. on Thursday morning, the same day you left Tokyo. You gain almost a whole day! Therefore, the rule is that when crossing the International Date Line, add a day going west and subtract a day going east.

This change in time from one day to another causes the common travel fatigue known as "jet lag," which most international travelers experience. Hotel Okura in Japan has introduced a jet-lag fighting plan for busy and frequent business travelers. This plan is supervised by Dr. Mitsuo Sasaki, a consultant for NASA. The plan consists of physical exercise and relaxation and nutrition programs, and it works well for both business and leisure travelers.[6]

The differences in world times and dates complicate international business operations in terms of communication and meeting arrangements. Hotel managers need to familiarize the front desk staff with time differences to better help guests reorient themselves. Display clocks showing international time zones at the front desk are always appreciated by international guests.

ABSOLUTE LOCATION AND RELATIVE LOCATION

Geographically, a location has two attributes that need to be examined before a hospitality business can be developed: absolute location and relative location. Absolute location refers to the precise location of a place, which can be pinpointed precisely by the measures of latitude and longitude. It is also known as the site, which refers to the physical characteristics of the place, including geological features, climatic conditions, bioresources, and cultural and economic characteristics, such as the ethnic makeup of the local population, their religious beliefs, and the level of living standards. The study of absolute location analyzes the internal characteristics of a place.[7]

Relative location refers to the situation of the place, the external characteristics, such as proximity to major tourist markets and easy accessibility for tourists. It therefore refers to the location of places with respect to other places in order to understand interdependence at regional or international levels.[8] In essence, relative location describes how this place is situated in relation to the major tourist markets.

Geographic location is thus made up of these two components: absolute location, which identifies the internal characteristics of a place; and relative location, which identifies the external characteristics of a place. This concept is important to international hospitality developers when planning global expansion. Demographic profiles of the local population and international tourists, and local physical and cultural attractions, can all be identified, as well as where the originating markets are, the distance of this destination from the originating markets, and the accessibility of the destination to tourists. Therefore, it is essential to understanding the internal and external aspects of a location for potential overseas hospitality expansion.

WORLD REGIONS

World regions are subdivisions of the surface of the earth. A world region is defined as "the grouping of like places or the functional union of places to form a spatial unit."[9] In other words, it is a geographic area that displays certain common features. This concept is widely used for organizing hospitality corporations' global structures and for reporting global hospitality performance and trends. Sometimes, world regions are organized differently by different hospitality corporations in international operations, and by research and professional organizations in reporting statistical data. A review of world geographic regions reveals the variations in regional divisions and tourism statistical reports.

The most common criterion to define a world region is geographic proximity on a continent. The grouping of countries on the seven continents has long been used by geographers. However, this method of dividing the world into regions does not reveal the cultural differences and economic disparity among countries on the same continent. Therefore, perceptual regions can be defined by the criteria of cultural similarities and degree of wealth. When considering cultural similarities, countries in the same geographic area that share the same cultural values and religious beliefs are defined as a region, such as the Middle East with its dominant Muslim culture or Latin America with its strong Spanish influence. By degree of wealth, the world is measured by per capita income and is traditionally divided into two regions: developed countries and developing countries. However, a new region is emerging in the world economy—the newly industrialized countries (NIC), such as Taiwan and Singapore in Asia.

The increased regional economic integration in many regions of the world is another example to illustrate the concept of world regions. Regional economic cooperation among countries was first organized in Europe with the establishment of the European Community (EC) in 1957. The first six EC members were Belgium, the Federal Republic of Germany (former West Germany), France, Italy, Luxembourg, and the Netherlands. Later, Denmark, Ireland, the United Kingdom, Greece, Portugal, and Spain signed the treaty and made a total of twelve member nations.[10] The objectives were to remove trade obstacles and stimulate trade, investment, and travel among member nations. The EC has since become a formidable force in the world economy and has now changed its name to the European Union. The new EU's objectives are to eliminate all boundaries among its member countries so that people, capital, and goods can move freely. Eleven EU countries have been participating in a new single-currency system, the euro, since January 1, 1999.

The EU has set a model for other countries in different regions to follow. There are now several other such regional groupings in the world. The European Free Trade Association (EFTA), including Austria, Finland, Iceland, Norway, Sweden, and Switzerland, promotes free trade and regional travel among its member countries. The North American Free Trade Agreement (NAFTA), consisting of Canada, Mexico, and the United States, aims to eliminate all tariffs on bilateral trade among the three countries and to promote intraregional travel among them. The Andean Pact was established when Bolivia, Chile, Ecuador, Colombia, and Peru signed the Cartagena Agreement to promote free trade. Another South American group, called MERCOSUR, includes Argentina, Brazil, Paraguay, and Uruguay. ASEAN in Asia includes Brunei, Indonesia, Malaysia, the Philippines, Singapore, and Thailand. The Asia-Pacific Economic Cooperation (APEC) group encompasses the entire Pacific region. By 1996, APEC included Australia, Brunei, Canada, Indonesia, Japan, Malaysia, New Zealand, the Philippines, Singapore, South Korea, Thailand, the United States, China, Hong Kong, Taiwan, Mexico, Papua New Guinea, and Chile. The twelve countries in the southern part of Africa have organized the Southern African Development Community (SADC) to improve this region's economic development through cooperative efforts.

Developers and managers who are familiar with them can take advantage of the favorable economic policies formulated by these regional economic organizations. Certain favorable economic policies and incentives can enhance the success of hospitality operations in these regions.

WORLD REGIONAL TRAVEL
AND HOSPITALITY PATTERNS

Regions are thus used as a basis for helping us understand the world as an integrated system of places. The concept of region is important for organizing the geography of tourism and hospitality development. Now let us use this world region concept to examine current international travel patterns and hospitality development trends.

International Travel by Region

An examination of international travel by region can reveal travel patterns in different parts of the world and identify potential opportunities for hospitality expansion. Such travel patterns can be analyzed by hospitality corporations to make market entry decisions for certain regions. Exhibit 2.1 illustrates international tourist arrivals and revenues by region for the years 1986 and 1997. It reveals that Europe had 59 percent of the total share of international tourist arrivals and received 49.3 percent of the total international tourist revenues in 1997. Clearly, Europe is dominant in both international tourist arrivals and revenues. This pattern can be explained by the high living standards enjoyed by the western and northern European countries, their long leisure time, high education level, and most important, relatively small countries that are close to each other. For example, Austria has a total area of 32,377 sq. mi.^{2} (83,855 km^2), slightly larger than the state of Maine in the United States, with a total land area of 30,995 sq. mi.^{2} (80,277 km^2). Clearly, Europe as a region is the world's most popular tourism destination.

The Americas, which include North, Central, and South America, accounted for 19.4 percent of the total international tourist arrivals and 27.1 percent of the total revenues in 1997. East Asia and the Pacific region made up 14.7 percent of the total international tourist arrivals and 18.7 percent of the total tourist revenues. This region demonstrated an increase in both arrivals and revenues between 1986 and 1997. Africa had a relatively small portion of the international tourism industry, receiving 3.8 percent of the total international tourist arrivals and two percent of total revenues in 1997. Though African countries are endowed with rich physical and cultural resources for tourism development, the opportunities are hindered by political and ethnic conflict, military dictatorship, and the relative location factor: isolation and inaccessibility to the major international tourist originating countries. Countries such as Burundi, Chad, and

EXHIBIT 2.1. International Tourist Arrivals and Receipts by Region

	Tourist Arrivals (thousands)		Tourist Receipts (US$ millions)	
	1986	**1997**	**1986**	**1997**
World	340,891	612,835	140,023	443,770
Africa	9,458	23,537	2,970	8,712
Americas	70,972	116,673	37,652	120,251
East Asia/Pacific	32,539	90,163	16,671	83,153
Europe	217,218	360,774	76,570	218,918
Middle East	7,973	14,759	5,003	8,585
South Asia	2,731	4,546	1,670	4,151

Source: Adapted from World Tourism Organization, *International Tourism Review—Highlights 1997* (Madrid, Spain, 1998), p. 5.

Rwanda, located in the interior of Africa, are separated from Western Europe by physical distance and lack of adequate transportation infrastructure. The internal conflicts in some countries, such as Sudan, keep international tourists away from the region.

The Middle East region is famous for its splendid history of human civilization. However, this region has long been suffering from political turmoil, religious and ethnic conflicts, and terrorist activities. Tourism to this region accounted for about 2.4 percent of the total international arrivals in 1997. However, with the gradual improvement of political relations between Israel and the neighboring Arab countries, this area has the potential for improving and expanding its tourism and hospitality industry.

South Asia received only 0.7 percent of the total international tourist arrivals and 0.9 percent of the total revenues in 1997. This region also suffers from political instability, drastic cultural differences influenced by Hinduism and Buddhism, and its relative location (situation) to the tourist originating countries. However, the political and economic systems are gradually improving, particularly in India. This region will be the best-kept secret for international travel in the twenty-first century.

Regional Hospitality Development

There is no doubt that the hospitality industry follows international tourist demand. Regional hospitality development patterns are parallel to regional international travel patterns (see Exhibit 2.2). Regionally, Europe had 5,462,000 hotel rooms by 1994, or 44.71 percent of the world total hotel rooms. The Americas had 4,493,000 hotel rooms in 1994, or 36.77 percent of the world total. East Asia and the Pacific area registered 1,557,000 hotel rooms in 1994, which accounted for 12.74 percent of the world total. Africa had only 3.14 percent of the hotel rooms in the world, with a total of 384,000 hotel rooms in 1994. The Middle East and South Asia respectively recorded 179,000 (1.47 percent) and 143,000 (1.17 percent) hotel rooms in each region.

The performance of the hotel business by region was investigated by a comprehensive study that surveyed more than 3000 hotels worldwide in the mid-1990s. This study found that world hotel occupancies reached 66.5 percent in 1994, with North America, Asia, and Australia showing the highest occupancy rates. Europe, Latin America/Caribbean, and Africa/Middle East recorded occupancy rates below the world average. By price range, luxury hotels showed the highest occupancy rate at 68.8 percent, followed by first-class hotels at 66.7 percent, midprice hotels at 66.2 percent, and economy hotels at 63.2 percent. It is interesting to note that the more expensive the hotels, the higher the occupancy rates.

EXHIBIT 2.2. Hotel Capacity by Region

	Total Rooms (000)		% Change
	1985	1994	1985-1994
World	9,199	12,218	32.8
Africa	267	384	43.8
Americas	3,462	4,493	29.8
East Asia/Pacific	813	1,557	91.5
Europe	4,425	5,462	23.4
Middle East	130	179	37.7
South Asia	102	143	40.2

Source: Adapted from World Tourism Organization *Tourism Highlights—1995* (Madrid, Spain, 1996), p. 13.

In terms of daily average room rates, the world average rate was $81.02 in 1994. By region, Europe recorded the highest average room rate at $89.84 in 1994. This shows that Europe is a relatively expensive destination for lodging accommodations compared to other regions. This can be attributed to the high cost of living and the strong European currencies (foreign currency exchanges will be discussed in Chapter 9). The second highest average rate was found in Asia/Australia. Consistently higher room rates are reported in the major cities in this region, such as in Tokyo, Hong Kong, Singapore, and now even in Beijing and Shanghai. The other three regions, North America, Africa, and the Middle East, recorded average room rates below the world average level. By price range, luxury hotels reported an average daily rate of $124.37 in 1994. First-class hotels recorded an average rate of $82.53, midprice hotels $63.83, and economy hotels $42.56 per day in 1994.[11]

A recent study of global hotel performance conducted by Pannell Kerr Foster Consulting and published in *Hotels* reveals that the highest average daily rates are found in London ($223.72), Geneva ($207.65), Moscow ($189), and Paris ($187) in 1997.[12] Exhibit 2.3 is a sample of hotel occupancy rates and average daily rates in some major cities in Europe, the Middle East, and North America. These data show worldwide hotel occupancy rates and average room rates for the five regions and for each of the four price categories. This statistical information allows hotel companies and developers to analyze the performance of various segments of the hotel industry within a specific region.

EXHIBIT 2.3. Hotel Room Occupancy and Average Daily Rate (ADR) in Selected Cities, 1997

City	Occupancy (%)	ADR (US$/C$)
Abu Dhabi	66.0	$105.38
Amman	65.0	69.27
Amsterdam	77.0	114.18
Atlanta	69.0	71.00
Berlin	62.0	100.57
Boston	80.0	160.50
Calgary	71.0	C$97.00
Cairo	76.0	74.76
Dubai	75.9	122.53
Frankfurt	68.7	111.32
Geneva	60.0	207.65
Jeddah	67.5	117.30
London	82.8	223.72
Los Angeles	74.0	94.00
Miami	75.5	123.00
Madrid	69.0	110.67
Milan	69.0	158.87
Moscow	61.0	189.00
New York	83.0	187.50
Paris	72.1	187.00
Riyadh	61.0	111.97
Toronto	73.0	C$104.00
Vancouver	74.0	C$123.00
Vienna	64.5	122.16
Waikiki	80.0	124.00
Washington, DC	71.0	130.00

Source: Adapted from Tony Dela Cruz, "Global Optimism Tempered by Regional Crises," *Hotels* (January, 1998), 49-50, 54. Reprinted by permission of *Hotels* magazine, a publication of Cahners Business Information.

THE MOST INTERNATIONALIZED HOTEL COMPANIES

As discussed at the end of Chapter 1, various motivations have driven large hospitality corporations to expand operations beyond their own national boundaries. In the race to globalize hospitality operations, some giant corporations have emerged, in both the lodging and food service businesses.

In each year's July issue of *Hotels* magazine, the leading journal of international hotel and restaurant management, the editors publish valuable statistical data concerning hotel performance and trends around the world. The most internationalized hotel companies are identified by the criterion of geographic distributions—in how many countries the hotel company owns, manages, or franchises hotel operations. Exhibit 2.4 lists the eleven most internationalized hotel companies in the world by 1997.

As Exhibit 2.4 shows, the Phoenix-based Best Western International expands its international presence through membership affiliations in seventy-seven countries (this concept will be discussed in more detail in Chapter 6). Besides the major North American and European markets, Best Western ventures into many emerging markets, including some that used to be regarded as risky, such as Laos in Indochina. It now has about 3,700 independently owned and operated hotels worldwide and its annual sales reached $65 million in 1997.

EXHIBIT 2.4. Most Globalized Hotel Companies by Geographic Distribution, 1997

Firm	Countries
Best Western International	77
Bass Hotels & Resorts	75
Accor	72
Starwood Hotels & Resorts/Starwood Hotels & Resorts International Inc.	68
Marriott International	53
Hilton International	52
Forte Hotels	50
Carlson Hospitality Worldwide	48
Choice Hotels International	40
Club Méditerranée SA	40
Hyatt Hotels/Hyatt International	37

Source: Adapted from *Hotels* Special Report, "Corporate 300," *Hotels* (July 1998), 51. Reprinted by permission of *Hotels* magazine, a publication of Cahners Business Information.

Bass Hotels and Resorts, a subsidiary of U.K.-based Bass Plc, operates and franchises more than 2,600 Inter-Continental and Holiday Inn hotels with about 450,000 rooms in seventy-five countries. Inter-Continental Hotels, one of the earliest hotel companies to develop internationally, was acquired by Bass Plc in 1998 for its strategic global development. Inter-Continental developed a creative program for expanding its international operations: Global Partner Hotels and Resorts. This program recruits independent hotel proprietors to use its marketing and reservation services for a fee, which gives the smaller and independent operators exposure to the global travel markets.[13] The acquisition of Holiday Inn in 1990 by Bass Plc was major news in the international hospitality industry. Holiday Inn has been one of the leaders in international hotel development, with its first European hotel established in 1968 and its first Asian hotel in 1973. As the hotel division of Bass Plc, Holiday Inn has a new global orientation and focus, moving its headquarters from Memphis, Tennessee to Atlanta, Georgia. It operates and franchises hotels worldwide and even has a property at the world's highest elevation—Lhasa in Tibet.

The Evty, France-based Accor operated 2,577 hotels with a total of 288,269 rooms in seventy-two countries in 1997. It has been aggressively developing hotels in Eastern Europe, Asia, and the Pacific region, particularly its midscale and budget brands, such as Novotel, Ibis, and Formular 1. It operates the Motel 6 chain in North America.

Starwood Hotels and Resorts became one of the largest global hotel chains by strategically acquiring the Westin hotel chain and ITT Sheraton Corporation in 1998. Starwood Hotels and Resorts is the largest real estate investment trust (REIT) in the United States while Starwood Hotels and Resorts Worldwide operates and manages the firm's properties. Since January 6, 1999, Starwood Hotels and Resorts has been a subsidiary of Starwood Hotels and Resorts Worldwide. Sheraton brand has been one of the leaders in internationalization and its presence covers many tourism destinations in the world. Westin brand is also highly recognized globally and it is currently developing new hotels and resorts in Puerto Rico, Grand Cayman Islands, British Virgin Islands, Malta, Bangkok in Thailand, Surabaya, and Jakarta in Indonesia.[14] Now Starwood Hotels and Resorts owns and operates 653 hotels with a total of 213,238 rooms in sixty-eight countries.

The splitting up of Marriott Corporation into Marriott International and Host Marriott in 1993 was a major strategic move for international growth. Currently, Marriott International is vested with the task of developing international operations.[15] It has been very aggressive in expanding hotel operations in developing countries and it was the first company to develop a joint-venture hotel in Warsaw, Poland. In May 1995, Marriott made a strategic move by obtaining a 49 percent stake in the famous Ritz-Carlton brand. Its goal is to grow the Ritz-Carlton brand worldwide. In early 1997, Marriott International acquired Renaissance Hotels to further its global development. Renaissance is a highly internationalized hotel company, known for its history and elegance. The copper dome of the Amsterdam Renaissance Hotel has witnessed three centuries of historical development, ranging from Napoleon's conquest of Europe to the invasion of popular music (see Exhibit 2.5). Headquartered in Bethesda, Maryland, Marriott International operates, manages, and franchises 1,477 hotels with 289,357 rooms in fifty-three countries.

Hilton International, based in Watford in the United Kingdom, is a separate entity from Hilton Hotels Corporation, headquartered in Beverly Hills, California. Hilton International was established as a separate subsidiary of Hilton Corporation in 1949 with the opening of the Caribe Hilton and Casino in San Juan, Puerto Rico. Hilton International now has the exclusive right to use the name Hilton for hotels outside the United States and Vista for hotels within the United States. Hilton Hotels Corporation now uses the name Conrad for its overseas hotels.[16] The present owner of Hilton International is Ladbroke Group, Plc, one of the United Kingdom's top 100 companies. Hilton International currently operates, manages, and franchises 165 hotels in fifty-two countries. It still shares Hilton Reservation Worldwide with Hilton Hotels Corporation.

Forte Plc, a British conglomerate headquartered in London, operates lodging, gaming, and restaurant businesses around the world. It operates and franchises 260 hotels with 47,814 rooms in fifty countries. It owns and operates Travelodge in North America. Its latest acquisition was Meridian Hotels in 1995, which doubled the number of Forte's upscale luxury hotels to ninety. This merger gives Forte a strong presence in many regions, especially Southeast Asia, where Meridian has ten hotels.

Radisson Hotels International, a member of Carlson Hospitality Worldwide headquartered in Minneapolis, Minnesota, is one of the fastest growing upscale hotel companies in the world. In 1994, it formed an alliance with SAS (Scandinavian Airlines System) International Hotels to become a major global hotel company. This alliance added twenty-eight SAS hotels to Radisson's portfolio and expanded Radisson's presence in Europe. By 1997, Carlson/Radisson/SAS operated, managed, and franchised hotels in forty-eight countries (Exhibit 2.6). It plans to increase the number of hotels to 715 by the year 2000.

Choice Hotel International is based in Silver Spring, Maryland. It has been very aggressive in internationalizing its hotel development and it now has hotel operations, management, and franchises in forty countries. Of the seven brands that Choice Hotel International operates, Quality Inns and Friendship Inns are primarily found in the United States. EconoLodge

EXHIBIT 2.5. The Seventeenth-Century Koepelkerk-Renaissance Amsterdam Hotel (Photo courtesy of Renaissance Amsterdam Hotel.)

EXHIBIT 2.6. The Olympic Penta Hotel in Moscow Managed by Radisson (Photo courtesy of Radisson Hospitality Worldwide.)

and Rodeway Inns are operated in North America, mainly in the United States and Canada. Comfort Inns, Sleep Inns, and Clarion Hotel and Resorts are distributed in more than thirty countries.

The Paris-based Club Méditerranée SA was first founded by a Belgium Olympic water polo champion named Gerard Blitz in 1950. The first Club

Med village was set up on the beautiful Mediterranean in Alcudia, Mallorca, Spain by using surplus army tents supplied by Gibbert Trigano, who later joined the company. In the past forty-eight years, the tents were replaced by thatched huts, and then the thatched huts were replaced by bungalows. Now, Club Med operates 134 vacation villages and resorts in forty countries and has become a large international hotel/resort company.

Based in Chicago, Hyatt Hotels/Hyatt International operates, manages, and franchises 179 hotels with 80,311 rooms in thirty-seven countries. Hyatt International has long been developing commercial hotels in major cities and resort hotels in the most desirable geographical locations around the world. Now it continues to increase its global presence in many emerging markets in Asia and Latin America.

This discussion of the eleven most internationalized hotel companies has highlighted the size and scope of these giant international companies. It has also identified their geographical distributions. However, there are many other aggressive international and regional hotel companies, such as Park Plaza International Hotels and Resorts, Sol Melia, Hilton Hotels Corporation, Four Seasons/Regent, Nikko Hotels International, and LTI International Hotels, just to name a few. These and many other international and regional hotel companies will be identified later in this chapter.

MAJOR INTERNATIONAL FOOD SERVICE COMPANIES

The internationalization of the food service industry was primarily pioneered by, and is now dominated by, U.S.-based quick-service restaurants (QSR), such as McDonald's, Burger King, KFC, and Pizza Hut. The decision by these companies to go international was made to tap the great potential of foreign food service markets and to service Americans traveling abroad. It is interesting to note that American fast food is embraced by young people in many foreign countries as "fashion food," an element of the popular Western culture. This contributed to the success of quick-service restaurant operations in many foreign countries.

According to the National Restaurant Association in the United States, there are approximately 160 U.S. food service companies operating internationally.[17] Most of these international operations are quick-service restaurants. Exhibit 2.7 shows the ten major fast-food, pizza, and sweets chains by geographical distributions.

With the overseas success of the limited-menu, quick-service restaurant operations, the casual and midscale food service operations have also entered the international markets, such as U.S.-based Denny's, Sizzler International, T.G.I. Friday's, U.K.-based Forte Restauranta, and Mexico-based Chi Chi's Restaurants. T.G.I. Friday's, a member of Carlson Hospitality Worldwide, is a very aggressive international restaurant company. Under the brand name Friday Hospitality Worldwide, it now includes T.G.I. Friday's, Italianni's, and Front Row Sports Grill restaurants, with a total of 56 restaurants in twenty-three countries. It plans to have more than 200 international restaurants in over fifty countries, including Australia, New Zealand, the United Kingdom, Spain, Mexico, Canada, China and others in the Asia/Pacific region, Western Europe, South America, and Eastern Europe.[18]

It is clear that the food service industry will follow the lodging industry in internationalizing its restaurant operations. As the population continues to grow and the economy continues to improve in the developing countries, foreign cuisine is affordable to the majority of the local population and more importantly, dining is considered a cultural experience by the younger generation in many countries. Foreign cuisine as an element of popular culture, just like blue jeans, pop music, and Hollywood movies, can penetrate many foreign markets. Such appeal can attract millions of potential customers worldwide.

REGIONAL EXPANSION AND COMPETITION

This section discusses the expansion potential of the six major world regions and identifies other international and regional hospitality companies as potential competitors in these regions. This brief analysis is based on current travel patterns and hospitality development trends in each region. Knowledge of the major regional hospitality players can help international hospitality companies know their competitors and develop successful market strategies.

Europe

This region will continue to be the leading international tourist destination. Its political and economic stability, close cultural ties with North America, and splendid cultural history will attract tourists from all over the world. The European hospitality industry has been performing well in the past few years. The trend will be toward more consolidation among smaller or midsize companies to compete in the highly globalized markets, such as the alliance between Radisson and SAS, or Dusit Thani and Kempinski. Exhibit 2.8 describes the major regional hotel chains that are well positioned in their own countries and Europe.

EXHIBIT 2.7. Ten Major U.S. Quick-Service Restaurant Chains in the World, 1996

Restaurant Chain	Total U.S. Units*	Total Foreign Units
McDonald's	21,022	8,928
KFC	9,863	4,784
Burger King	8,874	1,817
Baskin-Robbins	4,311	1,700
Subway	12,516	1,668
Dunkin' Donuts	4,452	1,252
Domino's Pizza	5,500	1,200
Dairy Queen International	5,716	681
Wendy's	4,933	564
Church's	1,282	292

* Total U.S. units include both company-owned and franchise-owned units.

Source: Personal communication, National Restaurant Association (Washington, DC, 1997).

EXHIBIT 2.8. Regional Hotel Chains in Europe

Country	Chain	Head Office	Total Hotels	Total Rooms
Cyprus	Sunotels	Nicosia	31	3,300
Denmark	Helnan Hotels	Aalborg	12	2,822
Finland	Sokos Hotels	Helsinki	44	7,139
France	Societe du Louvre	Paris	468	29,120
	Hotel & Compagnie	Les Ulis	362	18,939
Germany	Maritim Hotels	Bad Salzuflen	43	11,700
Greece	Grecotel SA	Rethymnon, Crete	18	4,580
Hungary	Hunguest Hotels	Budapest	40	4,000
Ireland	Doyle Hotel Group	Dublin	10	1,744
Italy	Jolly Hotels	Valdagno	38	6,453
Holland	Golden Tulip	Hilversum	23	3,141
Norway	Rica Hotels	Sandvika	29	3,945
Poland	Orbis Co.	Warsaw	47	9,946
Portugal	Pestana (GP) Hotels	Madeira	11	2,614
Spain	Husa Hotels Group	Barcelona	131	12,500
Sweden	Scandic Hotels AB	Stockholm	94	15,000
Switzerland	Movenpick Hotels	Adliswil	29	6,231
U.K.	Queens Moat Houses	Romford, Essex	140	15,821

Source: Adapted from Frances Martin, "*Hotels* Giants—Corporate 200," *Hotels* (July, 1995), 48, 50. Reprinted by permission of *Hotels* magazine, a publication of Cahners Business Information.

North America

The United States has become one of the top tourist destinations in the world. The implementation of NAFTA increased the flow of people and goods between the three North American countries. The lodging industry has been performing well since 1992. The top U.S. hotel chains are highly globalized companies, as described earlier in this chapter. Four Seasons Hotels and Resorts of Canada is a fine lodging company operating upscale properties globally. The alliance with Hong Kong-based Regent International gives the company a strong partner in Asia and Pacific markets. Canadian Pacific Hotels, formerly a domestically oriented company, acquired Delta Hotels and Resorts (a major global hotel company in Canada) in 1998 to strengthen its global lodging development. In Mexico, Grupo Posadas de Mexico is a major domestic lodging company with thirty properties and an estimated 8,000 rooms. Grupo Situr operates twenty-six hotels with 7,368 rooms.

The Caribbean and Central and South America

The Caribbean region has been a popular playground for international tourists. Its popularity will continue as demand for sun-sea-sand destinations grows. However, an ecologically sensitive development approach has been emphasized by local governments in recent years. Political stability and economic growth in Central and South America attract many international hotel and restaurant chains to jockey for market positions in this region. A few regional hotel chains have also been doing very good business, such as Othon Hotels SA in Rio de Janeiro with sixteen hotels (3,100 rooms), Cubanacan SA in Havana with thirty-six hotels (3,342 rooms), and EnturPeru in Lima with forty-seven hotels (1,883 rooms).

The Middle East

This region has potential for future expansion. Traditionally, the oil-rich countries in the Middle East have set their economic priority on oil production and exportation. Tourism, particularly leisure tourism, is not enthusiastically promoted by Saudi Arabia or other countries in the region. However, with the new political stability maintained between the Arab countries and Israel, travel to the region will increase and demand for lodging facilities will grow. Hotel development has been primarily controlled by major international chains, although Saudi Arabia's Prince Al-Walid purchased New York's Plaza Hotel and Singapore's CDL Hotels in

June 1995 and invested $400 million in Euro Disney.[19] Hilton International has been very active in developing and managing hotels in this region. Several regional hotel chains are worthy of mention: Dan Hotels Corporation in Tel Aviv, Israel, has seven hotels with a total of 1,872 rooms. Moriah Hotels in Tel Aviv also operates seven hotels with 1,760 rooms, and the Syrian Cham Palaces and Hotels in Damascus operates fourteen hotels with 4,300 rooms.

Africa

Africa's vast land mass and rich cultural and natural resources do not justify the paltry 3 percent of the total international tourism arrivals to the region. Physical isolation, poverty, and internal turmoil have kept many tourists from visiting the region. Now, as racial tension eases in South Africa and democracy is slowly introduced to some African countries, this region will attract hospitality developers' attention for inexpensive land and labor (see Exhibit 2.9). Several large hotel chains in South Africa are actively expanding their operations in the region, such as Sun International, Protea Hospitality Corporation, and Southern Sun Hotel Holdings in South Africa, and Zimbabwe Sun Hotels in Zimbabwe. The trophy property developed by Sun International features the world-famous architectural marvel of the 350-room Palace at the Lost City.[20] Inter-Continental, which has fourteen hotels in Africa, signed a joint-venture agreement in 1995 with Sun International to develop hotels in this region.

Asia and the Pacific

This region has two-fifths of the world's population, which surely has hospitality developers pondering its market potential. In the first part of the 1990s, the economies of many countries in East and South Asia experienced marked improvement. The emergence of Hong Kong and Singapore as world financial and business centers attracted global hospitality companies to jockey for positions in this region. The major international and regional hotel and food service chains are well represented in this region. European and American hotel chains face competition from regional giants. Hong Kong alone is home to eight of these regional giants in Asia (see Exhibit 2.10). They are well positioned in the major cities and are pushing into the secondary cities for expansion. The alliance between East and West, as seen in the merger of Four Seasons/Regent and the acquisition of New World by Marriott International, has been proven as an effective strategy to increase global presence.

EXHIBIT 2.9. The Hilton Hotel at Addis Ababa, Ethiopia (Photo courtesy of Addis Ababa Hilton International, Plc.)

EXHIBIT 2.10. Major International and Regional Hotel Chains in the Asia/ Pacific Region

Country	Chain	Head Office	Total Hotels	Total Rooms
Australia	South Pacific Hotels Corp.	Sydney	76	12,939
	Rydges Hotel Group	Sydney	21	2,981
China	Shanghai Jin Jiang Group	Shanghai	17	6,857
Hong Kong	Shangri-la International	Hong Kong	27	13,627
	Regal Hotels International	Hong Kong	10	5,432
	Mandarin Oriental Hotels	Hong Kong	12	4,155
	Park Lane Hotels	Hong Kong	6	3,370
	Peninsula Group	Hong Kong	6	2,537
	Century International Hotels	Hong Kong	8	2,085
India	Taj Group of Hotels	Bombay	50	8,045
	Oberoi Hotels	Delhi	23	4,888
	India Tourism Development	New Delhi	34	4,000
Indonesia	Sahid Group of Hotels	Jakarta	12	2,245
Japan	Prince Hotels Inc.	Tokyo	58	24,087
	Tokyu Hotel Group	Tokyo	107	23,836
	Fujita Kanko Inc.	Tokyo	71	15,941
	Nikko Hotels International	Tokyo	38	15,369
	ANA Hotels	Tokyo	43	10,440
South Korea	Hotel Lotte	Seoul	2	2,017
Malaysia	Dederal Hotels International	Kuala Lumpur	3	1,376
Singapore	SMI Hotels & Resorts	Singapore	9	4,259
Thailand	Amari Hotels & Resorts	Bangkok	9	2,780
	Imperial Family of Hotels	Bangkok	7	2,700

Source: Adapted from Frances Martin, "*Hotels* Giants—Corporate 200," *Hotels* (July, 1995), 48, 50. Reprinted by permission of *Hotels* magazine, a publication of Cahners Business Information.

Many of these regional hotel companies have become major global players with very high standards of services and operations. They compete with the global giants in their own regions and in some other world markets as well, contributing to the dynamics of the global hospitality industry.

SUMMARY

- Knowledge of geography is important for understanding physical and cultural attributes of places in the world.

- Latitude is an indicator of how far north and south of the equator a given location is situated. Meridians measure longitude. The meridian selected as the base point of reference is called the prime meridian, which is the longitude of the Royal Observatory at Greenwich outside London.
- The Northern and Southern Hemispheres divide the world at the equator. The Eastern Hemisphere includes all meridians of east longitude from 0 to 180 degrees, while the Western Hemisphere includes all meridians of west longitude.
- The world is divided into twenty-four time zones with the initial or zero zone beginning at the prime meridian at Greenwich. The International Date Line marks the change in time from one day to another because of the rotation of the earth. When crossing the International Date Line, add a day going west and subtract a day going east.
- Absolute location refers to the precise site of a place. Relative location refers to its situation.
- World regions can be defined by continents, political systems, cultural attributes, and levels of economic development.
- More and more countries in the same region tend to band together to develop their economy and promote travel and trade. Such cooperation is known as regional economic integration.
- The World Tourism Organization collects and compiles statistical data on tourism arrivals and revenues for six regions in the world: Europe, the Americas, East Asia and the Pacific, Africa, the Middle East, and South Asia. Europe is the leading tourist destination.
- World regional hospitality development correlates with regional international travel patterns, with Europe and the Americas having the most hotel rooms in the world.
- The most globalized hotel companies are defined by their geographic distribution of properties. These companies are well positioned in the global hospitality market and have established high standards for quality service.
- Approximately 160 U.S. food service companies operate internationally. Many foreign food service companies operate in the United States as well. Most of these international operations are quick-service restaurants. Casual and midscale restaurants are inspired by the success of the quick-service companies and are expanding their operations in different parts of the world.
- There are many well-established and well-positioned regional hotel companies. Many of these companies not only serve the regional

travel markets, but also become influential in international hospitality development.

STUDY QUESTIONS

1. Why is an understanding of world geography important to a global hospitality manager?
2. What are latitude, meridian, longitude, and prime meridian?
3. How is the world divided into hemispheres?
4. How is world time organized?
5. What time is it in Moscow, Beijing, Frankfurt, Delhi, Lagos, Lima, São Paulo, Tehran, and Tel Aviv when it is 10:00 a.m. in San Francisco?
6. Where is the International Date Line? What will happen when an international traveler crosses the line?
7. What are absolute location and relative location? Why are they important concepts for international hospitality development?
8. How can world regions be defined? Please substantiate your answers with some concrete examples.
9. What is regional economic integration? What do you think of the impact of the North American Free Trade Agreement (NAFTA) on the promotion of intraregional trade and travel among Canada, Mexico, and the United States?
10. Which six major regions in the world are included in the statistical studies by the World Tourism Organization?
11. Can you explain why certain regions in the world have always been top tourism destinations, and some others have only a very small share of the international travel business?
12. Which regions had higher hotel occupancies or higher room rates in 1997? Can you explain why certain regions had higher occupancy rates or room rates than others?
13. Who were the top most globalized hotel companies as ranked by *Hotels* magazine in 1997?
14. Do you know all of these global giants? Can you describe their national origins, ownership, and global operations?
15. What type of food service operation is the most globalized business? Who are the leading food service companies in international operations?
16. What factors can you identify that will continue to influence the rapid globalization of the food service industry?

17. What trends can you identify in Europe for regional hospitality development?
18. What potentials can you identify for developing and improving international hotel operations in the Middle East and Africa?
19. What suggestions can you make to regional hotel companies for competing successfully with the global giants in different areas of the world?

CASE STUDY: MCDONALD'S GLOBAL EXPANSION FORMULA

McDonald's is one of the most globalized food service companies in the world. By 1996, McDonald's operated and franchised 21,022 restaurants in 101 countries around the world. Restaurant sales from international operations reached $15.442 billion, about 48.54 percent of McDonald's system-wide sales of $31.812 billion in 1996. McDonald's vision is to dominate the global food service industry by being customers' favorite quick-service restaurant. Rapid global expansion will continue to be the development focus of McDonald's in the twenty-first century.

The world market has great potential for McDonald's growth, according to James Cantalupo, president of McDonald's International. Cantalupo has developed a formula to estimate the market potential for McDonald's growth worldwide. He divides a country's population by the number of people per store in the United States and adjusts for differences in per capita income, arriving at the following formula:

$$\frac{\text{population of host country}}{\substack{\text{number of people per} \\ \text{McDonald's store in U.S.} \\ \text{(25,000)}}} \times \frac{\substack{\text{per capita income} \\ \text{of host country}}}{\substack{\text{per capita income} \\ \text{of U.S. (\$23,120)}}} = \substack{\text{potential market} \\ \text{for McDonald's} \\ \text{in host country}}$$

Applying this formula to estimate the potential world market for McDonald's, *Fortune* magazine calculated that the potential number of McDonald's could reach 42,000, compared to the 21,022 McDonald's restaurants reported in 1996. Clearly, the world market has great potential for McDonald's global expansion. However, this estimate of global market potential simply demonstrates the mathematical formula for calculating the size of the market. It does not take into consideration other factors that can influence the success of a company's global development, such as food preference in different cultures, the ability to adjust to local operations, and increased competition in the global marketplace.

People in different cultures have certain dietary preferences. Some foods that are preferred in one culture may be avoided in another. For example, the Hindus in India regard the cow as a sacred animal. Therefore, Hindus do not eat beef, which is the main type of meat for hamburger in the United States and many other countries. When analyzing the market potential in India, diet preference needs to be carefully examined and understood. Menu modifications need to be made to accommodate the food preference of the local population; therefore, McDonald's emphasizes that the management must know a country's culture before they are assigned to work in a foreign country, and they must modify the standard menu appropriately to cater to the local diet.

The great success of McDonald's overseas operations is also attributed to their ability to adjust to the local business environment. The prototype of McDonald's operations is not rigidly transplanted from the United States to the host country. The operation is adjusted to respond to the local real estate market, sourcing of foodstuffs, and human resources. Satellite stores, or low-overhead mini-McDonald's, were invented in high-rent Singapore. In Saudi Arabia, the scarcity of local suppliers forced the purchasing directors to utilize an enterprising team of global suppliers. As a result, the Saudi Big Mac represents a truly international effort, including sesame seeds and onions from Mexico, buns made of Saudi wheat, Brazilian soybean oil and sugar, beef patties and lettuce from Spain, pickles and special sauce from the United States, cheese from New Zealand, and packaging from Germany. These creative solutions developed by management continue to keep McDonald's at the forefront of global food service expansion.

Any study of global market potential for quick-service restaurants cannot overlook the factor of global competition. There is no doubt that McDonald's is the market leader. However, many other quick-service restaurants are also expanding their operations rapidly in foreign countries. These competitors include other hamburger restaurants, fried chicken restaurants, pizza restaurants, and doughnut and ice cream operations. All these quick-service operations compete for market share of their products and services. Therefore, analysis of the competition is a very important factor for estimating the market potential for a particular company's operations.

In summary, Cantalupo's formula estimates a company's market potential by its total population and per capita income. This gives a general estimation of a country's market potential for possible McDonald's development. The analysis of a country's market potential also includes the examination of other factors such as diet preference, adjustment to local operations, and competition in quick-service operations in the host country. These factors all have a direct impact on the success or failure of quick-service operations in a foreign country.

Case Study Sources

Andrew E. Serwer, "McDonald's Conquers the World," *Fortune* (October 17, 1994), 103-104; *The Annual: McDonald's Corporation 1994 & 1996 Annual Reports* (McDonald's Corporation, Oak Brook, IL, 1995 and 1997).

Case Study Questions

1. Can you describe the size and scope of McDonald's international expansion and operations?
2. What is Mr. Cantalupo's formula for estimating a country's market potential for McDonald's restaurants?
3. Can you use Mr. Cantalupo's formula to estimate the market potential of Brazil, Turkey, Hungary, and Vietnam for McDonald's restaurants?
4. Why is the diet preference of a particular culture important for market potential analysis?
5. Can you explain the importance of competition analysis as a factor that influences the estimation of the market potential in a foreign country?

PART II:
DIFFERENCES IN CULTURAL, POLITICAL, AND ECONOMIC SYSTEMS

Part II includes three chapters that discuss the differences in cultural, political, and economic systems of different countries. Global hospitality managers need to recognize these differences because the international hospitality business is regulated and influenced by national governments and cultural custom. These different systems are also known as external factors in international hospitality operations because a manager has no control over them. Adequate knowledge of the cultural, political, and economic systems in different countries will enable a hospitality manager to adapt hotel and restaurant operations to the local ways of doing business quickly and gain the trust of the local managers and staff.

Chapter 3 discusses the cultural dimensions of international hospitality operations. It explains various pertinent cultural concepts and analyzes how management decisions and service performance are influenced by cultural values and norms in different countries. It emphasizes that hidden cultural codes can often handicap international hospitality managers' effective operations in a different cultural environment. The similarities and differences of cultural values and behaviors of various countries are summarized and contrasted. An effective cultural learning process is thoroughly explained.

Chapter 4 focuses on the differences in world political systems. Economic activities in any individual country are highly influenced by its political system—government control through regulatory functions. Different political systems complicate international hospitality operations and present great political risk for investment and development. This chapter therefore discusses national government's functions in tourism and hospitality development and examines potential political risks for international hospitality development and operations.

Chapter 5 analyzes economic systems. Business structures and organizations are influenced by the economic system of the country. The current trend of economic reforms in many developing countries is emphasized, and potential hospitality development opportunities are identified in some emerging markets. Useful economic data for making global hospitality expansion decisions are introduced in this chapter. The economic impact of hospitality development on a foreign country is thoroughly analyzed and presented.

These three chapters combine to outline the complexity of the external environment for international hospitality operations. The up-to-date information keeps abreast with the current cultural, political, and economic developments in the world.

Chapter 3

Cultural Environment

The hotel business is creative, not stagnant. There is not one "right way" to build and run a hotel. Each hotel reflects its region, surrounding culture, and general manager.[1]

James Harper
Former Editor in Chief
Hotels Magazine

LEARNING OBJECTIVES

In this chapter, you will study:

1. The four aspects of culture
2. Cultural influence on management
3. Differences in cultural values, and perceptions of certain sociocultural issues related to hospitality management and operations
4. The complex aspects of cross-cultural communications
5. The silent language
6. Cultural generalizations
7. Cultural learning through cultural awareness and cultural adaptation

INTRODUCTION

International business and hospitality services are to a great extent influenced by the cultural values and norms of different societies. In this people-oriented industry, international hospitality managers have to manage, interact, negotiate, and compromise with people of different cultural backgrounds. The differences, particularly the hidden cultural codes in other countries, often cause misunderstanding and management frustration, and eventually handicap international hospitality managers' effective operations in a different cultural environment. However, when understood and successfully managed, differences in culture can lead to innovative business practices and sustainable sources of competitive advantage.

This chapter explains how cultural differences can affect international hospitality management. It defines the concept of culture and discusses how cultural values and norms shape and affect social and business behaviors in different countries. The cultural differences reflected in management styles are analyzed through an extensive review of existing international management studies. The importance of cultural learning is emphasized, and the objective is to provide an analytical study of cultural dynamics in international hospitality management.

DEFINING CULTURE

Culture has been defined in many different ways by social science scholars. In this book, culture is defined as the ways of living built up by a group of people and passed on from one generation to another.[2] In other words, culture encompasses the learned patterns of behavior common to the members of a given society. The shared ways of life consist of beliefs, knowledge, law, custom, institutions, and artifacts.

Culture has four distinctive characteristics:

1. Culture is not innate, but learned.
2. The various aspects of culture are interrelated.
3. Culture is shared.
4. Culture defines the boundaries of different groups.[3]

Culture Is Learned

Individuals learn culture in the course of everyday living by interacting with those around them at home, at school, or in church. This learning starts at an early age and generally stays with people for the rest of their lives. Young children are very quick at learning different aspects of a culture, such as languages and eating habits. For instance, if a five-year-old Japanese child moves to the United States and lives in Kansas City for two years, this child will speak fluent English by the end of her stay, but will not know how to use chopsticks when her contemporaries in Japan eat with them.

The Aspects of Culture Are Interrelated

This means that one aspect of the culture can directly influence other aspects. A good example is the interrelationship of religion and diet, two important aspects of any culture. Due to religious beliefs, some groups prohibit the consumption of certain food and beverages. For instance, Muslims do not consume pork and alcohol and Hindus do not eat beef, as was already explained in the case study in Chapter 2 (religion and diet will be discussed in Chapter 13). Clearly, people's diets in different societies are influenced by their religious beliefs. This creates great challenges to hotel food and beverage directors, and commercial restaurant managers in countries with different religious practices. Ignorance of local religious beliefs and practices can cause serious cultural misunderstanding in food service operations in different countries.

Culture Is Shared

When all members of a group speak the same language or follow the same religion, they have a shared culture. Cultural elements are transmitted to the next generation through direct instructions and through the behaviors they consciously or unconsciously encourage and discourage. This aspect of culture can present a challenge to hospitality managers working in a different cultural environment, since some societies regard people who do not share their cultural values as outsiders. However, the local people will respect and trust you if you respect or share certain aspects of their culture, such as speaking their language, eating their food, and making local friends.

Culture Defines the Boundaries of Different Groups

As discussed in Chapter 2, world regions can be defined by similar cultural traits. The distinctive aspects of a society's cultural traits can be revealed in spatial patterns; for instance, many societies in the Middle East do not consume pork. This spatial distribution of shared cultural traits can be valuable market information for hospitality companies to make global expansion decisions on consumer behavior.

CULTURAL VALUES AND NORMS

The essence of a culture is its value system, upon which a society's norms are established and justified.[4] Values are the beliefs a society holds in regard to right and wrong, good and bad, ethical or unethical. These beliefs encompass a society's attitudes toward such issues as human rights, freedom, honesty, loyalty, individualism, collectivism, and so on. Societies with different cultural values may perceive the same issue very differently.

Norms are social rules and guidelines that prescribe appropriate behavior in particular situations. Norms shape people's actions toward one another. Certain behaviors are perfectly normal in one culture, but are abhorred in another. For example, it is common in the United States for a hotel manager to praise an employee of the same sex with a pat on the back. But patting someone on the back is avoided in Japan because this part of the body should not be touched by other people.

Cultural values and norms in a society evolve over long periods and are strongly influenced by the prevailing political and economic forces, religious influence, and education levels. Values and norms are not static; they may change as the political and economic orientation shifts, or as education improves. For example, getting rich was a shameful thing to do in China before the country's economic reform campaign in 1978. Now, "getting rich is glorious" is the prevailing cultural value under the current national economic reform policy. It needs to be pointed out that some societies tend to experience faster cultural changes while others tend to maintain their value system more tightly, and go through slower changes. These aspects will be discussed later in this chapter when we discuss the generalization of world cultures.

CULTURAL VALUES AND THEIR INFLUENCE ON MANAGEMENT

Cultural values are shared by the members of a society. The cultural value system is complex, and includes countless people's attitudes toward family, religion, work, leisure, and so on. It is beyond the scope of this chapter to discuss exhaustively the cultural values of a given society. However, it is essential to identify and study the cultural values influencing international hospitality management styles and service practices, and to distinguish the differences among cultures. For the purpose of organization, religion as an essential element of culture is not discussed in this chapter. This topic will be introduced in Chapter 13 on food service operations, since religion has strong influence on dietary preference in different cultures.

Group Affiliations

People are commonly grouped into various categories either by birth or by affiliation. Grouping by birth consists of ascribed group memberships, which include age, gender, ethnicity, nationality, and caste. These are the basic demographic profiles for market analysis. Grouping by affiliation consists of acquired group memberships, which include religion, political affiliations, professional, and social associations.[5] These groupings place people at the different levels of the society, and their places in the social stratification system reflect their class or status positions. Three groupings have a direct impact on international hospitality operations.

Grouping by Age

Societies in different cultures have different attitudes toward age. Youthfulness is commonly valued as a professional advantage in Western societies such as the United States and Western Europe. Generally, any individual in these societies can get ahead through talent, creativity, and hard work regardless of his or her age. However, some other cultures view age differently. In Asia and Africa, it is believed that age and wisdom are positively correlated; the older one gets, the wiser one becomes. Wisdom and experience are accumulated through years of work. Hence, age is an asset in Asian and African cultures.[6]

These cultures value seniority in workplaces, and respect the elderly. Managers need to consider the age factor when managing hospitality operations in these cultures. Promotion of younger staff may disrupt the harmony of the entire company's work environment, particularly in Japan and China where people believe "a nail that sticks out must be hammered down." Age even influences the way business cards are exchanged and greetings are made. In Japan, the younger person must offer his or her card first, and bend deeper in bowing to the older businessperson. When the younger person receives the business card from the older person, he or she must hold the card in both hands, and show considerable respect. In Africa, younger people cannot openly question management decisions made by older managers.

Grouping by Gender

Attitudes toward gender vary significantly from culture to culture. In the United States, female workers constitute a significant part of the hospitality industry, and women executives and managers are seen in all the levels and aspects of the industry. This demonstrates the equality between male and female with respect to job opportunities and education. However, deeply ingrained cultural values in the Middle East, Latin America, and Asia still hinder the employment opportunities and social life of women. Saudi Arabia has extremely rigid rules for females in its society. Separation between male and female is practiced at school, in the workplace, in social life, and in using hotel elevators. A Saudi woman is not allowed to drive a car, or to ride in a taxi without a male relative. The Saudi government often denies entry visas for businesswomen from foreign countries. In Saudi Arabia, foreign managers are advised to avoid any questions or comments about a Saudi host's wife, or any female children over the age of twelve.[7]

In East Asia, Chinese and Japanese attitudes toward gender are deeply influenced by the 2,400-year-old Confucian tenet "man is dominant and woman is subordinate." In China, male preference is still revered, particularly in the rural areas. The wives of government officials or business executives normally do not attend social functions in China or Japan.

Grouping by Kinship

Kinship is the system that guides family and clan relationships in a given society.[8] The family is the fundamental building block of the kinship system. In the United States, the typical family structure is known as the nuclear family, which is made up of the parents and their children, though single-parent families have been increasing in recent years. But in other societies, the concept of family differs. The structure of a family is generally described as an extended family in Latin America, Asia, and Mediterranean countries. An extended family includes all relatives by blood and by marriage, and span several generations. This extended and closely knit family emphasizes members' responsibility and loyalty. The extended family structure has a strong influence on international business practice, particularly in the areas of negotiation, cooperation, hiring, and sourcing of materials.

In Latin America, an individual's name has both the maternal surname (Marin) and the paternal surname (Diaz) to indicate both branches of the family, as in Pedro Diaz Marin. When two businesspeople meet, they will first explore each other's family background to see whether they have common relatives. If they find any kinship at all, the negotiation tends to be fruitful.[9] There is a high degree of cooperation within family business units in these societies. In Greece, for instance, staff in family restaurants cooperate and mobilize their efforts to attain success much more effectively than in large organizations where people are from many different families.[10]

A family business is generally passed on from one generation to another in this kinship system. The best and most important positions are normally filled by family members regardless of their professional competence, since the owners are distrustful of non-family members, or outsiders. Therefore, the hiring practice contrasts sharply with that of the United States, which focuses on an applicant's ability and competence. This management difference must draw international managers' attention when they work in a hotel or restaurant owned by a family business.

The trust that family members place in each other also motivates them to source materials internally. They may buy supplies from distant relatives even if the price is higher. A hotel proprietor in Kuala Lumpur, Malaysia might buy linen for his hotel from a relative's textile company in Hong Kong rather than buying it locally at a cheaper price.

Kinship is the root of *guanxi* in China. *Guanxi* is a personal relationship and connection with others in society. Extending from the kinship system, the Chinese consider one's existence in society to be influenced primarily by one's relationship with others. To survive and advance, individuals must connect themselves with as many friends as possible. These friends will support or protect them against social adversity. The individual can fulfill political, social, and business goals through a network of associates. International managers must understand the strong influence of *guanxi* in Chinese society, since the right connections can bring cheap and reliable material supplies, assistance when problems arise, better recruits through government job agencies, and more tour groups scheduled by government travel bureaus.

The kinship system presents a great challenge to international hospitality managers who manage or work for large family businesses. It is not uncommon for foreign managers to be locked out of decisions when dealing with important family business. International hospitality managers must be aware of the family influence and loyalties that affect job performance, business negotiations, hiring practice, and sourcing of material supplies in these societies.

Individualism and Collectivism

A society's attitude toward individualism and collectivism is clearly reflected in the way in which people perceive themselves and relate to one another in social and business settings. These cultural values influence people's behaviors and aspirations in workplaces in different cultural settings. Individual achievement is highly respected in the value systems of Western societies. Individuals compete openly in the workplace to get ahead of others for prestige rewards and recognition. This cultural emphasis on individualism has been the driving force for entrepreneurship in Western societies and has resulted in the high level of entrepreneurship, due to continued innovations and inventions. New products, services, and new ways of marketing these products and services are constantly being created and initiated, and thus have sustained the competitive advantage of Western societies as world economic powers.

In contrast to the emphasis on individualism in Western societies, collectivism is valued, as in group achievement and decision making by consensus, in many Asian societies. In the value systems of these societies, the group is considered the primary unit of business organization. An individual's social status is determined as much by the standing of the group to which he or she belongs as by individual performance.[11] In these societies, collective efforts are highly valued and individual achievement is downplayed in business organizations.

When operating a hospitality business in countries with a strong cultural emphasis on collectivism, managers need to build up and maintain a group identity and cohesiveness. Cooperation among employees and collective achievements are emphasized. This is particularly true in Japan, where thousands of KFC employees start each day's work by pledging their loyalty to the company, and Nikko Hotels International has developed a company song as a group identity for its employees worldwide.

Two famous studies have been conducted to identify and compare national cultural differences in perceptions of individualism and collectivism. The most widely known study was pioneered by Geert Hofstede on the four dimensions of work-related value differences, with a very large sample of over 100,000 employees from fifty countries and three regions working at IBM during the 1970s. The four cultural dimensions are power distance, uncertainty avoidance, individualism and collectivism, and masculinity and femininity.[12] The individualism and collectivism dimension focused on the relationship between the individual and his or her fellow workers. Each country was assigned a score between 0 and 100. At the high end of the scale were societies in which the ties between individuals were very loose, and individual achievement and freedom were highly valued, such as Australia, the United States, Great Britain, the Netherlands, Canada, and New Zealand.

At the low end of the scale were societies in which the ties between individuals were very tight and group achievements and consensus were highly valued, such as Guatemala, Panama, Indonesia, Thailand, Taiwan, Nigeria, Portugal, Kenya, and Mexico. In these societies, people are born into collectives, such as extended families, and everyone is expected to protect the interests of his or her collective.

A compelling, more recent study by Fons Trompenaars shed new light on national cultures in terms of broad value differences.[13] Trompenaars surveyed over 15,000 managers from twenty-eight countries over a ten-year span, and included twenty-three countries in his report with at least 500 responses from each country. He identified seven cultural value variables, five of which are relevant to international business operations, including individualism and collectivism. His respondents were all managers in both manufacturing and service industries. Trompenaars' findings regarding the differences in individualism and collectivism revealed some variations from Hofstede's report. However, his findings in general support Hofstede's study by identifying Western societies as more individualism-oriented and Asian societies as more collectivism-oriented.

International hospitality management can be affected by individualism- or collectivism-oriented cultural values. Recognition, promotion, and merit pay are normally based on individual achievements in Western societies. Singling out the outstanding performer for praise is a common management practice in the Western cultural system. But the same practice may cause embarrassment rather than motivation in collectivism-oriented cultures. However, in recent years, teamwork in hospitality operations in the Western countries has been on the rise. With the implementation of Total Quality Management, hospitality employees are encouraged to form work teams to solve service-related problems and to ensure service quality, such as the self-directed work team used at Ritz-Carlton hotels.

Superior and Subordinate Relationship

Cultural values also differ among countries with regard to superior and subordinate relationships. The hierarchical superior-subordinate relationships seem universal. However, autocratic management is practiced in some countries while participatory management is preferred in others. For instance, most executives and managers in the hospitality industry in the United States take an open-door management approach by constantly consulting subordinates' opinions, even from the frontline employees, for improving service quality and operating more effectively. The management of empowerment is now widely implemented in the hospitality industry, which gives service employees certain authority to handle guest complaints on the spot, and involve them in management decision-making processes. It is recognized that the frontline employees have direct contact with the guests on a daily basis, and they are in the best position to discover what the guests need and want. As mentioned earlier, the concept of the self-directed work team developed by Ritz-Carlton is an excellent example of employee empowerment.[14] Ritz-Carlton employees share leadership with the management and are vested with the authority to solve hotel guests' complaints. For instance, each employee at the front desk has a $2,000 budget per occurrence to spend for solving a guest problem. No approval is needed to spend this amount. By involving the employees in managing guests' needs, the managers can free themselves from the detailed day-to-day operations, and focus more on strategic management issues and concerns. This self-directed team approach has resulted in happier employees, lower turnover, and improved problem solving. All of these contribute to a high level of customer service.

However, in some other countries, subordinates display a high respect for superior authority, and they seldom question a superior's management decisions and styles. It is interesting to note that some cultural values hold that the superiors are paid to make decisions, and the subordinates only carry out the decisions. A manager who asks subordinates for management decision input will be considered incompetent. The respectful response of subordinates often results in a centralized business structure and autocratic management style. Obviously, the empowerment of employees as practiced in participatory management can be very difficult to implement in these countries.

In his study of IBM employees worldwide, Hofstede defined the superior and subordinate relationship as power distance—the inequality among people in physical and intellectual capabilities. Based on his 0 to 100 scale, he assigned high scores to countries that allowed inequalities to grow over time into inequalities of power and wealth, and low scores to those that attempted to remove such inequalities. In countries where people display low power distance, such as Austria, Denmark, and Israel, superiors and subordinates are apt to regard one another as equal in power, which results in a consultative management environment. But in Malaysia, Mexico, Panama, Guatemala, and Venezuela, autocratic leadership prevails because a large power distance exists between superiors and subordinates.

Hofstede correlated the two cultural dimensions of individualism/collectivism and superior/subordinate relationship to develop a revealing power distance-individualism plot for the fifty countries and three regions. High scores on individualism and relatively low scores on power distance are recorded in many developed Western countries, such as the United States, Britain, and Canada. Low scores on individualism and high scores on power distance are found in the developing countries in Asia and Latin America. These correlations clearly demonstrate the differences in cultural values, and have important implications for hospitality operations across cultural boundaries.

Mobility and Loyalty

The attitude toward employment mobility and loyalty is closely associated with the attitude toward individualism and collectivism. A high degree of employment mobility is common in countries where individualism is highly valued. Talented managers tend to move from one company to another to find better positions and gain a greater share of compensation. It is not uncommon to have a high managerial turnover in the hospitality industry in the Western societies. A major advantage of the high degree of managerial mobility is to create competition and bring fresh ideas into a business organization. This high level of managerial mobility in individualism-oriented countries is often criticized as a lack of employee loyalty and commitment to the company.

In collectivism-oriented countries in Asia, the high value placed on group identification can be expected to discourage managers and employees from moving from company to company. This value system holds that material rewards from an individual's work may be less motivating because these rewards are divided among every member of the group. Loyalty and commitment to a company are highly valued in these countries. In Japan, lifetime employment with one company is the norm in many sectors of the economy. It was estimated that between 20 percent and 40 percent of all Japanese employees have formal or informal lifetime employment guarantees.[15] Such a high level of loyalty and commitment to a company is considered a major advantage because managers and employees accumulate knowledge and experience and develop a network of interpersonal business contacts through time. These can enable managers to perform their jobs more effectively, and achieve cooperation with others in and outside the organization.

It is no wonder that a Japanese manager of ANA Hotels in Australia could not understand why an Australian supervisor resigned from his job, and accepted another managerial position at another hotel. This Japanese manager even asked a professor at Bond University in Queensland for an answer: Why did he resign even though he was well treated by the management? Obviously, the differences in cultural values of mobility and loyalty are the root of this particular situation.

But a high degree of loyalty tends to result in the lack of dynamism, creativity, and cross-fertilization of new ideas in a business organization. Since managerial mobility is discouraged, seniority and internal promotion are the normal practices, therefore, younger talented managers and employees often find it very hard to advance.

Work and Play

Another dimension for examining a society's culture is its attitude toward work and play. Work is defined as the extension or effort directed to produce or accomplish something.[16] Play refers to the activities people pursue during their leisure time, such as recreation and tourism. This is a very important factor for developing international hospitality business. Traditionally, work has been viewed as a means of salvation. This idea has been strongly influenced by the Protestant work ethic in Western societies. The Protestant society viewed work as a moral virtue, and looked unfavorably on the idle. A similar work ethic is also found in Asian societies, where Confucian and Shinto work ethics prevail in China and Japan. The Japanese are well-known as workaholics and for their loyalty to employers.

These days, few Western societies retain the strict Protestant work ethic. "Work hard and play hard" has become the norm in many Western societies as a result of growing prosperity and shortening of work days. As discussed in Chapter 1, Europeans now enjoy the longest vacation time in the world. The reason for the the three-day weekend in the United States, moving holidays occurring in the middle of the week to Monday, was to create longer leisure time for people to participate in recreation and tourism activities. As more countries improve their economy and their citizens' living standards, there will be a cultural shift to more leisure time. For instance, leisure and tourism were considered decadent activities in China before its economic reform program in 1978. After fifteen years of economic reform, China instituted a five-day work week in 1995. More leisure time gives the Chinese new opportunities for cultivating leisure and recreational interests.

CROSS-CULTURAL COMMUNICATIONS

Language, both spoken and written, is the primary tool for communication within a particular culture. Language is described as a cultural mirror since it reflects the content and nature of the culture it represents.[17] The most distinctive aspect of cultural differences a hospitality manager notices in international operations is the spoken and written language. Knowledge of a foreign language can enhance a manager's effective management of international operations.

But cultural meanings can also be conveyed through nonverbal and nonwritten forms, such as body language, the use of colors, or personal space. These different ways of communicating cultural meanings are described as hidden cultural codes, the most difficult for an outsider to decipher. Ignorance of these cultural codes often leads to misunderstanding and embarrassment in the cross-cultural contact. This section discusses three types of cross-cultural communication: spoken language, written language, and silent language.

Spoken Language

An ability to speak the local language can not only enable a manager to communicate with the local managers, staff, and guests directly and effectively, but also gives the manager a key to the local culture. Without it, a manager is often left out on a culture's perimeter. A manager who does not speak the local language has to rely on an interpreter to communicate with other managers, staff, and guests. Communication through an interpreter can reduce the spontaneity of interpersonal contact. In addition, spoken language is highly situational. Local managers and staff can discuss matters in their own language when they do not want the expatriate manager to know. A study on expatriate hotel professionals in China found that the expatriate professionals who speak Chinese had higher interaction with the local managers and staff at both the professional and personal levels than those who need interpreters.[18]

It needs to be pointed out that substantial regional differences exist in spoken languages in many countries. Unlike Japan or Portugal where almost everybody speaks Japanese or Portuguese, China has many regional dialects, some of which are mutually unintelligible. Currently the Chinese government promotes Beijing dialect, known as Mandarin Chinese in the West, as the standard spoken language for the entire country. Mandarin is now taught and used in all Chinese schools. However, people outside of the Beijing area use their own dialects whenever the situation permits them. This can make communication more difficult for expatriate managers with working knowledge of Mandarin, for example, managing a hotel in Guangzhou, where local people speak Cantonese, a very different spoken language.

Written Language

Learning written language is normally harder than learning spoken language. Many languages have two totally different systems of phonetic pronunciation and written symbols, such as Japanese and Chinese. Memorizing the written symbols can be very difficult for a person from a different language system. English is now commonly used as the international business language. Hotels in non-English speaking countries like to translate their marketing messages and service directories from their own language to English. The lack of true understanding of the meanings of the words in both languages often results in poor translation that renders totally different meanings in another culture. Mistranslations can cause humorous, obscene, offensive, or unexpected situations. Translation from one language to another deserves the manager's attention since translations are an inevitable part of international hospitality operations. Qualified translators can best deal with the written communication the hospitality company has with its various audiences.

Silent Language

The term "silent language" was first used by Edward Hall, a well-known scholar of cross-cultural communication, to describe the transmission of cultural meanings that are not expressed by spoken or written language.[19] Silent language includes body language, such as eye contact, touching, facial expressions, and various gestures; and the cultural perceptions of time, personal space, color, and numerology. These behaviors and perceptions are shaped by cultural values, either consciously or unconsciously. But they convey cultural meanings within a particular cultural system. Since international hospitality operations are people oriented, body language is unavoidable in working with local staff and guests. Misunderstanding the meanings conveyed through body language can result in communication problems for the manager. A basic knowledge of the silent language can make international managers aware of the hidden cultural codes in the host society.

Eye Contact

Eye contact signifies interpersonal communication and carries messages. Many cultural variations are found in eye contact. Keeping good eye contact is an expected normal behavior in many Western societies. Arabs normally have very direct eye contact because they believe "the eyes are the window of the soul." It is important to the Arabs to know a person's heart and soul in order to do business together. Therefore, intense eye contact between men is a cultural norm in the Middle East Arab countries. However, in Japan, children are told at young age to only look at the shoulder level of their teachers. Young Japanese always lower their eyes when speaking to an older person or a superior to show respect. Minimal eye contact is characterized as the cultural norm in East and Southeast Asia. People in most Western and Northern European countries, the United States, and Canada maintain moderate eye contact, showing interest in what is being said, but not appearing to be intrusive.[20]

Touching

Touching is a very sensitive issue in cross-cultural contact. As a general rule, touching should be minimized when meeting or managing people from different cultures. Inappropriate touching can cause serious misunderstanding that may result in embarrassment or offending the local people. There are many hidden rules about touching in different countries. A handshake is considered unhygienic in some societies, and the bow is preferred when greeting strangers. Handshakes in Western societies are usually hard-pumping and hearty. However, they are generally limp in many other societies, such as Russia and Saudi Arabia. The handshake in Malaysia uses both hands but without grasping.

In Latin America, it is common for males to hold each other by the lapel, shoulder, or forearms as a sign of good communication. In the Middle East and North Africa, the left hand is considered unclean—it is the "toilet hand." It is extremely impolite to touch Arabs or Nigerians with the left hand, even if the person is left-handed. In India, men should avoid touching women or talking alone with women. You need to apologize if your foot or shoe touches an Indian since feet are considered dirty.

Facial Expressions

One way to express emotion is through various facial expressions: a grin, a smile, or a stern look. It might seem that these facial expressions are universal, but this is not the case. In emotional expressiveness, people in some societies appear more effervescent and lively, while in others they seem coolly subdued and uninterested. Latins and Arabs display impulsive emotions while Asians tend to control their facial expressions to a remarkable degree. The "know nothing face" (*shirankao*) shown by the Japanese and Chinese reveals their reservedness and reluctance to display their true emotions.

Americans tend to have moderate emotional display compared to the expressive Latins, Arabs, and reserved Asians. In the United States, managers often express serious points with a stern and solemn facial expression. However, Asians may display the same emotion with a smile or a short laugh. This typical facial expression is an attempt to reduce the potential for confrontation, and treat the serious matter in a nonthreatening way. A smile can express different emotions for Filipinos depending on the cultural context. It can mean praise, showing poise, making an apology, or displaying embarrassment or anger.[21] The facial expression can be only comprehended in the appropriate cultural context.

Gestures

The motion of hand and arm can mean something different to people from separate cultures, or it can mean nothing to the person of different cultural background.[22] For example, joining one's thumb and index finger in a circle means A-OK in the United States, an obscenity in Brazil, money in Japan, zero in France, and "I will kill you" in Tunisia.[23] Cultural messages conveyed through gestures are very complicated, and can be easily misunderstood by persons from different cultures. Gestures used in different cultures to summon a waitperson in a hotel dining room or commercial restaurant are described below to demonstrate such variations. To get a waitperson's attention in the United States, simply raise a finger or call the waitperson quietly. But one will find the following in other countries:

- In Europe, people clink a glass or cup with a spoon or finger ring.
- In Africa, people knock on the table.
- In the Middle East, people clap their hands to get attention.
- In Colombia, people extend a hand with palm down and move the index finger back and forth in a scratching motion.
- In Japan, people extend an arm slightly upward with palm down and flutter their fingers.
- In Spain and Latin America, people extend a hand with palm down, and rapidly open and close their fingers.
- In Singapore and Malaysia, people extend the right hand with palm down, keep the fingers together, fold the thumb across the palm or extend it, and wave the hand.
- In Pakistan and the Philippines, people do not use any hand gestures, they just say "pssssst!"[24]

These different gestures in summoning a restaurant waitperson illustrate that few gestures are universal in meaning. This discussion focused on body language. Now let us examine the other components of the silent language: cultural perception of using time, personal space, color, and numbers.

Time Concept

Different cultures view time quite differently. This can cause confusion and misunderstanding in business correspondence, setting deadlines, arranging an appointment, punctuality at business meetings, and so on. A dichotomy of time concepts was developed by Hall: monochronic and polychronic time.[25] The monochronic time concept emphasizes that time is used and experienced in a linear way, and it is divided into segments. Once time passes, it is gone forever. In societies where monochronic time is used, time is highly valued in business operations, as reflected in the common saying "Time is money." This time concept focuses on doing only one thing at a time. Appointments are required to meet people, and punctuality is expected. Emphasis on deadline and speed is essential in countries that value monochronic time. The United States, Canada, and Western and Northern Europe generally adopt the monochronic time concept.

The polychronic time concept views time in a cyclical fashion. Time travels in a circular way, and it always comes back, as experienced in day and night and the cycle of four seasons. Polychronic time is characterized by the simultaneous occurrence of many things at once. This means that "first come, first serve" may not apply in these societies, since the hotel front desk clerk can serve several guests simultaneously.

The polychronic time culture includes Asia, the Middle East, and Latin America. A delay in returning business communication can be a sign of serious deliberation in Japan. In the Middle East, the time required for a decision is directly proportional to its importance: the more important the matter, the longer the decision-making process. Local people normally elevate the prestige or importance of their work by taking a long time to make a decision. If a foreign manager tries to speed things up, he or she is regarded by the locals as downgrading the importance of the work.

In the United States, giving a deadline is a way of indicating the degree of urgency or relative importance of the work. However, giving a deadline in the Middle East indicates that you are overly demanding, rude, pushy, and exert undue pressure. In Latin America, when the general manager is told by the hotel engineer that the repair work will be done *mañana*, it does not mean tomorrow, the literal meaning of *mañana*. *Mañana* in Latin America is customarily understood as "in the next few days." Punctuality is also not strictly observed in Latin America. Time has different meanings in each country.

Personal Space

Personal space as discussed in this text refers to the appropriate speaking distance between two persons. Such speaking distance varies from culture to culture, and reflects the common behavior in different societies. In the Middle East (between men), South Europe, and Latin America, speaking distance tends to be very close, normally less than eighteen inches. The normal speaking distance in Western societies ranges from eighteen inches to about three feet. But the speaking distance is usually greater in Asia, many African countries, and in the Middle East when men talk to women.[26] The large speaking distance in Asia often gives the person of different cultural background an impression that Asians "keep strangers at arm's length." Obviously, the speaking distance in different countries can make a foreigner feel uncomfortable or unwelcome. It is essential to know the variations and the appropriate speaking distance.

Colors

Why does the Dutch beer Heineken sell so well in the southern part of Nigeria? Why are Chinese restaurants throughout the world decorated in bright red and yellow colors? To answer these questions, one has to understand the meanings of colors valued by a particular culture. The popularity of Heineken in southern Nigeria is due to the green can—the color green is the symbol of life in Nigeria. The red and yellow colors found in Chinese restaurants are associated with good luck, fortune, and wealth in Chinese culture. Colors preferred or avoided by a culture are important for international hospitality managers to know because hotels and restaurants use different colors for interior decorations. Colors preferred by one culture may be avoided by another. For example, black is associated with death in Western societies, but in some parts of Asia, white is associated with death, and purple is associated with death in Latin America.[27] These perceptions are deeply ingrained in each society's cultural value system. The Chinese perception of colors, for instance, is part of their ancient cosmic view of the world. The primary colors are integrated into Chinese cosmology, associated with yin and yang, the cardinal directions, the four seasons, and the emotions. Examining the association of red with joy, and yellow with the geographic center (center of the universe, the color of imperial power), one would easily understand why red and yellow are favored in the Chinese culture. These colors indicate prosperity and happiness.

Numbers

Some societies also feel that certain numbers are lucky and others are unlucky. In Chinese culture, the number eight is frequently used in business (phone number, street number, vehicle license plate, etc.) since it sounds like the word for fortune in Cantonese. The Hong Kong government has raised more than $40 million from regular auctions of the lucky numbers to companies and individuals since 1973.

The number four is avoided in Japan, since it sounds similar to the word for death. In Japanese hotels, no guest room is number four. One hotel even turns the entire fourth floor into a Japanese garden. An international hotel manager needs to be aware of such cultural preference for or avoidance of certain numbers. Proper training in room assignment for the front desk staff can make the guests happy if they are given the lucky room number.

CULTURAL GENERALIZATION

Cultural differences exist throughout the world. But many attributes shared by certain countries can be generalized as a cultural guide for international hospitality managers. Cultural generalization identifies the similarities and differences of different countries. The division of world cultures into high-context and low-context cultures by Hall is primarily based on cultural communications.[28] Examples of the high-context countries include Spain, Greece, Saudi Arabia, Vietnam, Korea, and China. High-context cultures emphasize human interaction and unwritten, casual, and nonverbal communication. Cultural meanings are communicated implicitly among members of the society. The high-context culture implies heavily interpersonal communication orientation, emphasizing kinship and friendship rather than legal documents. Individuals feel deep personal involvement with each other, and relations are relatively long lasting. People in authority are personally responsible for the actions of subordinates, and a premium is placed on loyalty between superiors and subordinates. Insiders and outsiders are clearly distinguished. Cultural patterns are deeply ingrained and slow to change in high-context societies.

The low-context cultures emphasize explicit communication, and ambiguity is avoided in management. Relationships between individuals are relatively shorter, and greater social and job mobility is normal. Members of a low-context society depend less on nonverbal communication cues. Agreements tend to be written rather than spoken. Contracts are regarded as final and legally binding. Insiders and outsiders are less closely distinguished. Foreigners find it relatively easier to adjust in low-context countries. Cultural patterns change quickly. Examples of low-context cultures include Germany, Switzerland, Norway, the United States, and Great Britain.

LEARNING CULTURE

Culture is rich and diverse. Different cultures make our world colorful and meaningful, and stimulate people's desire to travel. However, global hospitality managers face great challenges for managing operations in different cultures. An effective manager needs to have a good knowledge of the host culture and its influence on the behaviors of the local employees and guests. Knowledge of other cultures can be accumulated through learning, as culture is learned. Culture learning generally involves two major processes: cultural awareness and cultural adaptation.

Cultural awareness, the initial stage of culture learning, involves acknowledging and learning about the differences among cultures. Provincialism and stereotypes are often the two major obstacles to cultural learning, since we often view other cultures with our own cultural spectacles. Such provincialism can blur our vision of the differences between cultures, and cause us to stereotype other cultures and criticize the different ways of doing things. This provincialism must be corrected first by realizing that there are cultural differences in the world. Once we realize the differences among cultures, we can study them more objectively and effectively, and we can appreciate them genuinely. Thus, cultural awareness leads to effective cultural learning.

The next process is cultural adaptation in the host countries. Cultural adaptation is about the efforts one makes to behave like local people, just as the proverb says: "When in Rome, do as the Romans do." There is no universal standard for the extent to which you should adjust to the local ways of doing things. It depends on your personality, comfort level with the foreign culture, or management needs. But, one thing is clear—cultural adaptation requires determination and effort, because your own cultural habits have been changed to fit the local ways of life and business practices. We realize that we just cannot behave totally like the local people, since we were not born and raised in that culture. However, making an effort to learn local cultures and interact with local people will be appreciated by the local managers, staff, and guests, particularly in high-context societies, where people place a large emphasis on interpersonal interactions. You can thus win their trust and support.

SUMMARY

- Culture includes the learned patterns of behavior commonly shared by the members of a given society. The various aspects of a culture are interrelated, and culture defines the boundaries of different groups.
- Cultural values are the beliefs that a society holds in regard to right and wrong, good and bad, and ethical or unethical. Cultural norms are the social rules and guidelines that prescribe appropriate behaviors in particular situations.
- Cultural values have a strong influence on international hospitality management and services. Awareness and knowledge of cultural differences enables international hospitality managers to adjust effectively to the local management practice and develop successful operations.
- People in different countries are grouped into various categories. Grouping by birth is defined as ascribed group membership, and grouping by affiliation is known as acquired group membership.

- A society's attitude toward individualism and collectivism is clearly reflected in the way in which people perceive themselves and relate to one another in social and business settings. The studies by Hofstede and Trompenaars reveal the attitudes toward individualism and collectivism in different cultures.
- Cultural values differ among countries in peoples' perceptions of superior and subordinate relationships, mobility and loyalty, and work and play issues.
- Effective communication between management and staff is essential to successful international hospitality operations. Knowledge of both the spoken and written language of the host country can enhance the effectiveness of a manager's operations.
- Cultural meanings can be transmitted through nonverbal and non-written forms, known as the silent language. The silent language includes body language and the cultural perceptions of time, personal space, colors, and numbers.
- Many cultural attributes shared by certain countries can be generalized. The division of world cultures into high-context societies and low-context societies is primarily based on cultural communication styles.
- Cultural learning is normally involved in two processes: cultural awareness and cultural adaptation. Cultural awareness is acknowledging and learning about the differences among cultures. Cultural adaptation is about the efforts one makes to behave like a local person.

STUDY QUESTIONS

1. What is culture?
2. Can you explain the four distinctive characteristics of culture with your own examples?
3. How are cultural values and norms defined?
4. What are ascribed group memberships and acquired group memberships?
5. What are the differences in cultural perceptions of age, gender, and kinship between the American culture and the Latin American culture, and between the American culture and the Japanese culture?
6. Based on Hofstede's individualism and collectivism dimension, compare and contrast the countries that emphasize individualism with the countries that emphasize collectivism.

7. Can you identify the management styles in different cultures by examining their superior and subordinate relationships in the workplace?
8. Can you explain why people in individualism-oriented countries tend to have high employment mobility while people in collectivism-oriented countries tend to have low mobility?
9. How are work and play viewed in different countries?
10. Why do we say language is the mirror of the culture?
11. Why are the spoken and written languages essential to successful hospitality operations in foreign countries?
12. What is the silent language? What aspects does it include?
13. Can you describe the differences in eye contact in the United States, Mexico, and Japan?
14. Why is touching such a sensitive issue when dealing with people from different cultures?
15. People in some cultures tend to have controlled facial expressions. Can you name some of these countries?
16. What are the monochronic and polychronic time concepts? In what countries can you find these time concepts practiced?
17. Can you describe the different use of personal space in Latin America, Western Europe, the United States, and Asia?
18. Why are colors so important to product marketing in different countries?
19. Why is the number four avoided in the Japanese culture?
20. What are the high-context and low-context cultures? Which countries have high-context cultures and which have low-context cultures?
21. What are the two major processes for culture learning?

CASE STUDY:
CULTURAL DIVERSITY AT NIKKO HOTELS INTERNATIONAL

Nikko Hotels International is a subsidiary of the Japan Airlines (JAL) Development Company, Ltd. It was created as JAL's diversification and globalization strategy to strengthen the company's marketing and financial position. Known for its aggressive global marketing and application of new technology in hotel operations, the company is determined to establish a worldwide network of hotels comparable in number to Hilton, Sheraton, and Inter-Continental. It had forty-four properties in its worldwide portfolio by 1997. Relating to the theme of this chapter, this case study focuses on the cultural diversity of Nikko's management team and the cultural adjustment made by Nikko's executives when they first entered the U.S. lodging market.

The decision to enter the U.S. hotel market was intended to establish Nikko's identity and reputation in the large and competitive U.S. travel market. But, Nikko's entry into the market presented some cultural challenges to the company, particularly the transfer of a corporate culture based on Japanese cultural values to a multicultural workplace in the United States.

The first hotel Nikko Hotels International acquired in the United States was the Essex House in New York City. The famous Essex House was to be a springboard for Nikko's future growth. Nikko's executives believed that if they could do well with the Essex House in the competitive New York market, they would do well in other markets in the United States. Nikko's strategy and management operations would be tested in this major world commercial city and adjusted to the competitive and changing requirements of the U.S. lodging market.

The Essex House was originally managed by Marriott Corporation. When Nikko took over the ownership and management, all on-site Marriott managers and staff were invited to stay with the new company. In response to Nikko's invitation, six managers decided to stay. These six managers consisted of a German general manager, a North American director of rooms, an Austrian director of food and beverage, an Irish director of human resources, a Lebanese chief engineer, and a North American director of marketing. A Japanese controller was later added to this executive management team, which represented a highly diversified cultural group of managers.

Because of the diverse group, the corporate office of Hotel Nikko (USA) Inc. decided to develop an executive team building program. With the assistance of several professors at Cornell University, Nikko Executive Team Development Program was formulated for executive leadership exercises and simulations. This program included an overview of the hotel development trends in the United States and a perspective on Japanese management. The end result of this four-day retreat was to create a Nikko Mission Statement.

The executive retreat was held in May 1985 in Ithaca, a city in upstate New York. The participants were divided into small working groups to discuss group leadership issues and the hotel's mission statement. The president of the company, Yasuyuki Miura, did not participate in the group work, which was natural for a Japanese company president. After the group sessions, the teams reconvened to present their discussion results. At this time,

Miura came to the presentations and commented on them in a manner that the non-Japanese executives found annoying.

The managers began to complain: "If you have already formed your own mission statement, don't waste our time and energy, just give it to us! We don't like being tested like students." "On the other hand, if you don't have one yet and would like to contribute, why didn't you join us from the start?"

Miura was shocked to hear these sharp criticisms from his subordinates. It took a few minutes before he could control himself. He then told the managers: "Okay, you guys go to the student pub and keep complaining and accusing me over as much as you can drink. It's on me. My poor Japanese executives will accompany you and listen to you patiently. Who knows, they may even agree with you. In the meantime, I will go to my room and do my homework like a good student. First thing tomorrow, I will tell you about my career, experience, management philosophy, and aspirations. If that is acceptable to you, let's begin again."

The managers drank happily that night, while Miura worked very hard. The next day, Miura began his speech to the executive team in a frank and humble manner. He described the global strategic development by JAL, and explained why Nikko had come to the United States. Then he shared with the executive team his twenty-seven-year experience with JAL, and concluded with an appeal for cooperation. After his speech, he joined the executive team as a working participant to develop the Nikko Mission Statement.

This executive retreat was a great experience for all the executives and managers since they all worked hard to find common ground. After heated discussions and sincere attempts to reach a consensus, the team formulated the Nikko Hotels Mission Statement in a most participatory manner. The statement reads:

> At Nikko Hotels, our guests always find:
>
> > dedicated employees,
> > attentive service,
> > quality facilities,
> > together in harmony.

Case Study Source

Yasuyuki Miura, "Success Strategy: Nikko Hotels International Smiles a Hearty Smile," In *World-Class Service*, eds. Germaine W. Shames and W. Gerald Glover (Yarmouth, ME: Intercultural Press, 1989), pp. 35–43.

Case Study Questions

1. Why did Japan Airlines Development Company decide to develop a hotel company in the mid-1980s?
2. Why did Nikko Hotels International choose the Essex House in New York City as its first property in the United States?
3. Can you describe the cultural diversity of the management team at the Essex House?
4. What was the purpose of the executive retreat?
5. When did Miura join the managers at the executive retreat?
6. How did he annoy the non-Japanese managers during their presentations?
7. Why was Miura shocked to hear complaints from his managers? What did he do after he regained control of himself?
8. What happened the next day?
9. What is the mission statement for Nikko Hotels?
10. Can you explain what cultural blunder Miura committed during the executive retreat and how he bridged the cultural gap and brought the team together?

Chapter 4

Political Systems

Political stability is an important factor in determining whether a country will be a good investment or not.[1]

Jeff Williams
Senior Vice President
International Development
Lodging Division of Cendant Corp.

LEARNING OBJECTIVES

In this chapter, you will study:

1. The democratic and authoritarian political systems
2. The four types of authoritarian political systems
3. International relations and their impact on international hospitality development and operations
4. National tourism policy
5. Business ethics in international hospitality operations
6. The impact of nationalism on international hospitality operations
7. Political risk assessment

INTRODUCTION

A country's economic and legal systems are to a great extent shaped by its political ideology. Its political system has a great influence over international business operations. Countries with different political systems have developed different economic systems, and enact different economic and financial policies to control and regulate international businesses. For instance, some governments may encourage foreign hotel developers to build hotels in their countries by offering attractive development incentives, or discourage foreign hotel investors by setting up some tough entry barriers. Furthermore, a country's political stability has a direct and significant impact on foreign hospitality operations. Hospitality investment and management risks are closely linked with the stability of a country's political system. Therefore, international hospitality corporations must examine and understand the nature of the different governments under various political systems before they expand hospitality operations into these countries.

This chapter therefore focuses on the political dimension of international hospitality operations. It identifies and discusses the different political systems in our rapidly changing political world. It examines the diverse political forces that have a direct influence on international hospitality operations. Knowledge of these political systems and forces can familiarize international hospitality managers with the different political processes, and assist them to navigate effectively within each political system.

DIFFERENCES IN POLITICAL SYSTEMS

Every country follows a particular political system. A political system is a set of institutions and activities that link together government, politics, and public policy.[2] It is a way of formulating and implementing public decisions that affect the general society.[3] It is this way of policy formulation and implementation that differentiates governments in different countries. Some governments believe that every citizen of the country should have the right to participate in policy making by electing public officials to represent them at the various political levels. In others, the formulation of public policies is controlled by dictators or a small group of people. The political systems of individual countries can be studied by examining the major institutions connected with the exercise of power and its management. The two major political systems, democratic and authoritarian governments, are further analyzed in this section.

Democratic Political System

Democracy is a political ideology that originated in ancient Greece. The word "democracy" originates from two Greek words: *demo* (the people) and *kratos* (power or authority).[4] Democracy therefore means government by the people. For a certain time in ancient Greece, democracy was practiced in Athens and some other city-states. Citizens came together to debate issues, pass the law, and the rulers were selected by lot.

Currently, democracy as a political ideology states that individual citizens should have the right to participate in public policy making, and enjoy wider political and social freedom in society. But since in modern times society has become too large to make its decisions by involving everybody in open meetings and debates, a few representatives carry on the affairs of the many. The relationship between the few leaders and the many followers is one of representation. The closer the correspondence between representatives and their electoral majority, the closer the approximation to democracy. This form of democracy is known as representative democracy. It is a means of selecting policy makers and of organizing government so that policy represents and responds to the people's preference. If selected policymakers fail to perform the job adequately, they can and will be removed from office by the people at the next election.

In democratic countries, citizens have greater freedom of expression, such as freedom of speech and the press. Each individual can freely and openly express his or her opinions. A free press can objectively present information to the public and check on the moral and professional conduct of the elected public officials. In this way, no one party or group can monopolize or distort information. A democratic society ensures the essential principle of one person, one vote. This equality in voting gives the citizens an equal opportunity to express their views, when they have different opinions concerning politics or political leaders.

Another distinctive characteristic of democracy is to practice majority rule and preserve minority rights. In a democratic society, choosing among alternatives means weighing the desires of the majority. In addition, pluralism is a cornerstone of the democratic society, in which different ideologies coexist, and groups compete with each other for control over public policy, with no single ideology or group dominating. Bargaining and compromise are essential elements of the democratic society.[5] Most Western developed countries have democratically elected governments. Twenty-one countries have been continually democratic since approximately the end of World War II (see Exhibit 4.1).

The differences among these democratic countries are reflected in the way their governments function. Two subcategories of democracy are identified to describe the variations: majoritarian democratic government and consensual democratic government.[6] The majoritarian democratic government is characterized as concentrating as much power as possible in the hands of the majority party, such as in New Zealand and the United Kingdom. The characteristic of consensual democratic government reflects the principle of sharing, dispersing, and limiting power in a variety of ways, such as in the United States, Canada, and Switzerland.[7]

EXHIBIT 4.1. Twenty-One Continuously Democratic Countries Since World War II

North America	Europe	Asia/Pacific
Canada	Austria	Australia
United States	Belgium	Israel
	Denmark	Japan
	Finland	New Zealand
	France	
	Iceland	
	Ireland	
	Italy	
	Luxembourg	
	Netherlands	
	Norway	
	Sweden	
	Switzerland	
	United Kingdom	
	West Germany	

However, the fundamental principle of democracy is strictly followed by these democratic countries. Government derives its power from its citizens, and citizens have wider political freedom. The political system of democratic countries is normally stable. For international business operations, market information is easier to come by, because the democratic governments regularly release demographic, social, and economic information about their countries. The vast amount of published data on the various aspects of the democratic countries can be utilized by international hospitality companies for market analysis and business decision making.

Authoritarian Political System

Of the approximately 187 independent countries that exist in the world today, the governments of more than 130 are considered nondemocratic.[8] These nondemocratic governments are traditionally defined as authoritarian governments. An authoritarian government or regime usually has the following five characteristics: (1) the presence of one leader or a small group that exercises power, (2) the power of the leaders or rulers is not clearly defined, (3) absent or low citizen participation in policymaking, (4) suppression of opposition, and (5) limited pluralism.[9]

In authoritarian societies, political power is monopolized by an individual, a group of individuals, or a single political party. Political leaders are not elected by all citizens. The power limit of the leaders and rulers is ill defined. The rules and procedures are intrinsic to authoritarian governments and regimes. Sometimes the words of a particular leader or ruler can be the country's law. There is little or no citizen participation in public policy making at all political levels. Citizens are deprived of the right to choose the candidates who can represent their political views. Some authoritarian governments may preselect the candidates for various political offices, and ask the citizens to vote as a token form of democracy. Authoritarian government does not recognize or allow opposition. Individuals and groups do not have the freedom of speech, press, and assembly. The press is strictly controlled by the government, and there is no free flow of information. It is hard to obtain objective and accurate information on population, society, and the economy in these countries.

Four principal forms of authoritarianism are identified on the basis of political ideology: communist, theocratic, military, and tribal. Communism is regarded as authoritarianism because it allows only one party to rule—the Communist Party. The Communist Party defines the guidelines of society's progress in every aspect. It does not permit any opposition to challenge its leadership of the country, and any attempt to do so will be dealt with by the ruling Communist Party.[10] Communism was the major threat to world democracy during the Cold War from 1945 to 1989. Since 1989, communism disintegrated throughout the former Soviet Union and Eastern Europe, and the Communist Party relinquished its vanguard role in this region. The notorious coercive intrusion of police and security agencies into citizens' lives was abolished. The collapse of the communist system in Eastern Europe demonstrated that single-party rule violated the basic democratic values: self-worth, truth, personal integrity, and justice. Today, only a few countries are run by communist authoritarian governments, such as China, Cuba, Laos, North Korea, and Vietnam.

Theocratic authoritarianism is government that follows strict religious beliefs and principles. This is seen in the Arab world, where the strict application of Islamic principles for governing a country is followed. Monarchy is not uncommon in the Middle East, and power is concentrated at the very top, such as in Bahrain and Saudi Arabia. In Saudi Arabia and Oman, there are no written constitutions; each country governs its affairs by Islamic doctrine. In Qatar, power is concentrated in the hands of the emir. No political parties exist in these Arab countries.[11] Clearly, political power is transferred through family lines, and ordinary citizens have no involvement in public policy decisions.

The third type of authoritarianism is military dictatorship. In this case, the supreme power of the government does not lie in the hands of civilian politicians, but is controlled by military officers. The road to power is not through election by citizens, but through military coup. Africa is now the continent with the highest incidence of military takeovers, and numerous military-dominated political systems.[12]

The fourth type of authoritarianism is described as tribal authoritarianism. Many ethnic and tribal groups coexist in some African countries. A political party that represents the interests of a particular tribe often controls political power in tribal authoritarian societies, such as in Kenya, Uganda, and Zimbabwe.[13] Power is highly concentrated in the hands of the ruling party that represents a particular tribe. Citizens have very limited freedom and involvement in the policymaking process.

International Business Implications

The differences in political systems present great complexity and difficulty to international hospitality corporations. In democratic countries, the political system is stable and public policies are predictable. Citizens have greater political freedom in speech, press, organization, and assembly. Individualism as a cultural trait, discussed in Chapter 3, is highly valued in democratic countries. Information on many aspects of the country is easily obtainable, since the government compiles and publishes economic and demographic data regularly.

Doing business in authoritarian countries is comparatively difficult. Some authoritarian governments have very strict policies on foreign investment, and the policies regulating international business are subject to constant change. Due to constant power struggles in some authoritarian countries, frequent changes of government are not uncommon. As a result, the policies on international business change constantly. Market information is very hard to come by, since many authoritarian governments do not allow free speech and press in their countries. International hospitality companies face greater political risk in the authoritarian countries.

Transition to Democracy

Democracy as a form of government has become widespread in the world in the past decade. A trend toward democratization is evident in most world regions. As discussed earlier, new democracies have emerged in Russia and the Eastern European countries. A long-standing dictatorship was ended by nonviolent popular movement in the Philippines. Civil war in Nicaragua ended with internationally supervised democratic elections. The most remarkable achievements have been made in most of Latin America, where military authoritarian governments were replaced with democratically elected civilian governments. During the 1980s, competitive electoral politics made a major comeback in Latin America. Throughout the region, elections became the principal avenue to gain political office.

In this region, Costa Rica, Venezuela, and Colombia have practiced uninterrupted political competition for several decades. In others, such as Uruguay and Chile, democratic elections represented a recovery of relatively long-standing democratic institutions and practice. In still others, such as Argentina, Bolivia, Brazil, Ecuador, Mexico, Paraguay, and Peru, the increasingly open nature of electoral contest brought new opportunities for building democratic institutions.[14] The reassertion of electoral politics as the legitimate way to achieve political office demonstrated the trend to democratization in the entire region.

This trend has drawn great interest and attention from international hospitality corporations and potential hospitality developers for future development in the region. This region will experience dramatic hospitality development with democratic governments and stable political systems. Countries such as Argentina, Brazil, and Chile have already attracted many international hospitality corporations to develop commercial hotels in the major cities and ski resorts in the mountain regions.[15] As an emerging destination, this region presents great opportunities for future hospitality development (see Exhibit 4.2).

INTERNATIONAL RELATIONS AMONG NATIONAL GOVERNMENTS

International relations refer to the relations among national governments. Since different countries follow different political ideologies and systems, these differences, democratic or authoritarian, influence the relations among national governments. Countries that share similar political principles tend to have closer relations. Countries that have different systems tend to keep a certain distance in their political relations.

International relations between two countries are established through the official normalization of political relations and by opening diplomatic embassies reciprocally in both countries. Once diplomatic ties are established, each government can permit its citizens to travel and to conduct business in the host country. For instance, the normalization of relations between the United States and Vietnam in 1995 officially ended the hostility that had existed since the start of the Vietnam War in the 1960s. Vietnam is now considered a potential market for international hospitality development.[16] The establishment of normal relations between the United

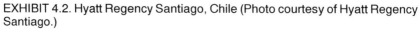

EXHIBIT 4.2. Hyatt Regency Santiago, Chile (Photo courtesy of Hyatt Regency Santiago.)

States and Vietnam paved the way for U.S. hospitality companies to conduct business there.

Established international relations between governments can also deteriorate for various political reasons. For example, the U.S. government responded to the way the Chinese government handled the student demonstration for democracy in Tiananmen Square in June 1989 by suspending high-level government contact and stopping the sales of high-technology equipment to China for eight years. At present, the United States has no normal relations with Cuba, North Korea, Iran, and Iraq. No direct business contact is permitted between U.S. companies and companies in these countries.

The U.S. government restrictions for doing business with Cuba can be traced back to the late 1950s, when Fidel Castro's communist government took over the country. A trade embargo was imposed on Cuba by the U.S. government then, and a new trade sanction was signed into law by President Clinton in 1996 after Cuba's military jets shot down two U.S. civilian airplanes. Therefore, there has been no direct contact between the two governments, and commercial business contact was strictly prohibited.

In recent years, to save its deteriorating economy, the Cuban government sought foreign investment to develop its hospitality industry, and attempted to regain its position as a tourist destination in the Caribbean region. In 1996, Cuba received 1.1 million foreign visitors, up from 810,000 in 1995. Tourist receipts reached $1.3 billion in 1996. With the expected increase in international tourist arrivals, only one-third of Cuba's 36,000 hotel rooms meet Western standards. In 1996, 5,000 new hotel rooms were built, and 5,000 new rooms are planned to be built per year until 2000.[17]

Many Western hotel companies are now developing and managing hotels in Cuba. The Paris-based Accor signed a contract to operate six existing hotels and construct another 1,300 guest rooms at a resort on the northern coast.[18] Recently, Canadians have been taking advantage of the fact that U.S. companies are prohibited from developing hospitality business in Cuba. Canadian hotel corporations have initiated several development projects in Cuba, since Cuba's tropical climate draws 140,000 Canadian tourists annually. Two Canadian hotel companies, Delta (acquired by Canadian Pacific Hotels in 1998) and Commonwealth, operate joint ventures with Cubanacan, one of the five state-owned tourism development companies in Cuba.[19] Currently, Delta operates nine properties in Cuba, and Commonwealth operates three, with new properties under construction (see Exhibit 4.3). Other European hotel companies are also aggressively developing and managing hotels in Cuba, such as Sol Melia of Spain, Golden Tulip of the Netherlands, and LTI and RIU of Germany.

Watching competitors' aggressive development in Cuba, the largest island in the Caribbean, the U.S. hospitality industry could only express its concern at being left out of the Cuban market, and hope the political relations could change soon, as they did between the United States and Vietnam. Clearly, the Cuban case demonstrates that international hospitality development is determined by international policies and relations. However, restrictions can come and go depending on the political relations of the two countries. Global managers need to keep abreast of the changing political relations in the world.

NATIONAL TOURISM POLICY

Many national governments, democratic or authoritarian, are actively involved in regulating and facilitating tourism and hospitality development. It is recognized that tourism and hospitality development has a major impact on international relations and foreign policy. Tourism can be

EXHIBIT 4.3. Delta Las Brisas Club Resort in Cuba (Photo courtesy of Delta Hotels and Resorts.)

used as a political tool for improving political relations between countries. For example, the Japanese government launched the "ten million campaign" in the 1980s to encourage more Japanese to visit the United States and Western European countries. The purpose of this travel campaign was to reduce the huge trade surplus Japan had in merchandise trade with those countries, in an attempt to defuse the harsh criticism from governments in the West. Tourism development is even recommended as a vehicle for unifying politically conflicting countries, such as South and North Korea,[20] and for improving relations between politically divided China and Taiwan.[21]

In many authoritarian countries, tourism promotion is intended to gain international media publicity and showcase economic and social achievements, or to defuse international criticism on certain political issues, such as human rights, dictatorship, and suppression of free press. International tourism can also be used as a political weapon by one country against another.

The political dimension of international tourism involves national governments in national tourism policy development. As international tourism development is embraced by most countries in the world as a significant part of their national economic development, national governments play major roles in planning, promoting, facilitating, and coordinating tourism and hospitality development and even operating facilities. Most countries have instituted national tourism administrations, which are vested with the responsibility of planning, regulating, and promoting the country's tourism and hospitality development.

National Tourism Development Plan

Many countries have formulated long-term tourism development plans, which are integrated into the country's overall national economic development plan. It is essential for any international hospitality corporation to review such development plans before they start expansion plans, because each country's tourism development plan may emphasize the development priority in certain geographic locations and restrict hotel development in other areas. For instance, the government of Egypt formulated a policy of diversifying tourist attractions and hotels in 1982 as a part of the country's first Five-Year Plan. This plan responded to development pressure on the historical sites along the Nile Valley, and called for geographical dispersion of hospitality development in other parts of the country. This policy of development diversification identified the sunny climate and splendid coastlines of the Mediterranean, the Red Sea area, and the Sinai Peninsula as new development zones. The Red Sea area has been a popular tourist destination for Arabs and young Europeans, and now attracts many international hotel companies for new development.[22] It is estimated that the Red Sea development zones, including Hurghada, Sahel Hasheesh, Ras Aub Some, and Safaga, need 9,000 additional hotel rooms for future development. Hilton International built a 200-room Hurghada Hilton in 1994, and has two more properties under construction in the Red Sea area.[23] A government tourism development plan can thus promote hospitality development in certain areas of the country, and control the development growth in other areas.

Tourism Legislation and Regulation

A national government is also involved in regulating international tourism and hospitality development in its country. However, the degree of involvement in tourism legislation and regulation differs between the democratic and authoritarian governments. Generally speaking, democratic governments are more concerned with the macro-level development policies, such as providing research data for the industry and coordinating the marketing and promotion activities of various segments of the industry. Authoritarian governments tend to be involved in both macro- and micro-level development policies and regulations. In addition to formulating development plans and coordinating marketing promotion for the country, some governments are also engaged in setting up operational standards for hotels and controlling prices. For example, the Mexican government has an agreement with the lodging industry for controlling room rates. The government has the right to restrain the lodging industry's prices in order to sustain the stability and economic growth of the lodging industry. In China, professional standards and qualifications for the various professions in the hospitality industry are determined by the government, such as certifying tour guides and rating hotels; in the United States, these responsibilities are handled by the industry professional associations and organizations, such as the American Hotel & Motel Association (AH&MA).

Government Entrepreneurial Ventures

Some national governments are even engaged in entrepreneurial ventures by owning and operating hospitality business. This is most common in the authoritarian countries, and is determined by the economic system of the country (Chapter 5 will discuss different world economic systems). In democratic countries where capitalism is practiced, government functions and private business operations are always separated. Governments at the various levels do not operate commercial lodging and food service businesses. However, this is not the case in many authoritarian countries, particularly the communist countries, where the government owns almost everything. This can present challenges to private foreign operations, since they have to compete with the local governments. This is why forming a partnership between a private foreign company and the local government is very popular in some authoritarian countries, such as the partnership between Canadian McDonald's Corporation and the City of Moscow for establishing a Moscow McDonald's restaurant, when Moscow was under communist rule in the 1980s.

Tourism Promotion

Another major function of the national government is to promote international travel to its country. Overseas promotion offices are established in key originating countries, and millions of dollars are spent in advertising to attract foreign tourists (see Exhibit 4.4). Overseas promotion by national

EXHIBIT 4.4. Top Tourism Promotion Countries (in thousands of US$)

Rank	Country	1994	1995	% Change
1	Australia	75,811	87,949	16
2	United Kingdom	77,885	78,710	1
3	Spain	77,457	78,647	2
4	France	62,729	72,928	16
5	Singapore	49,695	53,595	8
6	Thailand	42,907	51,198	19
7	Netherlands	43,800	49,700	14
8	Austria	45,694	47,254	3
9	Ireland	41,830	37,911	− 10
10	Portugal	34,904	37,271	7

Source: Adapted from Enco Paci, "Making Promotion More Effective," *WTO News* (March 1997), 10-11.

tourism offices can benefit private hospitality operations in the country. Sometimes the private business sector participates in overseas promotion campaigns sponsored by the national tourism administration to market their specific products and services in targeted foreign destination countries.

Infrastructure Development

Governments at various levels are normally responsible for infrastructure development in their jurisdictions, such as airports, seaports, public roads, railroads, and so on. These facilities are essential to enticing and facilitating hospitality development in a particular country. In 1969, a famous U.S. labor lawyer from New York, Theodore W. Kheel, along with some other investors, bought 15,000 acres of beachfront land in the Dominican Republic. They intended to build a beach resort there. However, there was no road access, and they could not build anything. Without the road infrastructure, the land was worthless. It was not until the Dominican Republic's government built a road to their property many years later that they started building a resort for international tourists. Since then, the resort has been very successful under Club Med's management.[24] Infrastructure development for tourism and hospitality operations will be fully discussed in Chapter 7.

Environmental Concerns

National and local governments are actively engaged in evaluating the environmental impact of hotel development. This aspect will be further discussed in Chapter 7 as an important international hospitality development issue. Government agencies also provide the following services to ensure the safety of international tourists: police protection, crime control, public health, and sanitary conditions in the destination countries.

National Tourism Agreement

Many countries have fostered international tourism policies through international representatives and bilateral negotiations with other countries. Tourism agreements are negotiated between countries as diplomatic arrangements prescribing reciprocal measures to reduce travel and hospitality development restrictions, and to establish the status of the two countries' official tourism promotion offices, such as encouraging international understanding, friendly relations, and goodwill.[25] In the tourism agreement between the United States and Venezuela, Item 5 in Article 3 clearly states that the two governments, through their competent authorities and other organizations, shall endeavor to develop new opportunities for commerce in tourism-related projects and for joint ventures in the establishment of tourism facilities and infrastructure. This item stipulates specifically the development for tourism facilities and infrastructure through competent authorities and organizations in the two countries.

POLITICS AND BUSINESS ETHICS

The different political ideologies followed by different countries give rise to various and complex ethical issues facing international hospitality operations. One of the major issues confronting companies from democratic countries is whether they should develop business in authoritarian countries that suppress their citizens' right to political freedom. Many view the development of business in an authoritarian country as economic support for repressive governments. For example, there has been strong opposition from Vietnam Veteran groups and M.I.A. (Missing in Action) organizations to U.S. corporations doing business in Vietnam.

However, many others contend that stopping business with authoritarian countries can only isolate those countries from the world economic community. The more isolated the authoritarian regimes are, the less flexible they are about political changes. Those who advocate doing business with such regimes view political freedom and economic development as positively correlated. They suggest that political change takes place when a country's economy and education are improved. Doing business with authoritarian countries can accelerate political changes from within.[26]

Unless it is mandated by the government, such as prohibition against the United States doing business with Cuba, it is very difficult to establish an ethical standard in regard to what an international company should do. Each company must make its own judgment regarding the ethical implications of developing hospitality business in authoritarian countries on a case-by-case basis.

Another important ethical issue concerns corruption and bribery. Government officials in some authoritarian countries are corrupt, since the political power is highly concentrated in the hands of this small number of individuals. Government officials at the different levels often seek personal gain from their power of approving and granting business applications and licenses. Bribery is a major ethical dilemma facing companies from Western democracies.

Bribery refers to payments in cash or gifts to induce local government officials to give favors to a foreign company. Business favors may include securing an ideal piece of government-owned beachfront land for hotel development, obtaining a management contract for a government-owned hotel, and receiving more tour groups organized by government-operated travel agencies. In addition to bribery, there is also extortion, which is payments made to local officials to keep them from harming the foreign company in some way, such as cutting off certain material supplies for hotel and restaurant operations. Two shocking bribery scandals were exposed in East Asia in 1995. The former president of South Korea, Roh Tae Woo, was arrested on the charge of taking $369 million in bribes from business corporations during his term in office.[27] In China, the mayor of Beijing, Chen Xi-tong, was removed by the central government for corruption charges. These cases clearly illustrate that corruption runs very high in some governments.

Bribery is, to U.S. law and cultural values, illegal and morally repugnant. The Foreign Corrupt Practices Act of 1977 forbids questionable payments by U.S. companies to obtain business abroad. These types of laws do not exist in other countries. For instance, French and German firms can write off payments to governments that were necessary to obtain foreign business. Payoffs to government officials are simply part of the routine business practice in many authoritarian societies. Again, it is impossible to generalize because of the complexity of the issue. International hospitality managers must use their own moral judgment and make appropriate management decisions by following the local normal business practice.

NATIONALISM

Nationalism is an important aspect of the political dimension of international business operations. Nationalism is the loyalty of citizens to their country. It emphasizes the pride of citizens in their cultural heritage and provides a basis for cohesion of a nation.[28] Nationalism can keep the citizens of a country together at times of military and economic emergency. Nationalism is a potent factor in international business, particularly regarding foreign companies and products. The emotion of nationalism can run very high among citizens when they feel that their economic well-being is affected by foreign companies and operations, or their cultural traditions are eroded by foreign cultural values. The ills of a society are often blamed on foreign companies when conflicts rise.

The early development of Euro Disney is a good example for illustrating this point. When the development of Euro Disney was first announced in Paris, an outpouring of opposition and criticism came from the French press and the public. The criticism focused on the invasion of American popular culture into the French cultural tradition. One French press went so far as to describe the development of Euro Disney in Paris as a "cultural Chernobyl."[29] Obviously, the French people strongly resented the development of Euro Disney, and this nationalist sentiment greatly affected the poor attendance at the theme park in the initial years of operation.

Nationalism usually leads to government intervention in certain economic activities to protect national interests. Government protection can be reflected in the following measures:

- Limit control of local hotel and restaurant business by foreign companies. Foreign companies are only given a minority stake in joint ventures. Solely foreign-owned business is restricted.
- Support national companies through government subsidies, such as providing subsidies to assist national airlines in European countries.
- Impose a fee on citizens who leave the country. This can discourage citizens from traveling to foreign countries, and keep out foreign currency. Israel charges a $400 exit fee for every Israeli who leaves the country;
- Make every effort to stop foreign takeovers of local companies, which is the so-called "French solution"—to find a French company rather than a foreign one to take over a French company.[30]
- Offer tax breaks or development incentives to domestic companies.

Government protection of domestic businesses resulting from nationalism can create extremely difficult competition for international companies. Government protection policy can be found in both democratic and authoritarian countries. Japan and France are known for their strong government protection of domestic business.[31] The degree of government protection of domestic business varies among authoritarian countries.

POLITICAL RISK ASSESSMENT

International hospitality development, especially hotel and resort development, is capital intensive. A hotel company needs to invest millions of dollars to build a hotel in a foreign country. When dealing with such large investments, the hotel company or individual entrepreneur has to consider the political risks. What political events can potentially harm hospitality operations in the host country and cause the company or individual investors to lose their initial investment? These potential risks can be analyzed and identified by using appropriate methods.

Types of Political Risks

One major political risk is the instability of the host government. A stable government maintains itself in power, and its political policies are predictable and are not subject to sudden and radical changes.[32] International business can prosper in a foreign country, if the host government is stable and its political and economic policies are permanent. Generally, Western democratic countries have stable governments, even though the head of the state changes every few years. The political and economic policies will continue, and no adverse impact will hurt international business operations.

But, in authoritarian countries, government instability often threatens and even ruins international business operations. The instability of authoritarian government can be caused by civil war, internal turmoil, and military coups. These political events can suddenly disrupt international business operations and cause heavy business losses.

The outbreak of civil war has catastrophic effects on both domestic and international business operations. International tourists are highly sensitive to travel safety, and always avoid countries with military conflicts. Civil war results in the destruction of hospitality facilities and the end of tourist arrivals. Lebanon, Somalia, Zaire, Serbia, Bosnia, and Croatia are some of the countries that have suffered from civil wars and have been shunned by tourists in the most recent past.

Internal turmoil can be caused by labor dispute, such as a major strike, or by an authoritarian government's open suppression of its citizens or opposition groups, such as the Tiananmen Square incident in China in 1989 when international hotels in China suffered a plunge of 27 percent in room sales.

Most hotels had to shut down certain buildings or floors and lay off many employees due to the sharp drop in room sales. Most hotels incurred heavy losses that year. Internal turmoil caused by strikes, demonstrations, and suppression has a short-term effect on international hospitality operations.

A successful military coup can cause a change of government, usually from a civilian government to a military dictatorship. This change then affects the country's political and economic policies on international business. For instance, the former civilian government might be pro-foreign investment and favor international hospitality development. But the new government ruled by military officers may make a 180-degree reverse of the former policy by showing an anti-foreign investment mentality and enacting very harsh policy for foreign hospitality companies.

The change of government, either through civil war or military coup, can result in the expropriation of foreign business assets in the host country. Expropriation refers to the confiscation of foreign-owned assets by the host government due to the abrupt change of government and its policies. Expropriation has been quite rare in the last decade, although it happened to Hilton International in Cuba in 1960 when Fidel Castro took power.[33]

Regional political and military conflict is another major threat to international hospitality development and operations. The Arab-Israeli conflict in the Middle East and the Serbian-Muslim-Croat conflict in the Balkan region both had devastating impact on hospitality development in these areas. Some countries, though not the focus of the conflict, are still directly affected in their tourism and hospitality development, such as Jordan in the Middle East. Potential tourists perceive the whole region as dangerous, and avoid it as a possible tourist destination.

Terrorism poses a severe and random political risk to international hospitality operations in some regions. Some terrorist groups specifically attack international tourists and hotels as targets to achieve political purposes.[34] The hijacking of commercial airplanes and cruise ships and the killing of innocent tourists were not uncommon in the past decade. The Al-Jihad terrorist group in Egypt attacked and killed sixteen Greek tourists in front of a hotel in April 1996. Another Egyptian terrorist organization, the largest and most violent militant Islamic group, killed fifty-eight international tourists at the 4,000-year-old Temple of Hatshepsut in Luxor in late 1997.[35] The Sender Luminoso (Shining Path) terrorist group in Peru deliberately targeted hospitality activities and international tourists. Many international tourists were attacked, kidnapped, and killed by this terrorist group from the mid-1980s to the early 1990s.[36] Hotels became their specific targets. A hotel accommodating primarily European tourists in Huarez was attacked in July 1990, and a hotel security guard was injured. The managers of the luxury El Pueblo in Lima received death threats from the Shining Path.[37] Because of such senseless attacks by the Shining Path terrorists, the British Foreign Office issued a warning to British tour companies, and advised them to stop sending tours to Peru in 1990. The Peruvian government had to use special trains for transporting foreign tourists from Cuzco to Machu Picchu with guards on board.[38]

Even though terrorist attacks are usually random, their impact is devastating and generates negative publicity for the destination. It is necessary to know about the major terrorist groups operating in major tourist destination areas. Exhibit 4.5 shows the main terrorist groups that are active in tourist destination areas.

Assessing Political Risk

Political systems are both complex and dynamic. Political changes are difficult to anticipate. The uncertainty in a country's political system entails a risk for international hospitality operations. International companies must conduct some form of political risk assessment to manage their exposure to political risk. Two types of risk assessments are normally used for political stability analysis.

One method is to conduct qualitative expert opinion analysis. Expert opinion analysis refers to the analysis of a country's political stability by people who are very knowledgeable about that country. They can be government officials in charge of foreign affairs, diplomats and media correspondents, scholars who are specialists in studying that country, and businesspeople who have operations there. Their opinions, which may be subjective, can give a general indication of the political stability of the country.

The second method of political risk assessment is to use the quantitative country ranking systems developed by consulting and publishing firms. These ranking systems are based on certain criteria deemed important by the research agencies. The political criteria normally used include the type of government (democratic or authoritarian), the continuity of political policy, and government corruption. A widely used country risk rating is published periodically by *The Economist*. *The Economist* Intelligent Unit, a research unit of *The Economist*, assesses the political, economic, and financial risks of more than eighty non-Western democratic countries, and regularly publishes the twenty-five countries with the highest risk ratings in *The Economist*. This rating system can be used as a good reference for evaluating the political stability of a particular country with a non-Western democratic government.

EXHIBIT 4.5. Major Terrorist Groups Operating in Tourist Areas

Terrorist Group	Area of Operation
Al-Jihad	Egypt
American Battalion	Bolivia
Arab Organization of May 15	Middle East
Arab Revolutionary Cells	Middle East
Armed Forces for National Liberation (FALN)	Puerto Rico
Basque Fatherland and Liberty Movement (ETA)	Spain
Committee for Solidarity with Arab Political Prisoners (CSPPA)	Middle East, France
Cuncolta	Corsica
Action Directe (AD)	France
Egypt's Revolution	Egypt
ETA Militar	Spain
Herri Batasuna Political Party	Spain
Hizbollah	Middle East
Islamic Jihad	Near East
Japanese Red Army (JRA)	Japan
Lebanese Armed Revolutionary Factions	Middle East
Liberation Tigers of Tamil Eelam (LTTE)	Sri Lanka
Manuel Rodriquez Patriotic Front (FPMR)	Chile
November 17	Greece
Red Army Faction (RAF)	Germany
Sendero Luminoso (Shining Path)	Peru
Sikh Terrorists	India, Pakistan
The People's Command	Bolivia
Terra Lliure (Free Land)	Spain

Source: Chris Ryan, "Tourism, Terrorism and Violence: The Risk of Wider World Travel," *RISCT* (September, 1991), 1-30. Used with permission from the Research Institute for the Study of Conflict and Terrorism, London.

A recent revealing study, published by the National Restaurant Association in early 1997, reported political risk analysis conducted by U.S.-based food service companies for global expansion decisions. Of the firms surveyed, more than two-thirds reported conducting in-house political risk analysis and one-third also used published ratings that were produced by specialized risk-assessment firms. Thirteen percent hired the consultants to perform political risk analysis.[39] Clearly, political risk analysis is a necessary study for making global expansion decisions.

Political Risk Insurance

The exposure to political risk in a foreign country can be insured in most Western developed countries. The Overseas Private Investment Corporation (OPIC) in the United States provides political risk insurance for new investment in friendly developing countries. Insurance covers a portion of the losses as a result of specific risks, such as expropriation by a foreign government. It also covers damages caused by war and terrorist attack. Another U.S. organization, the Foreign Credit Insurance Association (FCIA), also provides coverage for international companies to minimize losses caused by war and revolution. However, political risk insurance usually covers only the loss of a company's assets, not the loss of revenue resulting from expropriation.[40]

SUMMARY

- The political system is a set of institutions and activities that link together government, politics, and public policy. It is a way of formulating and implementing public decisions that affect the general society. It has a direct influence on international hospitality operations.
- Democracy as political ideology believes that individual citizens should have the right to participate in public policy making and enjoy wider political and social freedom in society. The two forms of democracy are majoritarian democracy and consensual democracy.
- An authoritarian political system is characterized by the presence of one leader or a small group that controls political power, poorly defined power of the leaders or rulers, absent or low citizen participation in policy making, suppression of opposition, and limited pluralism. Four types of authoritarian governments exist: communist, theocratic, military dictatorship, and tribal authoritarianism.
- Comparatively speaking, democratic governments do not interfere with private business operations, whereas authoritarian governments have tighter control over international business operations in their countries.
- Over the past decade, democracy has become more widespread as a form of government. Democratization occurred in Eastern Europe, Central and South America, and Asia.
- As countries adhere to certain forms of political systems, the relationships between countries are built on similar beliefs and political ideologies.

- National governments play an important role in their countries' international tourism and hospitality development. National governments' major responsibilities include: developing a national tourism plan, tourism development legislation and regulation, entrepreneurial activities by some governments, tourism promotion, infrastructural development, environmental regulations, and enacting national tourism agreements with other countries.
- The different political ideologies followed by different countries give rise to various and complex ethical issues facing international hospitality operations. Bribery and extortion are common in many authoritarian countries. Hospitality companies must make their own judgment on the ethical implications of developing business in authoritarian countries on a case-by-case basis.
- Nationalism is an important political dimension of international business operations, particularly regarding foreign companies and products. Nationalism can lead to government intervention in certain economic activities to protect national interests.
- As a capital-intensive investment, hospitality developers have to carefully evaluate the political risks of investing in a foreign country. Political risks include civil wars, internal political turmoil, military coups, the sudden change of a national government, the change of a country's economic policy, regional political and military conflicts, and terrorist activities.
- Political risks can be assessed by both qualitative expert opinion analysis, and the quantitative country risk rating method. Food service firms in the United States conducted political risk assessment for global expansion decisions. Exposure to political risk in a foreign country can be insured in most Western developed countries.

STUDY QUESTIONS

1. How is the political system defined?
2. What is the origin of the word "democracy"?
3. What are the distinctive characteristics of democracy?
4. Can you differentiate between majoritarian democracy and consensual democracy?
5. What are the five major characteristics of an authoritarian government?
6. Discuss the four major types of authoritarianism in the world.
7. What impact does the political system have on international hospitality operations in foreign countries?

8. What political system is now prevalent in Latin America and Eastern Europe?
9. Why are international relations important to the development of international hospitality business?
10. Can you describe the current international hospitality development in Cuba?
11. What are the major roles that a national government plays in developing international hospitality business?
12. How is tourism used as a political tool for improving political relations between countries or as a political weapon by one country against the other?
13. Why did the Egyptian government promote hospitality development along its Red Sea coast as a part of the country's first Five-Year Plan?
14. What are the differences in the degree of involvement in tourism legislation and regulation between the democratic and the authoritarian governments?
15. Under what political system does a national government often own and operate hospitality businesses?
16. What development problems did Kheel encounter when he first purchased beachfront land for developing a resort in the Dominican Republic?
17. What are the two different views regarding developing hospitality business in authoritarian countries that suppress their citizens' right to political freedom?
18. How are bribery and extortion defined? How can a hospitality manager deal with these issues in international hospitality operations?
19. How is nationalism defined? What political implications can nationalism have for international hospitality operations?
20. What will a national government normally do when the sentiment of nationalism is very strong toward foreign development and products?
21. Can you identify the various types of political risks?
22. What factors can trigger internal turmoil and disrupt normal hospitality business operations?
23. Why do certain terrorist groups specifically target international tourists and hospitality facilities?
24. How can you assess the political risks in a foreign country?
25. What does political risk insurance cover for assets and operations in a foreign country?

CASE STUDY: SONESTA INTERNATIONAL HOTELS— RESPONDING TO A CRISIS

Rob McCarthy, general manager of the newly opened Sonesta St. George Hotel in Luxor, quickly found out about a terrorist attack near his hotel. Shortly after the attack began, word came to him that there was an "incident" by the ancient monuments of Egypt's pharaohs. McCarthy walked out onto his office balcony overlooking the Nile and could hear the machine guns still roaring in the distance. It was November 17, 1997, when "a band of terrorists emerged from the ancient ruins along the Nile and slaughtered sixty-five people, most of them foreign tourists."

Although an international crisis of this magnitude is not routine, hotel companies are often confronted with events that can turn into public-relations nightmares—decreasing sales, destroying a positive public image, and ruining individual careers. Whether a crisis centers on a particular property or an entire area, it must still be addressed actively by a hotel company. This case outlines the events and subsequent actions taken by Sonesta in response to the human, public relations, and financial elements of the catastrophic event at Luxor.

Sonesta, which began operating decades ago as Hotel Corporation of America, currently owns two properties (in Cambridge, Massachusetts, and Anguilla) and manages sixteen others worldwide. The company's presence in Egypt is particularly strong. Sonesta opened its first Egyptian property in Cairo in 1998, and now runs six hotels and two cruise ships on the Nile. Although one-third of the company's hotels are in Egypt, Sonesta is not financially structured to be one-third dependent on Egypt because of fee structures and management contracts. Sonesta St. George was built by a local owner with a total investment of US$25 million. It opened in October 1997, just six weeks before the massacre.

The massacre outside the Temple of Hatshepsut in Luxor was not the first bloodshed in Egypt in recent years. Islamic militants have been waging a campaign to oust President Hosni Mubarak's secular government and replace it with strict Muslim rule. The militants have been carrying out terrorist attacks since 1992, but until November 1997 the majority of the attacks have been directed toward Coptic Christians and police, primarily in southern Egypt. Before the November massacre, over 1,100 lives had been lost in this conflict, among them thirty tourists. In September 1997 ten people, mainly German tourists, were killed when their bus was fire-bombed outside Cairo's Egyptian museum. Since tourism is the major foreign currency earner in Egypt, the militants have purposely selected international tourists as their target in an attempt to cripple Egypt's economy and force the government to yield to their demands.

The crisis of November 17, 1997, affected thousands of people worldwide. Fifty-eight foreign tourists, along with several policemen and terrorists, were killed that morning. Their families and friends are affected, as are the thousands of Egyptian citizens who rely on tourism for economic survival. The massacre also "killed" the business of international companies that depend on Egyptian tourism. The following discussion outlines three components that Sonesta had to consider when responding to this tragic crisis.

As reports of the attack came to McCarthy, he learned that twenty-three of the fifty-eight tourists killed were customers of the Sonesta, mostly members of a Swiss tour group that had been staying at the hotel for several days. That morning twenty-five members of the group and the tour operator went to the Temple of Hatshepsut at Luxor. Only three came back.

Facing an international crisis of this magnitude, Sonesta corporate office, regional office, and hotel management took effective actions to manage the crisis by focusing on the human, public-relations, and financial elements of the catastrophic event. The first crisis element was the human aspect concerning the tragic loss of guest lives, the surviving tourists, and the distressed hotel staff since many had become friendly with the tourists. The management identified three constituencies that required immediate attention: current guests, employees, and prospective customers. The emergency management team was immediately assembled. Rob McCarthy, an American expatriate general manager, made sure the three remaining Swiss tourists were settled—with access to any necessary medical attention, phone lines to call home, and any other requirements. He also assigned hotel staff members to stay with the tourists to reassure them and keep them as comfortable as possible. Then the emergency team coordinated with the American and Swiss embassies to get international tourists out of the country. The next day officials representing governments around the world sent planes to Luxor to evacuate their citizens. The hotel suddenly became empty, from 130 rooms occupied the previous day to only fifteen rooms occupied.

The regional vice president came to the property the next day to meet with the hotel staff. Two hundred fifty of the original 300 employees were able to keep their jobs. That was particularly important for the local employees since there is no welfare or unemployment system in Egypt. Even though there was little business to keep the hotel going, the owner and the management chose to support the employees. Employees were also offered counseling to cope with the terrible event.

The emergency management team also immediately contacted prospective customers who had already made reservations with the hotel. The company issued an Egypt-wide policy that all booking deposits would be returned—no questions asked. Customers were immediately notified to contact their travel agencies for cancellations and deposit refunds. All tour operators who had business with the hotel were very pleased with the way the hotel handled the cancellations and refunds.

The second part of the crisis was the public-relations element. The terrorist attack was reported worldwide, and thus created negative publicity for hotel operations in Luxor. McCarthy maintained close contact with the Sonesta corporate office, and a press release was issued by the corporate office to the media on the afternoon of the attack. Sonesta also implemented the crisis communication response plan, which detailed the steps to be taken in the first few hours after the crisis occurred. The essence of the plan was to communicate constantly and effectively with all constituencies.

The third part of the crisis was the financial element. The terrorist attack had a devastating impact on the Egyptian tourism industry. Hotel occupancy at the Sonesta St. George plunged from 40 percent to 8 percent after the attack. The hotel owner was losing considerable money because he kept the bulk of his employees when there was little business. Therefore, Sonesta had to implement a financial response for both Sonesta St. George and the region. For the property, Sonesta reconfirmed its commitment to the owner, because the owner was quite concerned that Sonesta might cancel the management contract. Instead, Sonesta forgave certain fees and deferred the remaining fees until business recovered. All advertising for the hotel was stopped for the short term. One month after the attack, Rob McCarthy returned to the United States for reasons of personal security and financial concern because it was costly to keep an expatriate manager at an overseas property when it did not make money. To deal with the loss of revenues from Egypt, in which Sonesta has considerable exposure, Sonesta reorganized its central office, laid off some corporate employees, reduced corporate training, and trimmed trips to the Egyptian properties from the corporate office.

This case demonstrates that hotel operations are vulnerable to political instability and random terrorist attacks. When a crisis occurs, corporate office, regional office, and hotel management all need to manage the crisis properly. Sonesta offers global hotel managers the following three suggestions for handling political crisis. First of all, management must keep a balanced perspective of the public relations aspect of the disaster. No one should blow the situation out of proportion or underestimate it. Second, management should focus on return to normalcy. When dealing with a crisis, the company should try whenever possible not to obstruct daily business operations, destroy the hotel's public image, or negatively affect the hotel's bottom line. Finally, the hotel company needs to develop a clear crisis plan that is simple to implement and it needs to ensure that managers and key staff members are trained for carrying out the plan effectively, particularly in countries with unstable political systems.

Case Study Source

Excerpts from Michael Oshins and Jacqueline Sonnabend, "Sonesta International Hotels Responding to a Crisis," *Cornell HRA Quarterly* (April, 1998), 38-45. Copyright Cornell University. Used by permission. All rights reserved.

Case Study Questions

1. Discuss why the management of international hotels needs to develop an effective crisis management plan.
2. Discuss the scope of Sonesta's development in Egypt and explain how Sonesta St. George's ownership and management are organized.
3. What were Egyptian terrorists' motives for attacking international tourists visiting Egypt?
4. Identify and discuss the three components that Sonesta management had to consider when responding to the terrorist massacre.
5. How did the hotel management and corporate office respond to the three crisis elements?
6. What are the three suggestions recommended for properly handling future political disasters? Do you think these are effective measures for managing political crisis?
7. What lessons can you draw from this case study on political risk of international hotel operations?

Chapter 5

Economic Systems

Every one thinks chiefly of his own, hardly at all of the common interest. . . . Everybody is more inclined to neglect the duty which he expects another to fulfill.[1]

Aristotle

LEARNING OBJECTIVES

In this chapter, you will study:

1. The different economic systems in the world
2. The economic reforms in the communist countries
3. The levels of national economic development by examining and analyzing economic data
4. Economic risk assessment
5. The economic impact of tourism and hospitality development on a foreign country
6. Economic policies on international hospitality development

INTRODUCTION

It may seem arbitrary that discussion of political and economic systems are separated in two chapters, since these two aspects are intertwined in any given society. However, because a country's economic system is normally determined by its political system, it is sequential to first examine political systems, and then study how these political forces shape and control economic systems and activities.

This chapter focuses on the differences in economic systems as they are influenced by various political ideologies. It discusses the levels of economic development in different countries, and identifies the economic factors that have a direct influence on international hospitality operations. It is emphasized that the economic system determines the business structures and organizations in a country. The complex economic systems and policy implications are summarized and analyzed.

DIFFERENT ECONOMIC SYSTEMS

An economic system "involves the interaction of organizations of participants engaged, according to rules and orders, in the production, distribution, and use of goods and services."[2] Economic activities comprise the production of goods, performance of services, and interaction among participants in the consumption of goods and services. A key aspect of the economic system is that it must have all the laws, rules, regular procedures, and customs constraining and sanctioning economic decisions. These laws, rules, and regulations determine the allocation of resources for production and the ownership of resources and assets in a country. Therefore, the differences in resource allocation and ownership of resources differentiate the economic systems of various countries. Three major world economic systems can be identified, and they are introduced in the following section.

Capitalist Market Economy

As mentioned earlier, a close link exists between political ideology and economic system. Capitalist market economies are commonly found in the democratic countries. The basic characteristics of a capitalist market economy are: (1) dependence on markets and prices to allocate resources and distribute income; (2) private ownership of the means of production; (3) the predominance of economic gain as the guiding force in decisions about investment, production, and sales; and (4) less government intervention in business operations.[3]

In a capitalist market economy, resources follow relative prices, which follow consumer demand. When demand for hotel rooms goes up, the hotel room rate will rise and more resources will be devoted to building more hotels to meet the demand. As discussed in Chapter 1, the basic resources for any production are capital, land, and labor. For hotel development, capital is required for buying the land and building the hotels, and labor is required to run the hotel with quality service.

Consumers are regarded as the "kings" or "queens" in the capitalist market economy. Their needs and wants are thoroughly studied by hospitality market researchers, and are met with a wide range of products and services. Private companies compete for travelers' dollars by providing the products and services guests desire. Competition forces companies to keep their prices as low as possible, because those who charge prices higher than necessary will be undercut by the competitors. Price signals and resource allocation go hand in hand, and require no government intervention. This allocation of resources based on the equilibrium of demand and supply is believed to be very efficient, since waste of resources is not tolerated. For example, in hotel and restaurant operations, more employees are hired during the peak tourist seasons to serve the increased number of patrons. But, the workforce is reduced during the slow seasons, since patronage is decreased. Many seasonal resorts even cross-train their staff to perform two or three different duties during the slow season. Human resources are thus maximized to respond to the seasonality of operations. This practice is known as a chased-demand strategy.

A capitalist market economy allows private ownership of resources and assets. Anyone can start up a business in capitalist societies. Entrepreneurs can seize any opportunity to develop a successful business with a sound business concept. Examples of successful hospitality businesses abound in capitalist countries. In the United States, Elsworth Statler, Conrad Hilton, the Marriott family, Ray Kroc, and Dave Thomas are some of the most successful entrepreneurs in the hotel and restaurant businesses. Owning a hotel or restaurant is the aspiration of many students in hospitality management education programs.

Less government intervention in business operations is evident in the capitalist market economy. Government regulatory function focuses primarily on macro-level economic and fiscal policies, such as interest rates and the control of inflation. Private business owners and corporations are left alone in developing new products and services. The freedom to operate in the market is a distinctive characteristic of the capitalist market economy.

Dynamism is another important aspect of this type of economy.[4] Capitalism is dynamic because competition among capitalists forces them to spend money in research and development (R&D) and to apply new inventions as soon as they are available. For instance, hotel and restaurant corporations in the United States spend millions of dollars to study travel behaviors and diet preferences of customers. The research findings are used by the hospitality companies to increase services and amenities in hotels or modify menus in restaurant operations. Therefore, as each company competes to lower its costs, rent more guest rooms, and sell more meals to gain a larger share of consumer market, economic growth will be stimulated.

Socialist Economy

A socialist economy is one wherein all the means of production are owned and run by the government or cooperative groups. It is also known as a centrally planned economy, since the central planners in the government develop comprehensive and detailed plans for almost all phases of economic life in the country. The formation of the central plan is based on planners' ideas rather than consumer sovereignty—consumers' demand for products and services. With socialist central planning, resources are allocated primarily by central planners' commands rather than by markets and prices.

Under the socialist economic system, the government has a greater control over the economic life of its citizens. The government appoints the head of a business organization and determines what and how much to produce. Waste of resources, both material and human, is notorious in the socialist economic system. Such systems are inefficient because of bureaucratic control and the lack of innovative entrepreneurs. The suppression of entrepreneurship leads to the lack of innovation of new products and services and the stagnation of economic growth. Consumers have little choice of products and services and they have to take what the hotels and restaurants have to offer. Service as a business is not well developed and emphasized in the socialist economy. Socialist economies operate under communist governments. Under such an economic system, everyone is dependent on the government, and the ruling party can easily establish a dictatorship. At present, North Korea is the only communist country that still strictly follows the socialist economic system.

Mixed Economy

Many countries integrate various aspects of both capitalist and socialist economic systems to develop systems that suit their own economic development. Such systems are described as mixed economies, with government control of certain means of production and market forces regulating the supply and demand equilibrium. Many governments own the means of production of certain industries, such as natural resources, transportation, and financial institutions, but let private entrepreneurs operate enterprises based on market demand and price signals.

This mixed economic system can be found in many developing countries, such as in Latin America and Asia. Many former communist countries are in a transition from the socialist system to the capitalist system. However, it is difficult to eradicate the old socialist system overnight as these countries adopt the new capitalist system from the West. Therefore, these countries demonstrate the mixture of both systems. The transition from the old system to the new one will take a long time, even if the political systems of these countries remain democratic and stable.

Economic Reform in China, Vietnam, and Cuba

These three countries are at present still ruled by communist parties. However, their socialist economic systems are undergoing fundamental changes of varying degrees. China started economic reform in 1978 by introducing some aspects of the capitalist market economy into its socialist system, such as permitting the establishment of small private businesses, allowing some enterprises to sell shares of ownership to raise capital for investment, and allowing foreign investment in some enterprises. The first joint-venture hotel, Jianguo Hotel, was built in Beijing in April 1982. It was used as a model for hotel development in China throughout the 1980s. In December 1987, Hilton International built the first international hotel in Shanghai that was solely financed and managed by a foreign company (see Exhibit 5.1).

The power of central planning is now reduced in China. Local governments have greater autonomy in controlling the means of production. The responsibility system has been established in business enterprises, in which every worker and manager is accountable for performance and productivity. Business enterprises will be closed and employees will be laid off if their operations cannot make profits. This measure makes the workers less demanding and more productive, as they are afraid that they may lose their jobs. Therefore, productivity and efficiency have been improved in China.

This market-oriented economic reform has been extensively carried out in China's economy. But China appears to retain more administrative controls, particularly through local government. The government tightly controls many key industries. The government still owns most of the hotels in the country and joint ventures in travel agency operations were only permitted in China in early 1998. Its fiscal and monetary policy needs to be modernized. However, the market-oriented economic reform has transformed the old central-planning system to a mixed economic system, and the Chinese government calls it the "socialist market economy."

This socialist market economy is now being emulated by Vietnam and Cuba. Under a communist government with central planning and government control of resources, both countries have been suffering economically, due to economic blockade by the United States and their nonefficient,

EXHIBIT 5.1. Hilton Hotel in Shanghai—The First International Hotel Solely Financed by a Foreign Company (Photo by Author.)

nonproductive socialist economic systems. Both relied on massive economic aid from the former Soviet Union in the past. After the disintegration of the Soviet Union, the economic aid stopped, and both countries had to find new ways to revitalize their economies. Therefore, they now copy China's economic reform model. This model allows some private ownership of business and seeks foreign investment for badly needed capital. It allows the communist party to stay in power, but also stimulates national economic growth. Fidel Castro even personally visited China in late 1995 to learn about Chinese economic reform firsthand. As discussed in Chapter 4, Cuba is eager to seek foreign capital for hotel and resort development and to upgrade its management and service by learning international standards of hospitality management. Vietnam is also seeking foreign investment and management know-how to modernize its hospitality management[5] (see Exhibit 5.2).

LEVEL OF ECONOMIC DEVELOPMENT

Differences in the levels of national economic development are essential information for global expansion decisions by international companies. A nation's level of economic development affects all aspects of hospitality development and operations: the type of property, the level of service, the marketing strategies, and so on. That is why Accor is actively building Formula 1, economical lodging facilities in Eastern European countries,

EXHIBIT 5.2. The Architectural Design of Delta Caravelle Hotel in Vietnam (Photo courtesy of Delta Hotels and Resorts.)

since the levels of economic development are considerably lower in these countries than in Western European countries. Most local people cannot afford luxury hotels. A study of economic development levels can enable international hospitality managers to understand the per capita income in different countries.

The widely used indicator of economic development levels of different countries is per capita gross national product (GNP). GNP is the market value of all the final goods and services produced by a national economy over a period of time, usually a year. Per capita GNP is thus used to compare countries with respect to the well-being of their citizens and to analyze market and investment potential for the hospitality industry. The World Bank classifies countries with more than one million population into three levels of economic development by measuring their per capita GNP. The per capita GNP cutoff levels for 1997 showed that countries with per capita GNP of $9,386 or more are described as high-income economies. This group consisted of twenty-six countries in 1997, including the Western developed countries, the oil-rich Arab countries, and the newly industrialized East Asian countries. Countries with per capita GNP ranging from $766 to $9,385 are categorized as middle-income economies. Fifty-eight middle-income countries were identified in 1997. However, the middle-income economies are further divided into two subcategories: upper-middle-income economies with per capita GNP between $3,100 and $9,385 (seventeen countries in 1997), and lower-middle-income economies with per capita GNP between $766 and $3,100 (forty-one countries in 1997). Countries with per capita GNP of $765 or less are classified as low-income economies. This group included forty-nine countries in 1997.[6] This classification of economic development levels by per capita GNP is a useful way to compare the purchasing power of different countries. It is generally assumed that the higher the per capita GNP, the more advanced the economy with a primary focus on the service industry.

It needs to be pointed out that hospitality companies are very interested in the rate of per capita GNP growth, since a high growth rate indicates a fast-growing economy, such as the emerging markets in Latin America and Asia. Hospitality companies are constantly searching for countries with high market growth potential for investment and development.

Another important economic indicator is often used to measure a nation's economy: gross domestic product (GDP). GDP is the total value of all goods and services produced domestically, not including the net factor foreign source income. The following formula shows the difference between GNP and GDP: GDP = GNP − net factor foreign source income.

Economic development performance of different countries can be reported in either GNP measures or GDP measures.

As used freely in the previous discussions, countries are also qualitatively classified as developed, newly industrialized, and developing countries. Developed countries include the high-income economies, the more industrialized and technologically advanced countries. The newly industrialized countries (NIC) include some high-income economies and some upper-middle-income economies, with large export volumes and a heavy concentration of foreign investment. Some of the NICs include Argentina, Brazil, Mexico, Hungary, Portugal, Taiwan, Singapore, and South Korea. The developing countries are the low-income economies with a low level of technological development and poor service industry infrastructure.

USEFUL ECONOMIC DATA

The examination of GNP or GDP gives a general indication of the economic development level of a country. Many other economic indicators can be used to measure economic performance and activities of specific market and consumption. Personal consumption, labor cost, and inflation will be discussed as useful economic data for making hospitality expansion and management decisions.

Personal Consumption

To the hospitality industry, the manner in which consumers allocate their discretionary income is very important for making global expansion decisions. As discussed in Chapter 1, discretionary income is the amount of income left after paying taxes and making essential purchases. When citizens have more discretionary income, they can spend more on travel domestically or internationally. Personal consumption of certain products and services can give a hospitality company an indication of market size and consumer behavior.

Consumers in some countries tend to spend more of their discretionary income than those in other countries. For instance, most Americans tend to spend most of their discretionary income, and some even rely on the easy credit extended by financial institutions. However, people in other countries, particularly in Asia, tend to save at least one third of their discretionary income. The personal saving rate is higher in these countries, and this can limit to some extent their purchasing power for travel products and services.

Clearly, consumption and saving patterns vary from country to country. Data on personal consumption are compiled by several international economic and financial organizations, such as the World Bank, the International Monetary Fund (IMF), the United Nations, and by various regional economic associations, such as the Organization for Economic Cooperation and Development (OECD), and the European Union (EU).

Labor Costs

Labor resources are the physical and mental talents that people can make available for production. Labor is typically measured by the time available for work during a given period. Hotel front desk staff, housekeepers, department supervisors, and general managers all provide labor service. Payments for labor services, such as salaries, commissions, fringe benefits, and so on, are called wages.

In making international expansion decisions, hospitality companies have to take unit labor costs into consideration. Unit labor costs are the total direct labor costs divided by units produced. This can be measured in the hospitality industry as the number of guests served, the number of rooms cleaned, the number of hours worked, or the dollar amount of sales per employee. Unit labor costs for the same job position are higher in the developed countries than in the developing countries. Typically, European countries such as Germany, Switzerland, Sweden, Norway, and Denmark have the highest unit labor costs, and many Latin American, African, and Asian countries have the lowest unit labor costs. International trends and standards in unit labor costs need to be examined, because each country has a different rate of increase in labor costs due to improvement in human resource development, such as education and technology development.

Labor costs are relatively low in countries with slower-rising unit labor costs. International hotels in some major cities of the developing countries charge room rates comparable to those in the major cities of the developed countries, but operations in the developing countries can be more profitable, since the hotel operators can pay lower wages.

Inflation

Inflation occurs when the average price level of goods and services rises.[7] It is a very important aspect of the economic environment, within which an international hotel operates. Inflation can cause two major losses for hospitality operations: real-income costs and social costs. Because of inflation, the real income of a hospitality company will be reduced by increased transaction costs and the unnecessary shifting of resources into repricing goods and services. Resources that could have been used productively elsewhere are used to reprice goods and services in order to keep the operations afloat. For instance, restaurant menus have to be reprinted regularly during an inflationary period. The constant reprinting cost chips away the real income of the restaurant operations.

Inflation can also have a social cost for the hospitality company and its guests: bad feeling can develop between the guests, who want low prices maintained, and the hotel, which has to raise prices to reflect rising operation costs. This may reduce the trust the guest and hotel have in each other.

It is important to know how to operate in some highly inflationary Asian and Latin American countries. Dealing with inflation requires both the art and science aspects of management skills. The pricing of room rates and restaurant menus cannot be too high or too low. Underpricing can severely limit the cash flow of the operations, but overpricing can scare away many customers. Adequate knowledge of inflation forecasts and following the market trend in pricing can enable the manager to stay competitive in a highly inflationary environment.

ASSESSING ECONOMIC RISK

Similar to the political system, the economic system of a nation can also pose certain business risks to international hospitality operations. The economic development level of a country normally determines its economic stability and its relative risk to an international hospitality company. Economic risk is normally higher in the developing countries, since the economic system is closely linked to a country's political stability.

The most sensitive economic risk is the change of a country's monetary, or fiscal, policies. A sudden change in foreign investment policy on repatriation of a foreign company's earnings can create a major financial problem, since the company cannot remit its income back to the home country. The risk of foreign exchange volatility brought about by currency translation exposures can have a major impact on the balance sheet of the company (the financial management of international hospitality operations will be covered in Chapter 9).

Economic risk can be higher if a hospitality operation is established in a country with high foreign debts. Many developing countries, particularly in Latin America, Asia, and Africa, seek financial aid from foreign governments and private financial institutions to develop their national economies. When a country has a heavy debt load, its economic development will be impeded, since a large portion of the nation's income is going to service the debt. Otherwise the money can be used for improving the infrastructure and promoting the hospitality industry.

As debts increase and the government is unable to fulfill its debt service obligations, financial crises are inevitable. Such financial crises occurred in Poland in the 1970s, in Mexico in 1982, and in several other Latin American countries in 1987.[8] The financial crisis in Asia in the latter part of 1997 and 1998 was also partially caused by the debt problem that shook international investors' confidence.[9] The restructuring of foreign debt can inflict heavy losses on banks and companies around the world. It always causes a sense of uncertainty for hospitality companies to operate in countries with high foreign debts, because the host government can initiate many macroeconomic measures to reduce debt. These measures may include curbing economic growth by introducing austere economic policy, and keeping tight control of hard currency. These measures obviously can impede the sales of hospitality products and services in these countries.

It is thus important to assess the economic risk of a country before making global expansion decisions. A country's economic risk can be assessed by: (1) the quantitative method, (2) the qualitative method, and (3) the checklist method.[10]

The quantitative method is to determine a country's creditworthiness over time through statistical analysis. This analysis is conducted by assigning different weights to economic variables to produce a composite index for evaluating a country's ability to fulfill its debt obligations, and comparing this country with other countries. The qualitative method, as used in political risk assessment, is to analyze the stability of the political leadership and examine the economic policies developed by the government. Based on the analysis, the future direction of the economy is projected. The checklist method is to simply check the vulnerability indicators that divide countries based on their ability to withstand economic volatility. The variables are measurable and illustrate the changes in the country's economic system. These methods assess the stability of a country's economic environment and the creditworthiness of a government from many different angles. Economic risk assessment methods can provide international hospitality companies with good indications regarding a country's economic stability for foreign investment and business operations.

ECONOMIC DIMENSION OF TOURISM AND HOSPITALITY

Tourism and hospitality development is accepted by most countries in the world as a major economic activity, regardless of the differences in economic systems. The industry has a profound impact on a country's national economy, such as generating more revenues, creating more jobs, balancing the payments, and improving infrastructure. It is also described as an invisible export, "clean," or "smokeless" industry. This section focuses specifically on the economic impact of tourism and hospitality development on the host country.

Land, Labor, and Capital

The development of hotels and restaurants requires the three basic factors of production: land, labor, and capital. Land availability and the cost of developing new properties vary from country to country. The allocation of land resources and the ownership of land differ from capitalist to mixed and to socialist economies. In the former communist countries in Eastern Europe, land title is still a major concern for potential hotel development. Under the communist regime, private land holdings were confiscated by the government. After the disintegration of the communist political system, individuals in these countries claimed their land and properties that had been taken over by the communist government. Therefore, land title remains unclear in many parts of Hungary and the former East Germany.[11] Many hotel developers are therefore hesitant to develop hotels in certain areas in those countries.

Hotel developers sometimes encounter opposition concerning the allocation of land resources, since hotel development, especially resorts, requires desirable land with beautiful, pristine, and natural locations. Land suitable for development may be requested by pressure groups for natural habitat or other land uses. Generally speaking, land is very expensive, and land use is highly regulated in the developed countries; land is considerably less expensive, and land use codes are not strictly enforced in some developing countries.

Labor is a major issue for international hospitality operations, since the industry is characterized as labor intensive. The availability of skilled service workers is crucial to successful hotel operations. Competent managers are not difficult to find in the developed or newly industrialized countries. But competent managers can be difficult to recruit in many developing countries. International hospitality companies have to bring in managers and supervisors from their own countries, or from a third country. Relocation of the expatriate managers can add costs to the company's operations.

Service employees are not hard to recruit in the developing countries, since labor is abundant there. Due to inexpensive labor, the employee-to-guest ratio can be higher and more personalized service can be provided. For instance, it is still common to use elevator attendants in some luxury hotels in the developing countries. Whereas the employee-to-guest ratio ranges from 1:2 to 2:5 in the United States and Western Europe, a similar property in a low-wage Asian country may have a ratio of 1:1 or higher.[12] That's why many U.S. and European business executives often give very high ratings to many Asian hotels for outstanding personalized service (see Exhibit 5.3).

International hospitality companies from the developed countries often bring capital investment to the developing countries. Capital resources are scarce in the developing countries, and they encourage foreign investment in hotel development. Capital resources are allocated by the government for many hotel and restaurant projects in socialist economies. Hotel developers in Western Europe and the United States tend to invest substantial capital in automation and labor-saving equipment, since labor costs are very high in these countries.

The Economic Impact and the Multiplier Effect

Hospitality development has a considerable economic impact on a particular destination. It can create more employment opportunities for the

EXHIBIT 5.3. The Oriental in Bangkok, Thailand (Photo courtesy of The Oriental Hotel.)

local population, generate more income for the local people and more tax revenues for the government, and improve destination infrastructure. Such economic impact can also spread to neighboring communities and contribute to the national balance of payments.

Many countries depend heavily on tourism. Tourism revenues represent a sizable proportion of their GNP and become the main source of national income. Hospitality development also generates an indirect economic impact on other sectors of the local economy. For instance, when an international corporation decides to build a new hotel in a foreign country, they need to hire the local builders to construct the hotel, and they may furnish the guest rooms with local furniture and fixtures. Therefore, the new hotel development creates additional employment and income for other local companies. After the hotel goes into operation, it still needs to spend a portion of the tourist revenues to pay local venders and contractors for various products and services. Tourist revenues are thus shared among the different sectors of the local economy. This recirculation of tourist revenues in the local economy is known as the multiplier effect. Since the initial injection of the tourism revenues can multiply to benefit many sectors of the local economy, such as the builders, furniture makers, farmers, and so on, hospitality development has a significant economic impact on foreign tourism destinations.

However, a portion of the tourist revenues has to be spent outside the local economy for various purposes. In some countries, hotels have to import products and services to satisfy international tourists' travel needs, such as certain food items that are not available in the local community. The proportion of tourist revenues that leave the local economy is known as leakage. Leakage can occur in four major areas. First of all, goods and services must be purchased to satisfy the needs of international tourists, such as importing wine and beer, or inviting a famous music band from a foreign country to entertain the hotel guests. Second, leakage can occur when expatriate hospitality managers remit a part of their compensation to their home countries. Many international hotel corporations assign expatriate managers to developing countries, due to the lack of competent local managerial personnel. These expatriate managers are highly compensated for overseas assignment, and they normally remit a portion of their wages to their home countries. Third, major leakage occurs when the international hotel company remits its earnings to the home country. To reduce such leakage, some host countries enact policies that international hotel companies are only allowed to repatriate a certain percentage of the earnings to their home countries. Lastly, hotels have to pay commissions to foreign travel agencies for referring international tourists to stay in the hotel. For example, when a hotel in Costa Rica receives many tour groups organized by several Dutch travel companies in Amsterdam, the Costa Rican hotel has to send commissions to these Dutch tour companies.

The size of the leakage is usually greater in the developing countries, and smaller in the developed countries. In the developing countries, goods of various kinds have to be imported to serve the international tourists, and many expatriate managers have to be employed. Therefore, a large proportion of the tourist revenues have to be spent outside of the local economy. On the other hand, goods and competent managerial personnel are readily available in the developed countries, since their economies are highly diversified and the labor force is highly educated. Little of the tourist revenues are spent to purchase goods and recruit expatriates from outside; therefore the leakage is minimized.

ECONOMIC POLICIES ON HOSPITALITY DEVELOPMENT

Since tourism and hospitality development plays a significant role in the national economy, many countries have developed favorable economic policies to encourage hospitality development by foreign companies. However, there are national differences in economic regulations that present more opportunities in certain countries than in others. International hospitality corporations need to study national economic policies before they expand operations into a particular country.

For instance, market monopolization via merger and acquisition is a very sensitive issue in some countries. Mergers and acquisitions of hospitality enterprises are more common in the United States (such as the bidding war over Sheraton between Hilton Hotels Corporation and Starwood Lodging Corporation in 1997), Britain, and the Netherlands than in Germany, France, and Japan. Regulations against monopoly and takeover by foreign companies are effectively exercised in the latter countries. Therefore, economic policies of different countries on hospitality business development need to be adequately analyzed before any expansion starts.

SUMMARY

- Economic systems are determined by political ideologies. An economic system involves the interaction of organizations of participants engaged, according to rules and orders, in the production, distribution, and use of goods and services.

- The basic characteristics of the capitalist market economy include: (1) dependence on markets and prices to allocate resources and distribute income; (2) private ownership of the means of production; (3) the predominance of economic gain as the guiding force in decisions about investment, production, and sales; and (4) less government intervention in business operations.
- A socialist economy is one wherein all the means of production are owned and allocated by the government or cooperative groups. It is also known as a centrally planned economy, since central planners develop comprehensive and detailed plans for almost all phases of the economic life in the country.
- Many countries integrate various aspects of both the capitalist and socialist economic systems to develop systems that suit their own economic development. Such a system is described as a mixed economy, with government control of certain means of production, and market forces regulating the supply and demand equilibrium.
- Dramatic economic reforms have occurred in several communist countries. Such market-oriented economic reform has been extensively carried out in China, and is now emulated by Vietnam and Cuba.
- Differences in the levels of economic development in different countries are essential information for global expansion decisions by international hospitality firms. The level of a particular country's economic development can be determined from the economic data compiled by various world economic and financial organizations. Major economic data include GNP, GDP, personal consumption, unit labor cost, and inflation.
- The economic development level of a country normally determines its economic stability and its relative risk for an international hospitality company. The most sensitive economic risk is the abrupt change of a country's economic policy, such as the monetary and fiscal policies.
- A country's economic risk can be assessed by using three research methods: (1) the quantitative method, (2) the qualitative method, and (3) the checklist method.
- Tourism and hospitality development has a great impact on the host country's economy. The economic impact is best illustrated by the concept of the multiplier effect.
- When initial tourist revenues have to be spent outside the host economy, the economic multiplier effect stops and leakage occurs. Leakage can occur in four major areas. The degree of leakage is usually greater in the developing countries and smaller in the developed countries.

• There are national differences in economic regulations that present more opportunities for international hospitality development in certain countries than in others. International hospitality corporations need to examine national economic policies before they expand operations into a particular country.

STUDY QUESTIONS

1. How is economic system defined?
2. What are the basic characteristics of a capitalist market economy?
3. What are the basic characteristics of a socialist economy or centrally planned economy?
4. What is a mixed economy? Can you list and discuss some countries that have a mixed economy?
5. Can you describe the current economic reforms in the communist countries, particularly in China?
6. Why do Vietnam and Cuba follow the Chinese economic development model?
7. Can you distinguish between GNP and GDP?
8. How does the World Bank identify and classify the levels of economic development of countries with more than one million population?
9. Why is the rate of per capita GNP growth important for making global expansion decisions?
10. What types of personal consumption data are useful for making global expansion decisions?
11. What is unit labor cost? What is the difference in unit labor cost between the developed countries and the developing countries?
12. What causes inflation to occur? What two major losses can inflation cause for hospitality operations?
13. What are the management strategies for operating hospitality businesses in highly inflationary countries?
14. What are the major economic risks a hospitality firm may encounter in a foreign country?
15. Can you explain why the economic risk will be higher for hospitality companies operating in a country with high foreign debts?
16. What are the three methods that are commonly used for assessing a country's economic risk?
17. Can you explain the relationship of the three major factors of production in international hospitality development and management?

18. Can you explain the multiplier effect of international hospitality development in a foreign country by using concrete examples?
19. What is leakage? Can you identify the four major areas in which leakage can occur?
20. Why is the degree of leakage usually greater in the developing countries and smaller in the developed countries?
21. Why do some countries restrict mergers and acquisitions of hospitality enterprises by foreign firms?
22. Why is it important for an international hospitality firm to examine the host country's economic policy before making expansion decisions?

CASE STUDY: THE CHANGE OF GOVERNMENT POLICY ON EXPATRIATE HOTEL MANAGERS IN INDONESIA

In 1997, the president of Indonesia issued a decree that required all star-rated hotels in the country to reduce their expatriate management staff to three by the year 2000. Indonesia first opened to foreign investment, including opportunities for expatriate workers, in 1967. Management at international chain hotels, some of which have a dozen expatriate members on their management and food and beverage staff, were unclear about the decree's meaning and nervous about its impending application.

"This included a mandate for transfer of technology and expertise, and training at least two Indonesians to take over every expatriate position," said Andi Mappisammeng, Indonesia's director general of tourism. "In thirty years, that has never happened. With about fifty international chains operating in Indonesia today, the tendency is not reducing positions occupied by foreigners, but enlarging the expatriate staff. This is not helping the country."

To qualify for work permits in Indonesia, all expatriates must supply documentation of qualifications that make them experts capable of transferring technology in their field. Calling all expatriate hotel staff files to his office, Mappisammeng said he made some interesting discoveries about the experts employed by international hotels in Indonesia.

"I found one so-called twenty-four-year-old 'expert,' who had a background in the fire brigade," he said. "How can he be an expert in tourism? This means that neither side—the hotel nor the government's approving authorities—has been honest in this case. So, enough is enough. We have implemented the decree, which will enforce what was originally outlined thirty years ago."

The decree makes no differentiation by hotel size or star rating. Hoteliers complain that the decree does not specify whether the restrictions apply to top management or all staff. Mappisammeng said management may choose where the three positions are, and they do not have to include general manager. "We have a few more years to achieve this, and international chains must push," he said. "Today, there are no Indonesian general managers at foreign chain hotels. I hope this deadline will give Indonesians opportunities for exposure and experience in overseas training, and will drive Indonesians to work harder to absorb what the expatriates can offer."

Jakarta's Casa Grande organization, representing forty-one top-rated hotels in the capital, stressed the difficulties of finding, for example, local sushi or teppenyaki chefs in its argument against the decree. The group said a company with multiple international outlets will have a greater problem. Mappisammeng said Casa Grande President Chris Green was supportive of the decree after the two discussed it.

"We have argued by emphasizing the lack of local management and technical personnel," said Green, general manager of Dusit Mangga Dua. "It would be difficult for a hotel with a Japanese or French restaurant to localize the position with an Indonesian. A sushi chef, for example, takes seven years to train in Japan. Mappisammeng has been very understanding of this position. Technical positions, such as chefs, are in a teaching mode anyway, and would have to have a technology transfer program," Green added. "While the Department of Tourism is committed to reduction of expatriates, we hope to review this technical aspect with the government. Hotel operators must be more committed to training and not expect the government to do the training for them."

The government has attached a $100 monthly fee for every foreigner on each hotel's roster to fund local management training programs. "The Department of Tourism has strong grounds, and we can understand their position," Green said. "The counterpart system is fair, and over the last thirty years, few companies have enthusiastically embraced this philosophy. There is now a shortage of qualified Indonesian management staff; that is no secret. There are valid reasons why the Department of Tourism says this has to stop."

Green estimated that the hotel industry in Jakarta alone will need 100,000 new staff by 2005 because of growth in hotel construction. "This growth is not restricted to Jakarta," he said. "Hotels are a weathervane of economic success. The government and the private sector have to roll up their sleeves and get on with some far-reaching training programs."

Case Study Source

Debe Campbell, "Government Enforces Old Expatriate Law," *Hotel & Motel Management* (October 6, 1997): 6, 67.

Case Study Questions

1. When did Indonesia open its door for foreign investment and expatriate workers?
2. What triggered the policy change and what does the new policy stipulate?
3. How are management and technology transfer concepts defined in this case?
4. What was the hoteliers' reaction to this new policy?
5. What would your opinion be concerning the new policy if you were the general manager of a major international hotel in Jakarta?
6. How will the local management training program be partially funded?
7. Discuss the issue of economic leakage and the employment of expatriate workers.
8. Discuss how a country's economy can be improved with increased training and education opportunities for its workforce.

PART III:
ORGANIZATIONAL STRUCTURES
AND DEVELOPMENT STRATEGIES

The two chapters in Part III discuss global hospitality organizational structures and development strategies. They demonstrate the complicated institutional arrangements for entering a foreign market and the processes for developing hospitality projects in a foreign country. Chapter 6 examines the six development strategies for entering a foreign market, and analyzes comparatively the advantages and disadvantages of these market entry modes. It also analyzes the influence of operational control, resource commitment, and political risk factors on the selection of market entry strategies. This chapter further defines the organizational structures for global hospitality operations. It emphasizes the importance of strategic planning as an integral part of international operations, and examines global hospitality operations organized by functions, product lines, and geographic regionalization.

Chapter 7 focuses on the global hospitality development plan and the building and construction of hotel properties in foreign countries. The conceptual development plan and feasibility studies are discussed. It introduces the essential aspects of infrastructure development as ancillary facilities for hotel operations. Hotel design principles and construction processes are presented with concrete examples. The chapter concludes with a detailed discussion of the growing popularity of ecotourism, ecolodge, and ecoresort development throughout the world.

Chapter 6

Market Entry Choice
and Organizational Development

Because of today's idea of the global hotel village, being an independent or regional player is hard to uphold. It is too costly to promote by yourself. . . . That is why more than 70% of U.S. hotels are branded. Yet only 30% in Europe are branded, which makes it the next big opportunity.[1]

Juergen Bartels
CEO of the Hotels Group
Starwood Hotels and Resorts Worldwide

LEARNING OBJECTIVES

In this chapter, you will study:

1. The mode of entry as an institutional arrangement for organizing and developing international hospitality operations
2. The advantages and disadvantages of the six market entry choices
3. Technology transfer as an important aspect of global hospitality expansion
4. The selection of market entry strategy based on operational control, resource commitment, and potential risk
5. Hospitality organizational structure in terms of the centralization, formalization, and complexity of a company
6. The development of strategic planning for international hospitality operations
7. Organization by business functions, product lines, and geographical locations

INTRODUCTION

This chapter focuses on two major aspects of international hospitality development: market entry choice and global organizational structure. As discussed in the previous chapters, international hospitality corporations face many external factors that are beyond their control, such as political and economic risks. Political and economic contingencies may pop up and foil well-prepared development plans, such as the expropriation of Habana Hilton by Fidel Castro's revolutionary government in the early 1960s. Global expansion plans take into consideration the uncontrollable external factors and prepare for possible political and economic crisis in the host country. One of the effective strategies for dealing with this issue is to choose a strategic market entry mode for overseas expansions. An appropriate market entry mode can enable hotel and restaurant companies to minimize vulnerability to potential political and economic crisis. The advantages and disadvantages of the six market entry strategies employed by international hospitality corporations are thoroughly analyzed in this chapter.

When international hospitality operations are expanded into many countries, the establishment of effective organizations is crucial to the communication between the corporate headquarters, regional offices, and individual properties. The flow of market information, the implementation of corporate policies and management decisions, and the assurance of service quality and standards can all be best facilitated through a well-organized global operational structure. This well-structured global organization can enable hotel and restaurant companies to operate effectively and successfully in foreign countries. Global organizational structures of hospitality corporations are examined and discussed in this chapter.

MARKET ENTRY CHOICES

Once a hospitality company decides to enter a foreign country for developing hotel or restaurant operations, it has to choose a mode of entry as an institutional arrangement for organizing and conducting international business transactions. Six market entry modes are commonly employed by hospitality corporations for global expansions: sole ownership, joint ventures, franchising, management contract, strategic alliances, and consortia. Since market entry modes have a major impact on hospitality corporation performance in foreign countries, their selection is always regarded as a critical international business decision.[2] Each market entry mode has its advantages and disadvantages in profit seeking and reducing potential risk in a foreign country. These six types of commonly used hospitality market entry modes and their advantages and disadvantages are analyzed and compared for hospitality expansion decision-making considerations.

Sole Ownership

A hospitality company can enter a foreign market by building a new hotel by itself, or by acquiring an existing hotel or an entire hotel company in the host country. These options give the expanding international hotel company the sole ownership of the properties and their operations. Building a new property in a foreign country thus allows the hotel company to have total control of the operations. The hotel company can gain all the profits, since no other owners are involved in decision making and profit sharing. However, building a new hotel in a foreign country requires substantial capital investment. The large investment exposes the hotel company to potential political and economic risks in foreign countries, particularly in the developing countries. When crisis occurs, the hotel company must take all the losses of its assets and operating revenues. Therefore, sole ownership as a market entry choice lets the company gain the greatest economic reward, but it can also present the greatest investment risk when political or economic crisis develops in the host country.

Acquisition of an individual property or an entire company is another major development strategy for entering a foreign market. The acquisition of local brand name hotel and restaurant chains or independent hotels with good reputations can enable the foreign hospitality company to gain instant market exposure and build on the existing market position for further development. The acquisition of Holiday Inn by British Bass Plc, Motel 6 by French Accor, and Travelodge by British Forte Plc in the early 1990s paved the way for these European hospitality firms to enter the U.S. market. Marriott International greatly strengthened its presence in Europe and Asia by acquiring Renaissance Hotels from New World in early 1997.

However, acquiring a foreign hotel company requires tremendous financial commitment. Bass and Accor each raised more than \$2 billion to acquire Holiday Inn and Motel 6 respectively.[3] As discussed in the previous chapters, some countries have policies restricting the acquisition of domestic hospitality firms by foreign companies. This will limit the entry choices a hospitality company can have for expanding operations into certain foreign countries. Sole ownership of hospitality operations through building new facilities and acquiring foreign hospitality companies or independent properties is a common market entry choice for overseas expansion in the developed countries. This is attributed to the stable political and economic systems in these countries, since sole ownership normally incurs the highest degree of foreign investment risk.

Joint Ventures

Joint ventures refer to a partnership between a domestic company and a foreign company for jointly developing and managing hospitality operations.[4] The structure of joint ventures varies from country to country. Some countries require that the domestic companies take the majority control of the operation, while the foreign company holds the minority stake. The 51 percent/49 percent majority-minority joint venture structure is quite common in some countries, such as France and China. Euro Disney was developed as a joint venture, with French partners controlling 51 percent of the stake, and the American counterparts the remaining 49 percent.[5] However, there are variations in ownership structures and the length of joint venture operations from country to country.

Joint ventures are commonly used as an effective market entry choice for hospitality development in most developing countries. When an international hospitality company is uncertain about the stability of a foreign government or unfamiliar with the business environment of a foreign country, it will normally seek local partners to develop and operate hospitality business together. Since the local partners know the host country's business rules, regulations, and cultural practices, they can assist the foreign partners in navigating the host political, commercial, and cultural environments. Local partners share business profits as well as investment risk with the foreign company.

On the other hand, host countries often seek foreign partners to gain new capital investment, technology transfer, and global exposure. As discussed in Chapter 5, many developing countries are badly in need of development capital for building hotels and resorts. They have to look for partners in capital-rich developed countries for financial assistance. Hospitality companies from the developed countries normally provide a portion of the capital investment for a joint-venture development. Technology transfer in international hospitality operations refers to the introduction of Western hotel management systems from the developed countries to the developing countries.[6] For instance, a joint venture between a hotel company from a developed country and a developing country results in the installation of a reservation system and the implementation of a cost control system and a human resources management system by the company from the developed country. Thus the hotel in the developing country benefits from Western management know-how. A joint venture with an internationally known brand hotel can also give the local partner instant global market exposure. The brand names of Sheraton, Hilton, Nikko, Club Med, and so on are recognized throughout the world.

Joint ventures are recognized as a win-win strategy for both foreign and local partners. This can be illustrated by hotel development in China in the late 1970s. The joint-venture policy was first initiated in July 1979 when China's National People's Congress passed the Law of the People's Republic of China on Joint Ventures with Chinese and Foreign Investment.[7] China's motivation for establishing joint ventures at that time was to attract badly needed development funds and to have better access to advanced hospitality technology, management expertise, and the world market.[8]

On the other hand, foreign investors were attracted to China by the size of the market, enticing tax and investment incentives, and low labor costs. The first joint venture hotel, Jianguo in Beijing, was built in 1982, with a total investment capital of $22.29 million, and proved to be an instant success. Its first six months' operation yielded a handsome gross income of $7.66 million.[9] The success of Jianguo stimulated a great number of joint-venture hotel developments in China in the last two decades.

It is clear that joint-venture development can benefit both local and foreign partners in international hospitality operations. The foreign partners can use it as a hedge against potential political and economic risk, and to take advantage of the local partner's knowledge and influence to develop a successful operation. The local partners can receive capital infusion, technology transfer, and brand recognition through a joint venture with a major international hospitality company.

However, business profits have to be shared between the two joint-venture partners. Sometimes, disputes concerning certain management provisions may arise between the two partners, particularly in countries where the legal system is not well developed (the legal aspect of international hospitality operations will be discussed in Chapter 8). It can be frustrating and costly for the foreign partners to handle the disputes, if the local government does not have a set of established legal procedures to follow, but deals with joint-venture disputes through bureaucratic or political means.

Franchising

Franchising is practiced by both hotel and restaurant companies as a market entry choice for overseas expansions. It is the major market entry choice for international restaurant corporations. By a franchising agreement, a hospitality company (franchiser) sells limited rights to another company or independent operator (franchisee) for the use of its brand name in selling certain standardized products and services, in return for a lump sum payment and a share of the franchisee's profits.[10] The franchiser normally provides the franchisee with its business format: standard operational procedures for making products and performing services. The franchisee has to deliver a product that conforms to the franchiser's standards and expectations that already exist in the minds of consumers. When Burger King enters a franchising agreement with a foreign company, it expects that company to operate its restaurants in a way identical to those with the Burger King name elsewhere in the world.

Franchising as a market entry choice can reduce the start-up costs of developing hotels and restaurants in foreign countries. It incurs minimal risk to the franchiser, since the franchiser only sells the brand name and its business format to foreign franchisees. The development costs and potential investment risk are thus borne by the local franchisees, because they must raise the capital investment to build and operate the hotels and restaurants. Therefore, an international hospitality company can build up global operations rapidly through franchising at low cost and risk.

The disadvantages of franchising include possible legal disputes between franchisers and franchisees, and quality control issues. Due to the differences in national cultural, political, legal, and economic systems, franchiser and franchisee disputes over certain operational provisions are inevitable. These disputes may severely affect the relationship between the franchiser and franchisee, affect the normal operations, and eventually lead to costly legal battles and the termination of the franchising agreement. Thus, when structuring a franchising agreement, hospitality companies need to consult experts who know both systems to protect the franchiser's interests and rights in the franchising agreement.

Quality control is a major concern for international franchisers. The essence of the agreement is to sell the franchiser's name and business format. The brand name is the franchiser's identity, which stimulates consumers' expectations of its products and services. For instance, when business travelers check into the Hyatt Regency in Singapore, they expect the same quality of room and food and the same level of service they would receive in Los Angeles. Therefore, the franchisers put their reputations on the line in overseas operations. If the foreign franchisee neglects the franchiser's operation standards and overlooks the quality of products and services, the inconsistency in product and service delivery may result in lost sales in a particular foreign market and tarnish the franchiser's worldwide reputation. Quality control is thus a major challenge for the franchiser, because of the geographic distance between the franchiser and the franchisee, and the large number of franchises developed by the major international hospitality corporations.

As hospitality franchising continues to grow, one way to handle the quality control issue is to decentralize by establishing franchising organizations in each country or region in which the company expands. These organizations can assume the rights and obligations to establish franchises in the area. For instance, the franchising agreements with Best Western International are all handled by Best Western International regional franchising offices (see Exhibit 6.1).

The regional franchising offices can thus oversee a small number of franchisees and ensure franchisees' operation standards. This franchising organizational arrangement has proven effective in international franchising quality control and has been practiced by many international hospitality companies such as KFC, Hilton International, McDonald's, and so on.

In international franchising, master franchising is the primary method used by many hotel and restaurant corporations. This involves franchising a business format and brand name to an established business enterprise that is familiar with doing business locally. For example, Domino's Pizza, Inc. established its international subsidiary, Domino's Pizza International, in 1982 for global expansion of its pizza business. Since then, Domino's Pizza International, Inc. has been using master franchising as a means of establishing international presence. The Domino's product and business system are thus combined with the master franchisee's expertise of the local market.

Domino's International now has a 150-member franchise body operating over 950 stores in forty-five international markets. These Domino's Pizza stores are all franchisee owned. Corporate regional staff serve as operations support for the foreign stores. Development of master franchises in foreign countries is the end result of many months and in some cases years of

EXHIBIT 6.1. Best Western International Regional Franchise Offices

Sales Offices:	Atlanta, Calgary, Chicago, Denver, Drieberge, London, Los Angeles, Milan, New York, Orlando, Paris, San Francisco, Seattle, Toronto, and Washington, DC.
Consolidated Reservations Offices:	Phoenix, Dublin, Milan, and Frankfurt

Source: Best Western International, Inc. (Phoenix, Arizona, 1997).

creating a suitable climate before opening a Domino's Pizza store. A training specialist from Domino's Pizza World Headquarters in Ann Arbor, Michigan spends up to four months working with the franchisee in the store, assisting in hiring and training employees. This direct contact has proven effective in providing consistent quality and service worldwide.[11]

In lodging franchising, Super 8 Motels and Howard Johnson International have expanded in Asia and the Pacific through a series of master franchise agreements with Singapore-based Hospitality Systems Asia-Pacific, Pte. This company oversees the development of Howard Johnson hotels in Indonesia and Thailand and Super 8 properties in Australia, India, and six other Asian countries. Many other international hotel operations all pursue franchising as a major market entry choice for global expansion.

Management Contract Companies

Hotel management requires specialized expertise and skills. Many inexperienced hotel owners, such as real estate developers and financial institutions, often find it very difficult to operate a profitable hotel. Hotels owned by the governments in the developing countries simply lack the professional managers to operate successfully. Therefore, these inexperienced hotel owners turn to professional hotel operators for assistance.

The original format of hiring professional hotel managers to run hotels for the owners was through leases. The hotel owners simply rented out the property to a hotel company for management, and the rental agreement was based on a percentage of total sales. Sometimes, the rent was based on a combination of a percentage of sales as well as a share of the gross operating profit (income before fixed charges). In 1954, Hilton International leased the Caribe Hilton Hotel in San Juan, Puerto Rico from the Puerto Rican government. The lease was structured as a two-third/one-third lease. Two-thirds of the gross operating profit went to the owner, and one-third went to Hilton International. Hilton later used the same lease agreement to expand its operations to Turkey, Mexico, and Cuba.[12]

The management contract concept was later developed by the Inter-Continental Hotel Corporation, with the signing of its first management contract with the respective owners of the Techendama in Bogota, Colombia, and the Tamanaco in Caracas, Venezuela in the early 1950s.[13] Inter-Continental Hotel Corporation did not pay rent to the local hotel owners. But the company collected a service fee and an incentive fee from the owners. The service fee was then based on a fixed amount per room, and the incentive fee was a percentage of the hotel's gross operating profits. In addition, Inter-Continental management's overhead expenses were reimbursed by the owners. Later, the management fee structure changed to a percentage of gross revenue plus a percentage of gross operating profit with no reimbursement of company overhead.[14]

Inter-Continental Hotels' pioneering effort in management contract was soon followed by other hotel corporations. A hotel management contract is now an agreement between a hotel owner and a hotel management company by which the owner hires the management company to assume full responsibility for managing the owner's hotel. In turn, the management company receives management fees for its service. Today, the management contract is popular as a market entry choice for international expansions, particularly in developing countries. The management contract incurs minimum risk to the company as compared to sole ownership and joint-venture development since the management company has little or minimal equity invested in the hotel. The hotel management company only assigns a group of professional managers to operate the property for the owner. If political crisis occurs, the management company can withdraw quickly without suffering heavy financial losses.

The host governments in developing countries also encourage management contract operations, since they are considered an important management technology transfer. Management contract companies in the developed countries send technically competent managers to manage the local properties and train the local managers and staff. If the management company is from a brand-name hotel chain, such as Forte or Marriott, it can introduce its long-established management system to the operations of the local hotel. The use of a management contract company can greatly enhance the local hotel's image and competitive edge in the international hotel market.

On the other hand, management contract operations can enable the company to expand its international operations by managing many foreign properties with relatively limited investment. But a major concern facing management contract operations in foreign countries is that the management company has to deal with an owner whose cultural, political, and economic values may differ from those of the operators. An owner and operator relationship needs to be cultivated, and a good working relationship can reward both the owner and the operator.

Two major types of management companies now exist: the brand-name hotel chains and the independent management companies. The brand name hotel chains, such as Accor, Red Roof Inn, Sheraton, or Holiday Inn, normally do not manage any other brands except their own.[15] Exhibit 6.2 lists the management companies operated by the brand-name hotel chains with the most managed hotels. Independent management companies, also known as second-tier management companies, operate franchise properties as well as independent hotels. Most of the independent management

EXHIBIT 6.2. Firms Managing the Most Hotels, 1997

Firm	Hotels Managed	Total Hotels
Marriott International	675	1,477
Société du Louvre	591	591
Accor	398	2,577
Promus Hotel Corporation	333	1,119
La Quinta Inns	271	271
Forte Hotels	260	260
Red Roof Inns	254	259
Tharaldson Enterprises	244	244
Wyndham International Inc.	233	241
Interstate Hotels Corp.	223	223

Source: Adapted from *Hotels* Special Report, "Corporate 300," *Hotels* (July, 1998), 54. Reprinted by permission of *Hotels* magazine, a publication of Cahners Business Information.

companies are based in the United States. Growth of management companies in Europe has not been as fast as in the United States. But some smaller European management companies have emerged to serve the need to operate troubled hotels that are repossessed by financial institutions.[16]

Management companies today typically receive a base fee and an incentive fee for managing a hotel. Base fees tend to range from 2 percent to 4 percent for full-service hotels, 2 percent to 5 percent for economy/limited service hotels, and 1.5 to 4 percent for luxury hotels. Incentive fees are frequently 15 percent of the increase in net operating income.[17]

The management contract concept is popular in Asia. Many developing countries in this region need the expertise of professional management companies. But owners are becoming more sophisticated and demanding. They expect the highest level of management performance and quick return on investment. Hong Kong-based Century International Hotels, operating three- and four-star properties in Hong Kong, Indonesia, and Vietnam, usually adds Century to the property's name when it gets the management contract. In Asia, small management companies are growing in number because larger companies have difficulty focusing on problems of properties in relatively remote locations. Large management companies are not geared to handle smaller properties in secondary locations, due to their economies of scale. Latin America is another region that is targeted by international management companies for management contract development. The Miami-based Carnival Hotels and Resorts is aggressively pursuing management contracts in the Caribbean and Latin American regions. It manages two independent hotels in Venezuela.[18] It continues to explore management opportunities from Colombia to Chile.

Strategic Alliance

The demands of globalization and the need to serve customers on a local level have brought more strategic alliances between hotel companies in different countries. Strategic alliance refers to a cooperative agreement between two hotel companies from two different countries. The two hotel companies band together for mutual support and expansion of their global presence. Several hotel companies have formed such alliances as a key strategy to provide entry to new and relatively unfamiliar markets.[19] The development of strategic alliances began in 1992 when Canada's Four Seasons and Hong Kong's Regent International announced an alliance to become one of the world's largest luxury hotel chains.[20] In 1994, Carlson/ Radisson launched a new global alliance with SAS International Hotels. This alliance resulted in Radisson's name being added to twenty-eight SAS hotels, and expanding Radisson's presence in Europe (see Exhibit 6.3). In turn, SAS benefited from the strength of Radisson's global brand.[21]

Hotel companies ally themselves for various strategic purposes. First, strategic alliances can give both hotel companies the instant exposure of a foreign market. Otherwise, it may take a considerably longer time for a hotel company to establish its presence in that foreign market. In particular, foreign hotel companies have always found it difficult to establish a U.S. presence and distribution system. Therefore, they prefer to form alliances with U.S. hotel companies rather than establish a new product from the ground up. Second, strategic alliances capitalize on the strengths of large multinational corporations while drawing on the benefits that tend to accrue for smaller, more differentiated companies.[22] This alliance gives both companies the benefits of global structure for marketing and reservation although the service is controlled and delivered at the local level. Third, strategic alliance allows the two hotel companies to share certain operational costs of promoting new markets. As Simon Johnson, hotel analyst for London's Kleinwort Benson Securities, explained, with limited funds for development, hotel companies are getting together on marketing.[23] Fourth, strategic alliances between two hotel companies can bring together complementary skills and assets that neither company could easily develop on its own. For instance, managing hotels in Asia differs from managing hotels in North America due to the differences in political, economic, and cultural systems. The alliance formed by Four Seasons and

EXHIBIT 6.3. Radisson SAS Plaza Hotel in Hamburg, Germany (Photo courtesy of Radisson Hospitality Worldwide.)

Regent International can thus bring their managers' talents together and complement each other's operations in two different cultural regions. Because of these strategic advantages, alliances between hotel companies will become more popular as a market entry choice and global strategic development.

In 1995, Scandic, based in Sweden and one of the leading Scandinavian hotel chains, formed a strategic alliance with Holiday Inn Worldwide, the largest single hotel brand in the world. The cooperation agreement between Scandic and Holiday Inn consists of two parts: (1) establishing a marketing alliance worldwide, and (2) a conversion to the Holiday Inn brand for the seventeen Scandic hotels located outside the Nordic region. Now Scandic represents Holiday Inn in the Scandinavian market, and Holiday Inn represents Scandic outside Scandinavia. As a result, Scandic offers its customers accommodation at more than 170 Holiday Inn hotels in Europe, or 2,000 Holiday Inn hotels worldwide, and Scandic hotels become the choice for Holiday Inn's customers during their visits to Scandinavia. As selected Scandic hotels are included in Holiday Inn's booking system, reservations for a Scandic hotel can be made at any of Holiday Inn's worldwide reservation offices. Scandic in turn handles reservations for any Holiday Inn hotel worldwide. Regular guests of both companies can receive benefits from the marketing alliance. All holders of a Scandic Club membership card staying at a Holiday Inn hotel are entitled to the same benefits as those offered to Holiday Inn's regular customers. This applies to any of the 2,000 Holiday Inn hotels worldwide. The same applies to Holiday Inn's regular customers whenever they stay at a Scandic hotel. However, Scandic's "bonus night's accommodation" system will only be offered at Scandic hotels.

This partnership enables both companies to strengthen their position in the European markets. Holiday Inn, which has not been well represented in the Scandinavian markets in the past, is now assured a comprehensive coverage of the Nordic countries. As for Scandic, the original seventeen hotels outside the region are now multiplied to hundreds. The Holiday Inn/Scandic alliance results in the largest single branded hotel chain in Germany. Therefore, both companies secure a stronger position in the European markets, with improved competitiveness and a greater potential for profitability.[24]

Consortia

The term "consortia" is used interchangeably with voluntary groups or membership affiliations in the lodging industry. Consortia offer global marketing and reservation services to independent hotels and some chain hotels. Consortia differ from franchises in that members of consortia are not mandated to follow standardized operational procedures established by the franchisors. Members pay initiation fees, and annual dues to use the marketing and reservation services, but remain autonomous in their management and operations. That is why they are also known as voluntary groups. Some consortia are nonprofit organizations, collecting fees from the members that are spent on membership services. Exhibit 6.4 is the latest list of the world's ten largest consortia ranked by the total number of rooms they represented in 1997.

REZsolutions was formed by the merger of the world's two largest consortia: London-based Utell International and Phoenix-based Anasazi Travel Resources in 1997. This merger created a giant consortium that provides reservation and marketing services to about 7,700 hotels worldwide, approximately 50 percent of the global consortium market. Currently REZsolutions represents 1,500,000 hotel rooms owned by independent hotels, and some international chain hotels in more than 180 countries (see Exhibit 6.5). REZsolutions is able to put travel agents in touch with hotels in different countries, from the Algiers Hilton to the Elephant Hills Hotel in Victoria Falls in Zimbabwe.[25] Its membership is also divided into different hotel segments, namely Summit International Group for deluxe city center hotels, Insignia Resorts for deluxe resort properties, and the Robert Reid division for Caribbean resorts. It plans to expand its leisure segment and seek new opportunities in emerging markets in Eastern Europe, Egypt, Israel, and Africa.[26]

EXHIBIT 6.4. Top 10 Consortia by Size, 1997

Firm	Rooms	Hotels
REZsolutions Inc. (United States)	1,500,000	7,700
Lexington Services Corp. (United States)	450,000	3,000
VIP International Corp. (Canada)	176,250	1,410
Supranational Hotels (England)	111,305	747
Leading Hotels of the World (United States)	89,800	312
Hotusa-Eurostar-Familia Hotels (Spain)	77,443	970
Keytel S. A. (Spain)	72,000	600
Logis de France (France)	71,822	3,966
SRS Hotels Steigenberger (Germany)	65,000	352
Golden Tulip Worldwide Hotels (England)	45,036	356

Source: Adapted from *Hotels* Special Report, "Consortia 25," *Hotels* (July, 1998), 76, 78. Reprinted by permission of *Hotels* magazine, a publication of Cahner's Business Information.

EXHIBIT 6.5. Hotel Regina in Paris—A Member of REZsolutions Inc. (Photo courtesy of REZsolutions Inc.)

Consortia have a special appeal to independent and small property owners around the world. In today's competitive lodging markets, independent operators find it very difficult to compete with the giant hotel chains. But they do not want to give up their management autonomy by purchasing a franchise, because the franchisers require them to follow a set of standardized operational procedures. Therefore, they turn to the consortia for marketing expertise and reservation referrals, but retain management autonomy.

Membership contracts with consortia vary from country to country, normally with a minimum of one year. New members need to pay a one-time initiation fee to join the consortium, and annual dues to receive marketing and reservation services. Consortia promote all members through a directory, at international and regional travel trade shows, and through tour operators around the world. A member hotel is normally given a plaque bearing the name of the consortium (see Exhibit 6.6).

EXHIBIT 6.6. Goodwood Park Hotel in Singapore—A Member of Preferred Hotels and Resorts Worldwide (Photo courtesy of Preferred Hotels & Resorts Worldwide.)

Consortium members are not mandated to follow a set of operation standards, and no architectural design uniformity is required for building a new hotel. Thus the members have management autonomy in operating their properties, but gain access to an international reservation system and global marketing programs. Since the membership contract can be signed for a short period of time, such as a one-year minimum contract by Best Western International, the independent operators can terminate membership at the end of the contract period, if they do not like the services provided by the consortium. This clearly differs from franchising operations since a franchise agreement is usually longer, ten or fifteen years. If the franchisees find out after one or two years of operation that they do not agree with the franchisers on some management and operation issues, the franchisees cannot terminate the contract easily. Therefore, consortia cater to the independent operators in the world by providing global marketing and reservation service with a flexible contract structure. Consortium development has been quite popular in Europe and the United States. European consortia are now growing rapidly in the United States. For instance, seven of the top ten consortia originated in Europe. Utell International strategically merged with Anasaza to further develop the North American market.

Which Entry Strategy to Choose

Market entry choices are used for organizing international hospitality operations in foreign countries. Each of these six market entry choices has different indications for the degree of control that an international hospitality company can exercise over the foreign operation, the resources it must commit to the foreign operation, and the risks that it must bear to expand into the foreign country.[27] Identifying the appropriate market entry choice for a given country is necessarily a difficult and complex task. But the choice is crucial to the likely success of the hotel operation in the foreign country.

Exhibit 6.7 analyzes the relationship between the six market entry choices and operational control, resource commitment, and potential risk. Operational control refers to authority over management decision making and strategic development. Resource commitment is the amount of equity invested in the property. Potential risk refers to the uncertainty of political and economic stability of a foreign country.

The analysis of market entry choices and the three development factors can assist international hospitality companies in identifying the appropriate strategy for entering a foreign market. The appropriate choice of entry strategy can have a major and positive impact on the success of a company's international operations in both developed and developing countries.

HOSPITALITY ORGANIZATIONAL STRUCTURES

As the hospitality industry is increasingly globalized, hospitality corporations have to go through fundamental organizational restructuring to meet the challenges of global expansions and overseas operations. An efficient global organizational structure can maximize a hospitality company's rates of survival and growth. Since the 1980s, most international hospitality companies have transformed their organizational structures in order to embrace the rapid globalization of the hospitality industry.

Hospitality organizational structure refers to the degree of centralization, formalization, and complexity of a particular company.[28] Centralization refers to the locus of control and power relations in the company. International hospitality corporations now operate with few corporate layers in an attempt not only to narrow the distance between executives/managers and employees, but at the same time put management and staff closer to the customer. Because of the differences in local cultural and commercial practices, hotel management in different countries is given the responsibility for operational decision making and quality control. The corporate headquarters are normally responsible for strategic development, finance, global marketing programs, legal affairs, and corporate human resources programs. The service is controlled and delivered at the local property level without headquarters interface, even if those services have been centrally designed.

Formalization refers to the policies, rules, and regulations that are formulated to keep the organization achieving its goals. As international hospitality organizational control is decentralized, fewer procedures exist that prescribe

EXHIBIT 6.7. Selection of Market Entry Choice

	Factors		
Choice	**Operational Control**	**Resource Commitment**	**Potential Risk**
Sole Ownership	high	high	high
Joint Ventures	medium	medium	medium
Franchising	high	low	low
Management Contract	high	low	low
Strategic Alliance	low	low	low
Consortia	low	low	low

management interaction between the headquarters and the local property. However, effective corporate policy guidelines are established to guide decision making at the property level. The policies, procedures, and rules are designed to provide hotel managers with sufficient guidance to operate individual property so as to achieve the goals set by the corporate headquarters.

One important aspect of formalization in international hospitality operations is the development of strategic planning. Most international hospitality corporations now require their managers to develop a comprehensive strategic plan for operations. The basic strategic planning framework, provided by the corporate headquarters, serves as a guideline for the managers to think strategically and develop a comprehensive management plan for their properties or units. After the strategic plan is formulated, the manager submits the plan to regional or corporate executives, and later presents the plan orally to a team of executives representing various operational areas of the corporation, such as finance, human resources, and marketing. During the presentation, the executives will ask various questions concerning the objectives, implementation schedules, and specific activities of the plan. The final plan is then accepted by both the executives and the unit manager, and is used as the guideline for management operations for a specific period of time. The manager's performance is then evaluated by measuring how successful he or she was in achieving the plan's objectives. This formalization in strategic planning allows managers to develop for themselves how to reach the goals specified in their strategic management plan.[29]

Complexity refers to the degree of specialization of operational functions within the corporation. As the hospitality industry is globalized, firms face increased specialization at the corporate headquarters. This specialization consequently increases the corporation's complexity. This is true of many international hospitality corporations, which feel the need to strengthen the corporate headquarters with individuals who are capable of understanding and managing new international operations. These specialists are also needed in the regional offices. These special management functions range from international finance, law, design, information technology, and engineering to marketing. International hospitality management employs highly skilled functional specialists in many top management positions, and this trend reflects the increasing complexity of the international hospitality industry.[30]

As hospitality corporations grow and expand into foreign countries, the management characteristics become more complicated. No standard approach to meeting these complex needs can be found in international hospitality operations. Hospitality corporations have to differentiate their tasks and products sufficiently and create subdivisions that can specialize and standardize the operating procedures for increased efficiency and profitability.[31] Three criteria are often used to organize a company's operations: (1) business functions, (2) product lines, and (3) geographical locations.

Functional organization is used at various operational levels, at the corporate, regional, and unit levels. The various corporate divisions and unit departments are normally organized by functions, such as human resources, accounting, marketing, and food and beverage operations. Organization by product lines is practiced at the corporate level. Most hospitality corporations today have multiple subsidiaries, each of which individually represents a distinct product of the travel and hospitality industry. These different hospitality products, such as Forte's Crest, Posthouse, and Travelodge, serve international tourists in particular niche markets (see Exhibit 6.8). Accor has also developed many hotel products that serve almost all possible target hospitality markets. Each product segment is led by its own general manager, who must conform to the budget and financial expressions of the corporate headquarters.[32]

Organization by geographic regionalization is an important strategy used by hospitality corporations to reduce the span of control over multiple subunits in many countries. Regional offices are thus established to oversee the operations in a particular region, such as the Sheraton Asia/Pacific Division, or Accor North American Division. Regionalization in international hospitality organization has two distinctive advantages. First, hospitality products and services can be adapted to the customers' needs and wants in the region, and management can respond more readily to con-

EXHIBIT 6.8. Hotel Branding by Forte

Brand/Collection	Market Level	Geographic Focus
Exclusive Hotels by Forte	5-star deluxe	worldwide
Le Méridien/Forte Grand	4-star international	worldwide
Forte Crest	4-star domestic	UK and Italy
Forte Posthouse	Midscale	UK
Forte Agip	Midscale	Italy
Forte Heritage	3- and 4-star	UK
Forte Travelodge	Budget	UK, Spain, and Ireland
Travelodge US	Economy	The Americas

Source: Press release, Forte Plc, London, 1997.

sumer demand changes in the local markets. Second, a regional organization can deal with the various different legal, economic, political, and social constraints more effectively, such as income fluctuation, consumer behavior change, or government fiscal and monetary policy change.

Organization by product lines and geographic regionalization can be employed at the same time. When Accor and Forte decided to expand their operations to the United States, they both entered the U.S. market by acquiring well-established economy hotel chains in the United States, Motel 6 and Travelodge. The acquisition of Motel 6 by Accor and Travelodge by Forte represented both a new product line and a new regional market for both corporations.[33] International hospitality corporations thus organize their overseas operations by providing products appropriate to the market niches existing in the new geographic location. For instance, Accor is now actively developing its economy hotel product, Formula 1, in many developing countries where there is a great demand for no-frill hotel services. But, Accor did not introduce Formula 1 in the United States because the economy/budget market segment is well developed in the United States.

SUMMARY

- Any global expansion plan by international hospitality companies must take into consideration the uncontrollable external factors, and prepare for possible political and economic crisis in the host country. One of the effective strategies for dealing with this issue is to carefully plan market entry strategies.
- Market entry mode is an institutional arrangement for organizing and conducting international hospitality business transactions in a foreign country.
- Six market entry strategies are commonly employed by international hospitality corporations: sole ownership, joint ventures, franchising, management contract, strategic alliance, and consortia.
- Sole ownership is the building of a new hotel or the acquisition of an existing hotel by one corporation. It requires total commitment of resources and gives the owner 100 percent ownership and total profits. But it has the greatest investment risk.
- A joint venture is a partnership between two or more investors for developing international hospitality operations. The ownership, profits, and risk are proportionally shared.
- Franchising is selling the business format and brand name by the franchiser to a franchisee in a foreign country. The franchiser can ex-

pand its global operations rapidly with minimal investment and at low risk, while the franchisee can gain a recognized global brand and established management know-how.

- A management contract is a contractual agreement between a hotel owner and a professional hotel management company. It is a common strategy for international hotel corporations expanding into developing countries where the political and economic systems tend to be unstable. It is considered a technology transfer from a developed country.
- Strategic alliance refers to a cooperative agreement between two hotel companies from two different countries. The two companies band together for mutual support and expansion of their global presence.
- Consortia are also known as voluntary groups or membership affiliations. Consortia offer global marketing and reservation services to independent hotels and some chain hotels. They differ from franchises in that members of consortia are not mandated to follow standardized operational procedures.
- The selection of market entry choices needs to be evaluated with operational control, resource commitment, and political risk factors.
- Hospitality organizational structure refers to the degree of centralization, formalization, and complexity of a particular company.
- An important aspect of formalization in international hospitality operations is the development of strategic planning. Strategic planning serves as a guideline for hospitality managers to think globally and strategically, and develop a comprehensive management plan for the property.
- Three criteria are used for organizing a company's global operations: business functions, product lines, and geographic locations.

STUDY QUESTIONS

1. How is the market entry choice concept defined?
2. Why is the selection of market entry choice such an important part of the global expansion decision-making process?
3. Can you explain the advantages and disadvantages of using sole ownership as a market entry choice?
4. How can joint ventures be structured as a mode of market entry for global expansion? Can you identify the advantages and disadvantages of a joint venture as a market entry choice?
5. What is technology transfer? Why is it so important to hospitality companies in the developing countries?

6. What are the advantages and disadvantages to a franchiser and to a franchisee if franchise is used as a market entry choice?
7. What is the master franchising concept?
8. Why is management contract often used as a market entry strategy by international hospitality companies to enter the developing countries?
9. Discuss the advantages and disadvantages of management contract to both the hotel owner and the management company.
10. What is the primary purpose of strategic alliance? Can you describe the strategic alliance between Scandic and Holiday Inn Worldwide, and the advantages to both hotel corporations?
11. What are consortia? How do consortia organize their global operations? What are the major consortia in the world?
12. Why does an international hospitality corporation have to consider operational control, resource commitment, and potential risk factors when selecting an effective market entry choice?
13. What are the three major components of hospitality organizational structures?
14. How is a strategic plan formulated and implemented?
15. What are the three criteria for organizing international hospitality operations?
16. Why didn't Accor promote its Formula 1 brand in the United States?
17. Can you think of some international hotel corporations that organize their global operations by function, product lines, geographical location, or any two of the above?

CASE STUDY:
FRANCHISING—A MARKET ENTRY CHOICE USED
BY CHOICE HOTELS INTERNATIONAL IN THE EARLY 1990s

This case study is based on an interview between Sally Wolchuk, editorial assistant of *Hotels* magazine, Frederick W. Mosser, Choice's managing director of Europe operations, and Brendan Edds, senior vice president of Choice's international division. The topic is global expansion strategies developed by Choice Hotels International in the early 1990s.

Choice Hotels International, based in Silver Spring, Maryland, is one of the leading global hotel corporations in the world. It has seven hotel brands in the United States: Comfort Inn, EconoLodge, Quality Inn, Clarion, Sleep Inn, Rodeway, and Friendship Inn. The following interview discusses how franchising was used by Choice Hotels International to expand its global operations in Europe.

Q. What brands will you promote in Europe?

A. We are represented in Europe with the Sunburst Group. Over the next two years we will focus primarily on the Quality and Comfort brands. In terms of our franchising activity, we see the opportunity to be in the broadly defined midmarket, midprice segment of the industry. Quality and Comfort fall into that category.

Q. Why? Is there an overabundance of upscale hotels? Is the upscale market more competitive?

A. That is part of it. You avoid going head to head with every other major hotel chain that is international. Virtually all of them are in the four- to five-star category, so we come in underneath them and avoid that head-to-head battle. Second, and most important, Choice has the greatest strength, expertise, and organizational skills in the midmarket range.

Q. Do European hoteliers understand franchising?

A. Once explained, they understand it. It is a relatively new concept and not instantly recognizable among hoteliers in Europe as it is in the United States. You have to start with the whole idea as to what franchising is. Then you have to explain what a franchiser does, what service a franchiser provides and what the obligations of the franchisees are. Finally, you get into the benefits of the franchise itself.

Standards in Europe will be consistent within Europe and somewhat different than in the United States, just as in other aspects of the hotel industry. We aren't taking over American cookie cutter designs, concepts, and room packages. We're not saying that this is what all the hotels around the world are going to look like. What we do is take hotels that meet our minimum standards but still reflect the local characteristics and nature of the region in which these hotels fall.

Q. Are the steps in helping the franchisees in Europe the same as in the United States?

A. Yes, our service package is the same.

Q. In Europe, who are your biggest competitors in franchising?

A. Holiday Inn has been in Europe for twenty years, and they have somewhat blazed that trail, so to speak. There are other European hotel chains that have franchised but not to any great extent. Accor, in France, does some franchising. In Europe, franchising is not totally foreign, and it is definitely a growing trend.

Q. Will your biggest competitor someday be Accor?

A. No, I think our largest competitor is the option to stay an independent hotel.

Q. Will independent hotels resist taking on a franchise?

A. I don't think someone voluntarily, without good market reasons, decides to buy a franchise. There has to be a compelling reason. A compelling reason becomes a competitive one, and to plug into the larger national and international worldwide marketing system is the way the industry is going. As an independent hotel you don't have the marketing resources of the reach, and that awareness is beginning to become more and more pervasive in Europe.

Q. What percentage of Choice properties will be conversion compared to new properties?

A. The first couple of years my projection is that we will have about 75 percent conversion to 25 percent new construction. As Europe continues to grow and expand, we will get plugged into that with our own new construction concepts. As our pipeline fills up, we will see a shift of that balance. In five years from now we can be looking at 60 percent to 65 percent new construction versus conversion.

Q. Does it take longer to build a hotel in Europe than in the United States?

A. In certain parts of the United States, such as the California coast, you are in for a long haul. There are many parts of Europe where that would be a good analogy. In general, the development process is slower in Europe. There are more hurdles. You are more restricted in terms of what sites are developable.

Q. On another subject, how does the European traveler differ from the U.S. traveler? Do Europeans expect more?

A. They expect different things—you can't characterize it as European. What do British, French, and German travelers expect? There are differences among each culture. Some like to have hot water to make coffee or tea in the morning. Others insist on pants presses and so forth.

One of the things that is different about their expectations is food and beverage service. There is more emphasis in Europe than in the United States on a hotel having a restaurant, or at the very least for the more economy type of properties, a full breakfast.

Q. Will this pose any problems for Choice?

A. No. Our concepts and designs are very adaptable to incorporate that sort of thing—to meet whatever the market needs. Generally, in Europe, you don't have suburban highway and commercial activity centers such as free-standing fast food restaurants or department stores within walking distance or a short drive from the hotel. A hotel has to be more of a self-contained unit in many cases, particularly in eastern countries.

Case Study Source

Excerpt from Sally Wolchuk, "How Choice Uses Franchising to Grow Worldwide," *Hotel* (April, 1992), 52-54. Reprinted by permission of *Hotels* magazine, a publication of Cahners Business Information.

Case Study Questions

1. Why did Choice Hotels International primarily focus on the Quality and Comfort brands in Europe?
2. How did Choice Hotels International explain the franchising concept to European independent hoteliers?
3. Are other international hotel chains expanding hotel operations in Europe?
4. How can you convince the independent hotel operators in Europe to purchase your franchise?
5. What proportion of Choice hotels were converted from existing European hotels and what proportion were new constructions?
6. Is there any difference between the United States and Europe in the length of time to build a new hotel?
7. What are the travel expectations of tourists from different European countries?
8. How did Choice accommodate European travelers' lodging needs?

Chapter 7

Hotel Development and Design

How much more down-to-earth can one get than the saving of 1.34 liter per individual flush achieved through the London Hilton's simple expedient of banging a brick into each and every cistern of the hotel! Today, we see the glamour of high-profile initiatives of this kind—but their success depends on the very unglamorous business of reducing environmental impacts step by step, pound by pound, flush by flush.[1]

The Prince of Wales

LEARNING OBJECTIVES

In this chapter, you will study:

1. The factors that influence the building of a hotel in a foreign country
2. The formulation and implementation of a hotel development conceptual plan
3. Tourism and hospitality infrastructure development
4. Hotel design and the integration of hotel building with the local natural and cultural environment
5. The environmental impact analysis statement
6. The complexity of hotel construction in a foreign country
7. The trends of ecologically sensitive development in hotels and resorts around the world

INTRODUCTION

When an international hospitality company decides to enter a foreign country by building a new hotel, it has to consider a wide range of development issues and concerns. Foreign hotel development is determined by various political, economic, financial, sociocultural, and environmental fac-

161

tors. This chapter focuses on the complicated development factors that influence the building of a hotel property in a foreign country. It first discusses the conceptual development plan for a new hotel, particularly the feasibility and viability of new development in a new foreign market. Second, it discusses infrastructure development as the essential ancillary facilities for a hotel property, and the complexity of infrastructure development in the developing countries will be analyzed. Third, it focuses on hotel design, particularly the integration of the physical building with the local natural and cultural environment. A great emphasis is placed on environmental impact analysis—a study hospitality firms have to conduct to have the proposed project approved by the host government. Selected hotel designs in different countries will be presented and analyzed. Fourth, the basic aspects of hotel building and construction will be introduced, and specific considerations for building a new hotel, such as environmental hazards, building materials, construction cost, and time are identified and discussed. Fifth, it discusses the new trend in international hotel and resort development that features ecological and sustainable development. Ecolodge and ecoresort development and its positive impact on the international travel and tourism industry are analyzed with selected examples. Finally, the chapter concludes with a case study on the growing popularity of ecoresort development in different countries. This case study integrates and reinforces the complex development concepts discussed in the chapter.

HOTEL DEVELOPMENT PLAN

International hotel products vary, and each type of hotel product serves a certain level of consumer demand. International tourists bring their own cultural expectations to the demand for provision of lodging facilities, quality, and service. The development of international hotels is thus concerned with identifying market demands for hotel facilities in particular locations.

In the past decades, international hotel companies concentrated on building luxury and upscale hotels and resorts around the world to serve tourists from the developed Western countries. Since the early 1990s, international hotel companies have noticed that growth at the high end of the hotel segment slowed down worldwide, but demand for two-star and three-star midscale hotels has been on the rise in many countries with emerging economies. For instance, the rush to build luxury hotels in Bangkok, Thailand, in the 1980s and early 1990s has pushed the hotel market to a glut. The average room rate of a five-star hotel in Bangkok in 1993 was only $79 per night.[2] However, there has been a shortage of two-star and three-star hotels in Bangkok to accommodate the increased number of tourists from South Korean, Taiwan, and China. Most Asian tourists are unable to pay for the luxury five-star hotels. Therefore, the demand for midmarket hotels is growing both in Asia and Latin America as their economies give rise to a growing middle class with a penchant for business and pleasure travel worldwide.[3]

The mid-1990s witnessed an intense competition among international hotel companies over middle market development around the world. Grupo Sol Melia built midmarket Sol Inn Hotels in Brazil and other south American countries. Days Inn signed an agreement to build three-star hotels with a total of 6,000 rooms in China by 2000. Accor Asia Pacific Ltd. is currently developing its three-star brands, Mercure and Ibis, in New Zealand, Australia, Indonesia, and Nepal. Holiday Inn Worldwide is aggressively pursuing franchise opportunities for its midmarket Holiday Inn Express and budget Holiday Inn Garden Court Hotels in Africa through a partnership with Southern Sun Group in South Africa.[4] The list can go on and on. The point is that international hotel development responds to international travel market demand, shifting development strategy from luxury hotels to midmarket hotels since the mid-1990s.

Identifying and quantifying market demands for hotel facilities in different regions or countries requires systematic market research and feasibility studies. A successful development project can be guided by a well-formulated conceptual plan. A conceptual plan for hotel and resort development normally includes seven phases: (1) establish need, (2) feasibility analysis, (3) statement of scope, (4) project construction, (5) commissioning report, (6) facility testing, and (7) evaluation report.[5]

The phases of establishing need and feasibility analysis are defined as the first planning process. The need for new hotel development is identified by quantifying the level of demand for hotel facilities in certain geographical locations, the characteristics of the markets involved, and the extent to which their requirements are being met by the existing supply of facilities. The need for midmarket hotels in Asia and Latin America, as discussed earlier, is established through extensive market feasibility analysis by hotel companies, government tourism agencies, and private consulting firms.

The feasibility analysis must be comprehensive, examining various factors that may affect the successful development of the new hotel project, such as future growth trend, estimated development budget, site evaluation, market analysis, room night analysis, competitive analysis, project recommendations, location maps, forecast of income and expenses, economic evaluation, and feasibility conclusion.[6]

Based on the feasibility analysis, the markets and the scope of the facility and operations are defined. In the second interface between feasibility analysis and statement of scope, the scope of the operation and the size of the property are clearly defined. For instance, many international hotel companies, in the current international competition over midmarket development, have developed a strategy to quickly build a cluster of four to five midmarket hotels in a primary city, not a "one here, one there" plan.[7] The scope of developing a critical mass of midmarket hotels in a foreign city can quickly establish the company's presence in this market, and help attract inbound international tourists and domestic tourists.

Once the development scope is defined, the implementation phase moves into the project construction phase. Constructing hotels in foreign countries can be a very complex task. Resources and supplies need to be carefully planned. In developing countries, certain building materials or guest room furniture and fixtures may have to be imported from other countries. Planning has to be established for the control of production, procurement scheduling, supplier appraisals, cost control, contractual agreements, and construction quality control.

As the new property is under construction, the project development progresses into the commissioning phase. This commissioning program is characterized by the preparation and implementation of training procedures for hotel management and in-house staff. These commissioning procedures are designed to train the management and staff how to use technological equipment and to explain design features and the plans that complement hotel functions and operational facilities. Efficient commissioning of the physical property to the hotel management and staff plays a crucial role in the future success of operations.[8]

When the hotel management and staff complete the commissioning procedures, the new property goes into an operation known as soft opening, which is to test all the functions of the new hotel. If functional problems are detected during the soft opening period, they can be corrected before the property is officially open for business.

The final phase is to evaluate the entire new property. A final inspection of the quality of the work is made, and supplies are checked against specifications. These evaluations are then compiled in a report, and the finished hotel project is handed over to the in-house management. The hotel is now ready for grand opening.

This conceptualization of the development plan explains the complexity and systematic organization of new hotel development. Hotel developers use this plan to conceptualize the entire development process, systematically organize the phases, and rationally allocate resources. Effective execution of the development plan can integrate well the various and complicated development phases and ensure the success of the project development.

INFRASTRUCTURE DEVELOPMENT

Infrastructure consists of all the underground and surface development construction of a place. The level of basic infrastructure development in a particular destination directly affects the smooth and successful construction of a new hotel and subsequent operations because the hotel is supported by various basic infrastructure needs. As discussed in Chapter 4, major infrastructure development is normally initiated by government at various administrative levels, and includes roads, water systems, sewage and drainage systems, transportation terminals, and so on. Thus, the development of infrastructure is almost always a public-sector responsibility.

Disparity exists in the level of infrastructure development around the world. In the developed countries, infrastructure is highly advanced, presenting little problem for hotel developers and managers. But, in many developing countries, hotel developers and managers have to spend more time dealing with basic infrastructure needs, as the systems in these countries are not fully developed. A comprehensive discussion on the basic infrastructural needs of international hotel development can illustrate the differences in the levels of development around the world.

Roads

The availability of first-class roads provides easy travel accessibility to the hotel properties, points of interest, and other transportation terminals. Every nation has invested heavily in upgrading its road systems to facilitate efficient movement of people for various purposes. In preparation for travel in the twenty-first century, the U.S. government passed legislation on the improvement of surface transportation infrastructure in December, 1991. Known as the Intermodal Surface Transportation Efficiency Act (ISTEA) [Public Law 102-240, 102nd Congress, H.R. 2950 (December 18, 1991)], this legislation promotes the intermodalism concept, which emphasizes the interface of mass transit, highways, railways, airports, and ports. This means that all different modes of transportation must come together to form a seamless transportation system that will allow tourists to move from one mode to another smoothly, with minimal congestion and intervention.

Under ISTEA, federal funds are earmarked for the planning, design, and development of a national system of highways and scenic byways. The

National Scenic Byways Program designates roads with significant scenic, historic, recreational, cultural, natural, and archaeological value as "National Scenic Byways" or "All-American Roads." The development of national highways and scenic byways is necessary to stimulate tourism, and hence hotels and resorts.

In the developing countries, road construction and improvement have been prioritized by many national governments as an incentive to attract foreign hospitality development. The Chinese government received construction loans from the World Bank to develop its national and regional highway systems. With this development, many secondary Chinese cities became accessible to foreign hospitality firms for midmarket hotel development.

At the local or property level, road development is essential to easy and efficient access to hotels and to circulation within the property. As Inskeep and Kallenberger reported in their case study of the Puerto Plata Resort project in the Dominican Republic, this resort is served with a loop road, with the only two entrances located at each end of the loop road. This road design limits public access to the beaches and promotes security in the resort. The loop road has many speed bumps to slow vehicular traffic, and it is adequate for limited traffic use in the resort complex. However, the roads in the nearby town are unpaved, and many are in poor condition. This inconveniences resort guests when they want to visit the town. The authors recommended that the local roads be improved by the local government.[9]

Water

Water supply and quality are essential for guest consumption and hotel operations. Typical daily consumption of water ranges from thirty-five gallons per guest in commercial hotels to eighty gallons in luxury resorts in developed countries.[10] Large quantities of water are used for housekeeping, food preparation, cooling, boilers, laundries, swimming pools, recreational use, and irrigation of grounds (see Exhibit 7.1).

The quality of water is always a major concern for tourists who travel to the developing countries. The media coverage of bacterial infection through drinking water in hotels and resorts in developing countries often generate negative publicity for some destination areas. In some Mexican hotels, the management posts a notice to assure the guests that the water in the hotel is safe to drink. In some countries, guests are advised to drink the boiled water provided by the hotel. It is very important that drinking water be pure, sterilized, and protected from contamination.

As large quantities of water are required for daily use, the supply must be guaranteed. Water supplies are normally obtained from three major

EXHIBIT 7.1. Burswood Resort Hotel in Western Australia (Photo courtesy of Burswood Resort Hotel.)

sources, depending on the physical location of the property: (1) underground aquifers extracted from wells and boreholes; (2) catchment surfaces draining to storage tanks and cisterns; and (3) sea water desalination using evaporation, freezing, or osmotic processes.[11] Many hotels and resorts have potable water that is treated in independent systems built to international standards.

Power

An efficient supply of electricity is essential to illumination, ambiance, decoration, directions, refrigeration, and security in hotel and restaurant operations. Brighter decor tends to make guest rooms appear more spacious and provides a comfortable, sociable environment. However, power supply, measurement of electricity usage, and supply voltages vary from one country to another. The power supply is not an operational concern in the developed countries. However, power shortages in some developing countries can be a major concern for hotel operations. Some hotels are often forced to shut down air conditioning during humid summer nights due to power shortages. To provide a comfortable lodging and dining experience, many hotels and resorts in developing countries are equipped with their own generators, since the main supplies are inadequate or unreliable. In emergencies, an automatic transfer switch enables generators or batteries to be used.[12]

Electric power is normally three-phase AC with a cycle frequency of 50 or 60 kHz. Supply voltages differ among countries. For instance, in the United States 120/208 V and 277/480 V are used. Voltages of 240/415 V are commonly used in Europe and Asia. International hotels need to provide electricity converters as a necessary amenity for guests to use electric appliances such as driers and shavers. Normally, the cost of electricity is measured by usage in many countries. However, in some countries, usage is not measured and hotels are billed with a fixed charge, as in the case of the Playa Dorada Resort in the Dominican Republic.[13]

Electrical installations and levels of illumination are often determined by national codes and regulations to ensure the comfort and safety of guests and quality service by hotel staff. In the United Kingdom, standards for levels of illumination are determined by the Illumination Engineering Society (IES) and the Institution of Building Service Engineers (IBSE). Appropriate levels of illumination in different areas of a hotel and restaurant provide employees with a safe working environment, the guests a pleasant and comfortable living and dining environment, and reduce and avoid excessive contrast and glare in guest and dining rooms.

Communications

When people travel internationally, keeping contact with their home offices or family members and relatives is essential. International direct dial phone lines, fax services, and access for a laptop computer are the basic services to business and leisure tourists in developed countries. However, telecommunication systems in many developing countries still cannot meet the needs of international tourists. Modern fiber optic cables are limited, and exchanges are often overloaded in many developing countries. It often takes hours for a hotel guest to place an international phone call. For instance, Choice Hotels in India cannot be effectively connected to the company's global reservation system. Much of the communication is still done by faxing. In Russia, the telephones in Moscow's few Western-run hotels can often prove unreliable.[14] Russia has a long way to go in improving its telecommunication system since it has about fifteen telephone lines for every 100 people. Western technology and financial investment are badly needed to upgrade the telecommunication system in Russia.

Telephone systems vary from country to country due to the differences in economic and technological development. Four basic types of telephone systems can be found in hotel operations around the world. Private automatic branch exchange (PABE) is now commonly used in hotels with more than fifty extensions. It provides direct dialing and metering functions and offers automatic connection of outgoing and extension calls. Private manual branch exchange (PMBE) is often used in smaller properties and in many developing countries. This system routes all incoming and outgoing calls through the operator, and it is often limited by a certain number of outside lines. Private manual exchange (PME) is an independent internal system for communications between extensions, for example, guest room to guest room, or office to office. It may be used in parallel with public telephones. Some hotels also use an intercom system, which is directly wired and radio controlled for internal communication among the various departments.[15]

Sewage

The discharge and treatment of sewage are necessary infrastructural facilities for hotel operations. Proper sewage treatment can prevent pollution of beaches and water sources, and enable recycling of effluent for land irrigation. Therefore, appropriate drainage systems provide for separation of foul water from surface water to facilitate sewage treatment. Sewage treatment provides for settlement, removal, and decomposition of sludge and oxidation of suspended organic matter. Tertiary treatment is often used to chlorinate the effluent.[16] If poorly designed and built, sewage treatment plants tend to produce odor and attract flies. Therefore, proper siting and design of plants can reduce environmental hazards. Plants should be located away from the building, beach, and leisure areas.

The treated water is normally reused for secondary-grade water requirements. The remainder passes through soil-activated bacteria to be absorbed by the ground or displaced by evaporation. In coastal resorts, treated sewage is discharged through sea outfalls. However, in tropical regions with high rainfall, the sewage system can be overloaded during periods of heavy rain. Hotel managers in different geographical locations need to be prepared for handling sewage-related infrastructural concerns.

Solid Waste Disposal

Hospitality operations generate a large amount of solid waste materials on a daily basis. Many national governments have enacted strict environmental codes for collecting and disposing of these materials. Hotel and restaurant operations have to comply with such codes and regulations. Recycling of paper, aluminum, glass, and plastic is now a normal practice in hotel operations around the world.

To develop an effective recycling program, hotels need to use modern equipment for collecting solid waste. Waste needs to be transported to local or regional disposal sites, and the recycled materials are sent to the recycling center. An effective recycling program can also enhance the hotel's image among the guests and in the local community. This can create positive word-of-mouth publicity for the hotel as a leader in resource conservation and environmental protection.

HOTEL DESIGN

Hotel design is influenced by many factors: the functions of the hotel and the local cultural and physical environment. Hotel functions reflect various travel markets targeted by hotel companies. If hotels are planned to serve the upscale travel market, the design must be luxurious and sophisticated. For the economical segment of the travel market, the hotel design is simply no-frill and functional.

Hotel design is also dictated by the local cultural environment. It is recognized that most international tourists like to experience different cultures when they visit foreign countries. Hotel design modeled after a local architectural style is particularly popular with resort hotels. Hotels featuring unique local traditional architecture can become tourist attractions themselves and thus, increase business.

Hotel design also needs to incorporate the surrounding physical features and blend the property harmoniously with the physical environment. Failure to integrate the hotel design with the physical environment is criticized as "architectural pollution," which spoils or destroys the physical amenities such as beachfront, lakefront, or valley and mountain views.

Hotel building is usually subject to zoning requirements in many countries, especially in the developed countries. These countries have strict planning regulatory controls that require beach areas, sensitive coastlines, and hillsides to be kept free from obscuring hotel development. Control measures include a longer setback distance from the beachfront, or a certain building height behind natural vegetation. Hotels are therefore creatively integrated into the background with appropriate landscaping, built into cliffs and among rocky outcrops to reduce the outline, stepped down slopes screened by planted terraces, or kept below the height of the indigenous trees (see Exhibit 7.2).[17]

EXHIBIT 7.2. Best Western Berjaya Mahe Beach Resort and Casino, Victoria, Seychelles (Photo courtesy of Berjaya Mahe Beach Resort and Casino.)

The interior design of hotels often reflects the local cultural traditions or cultural themes from other countries. Many European hotels currently attract travelers with new and elaborate interior designs. Hotels in Germany, Denmark, and Great Britain are all participating in this new trend. The 233-room Radisson/SAS Scandinavian Hotel Aarhus in Denmark has used different and interesting room styles to raise sales. Four different cultural themes are used for the design of the guest rooms: Scandinavian, English, Chinese, and Japanese.[18] The hotel not only offers the guests lodging facilities, but also a cultural experience. In another example, the lobby of London's 640-room Mount Royal has a Tiffany-style ceiling, and the restaurant is Charleston style. The guests can thus enjoy the grandeur of the American cultural theme.

Hotel design is therefore determined by these three major factors: the markets served, the cultural factors, and environmental factors. Hotel developers need to identify not only the travel markets, but also the prevalent cultural theme as reflected in the local architectural style and the natural environment. A good design will enhance the property's image, increase the hotel's business, and enrich guests' travel experience (see Exhibit 7.3).

The Environmental Impact Statement

The environmental impact statement is a study that analyzes the impact of hotel development on the local environment and on society both on a short-term and long-term basis. In most developed countries, hotel developers are required to conduct an environmental impact analysis of a proposed hotel project. The impact of development on the vegetation and wildlife in the area, and other aspects that may affect the quality of life of the local residents, such as noise, pollution, and aesthetic values are thoroughly analyzed.

The environment impact analysis must comply with the local city or regional government regulations, codes, and ordinances. When the analysis is submitted for formal approval of zoning and development, the authority may request that development be modified or scaled back, for instance, by restrictions of height, vehicular access, sewage disposal, and color schemes.

Requirements for environmental analysis in different states or countries usually vary in detail, but the main contents tend to be similar. Even in many developing countries that used to have lax or no environmental regulations, new regulations for hotel and resort development are now being formulated. For instance, Thailand has recently developed very strict environmental laws to regulate hotel and resort development. These laws are intended to guide sound development practice and minimize the negative impact of hospitality development on the physical and cultural environment of the country.

HOTEL CONSTRUCTION

A detailed discussion of hotel construction is beyond the scope of this text. However, some basic knowledge regarding hotel building in foreign countries can be useful to international hotel managers. Location selection, design, materials, construction cost, and time are the important aspects of hotel construction.

Land Costs

Unit density of hotels is normally determined by the land and building costs. If the land is very expensive, hotel design usually results in a high-rise

EXHIBIT 7.3. The Atrium of Osaka Hilton Hotel (Photo courtesy of Osaka Hilton Hotel.)

building, such as the high-density multistory hotels in New York, London, Paris, Tokyo, Honolulu, Miami, and Hong Kong. When land for development is inexpensive, more can be purchased, and the hotel structure can sprawl with lower height. Land cost is generally 5 percent of overall development costs for undeveloped rural areas, 10 percent for suburban and secondary cities, and 15 to 20 percent for prime city locations.[19]

Plot ratio is the aggregate of gross floor area divided by the net area of the site. This ratio is applied to building density. In Western Europe, the ratio of 1:1 is used in sensitive residential districts, 2:1 in mixed urban areas, 2.5:1 on shopping streets, and 3.5:1 and 5:1 in heavily built-up commercial districts in central London and Paris. Plot ratios of 4:1 have been applied in some resorts in Spain, with a balance of public open space in promenades and gardens.[20]

In some developing countries and Eastern European countries, clear land title can be a major concern for hotel developers. Land in these countries has no legally recognized owners. For instance, two-thirds of Mexico City's residents have no proper deeds. In Indonesia, onerous titling regulations add 10 to 30 percent to the cost of buying land. In Peru, getting a deed used to require 207 bureaucratic steps divided among forty-eight government offices, and usually took forty-three months.[21]

The uncertainty of land title in many Eastern European countries is one of the major obstacles for many Western hotel developers in the region. These Eastern European countries were formerly ruled by communist governments. Under the communist regimes, private properties were confiscated and controlled by the authoritarian governments. After the collapse of the communist system, former property owners were allowed to reclaim their properties in East Germany and Hungary. Thousands of people submitted claims for their former land and property. This process makes the land title very cloudy in these countries. If a developer purchases a piece of land and builds a hotel on it, it may be later claimed by a private citizen who demands the land back. Even though the present governments in these countries promise clear land titles to foreign developers, developers still see the land title issue as a major obstacle.

Environmental Hazards

The selection of a construction site has to take into consideration potential environmental hazards ranging from storms, hurricanes, flooding, and earthquakes to rock or mud slides. These potential environmental hazards can cause varying degrees of damage to the physical structure of the hotel, threaten guest and employee safety, and cause substantial investment losses for the investors. Therefore, a thorough study of the building site and its vulnerability to potential environmental hazards must be carefully analyzed. If environmental hazards are unavoidable, such as seasonal hurricanes in the Caribbean region, effective and functional building design and construction can prevent damage to the building and loss of guest and staff lives and personal property. Following is a discussion of the major environmental hazards that may pose potential threat to hotel buildings.

Low-Lying and Coastal Areas

Hotels in low-lying and coastal areas are subject to flooding. An interesting study reported that a resort development on Viti Levu Island in Fiji had to raise the height of the resort's foundation by dredging and filling. This massive dredge-and-fill plan was proposed to protect the new resort from inundation by storms and possible rising sea levels because of global warming.[22] Flood level and the high tide level must be carefully examined to avoid these hazards. A setback distance is required in coastal areas, which places the hotel at certain distance from the shoreline. This distance varies from country to country. However, as a general rule, the setback distance is 40 meters (about 130 feet) from the highest level of tidal waves. Thus, the hotel will not be subject to severe flooding.

Seasonal storms, such as hurricanes or typhoons, cause substantial damage to hotels and resorts. High wind velocities, often reaching 140 mph to 150 mph, can destroy structures and devastate hotel operations. In 1995, several islands in the Caribbean were severely hit by two hurricanes in about a week, Hurricane Luis and Hurricane Marilyn. St. Thomas in the U.S. Virgin Islands was hard hit by Hurricane Marilyn in September 1995. Many infrastructural facilities and hotels were badly damaged and electric power was out. Marriott's 423-room Frenchman's Reef, the largest hotel in St. Thomas, recovered fully from the hurricane damage after one year of renovation. The 169-room Caneel Bay Hotel in St. John sustained heavy damage, and had to spend more than half a year for complete renovation. In St. Croix, the forty-room Hibiscus Beach Hotel lost six rooms in Hurricane Luis and, in the same storm, the restaurant of the St. Croix-by-the-Sea was blown into the hotel's swimming pool.[23] Obviously, hurricanes can devastate the hotel industry, and damage infrastructural facilities for a substantial period of time.

Hillsides

Many hotels and resorts are built on scenic sites to get the best view of mountains or lakes. Hotels constructed on hillsides are subject to several environmental hazards. Building construction has to cut into the slope, and therefore disturbs the stability of the vegetation cover. Once the vegetation is removed, the building site is vulnerable to runoff and soil erosion. Severe erosion can cause mud slides. It is normally suggested that it is not feasible to build hotels on hillsides over 20 percent.[24] If hotels have to be built on hillsides, appropriate engineering and construction methods must be used, and adequate landscaping needs to be planned. Extensive landscaping can blend the hotel with the surrounding environment and stabilize the ecosystem to reduce potential erosion problems (see Exhibit 7.4).

Earthquakes

When building hotels in geologically active regions, developers must take earthquake hazards into account. Earthquakes can destroy buildings and tourism infrastructure and kill people. The massive destruction of the Japanese city Kobe by earthquake in January 1995 claimed more than 6,000 lives and destroyed thousands of structures. Many hotels were destroyed in the earthquake. Some hotels were originally built to withstand earthquake damage, but they suffered to varying degrees from power

EXHIBIT 7.4. Hyatt Regency Tahiti in Arue, Tahiti (Photo courtesy of Hyatt Regency Tahiti.)

shortages, loss of gas services, ceiling cracks, and problems with the drain pipes. It took almost a year for most of the hotels to reopen for business.[25] The famous resort destination of Acapulco, in Mexico, also experienced a severe earthquake in 1997, causing significant damage to many local resort properties.

Building heights need to be evaluated to minimize potential hazards of earthquakes. Structurally, the foundation of the building must be firmly anchored on the bedrock. The use of building materials needs to follow local practice to reduce the damage to people and hotel property. In a word, hotels must be built to withstand potential earthquake hazard.

Using Local Building Materials

As discussed earlier, hotel design and building need to reflect the local cultural and physical environment. To achieve this objective, hotel contractors avail themselves of local building materials. The use of local materials has several advantages to the hotel developers and the local community. First, it can reduce building costs. Hotel developers do not need to import building materials from other countries, unless certain materials cannot be found in the host country. Second, the use of local materials can generate more jobs in the local economy, ranging from brick makers and cement producers to wood cutters. Therefore, the hotel company and developers can be favorably accepted by the community as a major contributor to the local economy. Third, the hotel can be integrated harmoniously with the local cultural and physical surroundings, since the building materials are similar to what the local people use.

Construction Cost and Quality

Building a new hotel in any country requires substantial capital investment. Construction costs for hotels of similar type and size vary significantly between the developed and the developing countries. But even among developing countries, construction costs vary considerably. For instance, Manila in the Philippines and Jakarta, Indonesia are comparable in population size and per capita income, but they differ greatly in construction cost of commercial buildings and time needed to obtain a building permit.[26]

Construction quality is highly regulated and inspected by government agencies and professional associations in most countries. However, great attention must be paid to the selection of local architects, designers, and building contractors in the developing countries. Some of them tend to overlook the building codes and ordinances in order to make maximum profits.

Such negligence often results in the collapse of the building and causes great personal and property damage. On August 13, 1993, more than 100 hotel guests and staff died when the Royal Plaza Hotel in Nakhon Ratchasima, about 155 miles (250 km) from Bangkok, collapsed. This tragedy was caused by the negligence of the local architect, who ignored the building safety codes and illegally added four floors to a two-story building.[27]

THE TREND OF ECORESORT DEVELOPMENT

Resort development requires sites with outstanding and unique natural features, such as beachfront, remote islands, riversides, lakesides, or mountains. Resort hotels do not just offer guests luxurious lodging facilities and food services, but also rely on magnificent physical surroundings to create a relaxing and tranquil vacation environment, and provide a wide range of outdoor recreational activities to keep guests at the resort longer. Due to the heavy demand for spectacular physical attributes, the integration of the physical environment and resort development has been highly emphasized by the international hospitality industry, and highly regulated by many national governments. New names for such integrated development have recently appeared in the research literature and industry journals: ecolodge, ecotel, ecohotel, ecoresort, green hotel, green resort, green room, and green suite. The development of environmentally sensitive hotels and resorts thus responds to the fast-growing ecotourism markets, and the general public's awareness of environmental preservation and sustainability.

The International Hotels Environmental Initiative (IHEI) was thus launched in May 1993 in the United Kingdom. This initiative was originally set up by eleven of the world's leading hotel chains (see Exhibit 7.5). It exemplified the idea of sustainable global and local development of the hospitality industry. Sustainability is intended to improve the quality of our life today without destroying it for subsequent generations. Since the hospitality industry is a major consumer of land, water, energy, food, raw materials, and cleaning products, and a major producer of solid wastes and effluents, the industry has a great responsibility to develop and manage hotels and restaurants in a sustainable way.[28]

An ecoresort master plan for sustainable hospitality development has been forcefully articulated by Hana Ayala, president of Eco-Resorts International, based in Irvine, California. She carefully examined the scope of environmental performance in the hotel industry, and identified environmental sponsorship and ecotechnologies as the new development trends.[29]

Environmental sponsorship refers to the initiatives set up by individual hotel corporations to involve the global industry in achieving greater envi-

EXHIBIT 7.5. Charter for Environmental Action in the International Hotel and Catering Industry

---

Recognizing the urgent need to support moral and ethical conviction with practical action, we in the hotel industry have established the International Hotel Environment Initiative to foster the continual upgrading of environmental performance in the industry worldwide.

With the cooperation and active participation of individual companies, hotels, and related organizations, the Initiative, which will be coordinated by The Prince of Wales Leaders Forum, will endeavor to:

1. Provide practical guidance for the industry on how to improve environmental performance and how this contributes to successful business operations;
2. Develop practical environmental manuals and guidelines;
3. Recommend systems for monitoring improvements in environmental performance and for environmental audits;
4. Encourage the observance of the highest standards of environmental management, not only directly within the industry but also with suppliers and local authorities;
5. Promote the integration of training in environmental management among hotel and catering schools;
6. Collaborate with appropriate national and international organizations to ensure the widest possible awareness and observance of the Initiative and the practice it promotes;
7. Exchange information widely, and highlight examples of good practice in the industry.

Charter Signators*

Paul Dubrule and Gerard Pelisson, Co-Chairmen, Accor;
Rocco Forte, Chairman/CEO, Forte PLC;
Michael Hirst, Chairman, Hilton International;
Bryan D. Langton, Chairman/CEO, Holiday Inn Worldwide;
Barron Hilton, Chairman, Conrad International Hotels;
Robert Collier, President, Inter-Continental Hotels;

W. R. Tiefel, President, Marriott Corporation;
Rodolphe Frantz, CEO, Societe Des Hotels Meridien;
Edward Cheng, President/Managing Partner, Wharf Hotel Investments Limited;
Bill Grau, President/CEO, Ramada International Hotels and Resorts;
John Kapioltas, Chairman/President/ CEO, ITT Sheraton Corporation.

Source: Jonathan Porritt, "The Prince and the Hoteliers," *Lodging* (October, 1995), 48.

*As this charter was signed in July 1994, some of the CEOs today are no longer with the organizations they represented then.

ronmental sensitivity and sustainability. The environmental and sustainable development strategy was pioneered by Inter-Continental Hotels in 1990 when it commissioned an environmental manual for hotel development and management. This manual consists of two major parts: "Handy Green Hints for Around the Hotel," and a "Mission Statement for Sustainability." Hotel development and operations by Inter-Continental Hotels are required to follow the environmental manual, and managers' bonuses are partially based on their properties' environmental performance.[30] This pioneer foresight by Inter-Continental Hotels was the initiative for getting the world's leading hotel corporations together to define the international hotel industry's environmental and social responsibilities.

Forte Plc has a very strong commitment to the environment of host communities in which its hotels operate. The commitment is reflected in activities such as tree planting and conservation programs. ITT Sheraton has initiated the "Going Green" program in Africa and the Indian Ocean region. This program seeks to improve conservation and environmental education within this geographical region. Sheraton has developed a very effective fundraising program known as "Optional Dollar" at several of the corporation's city hotels. The donations from guests are used for the study of wildlife in Benin, protection of the black rhinoceros from extinction in Zimbabwe, and purchase of antipoaching equipment for Nigeria's Game Reserve. Ramada International Hotels and Resorts and American Express have formed a cooperative partnership to support The Nature Conservancy in its effort to preserve the Palau archipelago in Micronesia.[31]

Ecotechnologies include the engineering and maintenance techniques used in hotel construction, operations to reduce the consumption of energy and water, and recycling and reusing waste materials. These ecotechniques include the use of solar energy, rain water collection, bioclimatic design, and recycling solid waste. The workbook published by the International Hotels Environmental Initiative has emphasized the importance of applying ecotechniques to upgrade the environmental performance of hotels. This document demonstrates effective ecotechniques practiced worldwide in building a hotel's environmental culture through six Rs: rethinking, reusing, reducing, rationalizing, recycling, and recovering.[32] Successful use of ecotechniques can greatly enhance favorable corporate image and make a positive impact on the supply industries, the venders, through precycling—making purchasing decisions that favor environmentally friendly products.

It is now quite common in hotel development and construction for the developer to set aside a portion of the site as an environmental preserve. For example, Las Bahias de Huatulco, a multiresort project in Mexico, has set aside about 70 percent of the site's 51,900 acres for conservation.[33]

The design of ecoresorts requires practices and equipment that differ from those of conventional resorts. The objective of ecoresort development is to minimize the strain of the resort's presence on the environment. Therefore, new design guidelines need to be followed for developing ecoresorts.

The design of environmentally sensitive hotels and resorts demonstrates the hospitality industry's concerns for the environment, and sets an example for consumers. Well-designed ecotels and ecoresorts can be an imaginative extension of the natural world, and provide a participatory window on nature's creations.[34] The creation of this kind of participatory educational environment can heighten the experience of the visitors, and help to establish an attitude of appreciation for the natural world. The conservation of the natural environment and participatory education through the development of an ecolodge can greatly place a hotel in a very competitive market position, enhance the hotel's image, and improve the quality of a destination's physical environment—the very attraction that pulled international tourists to visit in the first place.

SUMMARY

- International hotel products are varied and each one serves a certain segment of the international tourism market. International hotel development is concerned with identifying market demands for hotel facilities in particular locations.
- Since the early 1990s, international hotel companies have discovered that growth at the upscale/luxury segment of hotel development slowed down, but there has been an increasing demand for midmarket hotels worldwide.
- Hotel and resort development and construction require well-conceived conceptual plans based on market demands. The conceptual development plan includes seven phases: (1) establishing need, (2) feasibility analysis, (3) statement of scope, (4) project construction, (5) commissioning report, (6) facility testing, and (7) evaluation report.
- Infrastructure consists of all the underground and surface development construction of a place. The development of roads, water, power, communication, and sewage and solid waste disposal directly affect the successful operation of hospitality businesses since the hotel and restaurant operations are supported by the basic infrastructure.
- Hotel design is greatly influenced by the functions of the hotel, local cultural motif, and physical environment. A well-designed hotel can enhance the property's image, increase business, and enrich guests' travel experience.

- The environmental impact statement is a study that analyzes the impact of hotel development on the local environment and society both on a short- and long-term basis. It thoroughly analyzes the building's potential effect on surrounding environmental conditions, both at the time of construction and in the future.
- Unit density of hotels is normally determined by land and building costs. If land is very expensive, the hotel is often designed as a high-rise building. When land for development is inexpensive, the design of the hotel tends to be spread out.
- The selection of a hotel construction site needs to consider various environmental hazards: storms, hurricanes, flooding, earthquakes, and rock or mud slides.
- Use of local building materials can reduce construction costs, generate more employment for the local economy, and blend the hotel harmoniously into the local cultural and physical surroundings since the building materials are similar to what the local people use.
- The development of environmentally sensitive hotels and resorts responds to the fast-growing ecotourism markets and the general public's awareness of environmental preservation and sustainability. Sustainability improves the quality of life today without destroying it for future generations.
- The International Hotels Environmental Initiative (IHEI) was established in May 1993 in the United Kingdom. This initiative was originally established by eleven of the world's leading hotel chains. It exemplified the idea of sustainable global and local development in the hospitality industry.
- Environmental sponsorship refers to the initiatives set up by individual hotel and restaurant management to achieve greater environmental sensitivity and sustainability in their development and operations.
- Ecotechnology includes the engineering and maintenance techniques practiced in hotel construction and operations to reduce the consumption of energy and water, and recycle and reuse waste materials.
- The conservation of the natural environment through the development of ecotels and ecoresorts can enhance the establishment's competitive market position and improve the quality of the host country's physical environment.

STUDY QUESTIONS

1. What do international tourists expect for provision of lodging facilities when they travel to different countries?

2. What type of lodging facilities did the major international hotel companies primarily develop globally before the 1990s?
3. What has been the new global development focus by international hotel companies since the early 1990s?
4. What are the seven phases of a conceptual plan for hotel and resort development?
5. How can you identify the needs for new hotel development in a foreign country?
6. Discuss the aspects of market research that are normally included in the feasibility study.
7. What will be the advantage of developing a critical mass of mid-market hotels in a foreign city?
8. What does the project construction phase focus on?
9. What is the commissioning phase in the conceptual development plan?
10. What is the function of soft opening?
11. How can you define infrastructural development?
12. What is the Intermodal Surface Transportation Efficiency Act (ISTEA)?
13. Can you describe the layout and functions of the road in Puerto Plata Resort, the Dominican Republic?
14. What is the typical consumption of water per person in commercial hotels and luxury resorts in the developed countries?
15. Can you describe the three major sources of water that can be used for hotel, resort, and restaurant operations?
16. What are the different measurements in electrical voltages between the United States, Europe, and Asia? What impact will this difference have on serving international guests?
17. What are the four basic types of telephone systems that are commonly used around the world?
18. What are the major operational issues concerning sewage and solid waste disposal?
19. What does a hotel developer need to consider in hotel design?
20. What is "architectural pollution"?
21. What is the function of the environmental impact statement?
22. In what way does land cost determine the height and layout of a hotel?
23. What are plot ratios? Discuss the different plot ratios of hotel and resort development in different areas in European destinations.
24. What are the problems of obtaining land title in some developing countries?

25. What are the major environmental hazards that need to be considered in hotel design, construction, and operation?
26. Can you explain the advantages of utilizing local building materials for hotel construction in a foreign country?
27. What is sustainable development in the hospitality industry?
28. What is environmental sponsorship in global hospitality development and management?
29. Can you describe the various ecotechnologies used in international hotel and resort development and operations?
30. How can a well-designed ecoresort be an imaginative extension of the natural world and provide a participatory window on creation?

CASE STUDY: ECORESORTS— DOLLARS, SENSE, AND ENVIRONMENT

Among the terraced hillsides and rice fields of the Petanu river valley near the picturesque village of Ubud, Bali, the Banyan Tree Kamandalu promises peace and tranquillity in the form of a private villa. In Guyana, along the black waters of the Kumuni River near the Native American reservation of Santa Mission, Forte Hotels offers a weekend getaway for weary business travelers at Timberhead, a rainforest retreat. In Tanzania's Lake Manyara National Park, where lions sleep among the trees and rhinos roam the range, the traveler on safari finds solace at Accor's 100-room Lake Manyara Hotel, high atop a western bluff.

Tourism and culture. Tourism and the environment. Tourism and wildlife. One word, "ecotourism" (ecology + tourism) ostensibly covers them all—where ecotourists visit ecoresorts. Fad or trend? Only time will tell, but in the meantime, environmentally sensitive projects in remote places have never been more popular—or profitable.

"Gone are the days of the mass market going somewhere to just lie on the beach," says Howard J. Wolff, vice president and principal at the international resort design firm of Wimberly Allison Tong & Goo (WATG), Honolulu, Hawaii. "People are seeking to transform their lives in some sort of way, through education, culture, and recreation. The design of the resort can enhance that kind of experience." On Hawaii's Kohala Coast, teenagers at the Mauna Lani Bay Hotel and Bungalows are invited to explore the hidden pools, waterfalls, ravines, and guava forest of the Big Island in a day-long trek.

At Praia do Forte, a resort 85 km (52 miles) north of Salvador, Brazil, where the Rio Pojuca meets the Atlantic Ocean, guests watch as baby turtles crawl to the sea from one of the largest nesting sites in the world.

On Vanua Levu, the northern island of Fiji, a naturalist and a marine biologist at the Jean-Michel Cousteau Fiji Islands Resort lead nature hikes, while certified dive masters invite visitors to explore the Koro Sea and Savusavu Bay.

"If you approach the resort as an educational experience, there are unlimited possibilities," says Michael Freed, a cogeneral partner at Jean-Michel Cousteau Fiji Islands Resort, open since Earth Day, April 19, 1995. "There are an infinite amount of things to learn in this world."

Economics of Ecotourism

"If you create a great experience, people will pay, whatever the cost," says Freed, who employs the same philosophy at his consortium's senior resort, the Post Ranch Inn at Big Sur, California. "Our average daily rate at the Fiji resort is $400, and there is not a television in sight." Statistics garnered from no less than four recent studies confirm the fact: a huge market exists for ecotourism. According to a Travel Industry Association of America study, an estimated 43 million people in the United States alone consider themselves ecotourists and are willing to pay an 8.5 percent premium to stay in what they perceive as an environmentally sensitive property.

"Basically, ecotourism is going mainstream," says Megan Epler Wood, executive director of The Ecotourism Society, North Bennington, Vermont, an association with more than 1,000 members in seventy-five countries. "It is a plum market when you study the data, with people willing to spend more money for less infrastructure." The studies describe the ecotraveler as educated and affluent:

> More than 50 percent of ecotravelers are college educated with mean incomes of $50,000 to $70,000.

> Only 28 percent of ecotravelers have children at home, compared with 40% of the general traveling public.

> About 50 percent of ecotravelers regularly take more lengthy vacations, from eight to fourteen days, compared with only 35 percent of other travelers.

"This sounds like the profile of a retiree," says Epler Wood, "but actually 56 percent of ecotravelers are between the ages of thirty-five and fifty-four, with a mean age that hovers around fifty." According to the Pacific Rim Institute of Tourism, Vancouver, British Columbia, these educated, affluent travelers are interested first in natural settings, second by activities. Accommodations are far less important than the overall experience, which can be enhanced by guides or interpretive programs.

"Just as hotel developers as a group are becoming more sophisticated, so are the travelers," WATG's Wolff says. "They know the difference between a well-designed and a poorly designed resort. As a result, it is much easier now to appeal to the conscience of the developer and explain why an environmentally sensitive design makes sense—because 'eco' also stands for economics. Now more than ever, hoteliers know that environmentally friendly strategies make sound sense."

The staff at the Chicago Hilton and Towers collects more than 14,000 lbs. (6,342 kg) of cardboard each month, while engineers at the Regent Jakarta installed an irrigation system to raise crops and water plants that has reduced water consumption by 33 percent. Food items are separated and returned to the sea, or composted at the Banyan Tree Maldives Vabbinfaru, Republic of Maldives, according to general manager Robert de Graaff. "No doubt, you can increase the profitability of any hotel or resort," says J. T. Kuhlman, president of Inter-Continental Hotels and Resorts' American Division. "Our big win has been the electric bill, where we were able to save $5 million around the world last year." Some programs are not profitable, such as the handling of toxic wastes, Kuhlman says. But improper disposal "simply does not make good business sense—or good citizenship."

Abused, Misused, and Ill-Defined

The term "ecotourism" continues to be extensively abused in resort advertising campaigns, while the word "ecoresort" has yet to be fully defined, says The Ecotourism Society's Epler Wood. The society defines "ecolodge" as a "nature-dependent tourist lodge" that offers "an educational and participatory experience. It is developed and managed in an environmentally sensitive manner and protects its operating environment." The ecoresort typically has some or all of the following components: flatlands, water, hills, forest, and local culture. Aspects of archaeology, history, architecture, anthropology, ethnicity, religion, arts, and crafts also should be included.

Culture and community increasingly are important aspects of the ecoresort. Both facets are featured extensively in The Ecotourism Society's guide for ecolodges, which will be published soon. Surrounding communities should have a say in how a resort will interact with the native culture. Programs also should be developed to hire and train locals for decision-making positions. Above all, communities should share in the success of the property.

The idea of sustainable nature tourism is being applied deep within the Amazon basin at the Amazon Jungle Lodge, a model for ecotourism near Manaus, Brazil. The low-impact development, a joint venture between the Foundation for the Future (FUTURO) and the Instituto Interamericano de Capacitacion Turistica (IICT), will include a Rainforest Lodge, a training academy, and a native crafts center. The academy, operated by IICT with curriculum provided by Hocking Technical College, Nelsonville, Ohio, will educate and train locals in fields associated with ecotourism such as forestry management and natural resources technology. The arts and crafts center will serve as a showcase for traditional culture and native wares. All profits from the project will be reinvested in education and conservation programs within the region.

Partnership in Paradise

Tourism means money, and to government officials of developing nations, money generated by ecotourism brings fresh water, waste treatment facilities, roads, and electricity to undeveloped lands. "Since 1991, there has been an effort to liberalize and diversify our economic base," says Tessa Fraser, director of tourism in Guyana. "One area we looked at to attract investment was tourism." Guyana's strategy shows some signs of paying off. Besides the successful Timberhead Lodge, there are plans for additional ecotourism facilities near outdoor attractions such as Kaieteur Falls, along the Potaro River. "As a tropical destination, we are still in the process of developing our product," Fraser says. "We have mountains and 75 percent of our rainforest is intact, but our infrastructure is relatively underdeveloped. Our airport may be OK for flights from within the Caribbean, but from an international point of view, it needs to be upgraded."

An international partnership can help. In Tanzania, Accor Resort Hotels, in a partnership with Tanzanian Hotel Investments Ltd. (TAHI), was awarded a management contract in return for a $20 million investment in five run-down, government-owned wildlife lodges: The Lobo Wildlife Lodge and The Seronera Wildlife Lodge on the Seregeti plain; The Ngorongoro Wildlife Lodge at the rim of Ngorongoro, the world's largest crater; The Lake Manyara Hotel, which overlooks glassy waters adjacent to Manyara National Park; and a hotel at the foot of Mount Meru in Arusha.

"It is a fifty-fifty venture. Accor brings the cash and the Tanzanian government provides the lodges," says Didier Rouge Biscay, vice president of sales and marketing for Accor, which, with TAHI, completed renovations at the lodges in December 1995. Accor, well-established in West Africa, receives a foothold in the potentially lucrative southern Africa market as well as a percentage of the revenues and gross operating profits. Tanzania, in return, enjoys a French hotel company that trains and feeds 170 employees per lodge and donates a percentage of revenues to the national parks and $1 per guest to surrounding communities.

The Final Frontier

As ecotourism grows, so does the demand for new resorts in faraway and pristine lands. From northeastern Brazil to the South Pacific, Africa to the Adriatic Sea, construction is underway. "We have got 5,000 hectares (12,500 acres) and 12 kilometers of beach, a mixed bag of cultural history, rivers, and a rainforest, but this market will not take off until the airplanes do—there are no direct flights from the U.S. to Salvador in Brazil," says Marc Van Steenlandt, managing principal at VOA Associates Inc., Orlando, Florida, designer of Praia do Forte. "So far, that is what is keeping operators at a distance." Beyond Brazil, Van Steenlandt has been involved with recent resort development projects near Cartagena, Colombia; Machu Picchu, Peru; and Tikal, Guatemala. What destination could be next in line? Van Steenlandt suggests Lombak, an island east of Bali.

"The South Pacific has tremendous potential," says Epler Wood. "It has the most pristine coral reefs in the world—even better than in the Caribbean." South Africa, with its first-rate system of national parks, has prepared for an onslaught in ecotourism since economic sanctions were lifted, according to Epler Wood.

In the Middle East, WATG has designed a desert oasis near the Dead Sea in Jordan. The firm also has plans for a hillside village resort that blends with the petroglyphs and rock house temples of the ancient city of Petra, Jordan.

"Other recent and perhaps surprising regions for ecoresort development are India and the islands off Croatia. "Some of the islands in the Adriatic Sea have twelfth-century monasteries," says Bierman-Lytle, executive director of New Canaan, Connecticut-based Sustainable Environment Associates, who is developing a plan to convert the monasteries into ecoresorts. "Coast to coast, Panama has some interesting opportunities," Inter-Continental's J. T. Kuhlman says. There are 10 km (6 miles) on either side of the Panama Canal that is in the hands of the government. The land is uninhabited and untouched . . . for now.

Case Study Source

Steven Shundich, "Ecoresorts: Dollars, Sense & the Environment," *Hotels* (March, 1996), 34-36, 38, 40. Reprinted by permission of *Hotels* magazine, a publication of Cahners Business Information.

Case Study Questions

1. What travel and lodging experience do most international tourists seek when they travel to foreign destinations?
2. How can hotel design enhance such experience?
3. What is the potential for ecotourism development around the world?
4. Can you explain why "hoteliers know that environmentally friendly strategies make sound economic sense" in resort development?
5. How is the term "ecolodge" defined by the Ecotourism Society?
6. What components does an ecoresort typically have?
7. Why should the host culture and community be considered as important aspects of the ecoresort?
8. Can you describe the low-impact development and operations at the Amazon Jungle Lodge?
9. What economic benefits can ecotourism bring to a local community?
10. How was the international partnership developed between Tanzanian Hotel Investments Ltd. and Accor for developing and managing the wildlife lodges?
11. Can you identify the emerging regions that have great potential for future ecoresort development?

PART IV:
HOSPITALITY MANAGEMENT
FUNCTIONS

The six chapters in Part IV focus on international hospitality management functions. Operating a hospitality business in a foreign country differs to some extent from domestic operations because of the legal, commercial, and cultural differences between the host country and the home country. These differences are identified in each of the hospitality management functional areas. Appropriate management skills are discussed for hospitality operations in the global environment.

Chapter 8 dwells on the legal aspects of international hospitality operations. National law reflects the cultural values of a country. Various legal systems follow different procedures for regulating business operations and resolving business disputes. Different legal systems are analyzed in this chapter, with specific attention to laws governing the operations of hospitality business.

Chapter 9 examines the financial aspects of international hospitality development and management. International hospitality operations deal with many foreign currencies; the conversion of one currency to another involves exchange gain or loss. This chapter explains the complex foreign exchange market and techniques for hedging foreign exchange risk. The availability of capital markets for global development is discussed. Chapter 9 describes a detailed financial budget planning process for developing international hospitality business.

International accounting and taxation issues are the focus of Chapter 10. International hospitality accounting has to deal with the transaction of foreign currencies and the recording of gain and loss. A standard translation method is introduced in this chapter. Each country has over the years developed its own tax structure. Knowledge of the host country's tax system and proper tax planning can reduce a firm's tax liability in a particular country. Different types of taxes and tax rates in selected countries are explained in this chapter.

Managing employees in a different culture presents a great challenge to global hospitality managers. Chapter 11 discusses human resources management in international hospitality operations. This topic is treated at two levels: management of expatriate managers and management of local managers and staff. Each function is thoroughly analyzed with multicultural considerations. Management and labor union relationships and expatriate compensation are also covered in this chapter.

Chapter 12 is about international hospitality marketing, which deals with three different markets: guests from the home country, guests from the host country, and guests from other countries. It is a great challenge for managers to understand consumer behavior in the highly diversified international markets. This chapter follows the traditional discussion of the four marketing elements: product and service, distribution, promotion, and pricing. Online marketing as a new marketing tool is extensively discussed in this chapter.

Food service operation is a major component of international hospitality business. However, dietary preferences and restrictions in a particular culture are greatly influenced by religious beliefs. Chapter 13 examines the impact of religion on diet and on food service operations. It discusses food service management issues encountered by hospitality companies in overseas operations. Dining etiquette in selected countries is described for better service practice, and for proper dining manners in the host country.

These six chapters combine to present a comprehensive discussion of international hospitality management functions. Each function is systematically discussed at both theoretical and practical levels. The case study at the end of each chapter demonstrates how the management concepts and skills can be applied to real-world management issues.

Chapter 8

Legal Environment

Because of the absence of a legal system, it takes a very experienced person to work in China, one with maturity and great patience. It has certainly been a lesson in life for me.[1]

An expatriate manager in China

LEARNING OBJECTIVES

In this chapter, you will study:

1. The major legal systems in the world
2. The common law system and where it is practiced
3. The civil law system and where it is practiced
4. The characteristics of the socialist legal system
5. Islamic law and its influence on business
6. Various aspects of international law
7. International franchise agreements
8. International dispute resolution

INTRODUCTION

Every hospitality manager is aware of the ubiquitous constraints of the law on business operations. International hospitality operations face an even greater maze of constraints, because the law of each host country is added to the problems faced when operating only in the domestic environment. However, law provides the ground rules for international hospitality investment and operations. An understanding of the ground rules for international hospitality businesses allows global managers to operate successfully in competitive global markets. Working knowledge of the international legal system thus enables global managers to make judgments about the political and business risk of hospitality operations in different countries. It allows managers to clarify their ethical values in a world of multiple ethical and legal paradigms.

This chapter therefore discusses and analyzes the complexity of the international legal system. It examines the nature and dimensions of the legal systems in which the hospitality business operates. It first describes the laws of nations, and discusses the essential legal aspects of the management and operations of international hospitality business. It then discusses the international law, treaties, and agreements that regulate international commercial undertakings. Finally, specific laws on tourism, hospitality investment, and operations in selected countries are highlighted, and strategies and assistance for legal disputes are discussed. The overview of the international legal environment enhances global managers' legal perspective on international hospitality management.

MAJOR LEGAL SYSTEMS

The laws of a society are one aspect of its culture. They are the rules established by authority, society, or custom. Collectively, these rules govern the affairs of people within a society. The laws of a nation are merely a more concrete manifestation of its attitudes and cultural norms, and usually reflect its religious tradition.[2] Laws of nations thus vary from country to country. However, most scholars who specialize in studying and comparing laws of different countries agree that there are at least four broad classifications of law in the world: common law, civil law, socialist law, and Islamic law. This section discusses these four major legal systems, and examines how each system accommodates international business undertakings.

The Common Law System

The common law originated in England, dating back to the conquest of England in 1066 when the Norman invaders centralized the administration of justice in the royal courts. The king's judges then determined the legal rights of disputing parties by examining similar cases from town to town. From the previous cases, a law common to the kingdom was developed.[3]

A major characteristic of the common law is that it reasons from the specific to the general.[4] Thus, the general principles of the common law are not based on a body of codes, but evolve through case precedent. Common law judges have never written a code to determine a myriad of specific problems. Rather, the judges solve a particular case in a certain way. When a similar problem arises, they have to decide whether to solve it in the same way as the earlier one, or whether it is different enough to justify another solution. The law thus grows through an organic process, adapting itself to changing conditions as the time requires.[5]

Clearly, the primary focus of the common law is the case. The law evolves over time as judges apply the reasoning of prior cases to new facts. A key concept in the common law is that similar disputes should have similar legal results. Therefore, parties to a dispute will search for similar earlier cases with favorable outcomes. Those earlier cases set a precedent for a current case. Precedents in common law are considered to provide the stability needed for citizens and business to plan future actions.[6] The common law system allows more popular participation than any other legal system through the use of the jury. It also allows more protection to those accused of crime than any other legal systems.

Common law countries are primarily English-speaking countries that were at one time English colonies. They include the United States, Canada, Australia, New Zealand, India, Hong Kong, Jamaica, Belize, Guyana, Ghana, Nigeria, Kenya, Singapore, and others. Countries following the common law tradition demonstrate similar legal systems in dealing with commercial undertakings. To illustrate, let us examine how business contracts are formulated in three common law countries: the United States, Britain, and Canada.

A commercial business contract is a legal document that binds the parties involved in the business transaction to their respective obligations. The business contract is vitally important in common law countries since legal judgment is not based on a body of codes, but on the court's interpretation of events. Therefore, contract law in common law countries tends to be very detailed, with all contingencies spelled out to protect each party involved.

Most of the American law governing the writing of commercial contracts is contained in the Uniform Commercial Code, adopted by all states except Louisiana (Louisiana follows the civil law system, which will be discussed later).[7] Following is the outline of the major components that are required by law for making a commercial contract:

1. A valid offer
2. A valid acceptance
3. The mutual assent of the parties
4. Consideration

5. Contractual capacity of both parties
6. A lawful objective
7. Sometimes, a written contract (a commercial contract must be in writing if a contract for sale of goods exceeds $500)

The parties to a contract are expected to perform as they agreed. Parties must do exactly what they promised on or before the time that was agreed. If a party does not do what was promised, and has no legally valid excuse for not doing it, the party is guilty of breaching the contract.

The remedies for breaching a commercial contract include restitution, damage, and specific performance. Restitution is used only when the breaching party has made partial performance or payment. The victim of a breach is entitled to recover the value of the performance or payment. Damages are the common remedy for breach of contract in the United States. The breaching party must pay the victim enough money to compensate for the harm caused by the breach. Specific performance is to force the breaching party to perform the contract.

Most of the English law of common contracts is contained in the Sale of Goods Act. It is similar to the American law except for a few minor variations. English courts are less likely to allow specific performance in case of breach of contract than are American courts. Canadian contract law has many of the same roots as U.S. contract law with similar terminologies and concepts. However, there are some marked differences in specific contract rules among Canadian provinces, particularly in the province of Quebec, which practices civil law.

The Civil Law System

The civil law system traces its origin to the Roman Empire. Justinian, one of the last emperors, compiled the *Corpus Juris Civilis* in the sixth century. This Justinian Code was a comprehensive legal document that was supposed to cover all necessary areas of the law. The code thus became the foundation document of the civil law tradition. It was intended to be a complete and exhaustive statement of the law, a concept that led directly to the modern idea of a civil code as an extensive and fully integrated body of law.

In some civil law countries, the civil codes attempt to cover every aspect of the legal system. In others, they cover more limited aspects, such as the obligations that individuals owe each other in tort and contract. In these countries, the codes will be supplemented by a substantial body of other statutory law. What ties the civil law countries together is that codes have a profound influence on the way law is shaped and on the way new law is made.

All the continental European countries have adopted civil law systems. The civil law tradition extends to Central and South America, parts of Asia, Africa, and Mexico, Puerto Rico, Quebec, and Louisiana. Clearly, there are historical links between the legal systems of many former European colonial powers, and those of their former colonies. The civil law system is practiced in more than seventy countries around the world.

There are many differences between commercial contract law under the civil law system and the common law system. Business contracts in civil law countries tend to be shorter and less specific compared to contracts written in common law countries. This is because the basic principles of contract obligations are covered in the contract in common law countries, but are included in the civil code in civil law countries.

In terms of accepting an offer, when the acceptance is effective varies from country to country within the civil law system. In Germany it is effective only when it is received by the offerer, not when it is sent to the offerer. In Switzerland it is effective when it is sent to the offerer. In France, it depends on the circumstances of the case because French law provides no general rule. An acceptance may be effective even if its items are not identical to those in the offer.

The concept of *consideration* does not exist in many civil law countries. In common law countries, a business contract must have a consideration component on both sides. Consideration takes four forms: (1) an act, (2) a promise, (3) a forbearance (a promise *not* to do something), and (4) a promise to a third party. The usual contract consists of an exchange of two promises: the service performer to perform the service duty, and the receiver to pay the performer for the service. These promises are called considerations in a contract. Therefore, most contracts in the common law system require a bargained-for exchange in order to be binding. But a promise is binding in the civil law system if there is a legal reason for making it. In Germany, agreements to make gifts and agreements to hold offers open are examples of legally enforceable expressions of will. This absence of consideration as a legal requirement can have a major impact on the process of negotiating complex commercial agreements in civil law countries.

German law also includes a statute governing the terms of standard-form contracts, such as those a consumer might have to sign when purchasing goods. Historically, such contracts between business providers and consumers have been one-sided, with the more sophisticated business providers using the contract form to disclaim responsibilities and liability. Currently, the law prevents them from disclaiming all liability for defective goods and protects consumers in situations in which historically they have not had real bargaining power.

In Austria, one party may rescind a contract when the value of his or her performance would be worth more than double the value of the other party's performance. In France, one party may rescind due to *Lésion Énorme*, a gross disparity in value between the two performances. Such rescission of a contract is criticized by lawyers in common law countries as inadequate consideration.

In terms of physical capacity, the age of adulthood is determined as eighteen in most civil law countries. However, the age of adulthood is twenty in Japan and Switzerland. Civil law generally considers the contract of a minor unenforceable if the minor's parents or legal guardian do not ratify it. Germany allows an adult to rescind a contract with a minor.

Civil law system gives contract parties much more flexible remedies for breach of contract than the commonly used remedy of damages in the common law system. For instance, in Germany, a hotelier has the option of making price adjustments for defective or lower quality goods with the purveyors, or of rejecting them. If the purveyor delivers goods to a hotel or restaurant, and the goods are of a lower quality than specified in the contract, the goods can often still be resold, but at a lower price. The law thus allows the hotel and restaurant to reduce the contract price and take the goods. This differs from the common law, which normally insists on acceptance or rejection.

In the civil law system, the victim has the right to force the breach party to perform if this is possible. The victim also has the option to claim damages. If relations between the parties have deteriorated to the point where court action is necessary, the victim usually prefers damages to specific performance just to get the argument settled.

The Socialist Legal System

The legal systems of the communist countries are based upon socialist law. The socialist legal system started with the Russian Revolution of 1917, and consequently has affected a number of other countries that adopted communism as their form of government, such as the former Eastern European countries, China, Cuba, and several countries in Asia and Africa. Since the socialist legal system originated in Western legal traditions, it resembles to some extent the civil law system.

In the late 1980s, the communist governments in the Eastern European countries and the former Soviet Union collapsed. The socialist legal system has been gradually replaced by the civil law system as these countries developed new, free-market economic systems. For example, jury trials, abolished by the Bolsheviks in 1918, resumed in Russia in 1994. However, the transition has not been a smooth one. Ubiquitous crime and corruption stand in the way. The murder of Paul Tatum, an investor in Radisson Slavyanskaya Hotel in Moscow, sent a chilling shock to the international hospitality industry in 1997.[8] The murder suspect has not yet been brought to justice. In addition, the judiciary system is still under the shadow of the old socialist influence, and the country has too few qualified lawyers: 28,000 public prosecutors and 20,000 independent lawyers for a population of 148 million compared to 800,000 lawyers in the United States.[9]

At present, a few communist countries remain in the world. Socialism still shapes the legal system in China, a major emerging economy that attracts many foreign investors. However, political ideology is deeply ingrained in the socialist legal system. China still looks to socialism for its formal legal institutions and methods. Even today, with its rapid economic growth, China is still cautiously experimenting with both its economic and legal systems, resulting in a highly unstable legal environment for foreign business.

Since 1979, China has enacted significant legislation in many areas affecting international business.[10] Among those laws are statutes regulating joint ventures, contracts, intellectual property, taxes, and product liability. Currently, the Chinese legislature is working on a comprehensive law for the travel and hospitality industry. Virtually all of the formal Chinese law a foreigner will encounter is in the form of statutes and regulations. China is working toward a civil law framework, with legislation as the primary source of law, and no real recognition of judge-made law or precedent.

Chinese contract law thus finds its sources in statutes and regulations, rather than in case law. The statutes governing contracts are all quite new, and some areas of law and regulation are still in the formative stages. Chinese contract law for domestic business is contained in the Civil Code, enacted in 1986. The Civil Code includes provisions on contract formation, legality, breach, and remedy. The Foreign Economic Contract Law, enacted in 1985, governs contracts between Chinese businesses, organizations, government agencies, and foreign investors.

Clearly, China's legal tradition is not yet fully developed. Some Chinese businessmen still do not consult lawyers for legal advice. They rely less on written contracts than do Westerners, and more on mutual trust, understanding, and the all-important *guanxi* (connection). Some Western lawyers and their clients, Americans in particular, find it very difficult to operate in such a legal environment.

Many government officials still lack legal concepts in business dealings with foreign companies. They tend to rely on bureaucratic or political methods for handling international business contracts and relations. Rescinding a promise in a business contract is not uncommon in international business operations. One of the major cases involved the city of Beijing and McDonald's Corporation in 1995.

McDonald's restaurant in Beijing was opened in 1992. It is the largest restaurant in McDonald's systemwide operations. Located in the busiest commercial section of downtown Beijing, just two blocks from Tiananmen Square, McDonald's was granted a twenty-year land-use agreement for the location by Beijing's municipal government. But McDonald's was shocked to receive an eviction notice from Beijing in late November 1994. City officials demanded that McDonald's vacate its central Beijing site to make room for a $1.2 billion commercial and residential complex called Oriental Plaza, which was proposed and would be financed by a Hong Kong billionaire, Li Ka-shing. Apparently, he had better connections with the municipal officials in Beijing. McDonald's was then guaranteed a place in the new building when it was completed in three years.

By late November 1994, much of the area surrounding McDonald's had already been demolished to make room for the new development. Only McDonald's and the sentimental notion of the rule of law stood in the way. McDonald's, understandably, did not care to leave, and quietly insisted that it should not have to leave according to the land-use agreement. Only after the McDonald's case drew international condemnation did the Chinese central government intervene, and McDonald's was allowed to stay at the same site. The proposed commercial and residential complex was scaled down.[11] This case demonstrated that contracts can be sometimes readily disposed of by authorities in communist countries, since they are used to solving legal disputes through bureaucratic and political means. Rescinding a promise in a contract with ease definitely sends a negative message to potential foreign investors.

The Islamic Legal System

The Islamic legal system is the most important non-Western legal system that is based on the teachings of a religion. The Islamic religion is widely distributed in the world. Its influence stretches from the Balkans through the Middle East, North Africa, India, and Southeast Asia. Understanding of the theocratic law of Islam is important for conducting hospitality business in the Islamic countries.

The Islamic religion began in the early seventh century when the Prophet Muhammad, a trader in the city of Mecca, began preaching his messages from God (Allah). God's commandments, as revealed to Muhammad, provide a path, or *Shari'a*, for true believers to follow (more detailed discussion on world religion will be presented in Chapter 13). Islamic law is primarily found in the *Shari'a,* which deals with the relationship of God to man, of rulers to ruled, and of man to man.

Islamic law recognizes four major types of contracts: (1) *bay,* or sale; (2) *hiba,* or gift; (3) *ijara,* or hire; and (4) *arriya,* or loan.[12] The hire contract is described in this section since it is relevant to hospitality management operations. Hire involves the selection and employment of a person. For a contract of hire to be valid, three things must be spelled out: the nature of the work to be performed by the employee, the wage of the employee, and the term of employment.

In financial management, Islamic banks used to pay no interest to depositors, and collect no interest from borrowers. This practice is strictly dictated by *riba*—the charging of any interest whatsoever on a loan is forbidden. If the Islamic bank is forbidden to lend money to borrowers for interest, how can it make loans and earn profits from them? The answer is found in a traditional Arab arrangement known as the *mudaraba*: the lender asks for partial ownership of the enterprise to which he lends. Instead of paying the lender interest, the borrower pays the lender a share of his profits. Lender and borrower thus become partners. The bank is not a creditor of its borrower, it is a co-owner of the borrower's enterprises. If the borrower's business prospers, the bank earns a larger return on its investment than it would by simply collecting interest. If the borrower fails, the bank will lose the lent funds.

INTERNATIONAL LAWS AND ORGANIZATIONS

International law is different from the laws of nations. The reason is that there is no international legislative body making laws that govern international business affairs. What does exist is a collection of agreements, treaties, and conventions between two or more countries, which constitute an important element of international law.

In addition, international organizations such as the United Nations, the General Agreement on Tariffs and Trade (GATT), the World Bank, and so on have a direct impact on the conduct of international business. International law is therefore an amalgamation of rules and obligations derived from a number of sources.

International treaties (agreements, conventions) are a source to which a court refers regarding international commercial relations and disputes between countries. A treaty resembles an international contract. A treaty between two countries is bilateral, and one between three or more countries is multilateral. A country is bound by the treaties to which it is a party, and it becomes a party by ratifying, approving, accepting, acceding, or adhering to the treaty pursuant to authority granted by the country's internal constitutional processes. For instance, the United States becomes a party to a treaty after it has been signed by the president, has received the advice and consent of the U.S. Senate, and has been ratified and proclaimed by the president.

International law regarding treaties is best summarized in the Vienna Convention on the Law of Treaties. Under Article 31 of the Vienna Convention, the terms of the treaty are to be given their ordinary meaning and interpreted in the light of the objective and purpose of the treaty. As aids to interpretation, the court may use the treaty's text, including its preamble and annexes, and any other related agreement made between all the parties at the conclusion of the treaty, and also any contemporaneous instrument accepted by the parties as related to the treaty. Subsequent agreements between the parties, and subsequent practices establishing such agreements, may also be used as interpretative aids.

Many international treaties govern international commercial undertakings between countries. The most widely used international treaty is known as the Treaty of Friendship, Commerce, and Navigation (FCN). This treaty is a comprehensive agreement providing equal treatment for foreign firms doing business in the host country. The agreement includes specific areas of business interest, such as trade, investment, property ownership and transfer, access to courts, intellectual property rights, and employment rights. In addition, FCN treaties open ports to the ships of other signatory countries, and provide navigation rights in each country's territorial waters. The purpose of FCN is to protect the right of a firm to do business in a foreign country and guarantee equal treatment to the foreign firm, so it will not be discriminated against by the host country's laws and judiciary. If there is no FCN treaty between two countries, these two countries cannot engage in any commercial relations. For instance, there is at present no FCN treaty between the United States and Cuba.

Agreement for the Sale of Services

International agreements involving the sale of goods and services have been developed over the years by various sources, such as the General Agreement on Tariffs and Trade (GATT). Signed on January 1, 1948, the purpose of GATT was to commit member countries to the principles of nondiscrimination and reciprocity. This means that if a bilateral trade treaty is negotiated between two GATT members, those provisions will be extended to other members. Member countries are granted most favored nation (MFN) status. All member nations must harmonize their laws with GATT or face sanctions. Currently, GATT has approximately 100 members.

These members bargain in multiyear rounds of discussion on tariff reduction, quantitative restrictions, and settlement of disputes. Thus, bilateral trade talks are replaced (not entirely) with talks with all contracting parties participating. The group offices are headquartered in Geneva, and a council made up of member representatives is responsible for enforcement and dispute settlement.

Countries that participate in the GATT are now bargaining to negotiate free trade provisions governing the sale of services. The United States-Canada Free Trade Agreement contains some innovative provisions on the sale of services between those two countries, particularly in banking and telecommunications. In sales of services, construction and engineering service contracts are commonly used in global development. Since construction and engineering service contracts include the building of hotels and restaurants in foreign countries, the formulation and provisions of this type of contract is discussed in detail.

The United Nations has promulgated a comprehensive set of construction contract provisions, known as the Legal Guide on Drawing Up International Contracts for the Construction of Industrial Works. While focusing on the construction of factories and similar projects, it is believed that this guide is helpful for virtually any kind of construction project. The guide includes an extensive list of elements that are normally contained in a construction contract:

Description of the construction
Guarantees
Technology transfer
Pricing
Payment
Scheduling
Role of the consulting engineer
Subcontracting
Inspection
Completion
Acceptance
Risk of loss
Delays
Damages (including liquidated damages)
Excusability
Changes
Suspensions
Terminations

Postconstruction obligations (such as the provision on training
  programs and spare parts)
Choice of law
Dispute resolution

Large-scale construction contracts are usually massive documents with exceptionally detailed provisions. Any hospitality company or individual developer who builds hotels and restaurants in foreign countries can follow this guide for writing construction service contracts.

As discussed in Chapter 6, an increasingly popular service contract for conducting hospitality business in developing countries is the management contract. A management contract is an agreement by which a company in the host country in essence buys expertise for the management of the purchaser's operations, such as managing a hotel for a local owner. The provisions for formulating a management contract normally include the length of the contract, control of operations, payment structure of management fees, termination, choice of law, remedy for legal disputes, and so on.

Another service contract that is commonly used in international hospitality operations is franchising. Franchising is a quintessentially U.S. form of doing international business. As popular as they are in the United States, franchise agreements are not uniformly admired elsewhere in the world. The primary concerns in foreign franchising operations include many complex legal issues, such as protection of trademarks and management know-how, specific regulations on termination of franchises established by the host government, any special matters of taxation, and any special controls on utilization of personnel.

At the heart of international franchise agreements lies a trademark licensing clause that conveys the trademark rights of the franchiser to the franchisee in return for a royalty payment. Trademarks are a form of intellectual property of great significance to international hospitality corporations. Since companies spend millions of dollars to develop product brands, others may use the name illegally if they are not protected by a trademark law. Trademarks must go through a national registration process to be protected internationally.

CASE STUDY:
THE USE OF THE CONRAD HILTON NAME

This case describes a legal fight between two major international hotel corporations for the use of a brand name. In 1991, London-based Ladbroke Group Plc, which bought Hilton International in 1987, filed a trademark-infringement lawsuit against the Beverly Hills-based Hilton Hotels Corporation. As explained in Chapter 2, when Hilton Hotels Corporation spun off Hilton International in 1964, the companies had agreed that Hilton Hotels Corporation could have the right to use the Hilton name in the United States, but that Hilton International would have the right to use the Hilton name abroad. In its lawsuit Ladbroke charged Hilton Hotels Corporation with trademark infringement for naming hotels in London, Dublin, Brussels, Istanbul, and Hong Kong "Conrad Hotels." The lawsuit was filed at a federal court in New York.

In a preliminary decision in May, 1995, a federal court judge in New York ruled that Hilton Hotels Corporation's use of the Conrad name had confused consumers in foreign countries. The judge also barred Hilton Hotels Corporation from using the Hilton name when advertising and promoting Conrad hotels outside the United States.

However, in late 1995, the preliminary ruling by the court was changed. The federal court in New York allowed Hilton Hotels Corporation to use the Conrad International name on overseas hotels and allowed those properties to participate in the Hilton Honors incentive program, in Hilton Reservations Worldwide, and in all other Hilton marketing programs. Therefore, the ruling ended a four-year legal battle between Hilton International and Hilton Hotels Corporations over the use of the Conrad Hilton name.

Case Study Source

Hotel & Motel Management, "Court OKs Use of Conrad Name," (Vol. 210, No. 20, 1995), 1.

*   *   *

The worldwide regulatory environment for franchising is very complex. Many countries have different regulations or legislation affecting contract terms and business practices. Since franchising involves licensing intellectual property rights, all of the considerations that apply to such licenses also apply to franchise agreements. In addition, an extensive body of antitrust law applies to franchise agreements. The European Union has developed comprehensive legal parameters for international franchising. They permit a franchiser to safeguard know-how and other trade secrets in the franchise relationship, permit termination of the franchise relationship on a number of grounds, yet prohibit price fixing and certain types of marketing-sharing arrangements.

The most significant area of regulation pertaining to franchising contracts relates to rules in various countries mandating financial and operational disclosure prior to beginning the franchise relationship. The United

States regulates franchising more extensively than most other countries, at both the state and federal levels. In the United States, for instance, the Federal Trade Commission requires extensive disclosure of financial and other information to prospective franchisees and limits the franchiser's predictions of future earnings. In Canada, the province of Alberta requires registration of all franchise plans and the filing of a prospectus before a franchiser may solicit franchisees in the province. France recently enacted a law requiring the delivery of extensive disclosure documents in French to prospective franchisees at least twenty days before the parties sign a contract or before the franchisee pays any money to obtain trademark rights.

Franchising regulations vary significantly in Latin American countries. Hotel and quick-service operations found franchising especially attractive there. Franchising can minimize investment risk and expand hospitality operations rapidly in the region. Exhibit 8.1 describes franchising regulations in Chile.

Franchise is a business relationship based on contract, but relying on flexibility, good faith, and mutual efforts toward success. The holder of trademark rights invests a lot of money and effort in making the product and service a success, and the franchiser relies on the franchisee's effort to achieve success in the foreign market. One of the difficult intersections of business and legal interests occurs when a franchisee is not meeting the terms of the franchise contract. If the franchiser allows the deviation, it may lose the legal right to rely on the contract terms in the future. It will also tarnish the image of its operations. Maintaining consistent service standards worldwide is a great challenge to international franchising operations.

Cultural clashes may develop between the local people and foreign franchise operations. In June 1994, McDonald's in England was accused by two British environmentalists of many wrongdoings ranging from ravaging the world's rain forests and serving unhealthy food to underpaying its British employees. These two young people, Dave Morris and Helen Steel, distributed in many public places thousands of leaflets listing all the accusations. McDonald's sued them for libel, which was legally allowed in Britain. In the United States, corporations cannot sue individuals for libel, because the First Amendment gives a special status to speech and publication freedom. But the courts in Britain can and do halt publication of materials. Clearly, there are legal differences between the countries even though they are under the same common law system.

The company first offered to end the case if the two defendants would retract their libelous statements and promise not to repeat them. But the defendants told McDonald's that they would not retract their words. This lawsuit involved McDonald's in the longest and most expensive libel trial

EXHIBIT 8.1. Franchising Regulations in Chile

Government Approval

Article 16 of the Decree Law No. 600 (The Foreign Investment Law) requires certain investments to be approved by the Foreign Investment Committee. The investments that need the Foreign Investment Committee's approval are:

1. those exceeding the value of 5 million U.S. dollars;
2. those relating to activities customarily reserved for the State;
3. those including the communications media;
4. those made by a foreign state or institution.

Those investments not covered by these categories can be authorized by the Executive Secretary of the Committee, provided the President of the Committee has given his approval. All foreign investments must be approved in some fashion by the Foreign Investment Committee. In reaching its decision on whether to accept the foreign investment, the Committee will consider the profitability of local employment, the effect on national development plans, and the effect of the imported technology on Chile's existing technology.

Other Considerations of Franchising in Chile

The Committee exercises unrestricted discretion in reviewing potential foreign investment in Chile. Apparently there are no explicit requirements for the foreign franchiser in Chile today. There are, however, certain things that the foreign franchiser should be aware of when considering contracting with a possible Chilean franchisee.

Patents and trademarks are both protected by Article 10 of the Constitution and Decree Law No. 958. A trademark application must be submitted to the national patent registration office. The trademark application must include:

1. Two copies of the label evidence that the name belongs to the applicant of consent of the owner, and
2. A notarized power of attorney if the applicant resides in a foreign country.

A summary of this application must be published in a local newspaper.

The Chilean Franchise Association (AFICH) was established in 1994 to promote franchising and serve as a clearinghouse for information.

Source: Chilean Embassy, Washington, DC, 1997.

in British legal history, which lasted from June 28, 1994 to June 19, 1997.[13] This long legal battle was highly publicized by the international media. Finally, McDonald's won $98,000 in libel damages from the two defendants, and McDonald's demonstrated its determination to stand up for and protect its reputation and image in the global markets.

Local laws sometimes respond to the cultural impact of foreign franchises, such as prohibiting the use of the large golden arch in the traditional city centers of Europe. Other nations require the use of local materials for food service, such as substituting olive oil in food preparation in the Mediterranean countries. This could alter the formula and value of fast food franchise operations.

Each country has its own specific laws governing hospitality operations. In some countries, the laws even vary from state to state, such as the laws for hotel, restaurant, and travel operations in the United States.[14] Global hospitality managers must understand their rights and those of others. They should be aware of the local laws and regulations pertaining to contracts, guests and employees' safety, alcoholic beverages, safety and product liability, labor relations, environmental regulations, and sexual harassment. The food service industry is highly regulated by each government because of health and safety concerns. The outbreak of "mad cow" disease (bovine spongiform encephalopathy or Creutzfeldt-Jakob disease) in the United Kingdom in the early part of 1996 caused great fear in Europe. The European Union banned imports of British beef for fear of contamination, which could be fatal. All the hamburger restaurants operated by international franchise chains in Britain had to import beef from other European countries. For instance, McDonald's in Britain had to import beef from the Netherlands.[15]

Some countries also have laws regulating product pricing and promotion. Managers need to know if the host country has a governmental price control authority that issues regulations on hospitality product and service pricing. Some countries may allow a standard percentage of profit on certain products and services. Most countries have some kind of law regulating advertising. Professional advertising groups in many countries have self-regulatory codes in addition to the law. In Germany, it is prohibited to use comparative advertising, and a hospitality company cannot use the words "better" or "best" to compare its products and services to those of the competitors. Britain allows no liquor advertising on television. France has a specific legal prohibition against door-to-door selling. This law can obviously restrict a common promotion practice used by some U.S. quick-service pizza chains—hanging discount coupons on doors. Peru imposes an 8 percent tax on all outdoor advertising, such as billboards.

INTERNATIONAL DISPUTE RESOLUTION

Legal disputes may still occur despite the most careful contract negotiations. Dispute management is the resolution of disagreement over a broad spectrum of different possibilities that may be encountered. In international operations, many additional factors, such as cultural and language differences, often affect the dispute resolution process. The most widely used form of dispute resolution in international contracting is arbitration. Arbitration is essentially the litigation of a dispute before an arbitrator rather than a judge. Each party chooses an arbitrator and the two party-appointed arbitrators then pick a third member, who normally chairs the panel and presides over the arbitration. The arbitrators may or may not be lawyers. For instance, engineers can be appointed for a hotel construction contract dispute.

An arbitral forum is often employed before a litigation forum. The advantages of arbitrating an international contract dispute are numerous. Arbitration is likely to be faster than most litigation. The arbitration process is not publicized. Unlike court proceedings, which are open to the public and often result in publicized decisions, arbitration is private. The final decision goes only to the involved parties. A business concerned about publicity will tend to try to solve disputes through arbitration.

Several organizations provide arbitration services for international business disputes. The best-known is the International Chamber of Commerce (ICC), based in Paris. Many commercial arbitrations are also heard by the London Court of International Arbitration and the American Arbitration Association in New York. These organizations may use their own rules of procedure, or may use a set of rules developed by the United Nations Committee on International Trade Law (UNCITRAL). The UNCITRAL rules are widely recognized in arbitration around the world.

Litigation is a formal proceeding conducted in an appropriate court in the host country, the home country, or in a neutral third country, to the extent that the third country agrees to hear the case. The process is expensive and often protracted. In many circumstances, litigation can cause additional hostility and antagonism between the parties. But litigation also has its advantages. It is generally final when concluded—that is, there is no other forum and no other resource for the losing party except to honor the judgment of the court. Some societies view litigation negatively, as evidence of personal failure by the parties. Thus, in these societies even parties with fundamental disagreements are motivated to reach an accord.

The manager facing a legal dispute in a foreign country often asks two questions: what court will hear this case and what law will apply? To control the site of any lawsuits regarding the dispute, the parties to a contract will often negotiate a contractual choice of forum and law. A forum is a place for litigation. Choice of forum clauses determines in advance where the case will be heard, thus reducing forum shopping by the parties' lawyers.

Parties to a contract can choose the law governing their contract relationship. A choice-of-law clause specifies which country's law will govern the obligations of the parties. Choice-of-law clauses have achieved wide recognition in international contracts. Generally, if that choice is reasonable, a court will honor it. Reasonableness is a matter of showing some kind of relationship between the body of law chosen and the contract. Within the European Union, the Roman Convention on the Choice of Law for contracts provides a number of rules for choosing law that are applied by many of the European nations. The Roman Convention sets out a number of detailed rules based on the subject matter of the litigation, for example, contract, personal injury, and so on. Though a firm's attorney will handle the legal procedures concerning dispute resolution, it is important for hospitality managers to have the essential knowledge of dispute management.

SUMMARY

- The laws of a nation are merely a more concrete manifestation of its attitudes and cultural norms and usually reflects its religious tradition.
- Law provides the ground rules for international hospitality investment and operations. International hospitality operations face a maze of legal constraints because of the different legal systems in the world.
- The general principles of the common law are not based on a body of codes, but evolve through case precedent. Common law countries are primarily English-speaking nations that were at one time English colonies.
- Business contracts are vitally important in common law countries since legal judgment is not based on a body of codes but the court's interpretation of events. Contract law in common law countries tends to be very detailed, with all contingencies spelled out to protect each party involved.
- The civil law system is based on a body of code. All the continental European countries have adopted the civil law system. This tradition extends to Central and South America, parts of Asia, Africa, and Mexico, Puerto Rico, Quebec, and Louisiana. Civil law is practiced in more than seventy countries.

- The legal systems of the communist countries are based on socialist law. Political ideology is deeply ingrained in the socialist legal system. Legal issues are often resolved through political or bureaucratic means.
- The Islamic legal system is the most important non-Western legal system that is based on the teachings of a religion. The body of Islamic law is found in the *Shari'a*. It deals with the relationship of God to man, of rulers to ruled, and of man to man.
- International law is a collection of agreements, treaties, and conventions between two or more countries. It is an amalgamation of rules and obligations derived from a number of sources.
- International agreements involving the sale of services have been developed over the years by various sources such as the General Agreement on Tariffs and Trade (GATT). Member nations of GATT grant most favored nation status to each other.
- Service contracts for hospitality development and management can range from construction and management contracts to franchising. Many countries have different regulations or legislation affecting contract terms and business practice.
- Legal disputes may still occur despite the most careful contract negotiations. Dispute management is the resolution of disagreement over a broad spectrum of different possibilities that may be encountered. Choice of forum and choice of law must be specified in the contract.

STUDY QUESTIONS

1. Explain why the laws of a society are one aspect of its culture.
2. What is common law? Can you name some countries that practice common law?
3. How are commercial business contracts written in the common law countries?
4. What are the remedies for the breach of a commercial contract in the common law countries?
5. What is civil law? What countries practice civil law?
6. Are there any differences in commercial contract law under the civil law system and under the common law system?
7. On what basis did the socialist legal system evolve?
8. Discuss the legal system and the current legal reforms in China.
9. What happened to McDonald's restaurant in Beijing in 1994 and 1995?
10. What is the Islamic legal system?

11. What are the four major types of service contracts the Islamic law recognizes?
12. How is international law developed? What is a treaty?
13. Explain management contract and franchising as sale of service contracts.
14. Discuss the laws in different countries that govern the practice of franchising.
15. Why do cultural clashes develop between the local residents and foreign franchise operations in some countries?
16. Do you know any legal restrictions foreign governments enforce on hospitality operations in their countries?
17. Why is dispute management so important in international hospitality operations?
18. What is arbitration and how is it carried out?
19. Where can you find arbitration services for international business disputes?
20. How are the choice of forum and choice of law determined?

CASE STUDY:
RAYMOND DAYAN V. MCDONALD'S CORPORATION

In October 1970, McDonald's negotiated with Raymond Dayan for a potential business partnership. McDonald's submitted three alternative proposals to Dayan. Proposal 1 was McDonald's standard license agreement with a 3 percent royalty fee on gross receipts, real estate to be bought and developed by McDonald's with rental rates comparable to U.S. leases. Proposal 2 was a joint venture with McDonald's and Dayan each owning 50 percent equity. Proposal 3 was a developmental license similar to the original Canadian franchises and provided for a 1 percent royalty fee, Dayan to develop his own real estate, and no McDonald's service except as ordered and paid for by Dayan.

In 1971 Dayan, the plaintiff, accepted proposal 1 and received an exclusive franchise to operate McDonald's restaurants in Paris, France. Under the standard McDonald's license, McDonald's was obligated to provide extensive services to Dayan in all areas of restaurant operations and Dayan would pay a correspondingly higher royalty fee. The 5 percent McDonald's contract consisted of a minimum of one annual full field inspection by a specially trained McDonald's consultant. The inspection process took two to three days to complete and was viewed by McDonald's as both a training opportunity for the operator and a process to ensure that minimum quality, service, and cleanliness (QSC) were being met by their franchisees.

The franchise agreement required that the franchisee meet all QSC standards set by McDonald's. Dayan acknowledged his familiarity with the McDonald's system, and with the need to maintain McDonald's quality standards and controls. The franchise agreement recited the rationale for maintaining QSC standards: "departure of Restaurants anywhere in the world from these standards impedes the successful operation of Restaurants throughout the world, and injures the value of its (McDonald's) Parents, Trademarks, Tradename, and property." Dayan agreed to "maintain these standards as they presently existed" and to observe subsequent improvements McDonald's might initiate. Dayan also agreed not to vary from QSC standards without prior written approval. After several years of quality and cleanliness violations, McDonald's sought to terminate the franchise. Dayan brought this action to enjoin the termination. The lower court found that good cause existed for the termination and Dayan appealed.

Presiding Judge Buckley said:

> Dayan also argues that McDonald's was obligated to provide him with the operational assistance necessary to enable him to meet the QSC standards.
>
> . . . Dayan verbally asked Sollars (a McDonald's manager) for a French-speaking operations person to work in the market for six months. Sollars testified that he told Dayan it would be difficult to find someone with the appropriate background that spoke French, but that McDonald's could immediately send him an English-speaking operations man. Sollars further testified that this idea was summarily rejected by Dayan as unworkable even though he had informed Dayan that sending operations personnel who did not speak the language to a foreign country was very common and very successful in McDonald's international system. Nonetheless, Sollars agreed to attempt to locate a qualified person with the requisite language skills for Dayan.
>
> Through Sollars' efforts, Dayan was put in contact with Michael Maycock, a person with McDonald's managerial and operational experience who spoke French. Dayan testified that he hired Maycock some time in October 1977 and placed him in charge of training, operations, quality control, and equipment.
>
> As the trial court correctly realized: "It does not take a McDonald's trained French-speaking operational man to know that grease dripping from the vents must be stopped and not merely collected in a cup hung from the ceiling, that dogs are not permitted to defecate where food is stored, that insecticide is not blended with chicken

breading, that past-dated products should be discarded, that a potato peeler should be somewhat cleaner than a tire-vulcanizer, and that shortening should not look like crank case oil."

Clearly, Maycock satisfied Dayan's request for a French-speaking operations man to run his training program. . . . The finding that Dayan refused non-French-speaking operational assistance and that McDonald's fulfilled Dayan's limited request for a French-speaking operational employee is well supported by the record. To suggest, as plaintiff does, that an opposite conclusion is clearly evident is totally without merit. Accordingly, we find McDonald's fulfilled its contractual obligation to provide requested assistance to Dayan.

In view of the foregoing reasons, the judgment of the trial court denying plaintiff's request for a permanent injunction and finding that McDonald's properly terminated the franchise agreement is affirmed.

Decision

Judgment is affirmed for McDonald's. McDonald's had fulfilled all of its responsibility under the agreement to assist the plaintiff in complying with the provisions of the license. The plaintiff had violated the provisions of the agreement by not complying with the QSC standards. The plaintiff is permitted to continue operation of his restaurants, but without use of the McDonald's trademarks or name.

Case Study Source

125 Ill. App.3d 972, 466 N.E.2d 958 (1984), Appellate Court of Illinois.

Case Study Questions

1. What were the important provisions written in the franchise agreement between McDonald's and Raymond Dayan?
2. What caused the legal dispute between the two parties?
3. What did McDonald's do in response to Dayan's request for a French-speaking person to work in his restaurant for six months?
4. How did Dayan violate McDonald's operation standards?
5. What was the judge's decision?

Chapter 9

Financial Management

It [the Mexican peso crisis in 1994 and 1995] came so suddenly, there was nothing we could do about it.[1]

Francisco Javier Gallegos
A restaurant waiter in Mexico City

LEARNING OBJECTIVES

In this chapter, you will study:

1. The functions of the foreign exchange market
2. Financial sources for global development
3. Government policy on foreign exchange
4. Foreign exchange exposures
5. Hedging techniques for foreign exchange exposure risks
6. Capital budgeting for international operations

INTRODUCTION

This chapter discusses financial management of international hospitality operations, focusing on the international monetary system. The financial activities of international hospitality corporations are much more complicated than domestic operations. The increased complexity and difficulty are the result of having to deal with more than one currency in international business transactions. Currencies of different countries do not maintain a fixed relationship to each other due to changing economic, social, and political factors. National currencies fluctuate in value, and such fluctuation can make a hospitality firm's investment or holdings of foreign currencies appreciate or depreciate against the home currency. It presents great uncertainty for hospitality firms to forecast accurately future net cash flows in capital budgeting, and incur potential financial risk in obtaining loans denominated in foreign currencies.

It is therefore vitally important to explain the basic financial concepts and management strategies commonly used in international hospitality operations. This chapter first presents the basics of the foreign exchange market and identifies various international financial markets and foreign exchange instruments. Government controls over foreign exchange and their implications for international hospitality operations are identified and thoroughly analyzed. The text then discusses foreign exchange exposures and the hedging techniques for minimizing such exposures. Finally, capital budgeting for international operations is discussed, and the forecast for future net cash flows for hospitality projects is introduced.

THE FOREIGN EXCHANGE MARKET

When an international hospitality company expands into a foreign country, the investment capital the company brings from its home country needs to be converted into the local currency. The trading of one country's money for that of another country is referred to as foreign exchange trading, which permits currencies to be exchanged to facilitate international business transactions.[2] The exchange of any two currencies is determined by the exchange rate, which fluctuates in accordance with market forces of supply and demand in the foreign exchange market. Exchange rate is thus defined as the number of units of one currency needed to exchange for one unit of another currency.[3] The exchange rates for the convertible currencies in the world are published in the major financial newspapers, and the financial section of major metropolitan newspapers. Exhibit 9.1 shows selected foreign exchange rates and the comparison of the fluctuations. Notice how stable the Saudi currency has been and the drastic devaluation of the currencies in Asian countries.

Two kinds of exchange rate quotations are shown in Exhibit 9.1: direct quote and indirect quote. Direct quotes show the number of U.S. dollars per unit of a foreign currency, such as $0.000118 equaled one Indonesian rupiah. Indirect quotes list the number of units of a foreign currency per unit of a U.S. dollar, such as 8450.00 rupiah were worth one U.S. dollar. The rule is that if you know the dollar price of the rupiah ($/rupiah), you can find the rupiah price of the dollar by taking the reciprocal (rupiah/$), or vice versa.[4]

EXHIBIT 9.1. Foreign Exchange Rate and Fluctuation Compared with U.S. Dollar

Country	July 18, 1994		January 18, 1998	
	Direct Quote	Indirect Quote	Direct Quote	Indirect Quote
Britain	1.5615	.6404	1.6335	.6122
Chile	.002442	409.51	.002181	458.50
Germany	.6466	1.5465	.5454	1.8336
Indonesia	.0004619	2165.00	.000118	8450.00
Mexico	.2943341	3.3975	.122100	8.1900
Saudi Arabia	.2666	3.7510	.2666	3.7510
South Korea	.0012392	807.00	.000618	1618.00
Thailand	.04005	24.97	.01951	51.25

Source: Thomas Cook Foreign Exchange Services, Washington, DC, 1998.

Different kinds of exchange rates are used to facilitate currency exchange transactions: mainly spot rate and forward contracts. The most common type of foreign exchange transaction is conducted at the spot rate. This is the rate at which a foreign exchange bank converts one currency into another currency "on the spot," which means the transaction is for immediate delivery. For instance, if a British tourist exchanges pounds for Hong Kong dollars at the foreign exchange service desk in the Hong Kong Marriott, the exchange transaction is determined by the spot rate for that day. For large-volume trading of foreign currencies, a spot exchange contract is used. A spot exchange contract is an agreement to buy or sell a foreign currency for delivery in two business days. This gives enough time for the verification of transactions, given the large differences in time zones involved in international transactions.[5]

Forward contracts will be discussed a little later with other foreign exchange contracts. Let us now examine the bid and ask spread. The exchange rate quotations listed in Exhibit 9.1 are called the selling rate, also known as ask quote. The ask quote is the exchange rate for converting your home currency into a foreign currency. However, commercial banks charge a service fee for providing foreign currency exchanges. This service fee is reflected in the bid or buying quote for converting the foreign currency back into your home currency. The bid rate is always less than the ask quote, and the difference between bid and ask is called the spread—the service charge collected by the banks to cover the costs involved in providing foreign currency exchanges.[6] The bid and ask rates are normally posted in the bank or at the foreign exchange service desk in major commercial hotels, or published in major financial or national papers.

Let us use a concrete example to further illustrate how a bid and ask spread could affect international tourists. On the first day of your four-day vacation in Japan, you exchanged $800 for Japanese yen at the ask rate of ¥1:$0.0074. At the end of the tour, you still had ¥18,000, and you decided to convert them back into U.S. dollars at the foreign exchange service at Narita International Airport. To your surprise, your ¥18,000 were converted back to U.S. dollars at the lower bid rate of ¥1:$0.0070, even though the ask rate had not changed in the past four days. If still using the ask rate, your ¥18,000 could be converted into $133.20, but the lower bid rate only gave you $126 back. The difference of $7.20 is the spread. For those who are interested in knowing more about the bid and ask spread in percentage terms, the following is the method for computing the bid and ask percentage spread.[7]

$$\text{Bid/ask spread} = \frac{\text{Ask rate} - \text{Bid rate}}{\text{Ask rate}}$$

Using your Japan travel experience:

	Bid rate	Ask rate
Japanese yen	$.0070	$.0074

$$\text{Bid/ask spread} = \frac{\$.0074 - \$.0070}{\$.0074} = .054 \text{ or } 5.4\%$$

Thus, the spread between bid rate and ask rate is 5.4 percent.

OTHER FOREIGN EXCHANGE CONTRACTS

Thus far, we have discussed foreign exchange trading in the spot market. As mentioned earlier, forward exchange rates are also used for several major world currencies, and foreign exchange transactions are also conducted in the form of futures, options, and swap contracts. Though they are not as common as the spot rate contract, adequate understanding of these foreign exchange contracts can enhance global hospitality managers' knowledge of the complicated global financial market. Following is a brief discussion of the functions of these foreign exchange contracts.

Forward Contract

A forward contract refers to buying and selling a certain amount of foreign currency at a specified rate for delivery at a specified date in the future, normally in 1, 2, 3, 6, or 12 months.[8] The advantage of the forward contract is that the exchange rate is established between two currencies, and the transaction does not need to take place until the foreign currency is needed at a future point in time. This is particularly important for international hospitality firms when they anticipate future need of foreign currencies, or future receipt of a foreign currency. For instance, a hotel in the United States will need 100,000 German marks in thirty days to pay commissions to several German travel agencies. The current spot rate is $.55 per mark. At this spot rate, the hotel would need $55,000 (100,000 German marks × $.55 per mark) for commission payment. The general manager of the hotel has to consider the following:

1. The hotel may not have the $55,000 to exchange for German marks at this time.
2. It could wait thirty days and exchange dollars for marks at the spot rate at that time. However, the general manager is concerned about the rise in exchange rate at that time. For instance, if the exchange rate moves up to $.58 by then, the hotel will need $58,000 to pay the German travel agencies 100,000 German marks: an additional $3,000 more for waiting thirty days to make the foreign exchange.

Therefore, it is advantageous for the hotel to "lock in" the preferable exchange rate to pay for marks thirty days from now without having to exchange dollars for marks immediately. International hospitality firms also use forward contracts to lock in the exchange rate at which they can sell foreign currencies. This strategy is used to hedge against the possibility of the local currency's depreciation over time.

Futures Contract

A futures contract is an agreement to buy or sell a standard volume of a particular currency at a price set today for delivery at a designated time in the future.[9] Many students are often confused by the forward contract and the futures contract. The futures contract differs from the forward contract in that a standard amount of a particular currency is specified, and trading occurs in standardized contracts and in specified markets, such as the International Monetary Market (IMM) of the Chicago Mercantile Exchange, the largest currency futures market.[10] The forward exchange contract can be arranged through commercial banks. The function of currency futures is primarily used by international hospitality firms to hedge drastic exchange rate swings. For instance, an international hospitality firm can hedge payables in foreign currencies by purchasing futures contracts to lock in the rate paid for a foreign currency at a future point in time. On the other hand, an international hospitality firm can hedge receivables by selling futures contracts to lock in the rate for receiving a foreign currency at a future point in time.

Options Contract

A currency options contract is an agreement that provides the right to buy or sell a specific currency at a fixed exchange rate any time during the life of the option.[11] This is also known as American options because currency options contracts in Europe can only be exercised at expiration. A currency options contract consists of calls and puts. A call option gives the right to buy a specific currency at a specific price, known as the strike price or exercise price, any time during the life of the option. A put option provides the right to sell a specific currency at a fixed exchange rate any time during the life of the option. Again, the function of the currency options contract is to hedge against foreign exchange fluctuation. A call option is often used to hedge future payables while a put option is employed to hedge future receivables.

Swap Contract

A swap is the simultaneous buying of a foreign currency at spot rate, and selling the foreign currency back into the initial currency at forward rate.[12] For instance, assume a U.S.-based hotel company needs French francs now. The hotel company could enter into a swap agreement wherein the hotel trades dollars for francs now at spot rate and trades the surplus francs back to dollars at forward rate in three months. The terms of the arrangement are closely related to conditions in the forward market. Swaps are an efficient way to meet hospitality firms' need for foreign currencies on a short-term basis because they combine two separate transactions into one.

In summary, these four foreign exchange contracts are not commonly used in international hospitality business transactions. They are also known as derivative contracts since they are normally used to hedge against potential exchange risk in international operations, and they involve the highest degree of financial risk. However, accurate forecast of exchange rate movements is difficult. Foreign exchange experts' advice is highly recommended if any of these hedging techniques are used.

CURRENCY CONVERTIBILITY

Convertibility of a currency refers to whether this currency can be publicly traded in the international exchange market. Many currencies can be publicly traded in foreign exchange markets around the world, and the heavily traded currencies include U.S. dollars, British pounds, German marks, Japanese yen, Swiss francs, and French francs. These six major currencies are also called hard currencies because their value tends to be stable, and they are the most widely held assets in the world. On the other hand, many other currencies cannot be circulated outside their own countries, such as the Russian ruble and the Hungarian forint. These currencies are called nonconvertible currencies. International hospitality firms operating in these countries have developed practical strategies to deal with the problem. In April 1990, PepsiCo reached a $3 billion deal with Russia to increase its production of Pepsi, and develop Pizza Huts in Moscow. Instead of accepting rubles, which were not convertible into dollars or any other world major currencies, PepsiCo accepted ten ships (mostly oil tankers) and vodka produced in Russia.[13] Many international hotels simply do not accept local currency, but accept different hard currencies as an effective way of diversification to reduce exchange risk.

FOREIGN EXCHANGE RESTRICTIONS BY GOVERNMENT

Governments in many developing countries do not allow free trading of foreign currencies, and impose many restrictions on foreign currency transactions. These restrictions include: (1) government licensing requirements, (2) travel allowance restrictions, and (3) prohibiting the repatriation of earnings by foreign firms to their home countries.

Government licensing simply requires all domestic business enterprises to apply for purchase of foreign currencies through the central bank. The central bank will approve or reduce the requested amount of foreign currency, or simply deny the application based on the nature of the business transaction. For instance, if the foreign exchange will be used to import certain goods from foreign countries, the government may disapprove the purchase of the foreign goods by denying the company's application for foreign exchange. Without foreign currency, the company cannot purchase the goods from foreign countries. Government licensing is an effective measure used to restrict import by domestic firms.

A travel allowance restriction limits the amounts of foreign currency that may be purchased by the local residents for overseas travel. For instance, many countries permit their citizens to purchase only a small amount of foreign currency for travel in foreign countries. Some countries even impose a limit on credit spending by their citizens in foreign countries, such as the maximum credit card allowance of $2,000 by the South Korean government. Such restrictions on foreign exchange purchase make it very difficult for citizens in many countries to travel overseas.

Prohibiting or limiting the repatriation of earnings by foreign firms is a way of controlling foreign exchange leakage. Some countries have policies that only permit foreign firms to remit a certain percentage of their earnings to the home country or permit repatriation only after certain years of investment. For instance, when McDonald's opened its first restaurant in Moscow, it was not allowed by the former Soviet government to remit all of its earnings back to the United States. It had to reinvest its profits locally in expanding operations by building a food processing plant outside Moscow.[14] In another example, the Dominican Republic also has similar restrictions on foreign repatriation of funds. When earnings of a foreign firm cannot be repatriated to its home country, the fund is called a blocked fund. One U.S. resort developer successfully borrowed blocked funds from several international companies to finance his resort development in the Dominican Republic, and later paid the funds back in the United States to these international companies.

Clearly, many countries have strict policies for controlling foreign exchange in their countries. As a result of government restrictions on foreign exchange transactions, illegal foreign exchange markets emerged to meet increasing demand for hard currencies. These illegal markets are called black markets, and are mostly found in developing countries where local people often wait outside the tourist hotels to exchange money with foreign tourists, and then sell the foreign currency in the black market for a profit. Sometimes even a business firm has to purchase a certain amount of foreign exchange in the black market if the central bank does not have enough of the foreign exchange. However, most countries have laws prohibiting illegal transaction of foreign currencies, and lawbreakers receive severe punishment when caught.

More countries now tolerate the existence of the free market in foreign exchange where the exchange rate fluctuates daily with market supply and demand conditions. Such a foreign exchange free market, known as a parallel market, is now considered an alternative to the official exchange market, and has flourished in many areas, such as Eastern European countries, Latin American countries, Russia, Vietnam, and China.

INTERNATIONAL FINANCIAL MARKETS

Hospitality development is capital intensive. Financial executives of international hospitality corporations face great challenges in raising capital for overseas expansions. They have to come up with creative solutions to secure financing for global development. This section discusses the major sources of global financing and analyzes the advantages and disadvantages associated with each financing opportunity.

Global hospitality development that requires substantial investment capital includes new development and acquisition. Investment capital for new development and acquisition derives from both equity and debt, and public and private sources, including C-Corp, real estate investment trusts (REITs), pension funds, insurance companies, commercial banks, government agencies, venture capitalists, and individual investors.[15] A revealing study by *Hotels* in 1997 thoroughly analyzed the financing opportunities for expansion in different regions. Exhibit 9.2 summarizes these financial resources for hospitality development in selected regions.

For new development and acquisitions, the primary sources of equity investment include C-Corp, REITs, entrepreneurs, and investment funds from public, private, or government sources—or any combination of the above. C-Corp, derived from its classification under Sub-Chapter C of the U.S. Internal Revenue Code, is used in the United States for raising hotel development capital in the equity market. C-Corp is the not-commonly used term for "corporation" in the United States. The C-Corp is recognized as a legal and tax entity separate from its owners, who are generally sheltered from any liability. Lodging corporations organized as C-Corp in the United States raised $3.4 billion in public stock offerings in 1996, and $1.2 billion during the first half of 1997.[16]

Real estate investment trusts are another popular and passive investment vehicle in the United States and Canada that raises funds for investments in mortgages and income producing properties through debt and equity gained from the sale of shares to the public. Unlike C-Corp, REITs avoid any double taxation. In accordance with U.S. federal tax codes, REITs are required to distribute 95 percent of their taxable income to shareholders who, in turn, must pay income tax on dividends, but are not personally liable should the REIT fail. The U.S. lodging industry witnessed a dramatic increase in REITs in the last few years, from 39 hotels and 6,634 rooms in 1993 to 562 hotels and more than 97,759 rooms controlled by REITs in 1996. REITs raised a total of $1.7 billion in equity capital from public markets in 1996 and about $1 billion in the first half of 1997.[17] Starwood Hotels and Resorts, one of the major REITs in the United States, successfully acquired Sheraton by outbidding Hilton Hotels in late 1997. Clearly,

EXHIBIT 9.2. Hotel Financing Sources in Selected Regions

Sources of Capital/ Terms	Debt	Equity
Southeast Asia		
Development	*Source:* Nonrecourse bank financing; *Term:* 5-10 years (7-8 avg.); *Interest:* 1.5-2.5% above cost; *Leverage:* 50-60%; *Amortization:* Accelerated schedule with maximum final principle payment; *Source:* Corporate guaranteed bank financing; *Term:* 10-20 years; *Interest:* 0.75-1.5% above cost; *Leverage:* 60-75%; *Amortization:* 15 to 25 years	*Sources:* Family, corporate, and funds; *Requirements:* A defined exit, particularly for fund investors; reasonable development and land premiums
Acquisition	*Source:* Nonrecourse bank financing; *Term:* 6-15 years; *Interest:* 0.75-1.75% over cost; *Leverage:* 60-70%; *Amortization:* 15-25 years *Source:* Corporate guaranteed bank financing same as development scenario	*Sources:* Family, corporate, and funds; *Requirement:* A defined exit; *Minimum IRR:* Singapore, Hong Kong, 11%; Malaysia, 13%; Thailand and Indonesia, 17%; Philippines, 18%; Vietnam, 21%; Myanmar, 25%
Europe		
Development	*Source:* Nonrecourse bank financing; *Term:* 8-15 years; *Interest:* 1.0-2.5% above LIBOR; fixed loans available; *Leverage:* 60%	*Source:* Real estate companies; corporations and public hotel companies; Middle Eastern and Asian investors
Acquisition	*Source:* Nonrecourse bank financing; *Term:* 8-20 years; *Interest:* 0.75-2.0% above LIBOR; fixed loans available; *Leverage:* 60-70%	*Source:* Real estate companies; U.S., Middle Eastern, and Asian investors; and public hotel companies; *Minimum IRR:* UK and key European cities, 12-15%; developing countries, 20-25%
Middle East		
Development/ Acquisition	*Source:* Nonrecourse bank financing; *Term:* Up to 10 years; *Leverage:* Up to 65%; *Amortization:* Equal installments, sometimes with a grace period of up to two years	*Source:* Family, corporate, and funds; *Requirements:* A defined exit; reasonable development and land premium; *Minimum IRR:* Variable, from 15 to 25%

Source: Adapted from Steven Shundich, "Art of the Deal," *Hotels* (September, 1997), 43-54. Reprinted by permission of *Hotels* magazine, a publication of Cahners Business Information.

public ownership of hotels is relatively high in the United States since many companies have obtained most of their financing from the public markets. It was reported that public ownership of hotels had risen to 20 percent in the United States by 1996.[18]

For debt financing, sources include commercial banks, small business associations, life insurance companies, pension funds, and investment banks. For instance, the Brasilia-based pension fund of Caixa Economica Federal in São Paulo purchased the new Renaissance São Paulo from the Encol Construction Co. in Brasilia for $100 million. Meanwhile, PREVI, Banco do Brasil's pension fund, paid $44 million for the Méridien Copacabana, Rio de Janeiro. This group planned to invest another $10 million to renovate the hotel.[19]

Raising capital globally needs to take into consideration geographic factors and foreign exchange risk since capital funds are moved from one country to another. Three major financing sources are identified: (1) the home country; (2) the host country, and (3) a third country. Financing from the home country means that a hotel corporation raises capital in its home equity market or borrows capital funds from various financial institutions, pension funds, or insurance companies at home to finance its overseas development. The advantage of securing financing in the home country is that the hotel corporation may receive low interest rate loans from domestic financial institutions based on its proven business success and credit history. However, the major concern will be the potential exchange risk. When the capital funds raised from domestic equity markets or borrowed from domestic banks are transferred to the host country, the funds need to be converted into the host currency since only the host currency is allowed to circulate in the country (though some countries allow international hotels to make transactions in hard currencies). The exchange of the home currency for the host currency might result in a certain loss of the capital due to the depreciation of the home currency against the host currency (although the opposite could just as well occur). Therefore, moving capital from home country to the host country can incur potential foreign exchange risk because of the fluctuations of exchange rates.

It is possible to raise capital in the local equity markets or to borrow funds locally. Raising equity capital in the host equity markets can be an effective means of sourcing development capital for some companies.[20] However, most hotel and restaurant companies are not listed on the local equity markets, and they often rely on local debt markets, borrowing funds from financial institutions in the host country. Many commercial banks are the major sources of financing for hotel and resort development projects. However, due to the financial crisis in Asia in 1997 and 1998, the debt market will be very tight in this region in the next few years. Generally, borrowing funds locally has obvious advantage of no foreign exchange risk, since the capital is denominated in the host currency. However, the trade-off for borrowing locally might be that the hospitality firm could face higher interest rates, which would increase the development cost in the long run.

Financing can also be secured from a third country. For instance, a Canadian hotel company may borrow capital funds from a German bank in Japan to finance a hotel development in Vietnam. This creative approach to borrowing capital for overseas hotel development has been successfully used by Marriott International to finance its first hotel in Warsaw, Poland. Warsaw Marriott is a joint venture partnership among three parties. Marriott is a 25 percent partner with ILBAU, an Austrian construction company that built the hotel and owns another 25 percent share, and LOT, the Polish international airline that owns the rest of the hotel. The total cost for the hotel was $65 million. To finance its share of the development, Marriott borrowed the capital from the Girozentrale Bank of Vienna in Austria. Girozentrale, a lending bank serving also as an escrow agency, receives all hard currencies, pays the debt and management fees, and ensures that working capital is available for the hotel.[21] International guests staying at Warsaw Marriott pay for their rooms only in hard currencies—such as U.S. dollars, German marks, Swiss francs, and Japanese yen. But they can pay for food and other services in zlotys, which are not usable outside Poland.[22] The financial structure and management operations have been proven effective, and Warsaw Marriott has become a very successful commercial hotel in Poland.

Financial resources for international hospitality development can be identified and obtained from various sources in the home country, the host country, and the third country. To further understand the complexity of the international financial markets, the functions of Eurocurrency markets and Eurobond markets are explained in the following section.

The Eurocurrency Market

A Eurocurrency is any currency banked outside of its country of origin.[23] The term evolves from "Eurodollar." Eastern European communist countries deposited many of their dollar holdings in Western Europe, particularly in London, in the mid-1950s. Eurodollar is thus defined as dollars banked outside the United States.

The growth of the Eurodollar market was also partially attributed to U.S. government regulations in 1968 that prohibited foreign lending by U.S. banks. Companies in need of dollars could obtain them in European banks.

Many Western European companies and major U.S. corporations also deposited their dollars in Eurobanks. The Eurocurrency market grew rapidly after the oil-rich Arab countries deposited their dollars with banks in London in the late 1970s.[24]

The main attraction for depositing and buying dollars in Europe is that Eurobanks offer higher deposit rates and lower lending rates because of liberal reserve policies and the lack of government regulations. The spread between the Eurocurrency deposit and lending rates is less than the spread between the U.S. deposit and lending rates. Therefore, it makes the investment very attractive for global investors. At present, Eurocurrency can be found anywhere in the world and in different currencies, such as Euro-yen, Euro-Swiss franc, and Euro-mark in the United States. The prefix Euro now only indicates the European origin of the market.

The International Bond Market

International hospitality firms can also obtain long-term debt by issuing bonds in the international bond markets. There are two kinds of international bonds: foreign bonds and Eurobonds. A foreign bond is issued by a foreign company, and is denominated in the currency in which it is sold.[25] For example, when Accor issues bonds in Canadian dollars and sells them in Canada, it is issuing foreign bonds. The nicknames Yankee bonds, Samurai bonds, and bulldogs refer to foreign bonds sold in the United States, Japan, and Britain.[26] Eurobonds are issued in countries whose currencies do not denominate the bond. For instance, a bond could be issued by a Hong Kong hotel corporation, denominated in British pounds, and placed in the Netherlands. Eurobonds are usually underwritten by a multinational syndicate of commercial banks and issued simultaneously in many countries. Eurobonds now make up the greater proportion of the international bond market.

FOREIGN EXCHANGE EXPOSURES

As an international hospitality firm expands into several foreign countries, it has a portfolio of properties or units that earn money in various foreign currencies. As discussed earlier, foreign exchange rates are not fixed and currency values change frequently according to market supply and demand. The host currency can either appreciate or depreciate in value against the firm's home currency. South Korea is the most recent example: South Korea's won lost more than 46 percent of its value against the U.S.

dollar in three and a half months, from $1:904.5 won on September 1 to $1:1202.5 won on December 13, 1997. Therefore, the firm's overseas operations are exposed to foreign exchange fluctuation.

Global hospitality managers must recognize that "a dollar earned may not appear to be a dollar" if it is earned in a foreign currency, especially if these earnings are not repatriated. The fluctuation of foreign exchange can have major impacts on: (1) a specific business transaction, (2) the firm's total earnings, and (3) the translation of foreign earnings into the corporation's consolidated balance sheet financial statement. These three foreign exchange exposures are known as transaction exposure, economic exposure, and translation exposure.

Transaction Exposure

Transaction exposure means that a specific cash transaction is affected by exchange rate fluctuations. This relates to the payables and receivables a company has to pay or collect since they are exposed to future foreign exchange rate movements. The amount of receivables and payables will change if the exchange rate changes at the time of the payment or receipt. Therefore, it directly affects the cash flows of the hospitality operations.

For example, assume Days Inn needed to pay a contractor in India who worked on the construction of a new Days Inn hotel in New Delhi. The payment was already negotiated at 14,135,000 Indian rupees based on the foreign exchange rate of $1:28.27 rupees. Thus, Days Inn had to exchange $500,000 for the 14,135,000 Indian rupees to pay the construction contractor. However, by the time of payment, the exchange rate between the dollar and rupee changed to $1:28.22 rupees. Days Inn now had to pay $500,886 to exchange for the 14,135,000 rupees as agreed upon in the original contract. For this particular transaction, Days Inn had to pay $885 more because of the exchange rate fluctuation between the time when the contract was signed and payable was disbursed. Therefore, in international operations, we may know exactly how many units of the foreign currency will be paid or received, but we do not know how many dollars will be needed to exchange for the foreign currency. This uncertainty remains because the exchange rates between the U.S. dollar and other currencies fluctuate over time.

Economic Exposure

As transaction exposure concerns the impact of exchange rate on individual transactions on a short-term basis, economic exposure concerns a company's total global earning power affected by exchange rate movements.[27] A good example is the decline of U.S. tourist arrivals to Canada in 1989 due to the strengthening of the Canadian dollar against the U.S. dollar. In 1988, Canada received 12.8 million U.S. tourists, and the average exchange rate was $1:CD$1.2318. In 1989, total U.S. tourists to Canada were recorded at 12.2 million, a 4.9 percent decrease over the previous year, and the average exchange rate was $1:CD$1.1624. Canada's total tourism receipts from U.S. visitors dropped by 5.6 percent in 1989. Many hotels in the major Canadian cities reported a flat business year. Therefore, many U.S. tourists changed their international travel destinations in 1989.

Another example is the decline of U.S. dollar value against most European and Japanese currencies since the mid-1980s. This fall in value of the U.S. dollar since then has made the United States a bargain travel destination for European and Japanese tourists. European and Japanese tourist arrivals increased during that time, and the hospitality industry in the United States benefited from the growing overseas travel markets. At the same time, this increase of tourists created a great demand for hotel expansion in the United States by foreign hotel companies, such as Nikko Hotel International's entry into the United States in 1986 to serve Japanese travelers.

Translation Exposure

Translation exposure refers to the impact of the exchange rate on the translation of each overseas hotel or restaurant's financial data into the corporation's consolidated financial statements. It does not concern the actual cash flow, but the exposed accounting gains or losses translated at the current exchange rate in the balance sheet financial statement. Translation exposure can have a significant impact on a corporation's consolidated balance sheet if certain countries in which the corporation operates hotels or restaurants devalue their currencies drastically against the corporation's home currency. For instance, the value of the Mexican peso tumbled from $.29:1 peso in December 1994 to $.13:1 peso in early 1995.[28] This drastic devaluation of the peso significantly reduced the dollar value of international hotel and restaurant equity as the earning power of the peso dropped by one third. This in turn reduced the dollar value of the corporation's equity reported in its consolidated balance sheet, and would consequently raise the corporation's debt ratio, and could increase the corporation's cost of borrowing and restrict its access to the capital market.

MANAGING FOREIGN EXCHANGE RISK

International hospitality corporations face potential foreign exchange risk as they expand operations into many foreign countries. As discussed earlier, the fluctuation of foreign currency exchange can have a direct impact on the earnings of a hotel or restaurant in a particular country, the cash flow of a particular transaction, and the unrealized accounting gains and losses translated from overseas operations into the corporation's consolidated balance sheet financial statement. To reduce or eliminate such exposures, international hospitality corporations have developed many sophisticated financial management strategies, commonly known as hedging techniques.

The best way to reduce economic exposure is to diversify a corporation's overseas development geographically as discussed in Chapter 1. By geographic diversification, the hospitality corporation's long-term financial well-being is not severely affected by adverse changes in exchange rates in one or two countries, such as the Mexican peso crisis in late 1994 and 1995, and the Indonesian rupiah crisis, when it lost 70 percent of its value against the U.S. dollar from mid-1997 to 1998.

There are many forms of hedging techniques for minimizing transaction and translation exposures. These techniques mainly focus on the protection of short-term cash flows from adverse changes in exchange rates. Futures contracts and forward contracts are sometimes used by large hospitality corporations that desire to hedge. Some corporations even use options contracts to hedge payables with currency call options, and hedge receivables with currency put options.[29] A detailed discussion of these sophisticated hedging techniques is beyond the scope of this text. Interested students are strongly encouraged to read a specific text on international financial management.

There are also some practical tactics that can be used to reduce transaction exposure. If a hospitality firm operates in a country with a weak currency (the local currency depreciates against the firm's home currency), it can employ several tactics to protect the value of its earnings in local currency. For example, during the Indonesian rupiah crisis in early 1998, if the transaction was made in local currency, a U.S. hotel company had to collect receivables as soon as possible and delay payables as long as possible. This was because as the rupiah depreciated against the dollar, the anticipated rupiah receivables would lose value as they were translated into dollars. On the other hand, the U.S. hotel company could use the strengthened dollar to purchase more rupiah as the company waited for the continuous devaluation of the rupiah. Thus the longer the wait, the more rupiah the dollar could buy, given that the rupiah would continue to depreciate. Therefore, the U.S. hotel company could use fewer dollars to make the same amount of liability payments. In addition, the U.S. hotel company must convert its earnings in rupiah into dollars quickly, and remit its earnings to its home bank immediately. If the host country has restrictions on the repatriation of a foreign company's earnings, the U.S. company has to invest the weakening local currency in fixed assets to prevent further loss of the value of the local currency.

Known as leads and lags, these hedging techniques are used to adjust the timing of disbursement and collection by anticipating future currency exchange movements. The lead technique advises that a firm needs to collect its receivables before the local currency weakens, and disburse the payables before the local currency strengthens. The lag technique says that a firm delays the collection of receivables until the local currency strengthens, and delays its disbursement of payables until the local currency weakens. Clearly, the lead and lag techniques attempt to predict foreign exchange movements by early collection and disbursement (leading), or lagging behind in collection and disbursement, hence the name.

CAPITAL BUDGETING

Considering the potential foreign exchange exposure and many other economic factors, international hospitality firms plan overseas operations by systematically developing a capital budget for each overseas property or unit. Capital budgeting examines the prospective investment alternatives, and the commitment of funds to desirable hotel or restaurant projects. Capital budgeting is essential to assessing a hospitality firm's cash needs on a long-term basis. But capital budgeting for international investment is very complicated because considerably more variables need to be analyzed than for domestic operations. Global hospitality managers must estimate and balance the risks and expected returns of investment in foreign countries. Capital budgeting for international investment in hotels and restaurants needs to forecast and analyze the following economic and financial aspects:

1. Initial investment
2. Consumer demand
3. Price
4. Variable cost
5. Fixed cost
6. Project lifetime
7. Salvage (liquidation) value
8. Fund transfer restrictions

9. Tax laws
10. Exchange rates
11. Required rate of return[30]

Initial Investment

No matter how the project is financially structured, such as by sole ownership or joint venture, sufficient funds and adequate working capital are required to start it, and keep it operating until revenues are generated to cover the expenses. Hotel investment is capital intensive, and cash inflows from hotel operations are normally insufficient to cover cash outflows during the initial three to five years of operations. Therefore, an accurate forecast of the initial investment is essential in avoiding potential financial shortfalls in the initial operations.

Consumer Demand

The forecast of anticipated hotel room occupancy and restaurant sales is important for scheduling cash flow for the operations. A higher room occupancy or high volume of patrons in the restaurants can make the return on investment sooner. Consumer demand can be examined through historical data and competition analysis. Most national and local governments collect and publish statistical data on both international and domestic tourism arrivals and receipts, and hospitality development trends in their jurisdictions. The World Tourism Organization and many regional economic or tourism organizations publish tourism development data by region and by country. Professional consulting firms such as Arthur Andersen, Pannel Karr Foster (PKF), Smith Travel, Hospitality Valuation Services (HVS), and PriceWaterhouseCoopers publish international, regional, and national travel, lodging, and food service trends on a regular basis. This quantitative and qualitative information on tourism development is useful data for analyzing consumer demand for a target country.

Price

The forecast of room rates and menu price is initially estimated by using competition-based pricing strategy. It simply investigates how the competition in the area charges for similar rooms and meals. If the hospitality company is the first company in the country and no other domestic companies offer comparable products, an examination of similar hotels and restaurants in comparable neighboring countries needs to be conducted. The long-term forecast of room rates and menu prices must consider the host country's inflation factor. Again, future inflation is difficult to predict and historical data have to be used to illustrate past patterns.

Variable Costs

The forecast of variable costs can be based also on assessing prevailing comparative costs of the various components, such as hourly labor costs. The projection of future variable costs needs to be adjusted to the inflation rate of the host country. Accurate forecast of consumer demand is essential to assessing variable costs since a hotel selling at only 50 percent occupancy employs fewer employees than when it has 85 percent occupancy. Therefore, variable cost is very sensitive to demand. Local government reports on consumer price index and labor trends are useful data for identifying and analyzing the factors that will influence the variable costs.

Fixed Cost

It seems that fixed cost is less sensitive to demand and is relatively easier to forecast. However, fixed costs also move in tandem with the future inflation rate of the host country.

Project Lifetime

Most hotel and restaurant projects are initiated for long-term development since it normally takes several years for the operations to break even. Some joint-venture projects may specify certain lifetimes, such as fifteen years or twenty years, at the end of which the property will be turned over to one partner or be liquidated. Some developers may specify a certain lifetime for the project, and liquidate the property at the end of its lifetime. Certain political and economic contingencies could force the hospitality company to liquidate the project earlier than planned. Generally, the capital budgeting for the project's lifetime is not difficult to analyze, but under certain circumstances, international hospitality companies may not have total control over the lifetime decision.

Salvage (Liquidation) Value

The after-tax salvage value of a hotel or restaurant depends on several factors: the quality of the hotel property or restaurant, level of service as determined by certain classifications or ranking, the location, and the reputation and success of the property or restaurant. If a war or revolution breaks out in the host country, the radical host government could confiscate foreign assets without compensating the international hospitality company, as in the case of Hilton Habana in Cuba in the early 1960s. The forecast of project salvage (liquidation) value can be difficult to analyze.

Fund Transfer Restrictions

As discussed earlier, many developing countries have restrictions or limitations on repatriation of foreign company earnings back to their home countries. The purpose of such policy is to prevent foreign exchange from leaking out of the local economy, and encourage additional local spending by foreign companies. Such policy makes it difficult for hospitality firms to project net cash flow from overseas hotels and restaurants to the parent company. Hospitality firms have to factor such fund transfer restrictions in their capital budgeting analysis, and only forecast the portion that is permitted by the host government for remittance to the parent company.

Tax Laws

After-tax cash flows are an important aspect of capital budgeting analysis. Tax liabilities of overseas operations need to be adequately forecast. However, the tax laws of different countries are very complicated. Some developed countries impose higher tax rates while some developing countries may offer tax concessions or credits to international hospitality corporations as an incentive to attract foreign investment. Tax laws of different countries will be fully discussed in the following chapter.

Exchange Rates

Any hospitality firm that operates overseas hotels or restaurants will be affected by currency exchange fluctuations as the value of the local currency can either move up or down against the value of the firm's home currency. Inaccurate forecast of exchange rates can result in improper estimate of net cash flows for the project. Therefore, knowledge of foreign exchange markets and hedging strategies are vitally important to the adequate forecast of net cash flows as affected by future exchange rate movement.

Required Rate of Return

The required rate of return on the project depends on the host country's existing economic conditions, the firm's cost of capital, and the project's potential risk. Once the cash flows for the hotel project have been determined, they need to be discounted to estimate the net present value by using an appropriate discount rate. The most commonly used discount rate is either the firm's cost of capital or some other required rate of return. The discount rate reflects the potential political and economic risk involved in investing in the project in certain countries. For instance, a firm might use a 6 percent discount rate for potential investment in the United States, Germany, or Switzerland, but apply a 10 percent discount rate or higher for potential investment in Russia or Vietnam (see Exhibit 9.3).[31] If the net present value of the discounted cash flows is greater than zero, the project is financially viable and should be implemented.

Analyzing the financial viability of a foreign investment opportunity is a very complicated process. It needs to forecast many different variables in the future and sometimes certain variables will be beyond the company's control. A good example is the failure of many Japanese financial investment projects in the United States in the 1980s. In the later part of the 1980s, many Japanese firms invested in the U.S. hotel industry by acquiring many expensive trophy properties in the United States. However, the buying spree ended when Japan's stock market and real estate markets collapsed in 1990, cutting off financing for the U.S. operations. Then the real estate market in the United States fell, and many Japanese firms found themselves facing losses of 50 percent or more on their U.S. holdings. The Dai-Ichi Kangyo Bank, the second largest bank in the world, sold its Ritz-Carlton Mauna Lani hotel in Hawaii to Colony Capital, a U.S. investment partnership, at a loss of $105 million in 1996.[32]

EXHIBIT 9.3. Discount Rates Applied by Hotel Investors in Asia

Country	Mean
Singapore	9.4
Malaysia	12.0
Indonesia	13.0
Hong Kong	13.3
Thailand	14.2
Vietnam	17.7
Philippines	18.5
China	20.0
Indochina	24.0

Source: Anna Mattila, "Investment Returns and Opportunities for Hotels in Asia," *Cornell H.R.A. Quarterly* (February, 1997), 74. Copyright Cornell University. Used by permission. All rights reserved.

Forecasting future cash flows in capital budgeting is often considered more art than science. International capital budgeting is a critical function in international hospitality development since it can distinguish the financially viable projects from those that are not. It can be effectively used to compare the benefits and costs of developing overseas hospitality projects and guide the financial success of the overseas operations.

SUMMARY

- International hospitality development and operations have to deal with complex financial management issues and concerns. The increased complexity and difficulty are the result of having to deal with more than one currency and different economic systems.
- The trading of one country's money for that of another country is called foreign exchange trading. The exchange of the two currencies is determined by the exchange rate.
- Foreign exchange rates are quoted directly and indirectly. The difference between selling rates and buying rates is called the spread.
- Foreign exchange transactions can be handled in spot, forward, futures, options, and swap markets.
- Capital financing for overseas development can be raised from the equity market and debt market in the home country, in the host country, or from a third country.
- The primary sources of equity investment include C-Corps, REITs, entrepreneurs, and funds of public, private, or government origin. For debt financing, sources include commercial banks, small business associations, life insurance companies, pension funds, and investment banks.
- A Eurocurrency is any currency banked outside its country of origin. At present, Eurocurrency can be found anywhere in the world.
- Currencies that can be freely traded at international exchange markets are called convertible currencies. The six major world convertible currencies, also known as hard currencies, are the U.S. dollar, German mark, British pound, Swiss franc, French franc, and Japanese yen.
- Some governments have strict policies on foreign exchange control, such as licensing requirements, limiting foreign travel allowance. Tight government control of foreign exchange often causes illegal trading of foreign exchange, known as the black market.
- Three types of foreign exchange exposures have a direct impact on a firm's overseas operations: transaction exposure, economic exposure, and translation exposure.

- Foreign exchange risk can be reduced through effective hedging techniques. Some of the commonly used hedging techniques include: geographic diversification, the use of futures and forward contracts, and lead and lag tactics.
- Capital budgeting examines the prospective investment alternatives and the commitment of funds to desirable hotel or restaurant development in foreign countries. Capital budgeting analyzes and forecasts economic and financial viability of the development project.
- Capital budgeting for international investment in hotels and restaurants needs to consider the following economic and financial aspects: initial investment, consumer demand, price, variable cost, fixed cost, project lifetime, salvage value, fund transfer restriction, tax laws, exchange rates, and required rate of return.

STUDY QUESTIONS

1. What is the function of the foreign exchange market?
2. How is exchange rate defined?
3. How are exchange rates quoted?
4. What is the spot rate?
5. How is the spread determined in spot market transactions?
6. What is the function of the forward exchange market?
7. What is the function of currency futures contracts?
8. How can you use a currency options contract to hedge potential exchange risk?
9. What is a swap contract?
10. How can you obtain capital funds for international hospitality development and operations?
11. Define the concepts of C-Corp and REITs. How are they used as the primary vehicle to raise public equity?
12. How did Marriott International finance its first hotel in Poland?
13. What is Eurocurrency?
14. What is the difference between foreign bonds and Eurobonds?
15. How is currency convertibility determined? What are the major world convertible currencies?
16. Discuss the major policy measures initiated by many governments to control foreign exchange in their countries.
17. What are the black market and parallel market for currency?
18. How can transaction exposure, economic exposure, and translation exposure affect international hospitality operations?

19. How can a hospitality firm minimize transaction and translation exposures?
20. What strategy should a hospitality firm adopt when operating in a country whose currency is weakening?
21. Explain the lead and lag strategies. How can these strategies be used to hedge foreign exchange risk?
22. Why is capital budgeting so important to the success of overseas operations?
23. Discuss the eleven necessary aspects of the capital budgeting process.
24. Can you describe the various economic and financial aspects that need to be considered in the capital budgeting process?

CASE STUDY: THE IMPACT OF RUPIAH DEVALUATION ON INTERNATIONAL HOTEL OPERATIONS IN INDONESIA

The drastic devaluation of the Indonesian rupiah began in the summer of 1997. Downward spiraling currency and political unrest plagued Indonesia's tourism industry in 1997 and 1998. Many hotels had to shift rates from U.S. dollars to local currency and dismiss U.S. dollar-salaried expatriates to make ends meet. Drastic measures to curb costs included from closing hotel wings and restaurants to laying off more hotel staff. It was estimated that 25 percent of Jakarta's 12 million population were unemployed in May 1998. Unemployment was forecast to reach 21 percent in 1998 and nearly 32,000 of 49,000 expatriate workers left the country from March to May in 1998.

The International Monetary Fund provided a $43 billion bailout package in January 1998 in return for government reforms to overhaul the banking system, open foreign investment, and end a system of patronage that has enriched the political leaders' children and close associates. The Indonesian government planned to peg the rupiah to the U.S. dollar, a plan strongly opposed by the United States, the IMF, and international experts. In March President Clinton sent Walter Mondale to Indonesia as his personal emissary to relay his concerns on the economic situation.

Indonesian Hotel and Restaurant Association chairman Pontjo Sutowo said the devastating financial crisis and political uncertainty further upset Indonesian tourism and increased tour cancellations. "Tourists may cancel or delay their trips to come here," Sutowo said. "Social unrest is the worst enemy of tourism." He predicted the dropping value of currencies in Asia also would contribute to dismal tourism prospects, at least for the first part of 1998. Tourists from Asia made up 40 percent of all foreign arrivals to Indonesia.

Sutowo said star-rated hotels—which charge rates in U.S. dollars—suffered more than nonstar hotels during the crisis. Star-rated hotels have lost their domestic market while nonstar hotels, charging in rupiah, have benefitted by grabbing the domestic market. Sutowo suggested using the Asian currency basket to lure visitors, adjusting the exchange rate to the average of Asian currencies against the U.S. dollar. The measure would be done in operation with other countries in the region, using instruments such as vouchers. "If we do not adjust to the decrease of arrivals from Asian countries, our market could be grabbed by other countries in the region which are more competitive," Sutowo said. The measure could make inter-Asian travel similar to domestic travel.

Many hotels in Indonesia were already calculating the "reasonable exchange rate" for the rupiah against the dollar. Director General of Tourism Andi Mappisammeng said, despite serious efforts to reach a reasonable rate, it was impossible for hotels to use 5,000 rupiah to the dollar, as suggested in the state budget and as the currency board peg. The actual rate at the time the budget was released in mid-January was already 8,000 rupiah to the dollar and by mid-March, hovered at 10,000 rupiah to the dollar.

When hotel managers come to a commonly agreed rate, they use it regardless of monetary fluctuations, Mappisammeng said. He said that setting a standard exchange rate, especially for star-rated hotels, was crucial. "Star-rated hotels must be denominated in U.S. dollars because the hotels' main business is international, and hotel investment is normally set in U.S. dollars," Mappisammeng said. He added that the government had never interfered in hotel rate formulation, leaving it to hotel management.

"Indonesia needs the foreign exchange," said Chris Green, chief of Jakarta's Casa Grande Association of star-rated hotel general managers. "If you go to rupiah rates, you have a major problem, but hotels are beginning to shift. This won't go on forever and eventually rates will have to return to dollars for the international stage. Rates can't be in rupiah on a daily basis for contracts. Casa Grande has agreed we should quote in rupiah for domestic business. It is up to each hotel to adjust rates for the market forces. For a customer who paid $200 a month ago, it equaled 500,000 rupiah. Now it translates to 2 million rupiah." Green said, "A two-tier system is essential and the domestic rate must be within the budget for the market. While the international market may not care, the domestic market does. The traveling international businessman on a corporate rate is not fighting. There is no change for this person except food and beverage is cheaper because it is in rupiah prices. Tour operators obviously are interested in getting rates adjusted to rupiah, but there is no tourism business in Jakarta right now."

Jakarta, as a business center, faces increasing decline in occupancy due to decline in business in the nation's economic crisis. Star-rated international hotels reported that occupancy was about 40 percent in January 1998, compared to 80 percent in the peak season and 60 percent in the second half of 1997. January's normal slowness is compounded because it is the Muslim fasting month.

Expatriate hotel staff are being pared down because their salaries are in dollars. "The general manager will still have a job, and maybe chef or specialty culinary staff," Green said, adding that his expatriate staff at Sahid Jaya Jakarta, the domestic Sahid Hotel chain's flagship, was cut from fourteen to three. Since January often was a contract renewal period, many contracts had not been renewed or escape clauses had been invoked by hotel operators. "It is not a question of getting over the situation," Green said. "It is a question of survival." Green added that some Jakarta hotels were considering mothballing restaurants and floors. "This is being considered with great gravity. It will mean possible layoff of staff. All general managers are reluctant to cause hardship on staff and family." He added that Sahid had put a freeze on casual employment, new hires, and contract renewals except in sensitive areas. "The strong will survive and the weak will go away," Green said. "In the long run, we will have a far better hospitality industry in Indonesia and will be forced to train Indonesian management and the Indonesians forced to take on responsibility." This is where the industry was headed anyway, with the government-enforced limit of three expatriates per hotel as of 2000 (see case study in Chapter 5).

Things look brighter for the industry in Bali, where tourism is the market focus. With the increase of rupiah to the dollar, employees were getting four times higher service charge payments, even when the occupancy was lower, said Bali Casa Grande chairman Erik Gangsted. Tourist arrivals are said to have dropped 40 percent and hotel occupancy rates have dived from 65 to 70 percent to 40 to 50 percent. The average rack rates for five-star hotels have plunged to $100 to $120 a night and $80 to $100 for four stars.

With the domestic carrier's mid-January overnight increase of airfares to Bali, local hotels saw an immediate 10 percent cancellation from the domestic market, Gangsted said. "It is not doom and gloom for the majority of hotels in Bali," he said. Restaurants' rupiah costs have not increased much yet, making food and beverage a true bargain for tourists in Bali. Casa Grande was encouraging hotels to keep their food and beverage rates in rupiah to eliminate any perception of "ripping off" tourists. Shopping, with discounts up to 70 percent on the already deflated rupiah prices, was also wildly attractive.

Case Study Source

Debe Campbell, "Crash Plagues Indonesian Hotels," *Hotel & Motel Management* (April 6, 1998), 6, 21.

Case Study Questions

1. Why did many hotels have to shift rates from U.S. dollars to rupiah?
2. What impact did the depreciating rupiah have on hotel operations in Indonesia?
3. Discuss the financial crisis and political unrest in Indonesia in the first part of 1998.
4. Do you agree with Mappisammeng on setting a reasonable standard exchange rate for star-rated hotels in Indonesia during the currency crisis?
5. What is the "two-tier system" suggested by Green?
6. What happened to business travel in Jakarta during the financial crisis and social unrest in early 1998?
7. What happened to hotel expatriate staff when the economic crisis continued?
8. What was the impact of airfare increases on travel to Bali?

Chapter 10

International Accounting and Taxation

Accounting reflects in each country the overall philosophy of the economy and the differences in the legal system. If we had a more uniform method of accounting around the world, we would have less uncertainty on the part of lenders and that might reduce borrowing costs. But it takes time.[1]

Arthur Wyatt
Chairman, International Accounting Standards Committee

LEARNING OBJECTIVES

In this chapter, you will study:

1. The differences in accounting practices among different countries
2. Generalized accounting models
3. The harmonization of accounting standards
4. Accounting for foreign currency transaction
5. Types of taxes imposed on international business
6. Relief for tax liabilities
7. Selected U.S. laws on international taxation
8. International tax planning

INTRODUCTION

Finance is the management of a firm's monetary resources and income. The financial affairs of any business organization need to be effectively managed, evaluated, and analyzed. The primary tool for doing this is through the organization's accounting system. Accounting as a financial management tool measures, records, and analyzes the receipts and disbursements of an organization. It reports on the resources (assets) controlled by an organization, and the claims (liabilities and equity) against those resources. Accounting is a financial representation of what the firm is.

However, there is no single unified accounting system in the world. Accounting standards and practices vary significantly across countries. These variations in accounting practice are strongly influenced by the political, economic, legal, and cultural systems of individual countries. The different accounting systems in the world greatly complicate international hospitality operations.

In addition, there is the common saying: "Nothing is certain but death and taxes." This also applies to international hospitality operations. As discussed in the previous chapter on capital budgeting, tax laws of different countries have a direct impact on net after-tax cash flows of a company's operations in a foreign country. International hospitality corporations face a complex array of changing rules of sophisticated and intricate tax laws. Knowledge of the host country's tax laws can enable managers to develop appropriate tax strategies to increase net after-tax cash flows.

This chapter thus combines the two important financial management topics and discusses the common themes underlying international accounting and taxation. It points out specifically the national differences in accounting and taxation practices and various financial accounting techniques used in different countries. Accounting for foreign currency transactions is also explained. It discusses the basic types of taxes, and several tax planning strategies that can be used by international hospitality firms to minimize tax liability both at home and abroad. It emphasizes that international accounting and taxation are an integral part of global hospitality development and operations.

INTERNATIONAL ACCOUNTING

The globalized world economy, the rapidly increasing volume of international business, and the emergence of multinational corporations have given an impetus to the development of international accounting. However, there is at present no universally accepted definition for international accounting. International accounting includes all varieties of principles, methods, and standards of all countries.[2] The differences in standards, policies, and techniques reflect varying geographic, social, economic, political, and legal influences of individual countries. This collection of all accounting principles, methods, and standards is considered the international accounting system.[3]

Accounting is thus shaped by the environment in which it operates.[4] In some countries, such as the United States and Britain, apart from assisting financial decisions by the management, accounting is primarily oriented toward parties external to the business organization who provide capital to it. Financial reports are very important for the investors and creditors for investment decision making. In some other countries, financial accounting has a different emphasis and performs other roles. For instance, accounting is mainly used by the government to ensure the collection of the proper amount of income tax in many Latin American countries.[5] Therefore, financial accounting practice in these countries is influenced by economic and political forces.

Accounting practice is also influenced by the cultural values of a particular society. The same accounting information can be perceived differently by different cultural groups, such as French-speaking Canadians and English-speaking Canadians.[6] The use of language in each culture has an impact on accounting practice. Accounting language may predispose users to a particular method of perception and behavior. Research has demonstrated that accountants in different countries have created different linguistic repertoires or codes for intra- or intergroup communications.[7]

Accounting practice in different countries is also influenced by the legal system of the country. In fact, accounting practices around the world have been divided by scholars into "legalistic" and "nonlegalistic" categories.[8] The legalistic group primarily includes countries under the civil law system, and the nonlegalistic group includes countries under the common law system. As discussed in Chapter 8, civil law is based on a body of codes that stipulate the minimum standard of behavior expected. In most civil law countries, accounting policies and principles are national laws. Accounting practice must follow closely detailed procedural rules, and financial accounting focuses on how much income tax a firm owes the government. Most continental European countries take a legalistic approach to accounting.

The nonlegalistic group is mainly represented by the United Kingdom and the United States, which practice common law. Common law establishes the legal limits of practice. But latitude is permitted within the limits. Accounting objectives and standards in common law countries are largely determined by accounting professionals rather than by legislators. Accounting principles and policies tend to be more innovative and adaptive in these countries.[9]

GENERAL ACCOUNTING MODELS

Financial accounting practice is therefore influenced by the political, economic, cultural, and legal systems in a given country. No two countries have identical financial reporting and disclosure systems. However, certain countries maintain some similar practices based on close political and economic ties, geographic proximity, and similar legal systems. The diffusion of accounting practice from Britain to former British colonies demonstrates close political and economic ties. Almost every former British colony follows British financial accounting practices. Practices in Canada and Mexico are heavily influenced by U.S. practice due to geographic proximity and close political and economic ties.

Then, as discussed earlier, countries under the same legal system share similar characteristics in accounting practices. Besides being used as a tool of internal control by managers on a daily basis, accounting in countries with civil law reflects an emphasis of government macroeconomic control, while accounting in common law countries is oriented toward providing detailed financial information to investors and creditors for decision making.

These similar characteristics can be used to classify countries into certain accounting models. A recent study classified 105 countries into four major accounting models: British-American, Continental, South American, and mixed economy.[10] These four models systematically generalize the similarities and differences among countries, and can be a guide for global hospitality managers to better understand the myriad of accounting systems.

British-American Model

This accounting cluster is represented by forty-three countries. It is the most influential model, dominated by the accounting practices used in the United Kingdom and the United States. Apart from being used as an internal control tool by managers on a daily basis, the accounting role is relatively oriented toward the decision needs of investors and creditors, since both public ownership and debt financing are greatest in these countries. Financial information users are highly educated and sophisticated in these countries. The Netherlands also has similar accounting practices. Together, these three countries have influenced many other countries in accounting practice.

Continental Model

Accounting in the continental cluster is influenced by the practices found in the continental European countries and Japan. In this model, most countries practice civil law and banks primarily supply capital to businesses. It is not the primary role of financial accounting to provide timely and sophisticated reports for investors' decision-making needs. Accounting policy is oriented toward the implementation of government regulations such as computing income taxes or illustrating compliance with the national government's macroeconomic plan. Twenty-eight countries are represented in this accounting cluster, including most French-speaking African countries.

South American Model

Nine South American countries are included in this accounting cluster. Spanish is a dominant language in this group except for Brazil, which uses Portuguese. The most distinctive aspect of accounting practice in this model is the persistent use of adjustment for inflation since all these countries experienced hyperinflation in the past. Accounting is used to satisfy the needs of government regulators and uniform practices are followed by all business organizations. Tax-basis accounting is often used as well for financial reporting purposes.

Mixed Economy Model

This cluster includes Eastern European countries and Russia. As discussed in Chapters 4 and 5, all these countries are now experiencing a transition from authoritarian to democratic governments, and from socialist to market economies. These countries also show dual accounting systems: the remnants of tight central economic planning and control and introduction of market-oriented practice. For instance, the uniform charts of accounting and budget used under the planned economy are still used by managers in some state-owned business organizations in Russia. On the other hand, many international businesses and local emerging private business entities try to follow the British-American model in order to provide adequate financial information for decision-making needs by investors from developed countries.

In addition to these four major models, two other general accounting practices exist: the Islamic model and accounting in communist countries. Financial accounting practice in the Arab nations is strictly dictated by Islamic religious doctrine. For instance, the Islamic religion prohibits any recognition of interest on money. Therefore, current market values are favored as measures of business assets and liabilities.[11]

As discussed in Chapter 5, the means of production and business are owned by the government in communist countries. In addition to the managers, government decision makers are the main users of the financial information. Uniform accounting is practiced for tight central economic control. Financial statements are not disclosed for outsiders, but are only used by management, government agencies, and government planners. The difficulty in obtaining timely and accurate financial information for decision making needs always frustrates international companies doing business in communist countries.

HARMONIZATION OF ACCOUNTING STANDARDS

The differences in accounting systems and practices discussed in the previous section complicate international hospitality operations. Since company financial statements impart different information, this lack of comparability may cause investors and creditors to make poor decisions. If accountants of different nations do not perform audits the same way, then the assurances they give about the reliability of financial information cannot be regarded equally by financial statement users. As international business continues to expand, more and more countries have realized the need for reconciling some of the accounting differences.

International accounting harmonization does not mean complete standardization of different accounting practices. Harmonization recognizes national differences in accounting systems and attempts to reconcile the differences to attain an acceptable degree of uniformity.[12] Various national and international accounting professional organizations have worked on developing a conceptual framework for establishing accounting and auditing standards.

Accounting standards are the guidelines for organizing and analyzing financial information. These standards specify acceptable practices in financial reporting. Auditing standards are the rules for professionally conducting an audit. An audit is performed by an auditor to examine a set of financial statements prepared by a particular firm, and determine if these statements are prepared in accordance with accounting standards and if the financial information provided in the statements is accurate and reliable.

To ensure that different countries can provide useful, reliable, and comparable financial information, various international, regional, and professional bodies have made substantial efforts to harmonize accounting standards across countries. Following is a brief introduction to some of the leading international, regional, and professional organizations that have made significant contributions to the harmonization of international accounting standards.

The International Accounting Standards Committee (IASC) is the leading organization in developing worldwide accounting standards. Founded in 1973, the IASC consists of representatives of 106 private professional accounting organizations in eighty countries. As one of the most influential international organizations in setting accounting standards for private business, the IASC has issued thirty-one International Accounting Standards (IASs) thus far. These accounting standards specify rules for reporting various financial transactions for international business.

The International Federation of Accountants (IFAC) is a professional organization for accountants around the world. The IFAC was established in 1977 and the membership now represents accounting professionals from over seventy-five countries. As IASC focuses primarily on setting accounting standards for private business, IFAC is more involved in formulating international accounting standards for the public sector. It develops standards for auditing, ethical conduct, education, and training in the international accounting profession.

The generally accepted accounting principles for U.S. companies to prepare financial statements are set by the Financial Accounting Standards Board (FASB) in the United States. Statements of Financial Accounting Standards (SFAS), written by the FASB, contain these principles. For instance, Statement 52 focuses specifically on the rules for foreign currency translation, which will be discussed later in this chapter.

In the United States, the American Hotel & Motel Association (AH&MA) issues the Uniform System of Accounts for the Lodging Industry in an attempt to standardize hotel accounting practice. In 1997, the Committee on Financial Management of AH&MA completed the *Ninth Revised Edition of the Uniform System of Accounts for the Lodging Industry.*[13] This revised edition will have a major impact on the standardization of accounting practice in the U.S. lodging industry.

Hospitality Financial and Technology Professionals (HFTP), formerly the International Association of Hospitality Accountants (IAHA), based in Austin, Texas, represents financial and accounting professionals in the hospitality industry worldwide. Its mission is to reduce accounting differences in hospitality operations across countries, establish standards in various areas of interest such as auditing, ethical codes, training, and education, and expand the use of technology in its profession. Its standard-setting efforts will greatly influence the harmonization of accounting practice in the international hospitality industry.

ACCOUNTING FOR FOREIGN CURRENCY TRANSACTIONS

Business transactions by international hospitality firms require the flow of money globally. These transactions include receiving royalties and management fees, payments for hotel rooms from foreign travel operators, purchase of foreign goods, commission payments to foreign travel agents, the payment or receipt of dividends, and so on. They are called foreign currency transactions because they require settlement in a currency other than the company's home currency.

For U.S. hospitality firms taking foreign currencies as receivables, foreign currency transactions must be translated into U.S. dollars for preparing financial statements for shareholders and creditors, and for measuring taxable income and tax liabilities. Therefore, accounting for international operations differs from accounting for domestic operations because accountants have to deal with foreign currency translation in preparing financial statements. This section describes the translation methodology and discusses its implications for managing international hospitality operations.

Import/Export Transactions

Import/export transactions refer to importing (buying) or exporting (selling) goods or services on credit with the payable and receivable denominated in a foreign currency.[14] As discussed in the previous chapter, payables and receivables denominated in a foreign currency are exposed to the risk of unfavorable changes in the exchange rate. Accounting for such transactions involves three major steps:

1. Initial transaction date: measure and record transaction at current exchange rate—the spot rate.
2. Balance sheet date, between initial transaction date and final settlement date: adjust recorded balances of unsettled receivables and payables that are denominated in foreign currency to reflect the current spot rate at the balance sheet date. This adjustment for the change in exchange rates results in foreign exchange gains or losses that are to be included in the income statement of the current period even though they are unrealized.
3. Final settlement date: adjust recorded balances of foreign currency receivables and payables to reflect spot rate at settlement date and recognize foreign exchange gains and losses.[15]

The following is a concrete example to illustrate these three accounting procedures. Assume a U.S. hotel company initiates a sale of franchise to a New Zealand hotel company. The franchise initiation fee is based on the size of the hotel in New Zealand, which is valued at NZD100,000. The initiation fee will be paid in New Zealand dollars within thirty days. The transaction exchange rate information is as follows:

Initial transaction date   December 21 19X7
   NZD 1 = $.50

Balance sheet date   December 31 19X7
   NZD 1 = $.55

Final settlement date   January 20 19X8
   NZD 1 = $.46

With the above information, the accounting procedure will be:

1. Date of initial transaction   December 21   19X7
   Accounts Receivable $50,000
   Sales $50,000
   (NZD 100,000 × 0.50)

2. Date of balance sheet   December 31   19X7
   Accounts Receivable $5,000
   Exchange Gains $5,000
   (Foreign exchange rate 0.55 − 0.50) This exchange gain will be
   included in the 19X7 income statement of the company as a
   nonoperating item.

3. Date of settlement   January 20   19X8
   Cash $46,000
   Exchange Losses $9,000
   Accounts Receivable $55,000
   (Exchange loss 0.55 − 0.46) NZD 100,000 × 0.46. This
   exchange loss will be included in the 19X8 income statement
   of the company as a nonoperating item.

Translation Methods for Financial Statements

If a U.S. company is involved in foreign business activities through the operation of a branch or subsidiary in a foreign country and the foreign entity maintains its books in a foreign currency, the accounts must be translated into U.S. dollars before the accounts are consolidated. Statement 52 (AFAS 52), "Foreign Currency Translation," issued by the U.S. FASB in 1981, specifies the standards for financial reporting by multinational companies. Statement 52 first defines the concept of functional currency and the nature of foreign operations. Functional currency is the currency of the primary economic environment in which the hospitality business is operated.

Statement 52 defines the U.S. dollar as the functional currency if the operation of a foreign entity is a direct and integral component of, or an extension of, the parent company's operations. If the foreign entity is self-sustaining or autonomous in a foreign country, the functional currency is the currency of that country.

If international operations depend on the parent company, these foreign entities tend not to customize their products and marketing strategies to local market conditions, because the entire corporation prefers to market a standardized product and service worldwide. Revenues and expenses are largely influenced by the parent, and the foreign entity's cash flows directly affect the parent's cash flows. For this type of operation, the U.S. dollar is the functional currency.

On the other hand, self-sustaining and autonomous foreign entities tend to establish product, service, and marketing functions in the host country. They tend to undertake some local customization of products, services, and marketing strategies. They operate relatively independent from the parent company, and revenues and expenses respond mostly to local conditions. Few of the foreign entity's cash flows affect the parent's cash flows. Most overseas hospitality entities are described as self-sustaining and autonomous operations, such as McDonald's.[16] The local currency is the functional currency.

If the foreign entity operates in a highly inflationary country (economies having cumulative inflation of approximately 100 percent or more over a three-year period), the local currency is considered too unstable to serve as the functional currency. In this case, U.S. dollars must be used.

The choice of functional currency is important for international hospitality operations. Once it has been determined, it must be used consistently over time unless economic change or other circumstances clearly indicate that the functional currency needs to be changed. Management judgment is required to determine which functional currency best captures the economic effects of a foreign operation's financial position.

Foreign Currency As Functional Currency

When foreign currency is the functional currency, the current rate translation method is used. Under the current rate method, revenues and expenses on the income statement are translated at the average exchange rate during the period. Balance sheet items are translated at the end-of-the-period exchange rate (see Exhibits 10.1 and 10.2).

Exhibit 10.1 illustrates a simplified income statement of an overseas hotel operated by a U.S.-based hotel corporation. All income statement items have been translated using the average annual exchange rate except for the dividends, which were translated at the spot rate when they were issued. Exhibit 10.2 shows the translation of balance sheet items at the current rate on December 31, 1997 except for capital stock, which was translated at the spot rate when the stock was issued, also known as the historic rate.

U.S. Dollar As Functional Currency

When the U.S. dollar is used as the functional currency, the temporal rate translation method is used. The temporal method specifies that accounts carried at past exchange rates are translated at historical rates and

EXHIBIT 10.1. A Sample Simplified Income Statement Using Current Rate Method, December 31, 1997

	Current Rate Method		
	Local Currency	Exchange Rate	U.S. Dollars
Sales	29,000	1.20	$34,800
Operating Expenses	22,000	1.20	26,400
Income before taxes	7,000	1.20	8,400
Income taxes	2,730		3,276
Net income	4,270	1.20	5,124
Retained earnings (12/31/96)	3,500		5,005
	7,770		10,129
Dividends	600	1.17	702
Retained earnings (12/31/97)	7,170		$ 9,427

EXHIBIT 10.2. A Sample Simplified Balance Sheet Statement Showing Current Rate Method, December 31, 1997

	Current Rate Method		
	Local Currency	Exchange Rate	U.S. Dollars
Assets			
Current Assets			
Cash	2,500	0.97	$2,425
Accounts Receivable	5,000	0.97	4,850
Total Current Assets	7,500	0.97	7,275
Property and Equipment	125,000	0.97	121,250
Total Assets	140,000	0.97	$135,800
Liabilities and Owners' Equity			
Current Liabilities			
Notes Payable	23,700	0.97	$22,989
Accounts Payable	8,000	0.97	7,760
Total Current Liabilities	31,700	0.97	30,749
Capital Stock	45,000	0.84	37,800
Retained Earnings	63,300		75,960
Accumulated Translated Adjustment			(8,709)
Total Liabilities and Owners' Equity	140,000		$135,800

accounts carried at current purchase or sales exchange prices or future exchange prices are translated at current rates. The temporal method retains the accounting valuation basis that is used to measure the foreign currency items.[17] Exhibit 10.3 summarizes the temporal method for various items listed in the income statement and balance sheet statement.

DETERMINATION OF APPROPRIATE TRANSLATION METHOD

It is clear from the above discussion that current exchange rates are used in translation when the foreign currency is the functional currency, while a mixture of current and historical rates is used when the U.S. dollar is the functional currency. Most international companies, particularly the self-sustaining and autonomous foreign entities, prefer to use the foreign currency as the functional currency because the current rate method generally results in fewer earnings surprises.[18] However, in some cases a hospitality company has to use the home currency as the functional currency, such as in high-inflation countries.

Because of the possibly significant and often unexpected effects of including the unrealized translation gain or loss in earnings, it is advantageous to neutralize its impact. Companies are advised to operate with a net monetary position as close to zero as possible. Any change in exchange rates when applied to the small net monetary position results in insignificant translation gains or losses.[19]

EXHIBIT 10.3. Summary of Temporal Method Applications

Income Statement	Balance Sheet
Revenue and expense are translated using the exchange rate in effect when the original measurements underlying the valuation were made. Revenues and most operating expenses are translated using the average exchange rate during the period. However, cost of goods sold and depreciation are translated using the historical exchange rate appropriate to the related asset such as monetary and fixed assets.	Monetary assets and liabilities, which include cash, accounts receivable, accounts payable, etc. are translated using the end-of-the-period exchange rate. Nonmonetary assets and equities, which include inventories, fixed assets, common stock, etc. are translated using the historical exchange rate.

Accounting standards are also established for preparing financial statements showing hedging transactions and using various foreign currency contracts. Discussions of accounting for hedging transactions are beyond the scope of this text. Those who are interested in this topic should consult a specific text on international accounting.

INTERNATIONAL TAXATION

Tax management is always a central part of international financial management. Taxation of different countries affects international hospitality firms' market entry decision, determination of net cash flows after taxes in capital budgeting (as discussed in Chapter 9), decisions on how to finance overseas development, when and where to remit cash, and how to maximize expected bottom-line profits after taxes.

International taxation is very complex and constantly changing since individual countries' laws, economic policies, regulations, and agreements between two countries often change. It is impossible in a general international hospitality management text to set out all the complexities of the tax laws of many countries. The discussion in this section is intended to give global hospitality managers an overview of the concepts and functions of international taxation management pertinent to international hospitality operations.

TERRITORIAL PRINCIPLE
VERSUS WORLDWIDE PRINCIPLE

Business taxation differs from one country to another. When an international corporation expands into a foreign country, it must examine its home country's tax rules, the host country's tax rules, and the interaction of the two. There are two general approaches to taxation: territorial principle and worldwide principle. Countries that follow territorial principle believe that they have the right to tax income earned inside their borders, while income earned outside their borders should not be taxed. Examples of countries that follow the territorial principle include Switzerland, Panama, Hong Kong, Argentina, Venezuela, and many Central American, and Caribbean island countries.[20]

Many countries adopt the worldwide principle that they have the right to tax income earned inside their borders, but also income earned outside their borders by companies registered in the country. This worldwide

approach can cause double taxation since the international company registered in the host country has to pay income tax both to the host government and its own government when the earnings are repatriated to the
home company. However, most countries following the worldwide principle grant some forms of relief for foreign companies to reduce or eliminate
double taxation. The different forms of tax relief will be discussed later in
this chapter.

TYPES OF TAXES

International hospitality firms face various tax liabilities when they
operate in different foreign countries since hospitality operations with
different forms of business organization may be subject to different taxes,
such as the different tax liabilities in the United States for corporations,
C-Corps, and REITs discussed in the previous chapter. In addition, hospitality firms have to consider the local sales tax, room tax, and beverage
tax. A recent survey of fifty tourism destinations by the World Tourism
Organization found more than forty different kinds of taxes levied on
tourism worldwide.[21] However, the most important characteristics of a
country to be considered within a hospitality firm's international tax assessment for entry decision include: (1) corporate income taxes, (2) withholding taxes, and (3) provision for carrybacks and carryforwards.[22]
These three major forms of international taxes are described in the following sections.

Corporate Income Taxes

The corporate income tax is the most widely used type of tax in the
world. Many countries rely heavily on corporate income tax as a major
source of government revenue. International hospitality firms planning
overseas investment and development must determine how the anticipated
earnings from direct foreign investment and operations will be affected.
Each country varies significantly in the amount of income taxes it levies
on business operations. Many developed countries impose corporate income tax rates above 30 percent, such as 46 percent in Germany, 37
percent in Japan, 33 percent in the United Kingdom, and 34 percent in the
United States. However, other countries may offer lower corporate tax
rates to attract foreign hospitality companies, such as 25 percent in Brazil
and 17 percent in Hong Kong. The Cayman Islands and the Bahamas have
a zero corporate income tax rate. However, even in countries with high

corporate taxes, many offer various tax deductions and incentives for international companies to reduce tax liability. Finding these tax incentives in different countries can help minimize the company's tax liability.

Withholding Taxes

When a foreign hotel property or restaurant transfers various funds to the parent company, such as earnings or royalties, these outflow funds can be subject to withholding taxes levied by the host tax authorities. Withholding taxes are assessed on dividends, interest, and royalties. Like the corporate tax rates, the withholding tax rates also differ from country to country. For instance, New Zealand imposes 15 percent tax on dividends, 10 percent tax on interest, and 10 percent tax on royalties, and Argentina levies no tax on dividends, but 12 percent tax on interest and 18 to 24 percent tax on royalties. The Bahamas, Greece, and Hong Kong do not impose any taxes on dividends, interest, and royalties.

Even within a country, the withholding tax can vary according to the purpose of the fund transfer. As overseas operations regularly send dividends, interest, and royalty fees to home countries, each of these fund transfers may be subject to a different withholding tax rate. Withholding taxes can be modified by using tax treaties between the host country and the home country. The use of tax treaties will be discussed later in this chapter.

Laws on Carrybacks and Carryforwards

If an overseas hotel property or restaurant has negative earnings in a particular year, it must consult the host tax laws to find out whether the net operating loss can be carried back or forward to offset positive earnings in other years. The provisions for net operating loss carryback and carryforward can vary among countries. Most countries do not permit net operating loss carrybacks. However, every country has some form of flexibility to allow foreign companies to carry operating losses forward to the next year. Therefore, it is always important to check the availability of net operating loss carrybacks and carryforwards.

RELIEF FOR TAX LIABILITIES

Most countries grant some form of relief for foreign companies to reduce double taxation. These relief measures include tax credit, tax treaties, tax haven, the deferral principle, and tax exemption.[23]

A tax credit allows a hospitality company to reduce its tax liability to the home government by the amount of tax that has already been paid to the host country government. This form of tax relief is a direct reduction of the tax liability and reduces double taxation to a certain extent. For instance, assume a U.S. hotel company pays income tax of $80,000 on yearly earnings to the Mexican tax authorities. In the United States, the company owes U.S. income tax of $150,000 for the operations of the hotel in Mexico. After deducting the $80,000 already paid to the Mexican government, the company only needs to pay $70,000 to the U.S. government.

A tax treaty is a bilateral agreement between two countries (or a multilateral agreement among several countries) to specify what items of income will or will not be taxed in the country in which the income is generated. Knowledge of tax treaties between the home and host countries is very important for avoiding higher income taxes and withholding taxes. For instance, a hotel company from Country A operates business in Country B. The tax treaty between Country A and Country B specifies that each country imposes a 15 percent withholding tax on dividends when they leave each country. Then the financial executive of the hotel finds out that there is a tax treaty between Country B and Country C with only 5 percent withholding tax, and a tax treaty between Country A and Country C with the same 5 percent withholding tax. After such treaty shopping, the hotel financial executive decides to use an intermediate company in Country C to receive the dividends from Country B with 5 percent withholding tax, and the dividends would flow from Country C to the home country, Country A, with another 5 percent withholding tax. Such procedure saves the hotel 5 percent withholding tax compared to the direct transfer from Country B to Country A.

A tax haven is a country with virtually no income tax, or a relatively low tax rate. Most tax haven countries follow the territorial principle, imposing low income tax only on income earned within their borders, but imposing no tax on income generated outside their borders. International hospitality corporations can shift income from a country with a high tax rate to the tax haven.

Some countries tax a firm's foreign-source income only when the earnings are remitted to the parent company in the home country. If the company's foreign-source income is not sent back to the parent company, the income will not be taxed by the home government. This is known as the deferral principle. Therefore, many multinational corporations take advantage of this principle by delaying the remittance of overseas income, or using the income for new development in other countries.

A tax exemption relieves a foreign company's tax liability by eliminating tax on certain income or even total income. This is often used by the developing countries to lure foreign hospitality companies to develop hotels and resorts in their countries. For instance, China offered foreign hotel companies total tax exemption for the initial three years of operations in the late 1970s and early 1980s. This tax exemption was one of the major motivating factors for foreign hotel companies to enter the Chinese hospitality market.

U.S. LAWS ON INTERNATIONAL TAXATION

The U.S. government imposes taxes on income earned outside the United States by U.S. citizens, residents, and business entities, or income earned by non-U.S. citizens and foreign business entities within the U.S. border. This section will briefly discuss the tax liability at home for U.S. citizens, residents, and corporations involved in international business activities.

U.S. Taxpayers Abroad

As more and more U.S. hospitality corporations expand their operations overseas, more expatriate hospitality managers and professionals will work and live in foreign countries. Citizens and residents of the United States are subject to federal taxation on their worldwide taxable income. U.S. citizens and residents who earn income from foreign countries must include foreign-source income in gross income for U.S. tax purposes. They are allowed for a deduction for related expenses and losses.

To avoid double taxation, U.S. citizens and residents are entitled to claim the foreign tax credit enacted by the U.S. Congress. Under this provision, a qualified taxpayer is allowed a tax credit for foreign income tax paid. The credit is a dollar-for-dollar reduction of the U.S. income tax liability. For example, an expatriate hotel manager owes $25,000 in U.S. income taxes on his foreign-source income. But he is also taxed by the foreign government for an equivalent of $18,000 in income taxes. Thus, his U.S. tax liability will be reduced to $7,000.

The U.S. government also grants an exclusion for a certain amount of qualified foreign earned income. The purpose of this exclusion is to reduce the tax burden on a U.S. taxpayer working abroad. Currently, the Foreign Earned Income Exclusion—§911 allows a foreign earned income exclusion for (1) a qualified housing cost amount, and (2) foreign earned income not in excess of $70,000. Any U.S. citizen or resident who works in a foreign country or countries for at least 330 consecutive full days is entitled to this tax benefit.

The housing cost amount is equal to the qualified housing expenses of an expatriate manager for the tax year less a base amount. The base amount is 16 percent of the salary of a U.S. government employee, and is determined on a daily basis. For instance, if the base amount for a full year was $8,737, and a qualified expatriate hotel professional was employed in a foreign country for 350 days of the year, the applicable base amount would be $8,778 ($8,737 × 350 days/365 days).

Tax Reporting for U.S. Corporations

Tax reporting methods for foreign-source income earned by U.S. corporations are specified in the Tax Reform Act of 1986. The amount included in the U.S. tax return of a parent company for the earnings of a foreign unit depends on whether the foreign unit is operated as a branch or a subsidiary of the parent company. A foreign branch is a separate and clearly identified unit of the parent corporation's business. This is also known as a qualified business unit (QBU). Most overseas hotel properties and restaurant units are considered foreign branches. Exhibit 10.4 describes income tax reporting methods for both branch and subsidiary operations.

EXHIBIT 10.4. Tax Reporting Methods for Overseas Branch and Subsidiary Operations

	Foreign Currency As Functional Currency	**U.S. Dollar As Functional Currency**
Branch	Revenues and expenses as measured in foreign currency are translated into U.S. dollars using the average exchange rate during the period. Income includes: (1) realized transaction gains and losses, and (2) realized transaction gains and losses when the foreign unit remits dividends or is liquidated.	The translation procedure is the same as for financial reporting. However, only realized transaction gains and losses are included in taxable income. Unrealized transaction and translation gains and losses are not included, nor is any gain or loss on dividend remittance.
Subsidiary	Only dividends are included in taxable income, translated using the exchange rate on the date of dividend distribution.	Only dividends are included in taxable income, translated at the exchange rate on the date of dividend distribution.

INTERNATIONAL TAX PLANNING

To maximize profits after tax is the prime objective of all global hospitality financial executives and managers. Managers must be aware of host country taxes on operating profits and fund transfers. Good international tax planning ensures that the company is not more heavily taxed than its domestic or third-country competitors. The initial step is to take advantage of the existing tax breaks and tax treaties. It is essential that the corporation does not pay tax twice on the same profit. Since tax systems and tax rates are unique to each country, international hospitality firms need to compare the various tax provisions of each country.

If an international hospitality firm plans to develop a hotel in a high-tax country, it can let the overseas property to finance the development itself by issuing bonds locally or within the Eurobond market. The interest expenses from bond payments can offset part of the income earned by the overseas hotel, and thus reduce income taxes.

Shifting income from overseas properties in high-tax countries to properties in low-tax countries is another commonly practiced strategy. These excess funds are often invested on a short-term basis in a tax haven country, and transferred to a particular development in a foreign country when needed. Otherwise the new development has to be financed from some other source, such as a local bank. Generally, such movement of funds from a high-tax to low-tax country can increase the after-tax cash inflows of the international corporation as a whole.

SUMMARY

- International accounting includes all varieties of principles, methods, and standards of all countries. The differences in standards, policies, and techniques reflect varying geographic, social, economic, political, and legal influences of individual countries.
- The legalistic group mainly includes countries under the civil law system and the nonlegalistic group includes countries under the common law system.
- Some countries have similar accounting practices because of their close political and economic ties, geographic proximity, and similar legal systems. The four major accounting models include the British-American, Continental, South American, and mixed economy.
- The harmonization of accounting standards recognizes national differences in order to achieve an acceptable degree of uniformity.

- Accounting standards are the guidelines for organizing and analyzing financial information. Auditing standards are the rules for professionally conducting an audit.
- Import/export transactions refer to importing or exporting goods or services on credit with the payables and receivables denominated in a foreign currency. Accounting for such transactions involves three major procedures: initial transaction date, balance sheet date, and final settlement date.
- Functional currency is the currency of the primary economic environment in which a firm operates. When foreign currency is used as the functional currency, the current rate translation method is used. When the U.S. dollar is used as the functional currency, the temporal rate translation method is used.
- Tax management is always a central part of international financial management. Taxation of various countries affects hospitality firms' market entry decisions, determination of net cash flows after tax in capital budgeting, decisions on how to finance overseas development, when and where to remit cash, and how to maximize expected bottom-line profits after tax.
- Countries that adopt the territorial principle believe that they have the right to tax income earned inside their borders, while income earned outside their borders should not be taxed. Countries that follow the worldwide principle believe that they have the right to tax income earned inside their borders, but also income earned outside their borders by companies registered in the country.
- The major types of taxes include corporate income tax and withholding taxes on dividends, interest, and royalties. Foreign governments may impose various taxes on tourism and hospitality operations at different administrative levels.
- Most countries grant some form of relief for foreign companies to reduce double taxation. These relief measures include tax credit, tax treaties, tax haven, the deferral principle, and tax exemption.
- The U.S. government imposes taxes on income earned outside the United States by U.S. citizens, residents, and business organizations, or income earned by non-U.S. citizens and foreign business entities within the U.S. border. Tax reporting methods for foreign source income earned by U.S. corporations are specified in the Tax Reform Act of 1986.
- To maximize profits after tax is the prime objective of all global hospitality financial executives and managers. Managers must be aware of host country taxes on operating profits and fund transfers. Effec-

tive international tax planning ensures that the company is not more heavily taxed than its domestic or third-country competitors.

STUDY QUESTIONS

1. How can you define international accounting?
2. What factors influence accounting practice in different countries?
3. What major differences in accounting practice are found between the legalistic group and the nonlegalistic group?
4. Discuss the four major accounting models in the world.
5. What are the other two accounting systems in addition to the four major accounting models?
6. Why is the global harmonization of accounting standards important to international business operations?
7. What are the functions of IASC, IFAC, AH&MA Financial Committee, and HFTP?
8. How are import/export transactions accounted for?
9. What is the functional currency?
10. Under what circumstances is the current rate translation method used?
11. How is the current rate translation method used in income statement and balance sheet financial reports?
12. Under what circumstances is the temporal method used in foreign currency translation?
13. How is the temporal method used in income statement and balance sheet financial reports?
14. Why do we say tax management is always a central part of international financial management?
15. What is the key difference between territorial principle and worldwide principle?
16. What are the major types of taxes a global hospitality firm has to pay in foreign countries?
17. What are carrybacks and carryforwards?
18. How can a hospitality firm or individual expatriate manager take advantage of tax credit to reduce tax liabilities?
19. What is the function of a tax treaty?
20. Where can you find the popular tax haven countries?
21. Explain the concept of tax exemption.
22. What are the U.S. laws governing U.S. taxpayers who earn income from foreign countries?

23. What is the tax reporting method for foreign source income earned by U.S. firms?
24. What are the major aspects you need to consider for international tax planning?

CASE STUDY: CAN YOU JUDGE
YOUR OPERATION FROM THE BOOK?

Accounting practice differs from country to country. But even in one country, there are also marked variations in preparing financial statements and reports.* The following case is based on an article written by Patrick Quek, president/CEO of PKF Consulting, an international hospitality consulting firm headquartered in San Francisco. This article reveals marked differences in the format and layout of accounting books in the hospitality industry in the United States. This can be an important management aspect for foreign investors, developers, and operators to know with regard to developing hotels in U.S. markets.

PKF Consulting (a major international accounting and consulting firm specializing in travel and hospitality management) recently finished processing over 2,500 hotel financial statements for our annual *Trends in the Hotel Industry* publication. After sorting through all these financial data, I am amazed by the variety of financial statement formats we see. Some statements contain more than 100 pages of management notes and detailed subschedules, while others are only slightly more detailed than a bank statement for a personal checking account.

Essentially, a financial statement is the organized recording of historical data. If prepared properly, however, the document can serve as a management tool for the future. To accomplish the latter, the preparer must develop a statement that provides the proper information for a wide variety of readers, without the threat of information overload.

Property-level department heads need the detail of the respective revenues and expenses. The controller needs amortization and depreciation schedules, payroll information, and a breakdown of room revenue to prepare monthly, quarterly, and annual tax returns. Ownership needs the data to measure its cash position and ability to cover debt service.

---

*As discussed in this chapter, the Committee on Financial Management of the American Hotel & Motel Association completed the *Ninth Revised Edition of the Uniform System of Accounts for the Lodging Industry* in 1997.

Uniform Format

Back in 1926, the Hotel Association of New York City published the first edition of the *Uniform System of Accounts for Hotels* to establish a "common language" for the preparation and presentation of hotel financial statements. Every few years, a selected committee of accountants and financial executives gather to update the *Uniform System of Accounts* (the book is currently in its eighth edition). I would estimate that 75 percent of the statements we receive follow the Uniform System to one degree or another.

Here, we've interviewed financial executives from selected hotel companies to examine the reasoning and degree of precision that go into preparing operating statements for their properties.

"The statement of income format used by Rosewood Hotels & Resorts summarizes each department into revenue, cost of sales, wages, other expenses and departmental profit," says Scott Blair, vice president and corporate controller. "From the departmental profit, we subtract the overheads (A&G, management fee, sales and marketing, maintenance, energy) to get our gross operating profit. Fixed charges are identified as insurance, taxes, depreciation, replacement reserve, and amortization. This gives us a bottom-line net profit or net available for debt. This setup varies significantly from the statement of income given on page nine of the eighth edition of *Uniform Systems.*"

For Omni Hotels and Waterford Hotel Group, the financial statements closely follow the *Uniform System*; however, both companies include all insurance (umbrella, property, and general liability) in one line item under fixed charges. Other deviations from the standard format revolve around the tracking and presentation of operating statistics. This approach enhances the use of the financial statement package as a management tool.

Custom Reports

Director of Finance and Development Robert Winchester emphasizes that Waterford customizes its report to suit the needs of a variety of readers. "We have various management reports which provide financial and operating statistics for both the current period and year-to-date for actual, budget, and prior year. Special reports are prepared for: room revenue, occupancy, and ADR by market segment, costs on a per-occupied-room basis; payroll dollars, hours, and average wage; food covers and average check; and utility costs and units on a pre-occupied-room basis."

"We've developed key customized reports to track weekly room revenue and statistics, labor productivity, and market segmentation," says Mike

Mahokin, corporate director of budgets for Omni Hotels. "In addition, for the summer P&L, we update our forecasts on a monthly basis for the subsequent 90 days and year end, showing variances to budget and prior year."

Proper Presentation

While a wealth of detail is good, presentation also counts, especially for owners, who are probably the most interested readers of the financial statements. One hotel company I've reviewed prepares extremely detailed statements; nevertheless, the format and layout make the document virtually incomprehensible. In my view, the quality level of these statements is so poor that, if the management company did not provide me with an alternative format, I would consider finding someone else to manage my property.

In general, however, management companies do try to make these documents user-friendly. "The owners of our properties like to see lines for capital replacement reserves, principle payments on debt and leases, and capital costs," says Waterford's Winchester.

Creative Accounting

As we know, the hotel business is dynamic. New sources of revenue and expenses emerge and old items grow in importance. How are these changes handled?

"Most new small revenue items are accounted for by adding a line to the miscellaneous revenue department (i.e., fax revenue)," says Mahokin. "If an item is significant to the statement of operations and/or has significant costs associated with it, we have added a new departmental schedule (i.e., honor bars, audiovisual)."

Blair adds that "new items are incorporated into our P&L based on common sense or discussion with fellow industry executives. The overall objective of matching revenue and expenses within a department is the overriding factor. Whether honor bars are separated out of room service or not would depend on the magnitude of the operation. The same for revenue."

For the next edition of the *Uniform System*, Winchester would like to see the franchise fee line item include all royalties, reservation assessments, and marketing assessments. "In addition, management fees should cover all base fees, accounting services, and other chargebacks," he says.

Hotel management spends enough time and invests enough money to track every single dollar and doughnut. And, judging by the thickness of the budgets and marketing plans I've seen, it's obvious hotel companies know the importance of proper data collection and analysis. Therefore, why limit such a valuable analytical exercise to just once a year? My suggestion is that monthly financial statements be prepared with the same incisive management commentary found in the annual version. That means the same detailed, yet readable formats, and the same customized schedules and reports. A little extra effort would aid management immeasurably in preparing for both short- and long-term future operations.

Case Study Source

Patrick Quek, "Can You Judge Your Operation from the Books?" *Lodging* (Number 1, 1995), 21-22.

Case Study Questions

1. What did Quek find after processing over 2,500 hotel financial statements for *Trends in the Hotel Industry*?
2. What is the primary function of a financial statement?
3. Can you explain the importance of using the Uniform Format to standardize accounting procedures in the U.S. lodging industry?
4. Why do some properties customize their financial reports?
5. Why is it so important to present financial statements properly?
6. What is creative accounting?

Chapter 11

Human Resource Management

The labor situation around the world is an issue. Having highly skilled employees is a problem everywhere.[1]

Curtis Nelson
President and CEO, Carlson Hospitality Worldwide

LEARNING OBJECTIVES

In this chapter, you will study:

1. Cultural orientations in hospitality human resources development
2. Recruitment sources for managers and service employees
3. The selection process in international human resources management
4. Techniques for training competent managers and skillful service employees
5. Management functions of motivation and performance appraisal
6. The design of compensation and benefit packages for expatriate managers and local employees
7. Handling employee termination in foreign countries
8. Management and labor union relationship

INTRODUCTION

This chapter discusses human resource management issues facing international hospitality operations. The hospitality industry is characterized as a labor intensive, people-oriented operation since many workers are needed to personally deliver high-quality lodging and food services to the customers.

The service skills, motivation, and dedication of the employees have a direct impact on the service quality and the operation success of a hospitality firm. It is an essential concern for the hospitality human resources executives regarding how to select employees with the right service attitude, train them with competent service skills, and motivate them to be consistently productive and courteous service providers.

Managing service employees in international hospitality operations presents an even greater challenge to global hospitality managers since they work with employees whose cultural background and professional training are different from theirs. In some cases, an expatriate manager may have to work with several different cultural groups. Under such circumstances, a manager has to be familiar with the employees' cultural beliefs and the legal aspects governing employee relations in the host country.

This chapter thus focuses on the fundamental aspects of hospitality human resource development in international operations. It discusses the conceptual organizational orientation an international hospitality company may adopt for human resource development in foreign countries. It describes recruiting sources for hospitality managers and professionals eligible for overseas assignment. The procedures for predeparture training for expatriate managers are outlined. Legal requirements for employment and compensation in selected countries are reviewed. It discusses in depth training programs and human resource management functions used by different hospitality corporations in overseas operations. The chapter ends with a discussion on labor relations and the characteristics of labor unions in selected countries, and examines the relationship between management and unions in some countries.

CULTURAL ORIENTATIONS

Three major theoretical approaches toward human resources management by international firms have been identified: ethnocentric, polycentric, and geocentric.[2] Each approach reflects the cultural orientation in human resource development that is pursued by international companies. These cultural orientations directly influence how each company selects managerial professionals for managing overseas operations. The following discussion is an overview and analysis of these three corporate cultural orientations and their influence on the strategy pursued by different companies.

The ethnocentric approach places the emphasis on appointing managers from the home country to all key positions in overseas operations. The rationale for a company to pursue the ethnocentric approach is threefold. First, there may be a shortage of qualified management personnel in the host country to fill hospitality management positions. Managers from the home country have to be transferred to the host country to assume managerial responsibilities. This approach is most often pursued when companies have operations in developing countries. Second, the ethnocentric policy is perceived by some companies as an effective measure to maintain a unified corporate culture. These companies argue that managers who have worked in the home country and are familiar with the corporate culture are best qualified for managing the corporate culture in overseas operations. Third, the ethnocentric approach is followed due to hospitality management competency transfer. Many hospitality operational functions require a high degree of management knowledge and skills, such as finance, accounting, and marketing. The knowledge underlying a particular management function cannot be easily written down and simply handed over to host country managers to read and follow, since management knowledge is accumulated through years of experience. Therefore, managers with operational competency need to be transferred to overseas hotels and restaurants to ensure a successful operation.[3]

The ethnocentric approach has been increasingly criticized as having two major drawbacks. Such a human resource development policy can lead to ignorance of the host cultural system, since all the top managers are from a different culture. These managers may take longer to adapt to the local cultural and business environment, and they may be slower in anticipating local market changes due to cultural differences. This policy can also lead to fewer advancement opportunities for the local managers. This limitation of opportunities and less remuneration can cause the local manager to resent the expatriate managers. A study examining the perceptions of both foreign and local hotel managers in Hong Kong found that the local managers viewed their advancement opportunities and remuneration as negatively affected by the presence of the expatriate hotel managers.[4]

The polycentric approach seeks to recruit managers in the host country. These host country managers are given real authority in management, since they know the local cultural, political, and business systems. Thus, the polycentric approach has two major advantages. The host country managers can avoid cultural mistakes in marketing and service operations, and the relocation costs and other associated expenditures for expatriates can be reduced (the compensation package for expatriate managers will be discussed in detail later). One major shortcoming of the polycentric policy is the possible lack of integration between the home office and the overseas property or unit. The host country managers may run the operations almost independently of the home office. Thus, the corporate headquarters may lose control over operations.

The geocentric approach integrates the ethnocentric and polycentric approaches by selecting the most qualified managers for key positions regardless of their nationalities. An international hospitality corporation thus takes a worldwide outlook in selecting the best people throughout the organization. The geocentric policy enables the hospitality corporation to make the best use of its human resources at the global level, and develop competent global managers who feel comfortable working in foreign cultures. The development of these managers can build a strong unifying corporate culture in overseas operations. The entire international hospitality corporation is treated as a single entity with overall development planning and global strategy.

Implementation of the geocentric policy encounters two major obstacles. First, many countries, particularly in Western Europe, have very strict immigration laws regarding the employment of foreign nationals since these countries want foreign companies to employ local people. Therefore, the immigration laws make it difficult for international hospitality corporations to transfer managers from the home country or from a third country. Second, recruiting globally tends to be very expensive. There are increased training costs, relocation costs for managers and sometimes their families, and high compensation for managers working in foreign countries. These factors often hinder a hospitality corporation's effort to aggressively pursue the geocentric approach.

In summary, there is no standardized model for global cultural orientation in human resources development. Each hospitality corporation adopts a policy or integrates different approaches to best suit its global development needs. However, each corporation has to consider the following factors: availability of competent managers and skilled employees, managers' ability to build a unified global corporate culture, efficient use of human resources globally, control of overseas operations, resentment of local managers, and the cost of transferring and relocating expatriate managers. These factors usually influence a corporation's decision on global human resources development policy.

RECRUITMENT

Recruiting competent managerial personnel for overseas operations is a main challenge facing the human resource recruiting executives of hospitality corporations. At the unit level, the managers in different countries face the challenge of finding courteous and dedicated employees for serving hotel and restaurant guests. This section identifies the potential recruiting sources for qualified managers and service employees for international operations.

Sources of Managers

A general manager of an overseas hotel property or restaurant is vested with a very important responsibility to implement corporate culture and run a profitable operation. Finding qualified managers for operating overseas hotels and restaurants is crucial to the success of any hospitality corporation's global strategic development. Competent managers are often identified in the home country, the host country, or a third country. Managers in the home country are primarily identified through internal sources, the corporation's present management pool. This recruitment method benefits from internal promotions, since the qualifications of the managers are known to the corporation. Most hospitality corporations announce overseas positions in their internal publications and keep a list of potential candidates who expressed interest in overseas assignments. Hospitality corporations can also search externally for qualified managers, such as from other hotel companies and restaurant chains, or from other businesses. For example, the founding chairman of KFC's operations in Japan was originally hired from IBM.

External search in the home country can be facilitated through advertising in the national business and financial papers and journals, and international executive search agencies. These managers, identified either internally or externally, are referred to as expatriates.[5] Expatriate managers are those who work and live in a foreign country. These global hospitality managers will continue to increase as more hospitality corporations have planned to expand their operations in foreign countries (see Exhibit 11.1).

In countries where the service industry is well-developed, international hospitality firms have a larger pool from which to select competent local managers. These local managers can quickly learn the corporate culture and manage hospitality operations effectively. However, it can be very difficult to find competent local managers in many developing countries.[6] Systematic training and education for service management functions, such as marketing, finance, and human resources, are still in the initial stages in many developing countries. Therefore, the competence of many local managers is not quite up to Western service standards. In most cases, local managers assume assistant manager positions and are trained on the job. Obviously, international hospitality firms have to devote more resources to training local personnel to be effective managers.

Qualified managers can be found in a third country and assigned to the host country for hospitality operations. For instance, a U.S. hospitality

EXHIBIT 11.1. Local and Expatriate Managers at Jianguo Hotel in Beijing—The First Joint-Venture Hotel in China (Photo courtesy of Jianguo Hotel.)

company can find managers in Belgium and assign them to manage hotels in France. These third-country expatriates are recruited for their intimate knowledge of the host country's business practices and cultural customs, and for geographic proximity of the third country to the host country, such as transferring managers from Singapore to China, since most Singaporeans speak Mandarin Chinese and the distance between the two countries is not great. The assignment of third-country expatriates can be an effective human resources development strategy since it can reduce the emphasis on the ethnocentric approach and reduce the cost for transferring managers from the home country.

Major international hospitality corporations are increasingly searching for foreign students studying in the hospitality management programs in their countries as potential future management professionals. Campus recruiting methods can identify future managers who are from a foreign culture but educated in the Western school of service management science. After appropriate training at corporate hotels, these foreign nationals can be assigned to their native countries to assume various levels of management duties. However, not every foreign student wants to go back after graduation and work in his or her native country. Hospitality companies need to find those who are motivated to go back and work for foreign hospitality companies.

Sources of Service Employees

General managers and human resources managers, no matter whether they are home country expatriates, third-country expatriates, or local nationals, must know where to find competent employees in a particular country and be familiar with the host government's employment regulations. Labor markets exist in most noncommunist countries, and are driven by supply and demand in each specific sector of the country's national economy. The hospitality industry is labor intensive and is dominated by semiskilled jobs. Various kinds of labor recruitment sources are available in different countries, and qualified employees can be recruited internally and externally.

Internally, current hotel and restaurant employees can serve as recruiters to refer new employees. Many hotels and restaurants post new job opportunities in employee lounges, and encourage employees to recommend new recruits. This internal recruiting method can be effective, low cost, and can boost morale. However, in many developing countries it is common for employees to try to help family and relatives. An employed member of the extended family may be under pressure to help other members find jobs. Thus, family considerations are usually more important than qualifications for the vacant position. This is the major disadvantage of internal recruiting in many developing countries where extended family and personal relationships are highly valued.

Externally, most Western hospitality companies tend to employ the same kinds of recruiting methods and sources as they do in their home countries. These methods include (1) advertising in local newspapers, (2) trade schools, (3) "help wanted" sign on the door or window (mostly used by restaurants), and (4) employment agencies. Employment agencies are used much less in developing countries because of the lack of such job search services. In communist countries, a hospitality company may have to rely on government-controlled job agencies for a labor supply. A labor contract is negotiated between the government job agency and the hotel management. The hotel then disburses employees' salary to the government job agency, not directly to the employees. The government agency deducts a certain percentage of the employees' salary as service charge, and gives the rest to the hotel employees.

There is a shortage of unskilled and semiskilled workers in some countries.[7] Hospitality companies in these countries have to rely on global labor markets. The recruitment of labor from foreign countries to meet low skill requirements in the hospitality industry is commonly practiced by some international hospitality companies in the United States, Western Europe, and the Gulf States. The 922-room Hyatt Orlando contracted thirty-five workers from Russia, Bosnia, Poland, and the Czech Republic to perform entry-level services in 1997. These foreign workers were recruited through a labor contracting company and paid $7 per hour.[8] In Western Europe, labor flows from the peripheral countries such as Ireland, Italy, Portugal, and Spain to work in hotel and restaurant businesses in England, France, and Germany. Countries such as the Philippines and Sri Lanka have been the traditional sources of labor for hotel industries in Europe and the Gulf States.[9] As the world economy continues to be integrated, the globalization of labor will increase in many parts of the world. More countries will lower the barriers to labor immigration, such as the free movement of labor in the European Union. When there is a scarcity of labor, hospitality managers have to search for effective methods to train local employees, or look beyond country boundaries for service employees.

SELECTION

The selection process chooses the applicants whose qualifications seem most nearly to match the job requirements. In this section, the selection criteria for both expatriate managers and service employees are discussed.

Selection of Expatriate Managers

The selection procedures for screening candidates for overseas management assignment are crucial to the success of overseas operations since the expatriate managers are vested with the responsibility for achieving the company's objectives and maintaining its management standards in overseas operations. If unqualified applicants are chosen and assigned to overseas management, these individuals will not thrive there, which will lead to expatriate failure. Expatriate failures in overseas management are very costly.[10] One study reported that the average cost per failure to the home office can be as high as three times the expatriate's annual domestic salary plus the cost of relocation.[11]

The causes for expatriate failure are various. For American expatriates, inability to adjust to the local cultural environment is a major problem.[12] When expatriate managers from the home country or a third country are assigned to the host country, they are coming into a new business and cultural environment, and are often shocked to discover the many complications of local business and cultural practices.[13] The differences in manageri-al values and practices among countries often confuse and frustrate expatri-ate managers and lead to the failure of the overseas assignment.

To reduce expatriate failure rates, international hospitality corporations use two criteria for selecting managers for overseas assignment: manage-ment competence and cultural adaptability. Management competence refers to a manager's competence in various functions of operating a hotel or restaurant. These functions include human resources management, account-ing, financial planning and analysis, marketing, and so on. Knowledge of these hospitality management functions is very important to successful hospitality business both at home and abroad.

Cultural adaptability refers to the manager's ability to adjust to the local cultural environment. It also includes the spouse's ability to adjust. As discussed in Chapter 3, cultural values can influence international business management in many aspects, including different perceptions of business behaviors such as decision making, superior and subordinate relationships, individualism and collectivism; body language such as eye contact, facial expression, touching, and gestures; and silent language such as concepts of time, color, and personal space. These perceptions and behaviors are condi-tioned by cultural values. Without prior knowledge of the host culture, expatriate managers will find it very difficult to manage the local staff due to the differences in cultural perceptions and behaviors. Therefore, there must be a balance between management competence and cultural adaptabil-ity when selecting a manager for overseas assignment.

Selection of Service Employees

In developed countries, the selection of hotel and restaurant employees follows rather standard procedures of requesting information regarding the applicants' qualification and work experience to be given on an application form and during interviews. Laws in many countries prohibit the employer from asking personal questions, such as marital status, religious beliefs, and so on. Applicants are protected by law from any discrimination based on age, gender, ethnic origin, and disability. Knowledge of the local laws governing the hiring of employees is essential to an effective selection process. In some countries, the applicant carries an identification book, or resume, which must be presented when seeking employment. The book entries constitute a record of employment, including jobs, wages, and em-ployer comments. Most companies in the United States and United King-dom use references.

In most developing countries, the selection process is usually less formal. In the eyes of the local people, working for foreign hospitality companies means high prestige and higher pay. Normally, there is a larger labor pool to draw from for hospitality service employees. However, as discussed in Chapter 3, family ties and personal connections are more likely to be the elements of selecting decisions in many developing countries.

Culturally, selection methods vary from country to country. There are differences not only in the priorities that are given to technical or interpersonal capabilities, but also in the ways that candidates are tested and interviewed for the desired qualities. In Western Europe and North America, the employers are most interested in how much the applicant can contribute to the tasks of the organization. In these regions, competencies for performing the job are carefully examined. For instance, the selection emphasis is more on the quality of education in a particular function in Germany. However, the selection process in Latin America and Asia focuses on how well the person can fit in with the larger group.

Expatriate managers conducting a job interview need to take the cultural background of the job applicants into consideration. In some cultures, people tend to be conservative, and they are hesitant to show or talk about their strong points. They tend to present themselves to the interviewer in a rather moderate manner. In other cultures, people are direct and aggressive. They tend to overstate their qualifications for a particular position. With such cultural understanding, an expatriate manager can probe patiently for the true qualifications of an applicant in the conservative culture and carefully evaluate the true qualifications of an applicant in the aggressive culture.

TRAINING

As selection matches a manager or employee with a job, training prepares managers and employees to perform a specific job effectively. Training methods for expatriate managers and service employees are discussed in the following section.

Predeparture Training for Expatriate Managers

As discussed in the previous section, an expatriate manager's ability to adjust to the local cultural environment affects directly his or her effective management performance. Predeparture training on the host culture can assist the expatriate manager (and his or her spouse) to get mentally prepared for a new cultural environment. Effective predeparture training can minimize the culture shock an expatriate manager will experience in a foreign culture and reduce expatriate failure. Culture shock is caused by the amplification of negative feelings about the new culture. When an individual suffers from culture shock in a foreign country, he or she is disoriented in the cultural environment and cannot function effectively as a manager. Therefore, most predeparture training for expatriate managers and their families focuses on cultural training, language training, and practical training.[14]

Cultural training seeks to make expatriate managers aware of the major differences between the home and host cultures, and foster an appreciation for the host culture. The belief is that understanding a host country's culture will help the expatriate manager empathize with it, which will in turn enhance his or her effectiveness in dealing with host country employees and guests. Cultural training normally includes workshops on the host country's culture, history, politics, economy, religion, and social and business practices. If possible, it is often recommended that expatriate managers be sent to the host country for a preassignment tour to experience the host culture firsthand before actually working there. This method seems to reduce culture shock and smooth the relocation transition.

Language training focuses on the teaching of the host language to the expatriate managers. It is believed that an expatriate manager who relies on an interpreter diminishes his or her ability to interact with local employees and guests. A willingness to communicate in the host language, even if the expatriate manager is far from fluent, can help build rapport with local employees and improve the manager's effectiveness. As Ronaldo Flores, personnel director at the Condado Plaza Hotel and Casino in San Juan, Puerto Rico, succinctly stated: "Puerto Ricans are basically warm and sociable. We smile and will move heaven and earth for someone whom we like. . . . This executive who sits down in the employees' cafeteria, eats one of our local dishes, and tries to speak Spanish (even though it may sound completely ridiculous) will win over the staff."[15]

Practical training is designed to help the expatriate manager and his or her family ease themselves into day-to-day life in the host country. The sooner a routine is established, the better are the prospects that the expatriate manager and the family will adapt successfully. Some hotel corporations switch general managers from properties in two different countries for a short period of time to let them gain firsthand experience working and living in a different culture. Expatriate managers found that mentoring by someone who has worked in the host country before can be very helpful as practical training. The expatriate community can also be a useful source of support and information, and can be invaluable in helping the family adapt to a foreign culture.

Hilton International was one of the first major international hotel companies to implement a company-wide predeparture training program for expatriate managers. Particular attention is devoted to the orientation and support of expatriate managers and their families. Hilton International's program takes full advantage of its existing training framework and staff. The training program for expatriate managers and their families is known as Meeting the Transfer Challenge. The program is a product of corporate concern for the well-being and effectiveness of its international mobile key personnel. Implemented companywide in December 1985, the training program incorporates cultural, language, and practical training. This program has been used by human resources managers and expatriate managers in Asia, the Middle East, and Europe.[16] It has been proven effective as a predeparture training program.

Training for Local Managers and Employees

Training for local managers and employees is normally conducted in two different ways: in-house and off premises. International hospitality companies in both the developed and developing countries offer several kinds of in-house training programs. In-house programs are developed by the companies' human resources department for training employees on hotel or restaurant premises. The programs include on-the-job training, classroom sessions, conferences, and role plays.

On-the-job training is most common in the hospitality industry for service employees. New employees, such as housekeepers, dining room servers, or front desk clerks, learn by doing the job under the supervision of an experienced employee.[17] Normally, a new employee can perform the duties independently after two weeks of on-the-job training.

Because of technological or market changes, managers and employees need to constantly update their skills through training. After ascertaining each hotel or restaurant's training needs, the human resources department will prepare and supervise in-house training programs for certain levels of managers or specific service functioning areas. These training programs can be conducted as classroom lectures, problem-solving case analysis, and interactive role plays. Not only can effective training programs train productive employees, but also serve as the recruiting edge to attract new employees.

Off-premises training sends managers and employees off the hotel or restaurant premises to a school or other training site. There are three major forms of off-premises training methods: hospitality and tourism management schools, a hospitality corporation's regional training center, and training at a particular hotel or restaurant in a foreign country. Many countries now offer four-year college education in hospitality management and professional training in hospitality services. Employees are encouraged to attend these academic and professional training programs to enhance their knowledge of hospitality management and service. Some countries have laws to encourage workers in various professions to take some time off and attend training programs offered at universities and professional schools. For instance, France has a particularly innovative law that permits workers to apply for a one-year leave of absence to enroll in an approved training program if they have been employed for at least two years. The French government and the employers share the expenses, which include the employees' salaries while they are in training. Most hospitality companies in the United States offer their employees partial tuition reimbursement annually. For instance, Choice Hotels International reimburses $1,500 of employees' tuition per pear.

International hospitality firms often hold training sessions for different levels of managers, supervisors, and service employees at their regional training centers. For example, Sheraton organizes regular training sessions on current management trends and issues in Hong Kong for all the managers in its Asia and Pacific division. Local managers and key service employees are sometimes sent to the corporation's hotel or restaurant at the home country for technical training. This overseas training program gives the local managers and employees an opportunity to experience firsthand how hotels and restaurants are operated in the home country. Operation standards and corporate culture can thus be learned by the managers and employees from the host country, and implemented and maintained in the host country when they return. The Essex House hotel in New York, owned by Nikko Hotels International, once organized a "seeing is believing" employee orientation tour to Japan. This tour included executives, managers, and selected employees from each department. Upon arrival at the Hotel Nikko Osaka, each of the twenty-five visiting members was assigned an exact counterpart as host or hostess: bellman to bellman, security guard to security guard, front office manager to front office manager, and so on. One of the positive experiences from this tour was the learning of the Total Quality Control management practiced in the Japanese hotels. Upon the group's return to New York, the managers and employees implemented Total Quality Control management and received very positive results.[18] In another example, McDonald's restaurant in Moscow sent its four local managers for extensive management training in the United States before the store was opened.

MOTIVATION

A major function of the human resources manager is to assist the general manager in keeping the employees satisfied with their jobs. If the employees are not satisfied, they will not perform productively. This dissatisfaction usually leads to high employee turnover in the hospitality industry, particularly in developed countries. According to Hotel and Catering Training Company in the United Kingdom, turnover in the United Kingdom was estimated to have cost the hotel and catering industry £430 million, and turnover was higher among men than women.[19] McDonald's in the United Kingdom reported an annual employee turnover of over 200 percent.[20] The Hong Kong Hotels Association found in its 1994-1995 annual survey that 41.26 percent of the employees in sixty-three hotels changed jobs or resigned. It remained one of the highest turnover rates in the region.

To reduce labor turnover and retain productive employees, management has to improve working conditions and keep the employees properly motivated. Human resources managers need to understand the motivational processes and human needs in different cultures. Without an understanding of these needs, managers cannot determine the kinds of employee motivation needed to induce employees to work toward the organization's goals.

Human resources managers in Western developed countries often turn to Maslow's hierarchy of needs model to explain the complexity of human needs. This theory explains that an individual's motivation is determined in response to a hierarchy of needs. On the basis of this hierarchy, an individual will only be motivated by a particular level provided that needs with respect to all levels below have been met.

As an employee is concerned with "making ends meet," his or her prime motivation is to pay for rent, food, and clothing, or school tuition for children. Once this basic level of human need is satisfied, the individual will start thinking about the security of his or her employment. An assurance of job safety from the management can motivate this employee to perform productively. Once the second level of human need is satisfied, the individual will develop a sense of belonging to the company. The company must make them feel like valuable members of the family. A mutual trust is thus fostered between the organization and the individual employee.

The next level of human needs is esteem. Every human being has an ego that calls for recognition. Management must recognize employees' fine performance by praise and material awards. Once an individual's esteem is recognized, he or she is motivated to work harder and contribute more. The highest level of human needs is self-actualization, which simply means to reach an individual's full potential. At this level, individual employees want to be involved in management decision-making processes, and express their views concerning how to improve guest service. Therefore, motivational strategies such as quality circles, empowerment, and self-directed management teams are practiced in the hospitality industry. Clearly, the real challenge to the hospitality manager is to identify the different levels of employee needs and then respond to these needs accordingly. If the constantly changing needs of the employees are recognized and satisfied, the employees will be satisfied with their employers and working environment, and they tend to stay longer with the company.

In most developing countries, employee expectations focus primarily on the two lower levels of needs in Maslow's hierarchy. Making a living and worrying about job security are the primarily motivated needs for most employees. Therefore, monetary awards are often used to motivate employee performance. Radisson Hotel in Russia even pays half of its employees' wages in foreign currency as a motivational tactic (see the case study at the end of this chapter). In some countries, working for a foreign hospitality company is a prestigious job. Many individuals express self-esteem by seeking employment with foreign hotel and restaurant companies.

A recent revealing study on what motivates Hong Kong's hotel employees found that the top three factors are: (1) opportunities for advancement and development, (2) loyalty to employees, and (3) good wages. These motivational factors suggest that hotel employees in Hong Kong have a strong concern for career development, and they want to grow with the company. They also want respect and trust by the management. Then they want good wages since Hong Kong has very high living standards.[21] Applying Maslow's hierarchy of needs model to Hong Kong hotel employees, one can clearly see that hotel employees in Hong Kong have the highest levels of motivation needs.

The implementation of Maslow's hierarchy of needs at the global level must take into account cultural differences across countries. For instance, as discussed in Chapter 3, employees in certain countries tend to be loyal to their employers, and a sense of belonging to a particular firm is stronger in these countries. Self-actualization as the highest need level may be absent in some cultures because of their cultural perception of superior and subordinate relations.[22] These cultures view superiors as decision makers who are paid to make management decisions. Seeking opinions from subordinates may indicate the incompetence of the manager. Therefore, efforts to practice empowerment of self-directed work teams as a motivational strategy will not be effective in these cultures.

PERFORMANCE APPRAISAL

Consistent and systematic evaluation of employee performance is a very important human resources management function. Performance appraisal is used to analyze and identify individual employees' strengths and weaknesses in performing the functions of a particular job. It can identify the needs for training employees, if the employees are found to lack certain job skills. The results of performance appraisal are also used as the basis for promotion, pay increase, and disciplinary action.

Because of the intangible nature of the hospitality service industry, management often finds it very difficult to measure employee productivity, since service performance cannot be measured by unit output as in the manufacturing industry. Several factors are taken into consideration for objective service employee appraisal: manager and supervisor observations, peer evaluations, guest feedback, and public interview of guests.

Managers and supervisors work closely with their employees in daily operations and help them develop professionally. They therefore know the employees very well and are able to render opinions regarding individual employees' strengths and weaknesses. Co-workers are another important source for performance appraisal since these employees work together in the same department. Guest feedback systems are widely used in hospitality operations. Guest feedback is solicited by every hotel and restaurant in various forms: guest comment cards, postvisit surveys, public interview of guests, and so on. Many international hotels and restaurants provide guests and customers with comment cards in foreign languages. A major purpose of the guest feedback survey is to find out guests' experience with and opinion of the quality of employee service. Therefore, guest feedback can be considered one source for employee appraisal.

A comparative study of human resources management in hotels in Australia and Singapore found that Singaporean hotels are more inclined to use passive guest feedback systems, particularly in-room questionnaires, than their Australian counterparts. Australian hotels tend to frequently utilize active strategies such as peer feedback mechanisms and public relations interviews of guests.[23] Obviously, hotel management in different cultures take different approaches in soliciting opinions for employee appraisal.

A final important note for expatriate managers is to be aware of and avoid unintentional bias toward evaluating the performance of local managers and employees. Bias is often conditioned by different cultural values. Due to such biases, many local managers and employees feel that expatriate managers evaluate them unfairly, and do not fully appreciate the value of their skill and experience. This could lead to resentment by local managers and staff, and consequently a high management and employee turnover. Therefore, expatriate managers need to be fully aware of unintentional cultural bias in evaluating employee performance.

EXPATRIATE MANAGER COMPENSATION

An appropriate compensation and benefit package is very important for attracting, retaining, and motivating expatriate managers for overseas assignment. Designing and maintaining an appropriate compensation package is more complex than it would seem, because of the need to consider and reconcile home and host country's financial, legal, and customary practices.[24] In designing compensation and benefit packages for expatriate managers, the challenge to human resources management executives is to maintain a standard of living for expatriates equivalent to their colleagues at home plus compensating them for any additional costs incurred.

The primary purpose of designing attractive expatriate compensation and benefit packages is therefore to ensure that expatriate managers do not lose out through their overseas assignment, and to provide financial incentives to offset qualitative differences between assignments in different countries. The financial outlays for managers in the home country normally include income taxes, housing expenses, expenditures for goods and services such as food, clothing, entertainment, and so on, and reserves such as savings and pension contributions, etc. Thus the compensation package provides expatriate managers with the same standard of living in the host country as they enjoy at home plus a financial incentive such as premiums. In designing such a compensation and benefit package, a human resources management executive has to consider five major components: base salary, foreign service premium, allowances, taxation, and benefits. Each component is discussed in the following sections.

Base Salary

The base salary for an expatriate manager is about the same as the base salary for a comparable position in the home country. The base salary is normally paid in either home-country currency or in the local currency; typically in home-country currency when working in developing countries, and in host-country currency when working in developed countries. The 1997 Worldwide Salary Review, conducted by Renard International Hospitality Consultants in Toronto and published in *Hotels*, reported the average salaries for hotel managerial positions worldwide. It compiled estimated median salary scales for most hotel managerial positions in ten regions and countries. Exhibit 11.2 lists a sample of salary scales for three selected regions. Clearly, salaries are determined by the types and sizes of properties, and regional differences reflect economic development levels of different regions. However, the survey report pointed out that salaries for hotel management professionals tend to be standardized as the industry

EXHIBIT 11.2. Average Salaries for Hotel Professionals in Selected Regions (in Thousands of U.S. Dollars)

Position	Latin America			East Europe		Middle East		
	125-250 rooms	250-475 rooms	475+ rooms	150-400 rooms	400+ rooms	125-250 rooms	250-475 rooms	475+ rooms
General Manager	60	75	120	70	95	62	70	90
Executive Assistant Manager	45	60	70	50	65	44.9	48	65
Rooms Division Manager	24	31.7	35	34	42	33	36	41
Front Office Manager	12.1	18	22	27	32.6	24	31	33
Executive Housekeeper	13	20	23	32	38.4	28	31	36.1
Chief Engineer	30.8	35	52	36	50	35	35	43
Food and Beverage Director	45	60	70	40	54	36	39.3	46.3
Executive Chef	36	55	65	39	56	31	38	40
Pastry Chef	7.4	12.5	18.6	26.4	38	28	28	31.7
Comptroller	48	60	70	37	53	35	41	46
Personnel Manager	30	40	42	28	45	31	33	31.7
Sales and Marketing Director	35	43	63	42	54	40	45	48.9

Source: Adapted from Jeff Weinstein, "1997 Salary Review," *Hotels* (October, 1997), 63-68. Reprinted by permission of *Hotels* magazine, a publication of Cahners Business Information.

becomes more globalized. Salaries are now based on a worldwide perspective as opposed to a local one since the global corporations know what others are paying and can control benefits and bonuses. Job-hopping for a higher salary in the same position will become more difficult for hotel professionals.[25]

Foreign Service Premium

A foreign service premium is an incentive to expatriate managers for working outside the home country. It compensates the expatriate for having to live in an unfamiliar country isolated from family and friends, having to deal with a new culture and language, and having to adjust to new work habits and practices. Therefore, foreign service premiums are offered to attract managers to accept overseas assignment. Foreign service premiums are normally paid as a percentage of base salary.

Allowances

Four types of allowances are often offered to expatriate managers and their families depending on the nature and destination of the assignment: cost-of-living differential, hardship, housing, and education.

A cost-of-living differential allowance ensures that expatriate managers will enjoy the same standard of living in the foreign country where the cost of living is higher than at home. The cost of living is very high in many cities in the world. In order to maintain the same standard of living, the cost-of-living differential needs to be calculated and adjusted in the expatriate manager's compensation package. The U.S. State Department publishes such cost-of-living differentials regularly, and these can be used as a guideline for designing an expatriate manager's compensation package. For instance, the composite index figure for a city is an estimate of the cost of living in that particular city. The following are the cost-of-living index figures for three major world cities: Washington, DC = 100, Hong Kong = 155, and London = 163. Clearly, Hong Kong and London have much higher costs of living than Washington, DC. Therefore, expatriate managers from the Washington, DC area need to be compensated for the 55 percent and 63 percent difference in cost of living in Hong Kong and London, respectively.

A hardship allowance is given when the expatriate manager is assigned to some developing countries, where the basic living standards such as health care, education, shopping, and entertainment are grossly deficient by the standards of the expatriate's home country. Therefore, an allowance is paid to compensate for this hardship.

A housing allowance is another type of allowance that needs to be considered. It is common that many expatriate hotel managers live on the premises in foreign countries. If the expatriate manager has a family, he or she may negotiate a housing allowance to cover the living expenses in the foreign country. In foreign cities where housing is very expensive, such as Hong Kong, Tokyo, and London, the housing allowance can be substantial.

As with housing allowance, expatriate managers with family and children may negotiate an education allowance for their children. This allowance ensures that the expatriate's children receive adequate education by home-country standards. Expatriate managers like to send their children to private schools in the host country, which are more expensive than the public schools.

Taxation

Taxation laws, as discussed in Chapter 10, require an expatriate manager to pay income tax to both the home and host country governments. If there is a reciprocal tax treaty between the host and home countries, the expatriate manager does not need to worry about double taxation. But when a reciprocal tax treaty is not in force, the company typically pays the expatriate's income tax in the host country. In addition, companies normally make up the difference when a higher income tax rate in a host country reduces an expatriate's take-home pay.

Benefits

Many companies also provide the same level of medical and pension benefits to expatriate managers as to domestic managers. Sometimes, companies have to provide expatriate managers with local benefit programs required by the host government. Clearly, sending expatriate managers for overseas assignment can be very costly for the company. That is why the expatriate hotel managerial staff had to be dismissed first when the financial crisis and social unrest hit Indonesia (see the case study in Chapter 9). All components of the compensation package must be considered in light of both home and host country legalities and practices. To be strategically competitive, the compensation package must be comparatively attractive to the qualified managers the company wishes to hire for overseas assignment.

EMPLOYEE PAY

Wage structure varies from country to country. Knowledge of the host country's wage structure, benefits, and compensation practice is important for expatriate managers to hire the best employees, motivate them, and retain them. Governments of many countries have regulations or influence regarding wage structures of various professions. To ensure adequate living standards of American hourly wage earners, the U.S. government raised the minimum wage to $4.75 in 1996 and to $5.15 in 1997.[26] About 10 million Americans received this increase, many of them in the hospitality industry.

National minimum wages (NMW) are used in the EU countries and have a major impact on the hospitality industry. It is reported that only Ireland and the United Kingdom do not operate legally enforceable NMW. The following EU countries practice NMW:

- France, Luxembourg, the Netherlands, Portugal, and Spain all have a statutory minimum wage
- National collective agreements create a legally enforceable general minimum wage in Belgium and Greece
- Denmark, Germany, and Italy set minimum rates through legally binding industry-level agreements[27]

In addition to the basic wage and gratuity (tipping is not customary in a few counties such as Japan), employee compensation and benefits also vary from country to country. The compensation and benefits typically include meals, incentives, and fringe benefits. In some countries, employee pay may not be very high, but the benefits can be extensive. In South Korea, the wage structure is believed to be one of the most complicated in the world.[28] Wages in South Korea are made up of various types of allowances and bonuses (even though these may be temporarily affected by the current financial crisis in the country). So many expenses are paid for employees other than wages and bonuses that it is hard to determine the total labor cost in South Korea. For instance, Korean companies give special bonuses for vacation, special holidays, and *kim chang* season (when Koreans make kimchi, Korean pickled cabbage, which will last throughout winter). Many companies provide a transportation allowance and a meal allowance. Some companies now even offer recreational funds. Many Korean companies send money to each employee's parents who celebrate a sixtieth birthday. To attract the best workers, many foreign companies adopted the Korean system, and now give employees transportation, lunch allowances, children's education support funds, and other amenities. South Korea also has a minimum wage policy that applies to all companies with ten full-time workers. Since September 1994, the minimum wage for an eight-hour work day has been $11.70.[29]

The above examples provide a sample of national differences in wage structure and benefit offerings. Expatriate managers must be aware of the government regulations and local practice in determining employee wages, such as education, experience, and seniority. A competitive wage structure and attractive benefit package can attract and retain the best employees in the hospitality industry.

MANAGEMENT AND LABOR UNIONS

In countries where labor is organized, one major function of the human resources management is to foster harmony and minimize conflict between management and labor unions. Managing labor relations effectively is essential to minimizing labor disputes and to overall operation success.

Workers in different countries are typically concerned about pay, job security, working conditions, and retirement benefits. Labor unions represent the individual workers by negotiating through collective bargaining with the management for better pay, greater job security, better working conditions, and better benefits. The working relationship between labor unions and management differs from country to country. For instance, the relationship tends to be confrontational in the United States and some Western European countries. The unions' bargaining power is derived largely from their ability to threaten to disrupt operations either by a strike or some other form of work protest, such as refusing to work overtime. Such a relationship can be disruptive if unions and management cannot reach a labor agreement. The relationship is built on consensus in Japan. Such an approach is directly influenced by the Japanese cultural value of group harmony and face saving. Labor issues and disputes are always resolved by consensus between the labor union and the management.

In communist countries, labor unions in joint-venture foreign companies are used as a way for the communist organization to monitor operations. For instance, the labor union in a joint-venture hotel in China may be headed by the secretary of a communist party branch. His or her responsibility is to monitor whether hotel operations deviate from government rules, and to ensure that the local staff are fairly treated by the foreign management.

In a unionized environment, management has to get along with local labor unions. A cooperative labor relationship can be a very positive force for effective operations. For instance, management can work with labor unions to reinforce employee discipline because labor unions establish, with the management, a set of disciplinary procedures through collective bargaining. Understanding the nature of the local labor organizations and working closely with labor unions will create a win-win situation for both the management and the labor organizations.

EMPLOYMENT TERMINATION

Employment rights and duties are in many countries based on the individual's contract of employment. One subject probably covered in every employment contract is termination. Many different issues have to be carefully evaluated before a termination decision is made. In many countries, termination of employment is a complex subject that is controlled by a range of different statutes and regulations. In England, all hospitality employees' right to dismissal notice is protected by law. A hotel or catering employee on a weekly contract is entitled to at least one week's notice. Wrongful dismissal may rise most typically where an employee is dismissed with no or inadequate notice.

When managers feel that a worker is not performing up to the service standards, management must consult with union representatives (if the hotel is unionized) before firing the worker. The union representative may agree that the worker is not performing adequately and should be discharged, or may suggest a transfer to a different job. If management and the union disagree, the contract contains a provision for grievance procedures or arbitration to resolve their differences.

Some countries have laws that oblige companies to give severance pay to terminated employees who have obtained permanent status, usually after a sixty- to ninety-day trial period. The Redundancy Act of 1965 in the United Kingdom requires employers to compensate workers for dismissals in quite specific circumstances. In Mexico, employees who have been employed for even one day after the trial period must be paid three months' wages if they are discharged. That amount is increased by twenty days' wages for each additional year of employment. In Chile, a company has to give a permanent employee thirty days' notice for dismissal and thirty days' severance pay.

Obviously, a hospitality manager needs to have adequate knowledge of the host country's rules on employment termination, and needs to seek advice from the local managers and labor lawyers. Such knowledge and advice will assist expatriate managers to make right personnel decisions and avoid potential costly mistakes.

SUMMARY

- Three cultural orientations in human resources management are pursued by different international hospitality firms: ethnocentric, polycentric, and geocentric orientations.

- These cultural orientations directly influence how each company selects managerial professionals for managing overseas operations.
- Managerial personnel can be identified and recruited in the home country, in the host country, or in a third country. Expatriate managers are those who work and live in a foreign country.
- Service employees can be both recruited from internal and external sources in the host country. Hospitality companies in some countries have to rely on global labor markets for service employees.
- Expatriate failure results from poor selection of candidates for overseas assignment. The two important criteria for selecting expatriate managers for overseas assignment are: management competence and cultural adaptability. The selection of service employees needs to follow the host government rules on employment and local cultural practice.
- Culture shock is caused by the amplification of negative feelings toward a new culture. Culture shock can disorient a person in the new cultural environment and make the person ineffective in management functions.
- Effective predeparture training can minimize the culture shock an expatriate manager will experience in a foreign country and reduce expatriate failure. Most predeparture training focuses on cultural, language, and practical training.
- Training for host managers and employees are conducted in-house, on-the-job, and off-premises in the firm's regional training centers or overseas properties.
- Effective motivation can reduce turnover and increase employee satisfaction. Maslow's hierarchy of needs model can be applied, with modifications and some limitations, to motivating employees in both developed and developing countries.
- Performance appraisal is used to analyze and identify an individual employee's strengths and weaknesses in performing a particular job function. Employee performance evaluation is normally based on manager and supervisor observations, peer evaluations, guest feedback, and public interview of guests.
- An appropriate compensation and benefit package is important for attracting, retaining, and motivating expatriate managers. Expatriate compensation and benefit packages include base salary, a premium, benefits, and various negotiable allowances.
- Wage structure varies from country to country. Adequate knowledge of the host country's wage structure, benefit, and compensation prac-

tice enables expatriate managers to hire the best employees by offering the most competitive wages and benefits.

- The working relationship between labor unions and management tends to differ from country to country. In a unionized environment, management needs to understand the characteristics of the local union organization and work closely with the local union to achieve effective operations.
- Employment termination in many countries is a complex subject regulated by a range of different statutes and regulations.

STUDY QUESTIONS

1. Discuss the pros and cons of the three cultural orientations adopted by hospitality firms in international human resources development.
2. Where can you recruit managerial personnel for overseas operations?
3. Are there any differences in recruiting hospitality managers in developed and developing countries?
4. Analyze the pros and cons for recruiting managers in the home country, in the host country, and from a third country.
5. How can you find and recruit service employees in different countries?
6. How did some hospitality firms cope with labor shortages in certain countries?
7. What will cause expatriate failure in international hospitality management?
8. What is culture shock?
9. Why are management competence and cultural adaptability vitally important criteria for selecting expatriate managers?
10. How are hospitality service employees selected in developed and developing countries?
11. What do expatriate managers need to know when interviewing a job applicant in different cultures?
12. What are the main components of predeparture training for expatriate managers?
13. Can you think of any new ways to enhance the practical training for expatriate managers?
14. What are the commonly used training methods for service employees?
15. What will normally happen when employees are dissatisfied with their jobs or the organization?

16. How can you apply Maslow's hierarchy of needs model to explaining the complexity of human needs, and the motivation factors expressed by hotel employees in Hong Kong?
17. Can you apply the hierarchy of needs model universally to employee motivation issues in different countries? Why?
18. What are the bases for employee performance appraisal?
19. How can you avoid unintentional bias in evaluating the performance of local managers and employees?
20. Discuss the importance of an appropriate compensation and benefit package for expatriate managers.
21. How can you design an appropriate compensation package for expatriate managers?
22. What are the allowances that need to be considered in an expatriate compensation package?
23. How did the countries mentioned in the text determine their minimum wages?
24. In addition to their wages, what benefits do most Korean employees receive from their companies?
25. What are the main functions of labor unions in different countries?
26. Why is it important to maintain a good working relationship between management and labor unions?
27. How should an expatriate manager handle the issue of employment termination in a foreign country?

CASE STUDY: IN MOSCOW, BUSINESS BEGINS WITH BASIC TRAINING

Around the corner from the Metropol in Moscow, people stand in line at the supermarket for several hours to buy a kilo of meat. Inside the hotel, Russian staff find it hard to accept customers who reject a dish in the restaurant because it is not what they ordered or not to their taste. Teaching waiters to take a dish away and replace it without question has been one of the challenges the hotel has faced since it opened in March 1991.

Hugh Hallard, sales and marketing director, said, "Traditionally, the staff would have argued. They have to learn to replace it with whatever the customer wants. It is hard in a country where food is such a high priority. We certainly don't want to waste food, but staff have to respect the guests."

When the Metropol opened (it is owned by Intourist, managed by Inter-Continental), it inherited about 200 former Intourist staff and took on 550 new people. Those joining the hotel business for the first time were the easiest to train. Initially, the staff had a three-day induction course. They toured the hotel, sat in a classroom, and met key managers. They had to forget they were in Russia.

"They were told they would be compared with the Ritz in Paris or the Dorchester in London, not another hotel in Moscow," Hallard said.

About ten staff (in sales, marketing, and food and beverage) already had had some training in London and Paris. Besides instilling the notion that the customer is always right, it is equally difficult to get staff to take responsibility and initiative rather than just follow rules.

Every hotel gets little disputes in the front office about telephone or minibar charges. "We give authority to rebate up to $10. We want them to take responsibility," Hallard said.

Like most other Western hotel managers, Hallard is impressed with the standard of education and the ability of the vast majority of the staff. He called their qualifications extremely high and said they are well educated with a university degree. Many can speak one or two foreign languages. Most Western hotel companies pick young people, ideally between the ages of sixteen and twenty-five, whom they can mold to give the service they demand. They avoid, if they can, anyone who has ever worked for a hotel before, particularly Intourist, and start from scratch.

Training in St. Petersburg

Sven Wermelin, general manager of the Grand Hotel Europe, spent more than two years training Russian staff for the opening of this beautifully restored turn-of-the-century hotel in the heart of St. Petersburg. They spent the time on a floating hotel, the Olympia, before moving to the Grand in December 1991.

Wermelin employs about twenty-three foreign managers with international experience and reckons it will be ten to fifteen years before the Grand can be run by Russian staff alone. "Our training is on the job. Some of them don't know how to hold a tray, so we have to begin with basics. We teach them poise, deportment—it is like model school."

Many Russians can barely identify everyday foods because the food shortages are so great in St. Petersburg. At the Grand Hotel Europe, training included tasting the food and entering cocktail competitions to demonstrate that staff knew which ingredients to use.

Moscow Bonus: $300

Western hotel companies have launched incentive schemes to motivate staff and encourage them to work hard and move up the ladder. At the

Hotel Savoy in Moscow, staff on average earn 1,000 rubles a month ($10), or two and a half times the Russian average. They also get a hard currency bonus of 30 cents for every ruble earned, so that on an average wage, they would get $300 a month to spend in a hard currency shop—a small fortune to most Russians. This amount dips if the hotel's profitability falls or the individual's performance is not up to snuff.

The Metropol, which pays at least double the average Russian salary, also has a bonus-points system. Each month staff—from pot washer to sales manager—are awarded a number of points based on their performance. At the end of the six months, the points will be totaled and exchanged for vouchers to be spent in hard currency stores for food, clothing, or electrical goods.

The Penta Hotel, Moscow, started with a similar productivity bonus but now gives a straight payment of 25 percent of salary in hard currency, using a voucher system. Assistant executive manager Paul Dalrymple questioned the effectiveness of productivity bonuses. In his view, if staff are not performing, they should not have been hired in the first place.

Many Western-managed hotels have several Russian staff in key positions working opposite an expatriate. Dalrymple, for example, has an opposite member who is a Russian. At the Metropol, Hallard is confident that in areas such as sales and marketing, Russians will be quickly promoted. "We have thirty expatriates at the moment. That will come down to about fifteen in the future. In sales and marketing, people will move quickly because there is particular local talent."

Case Study Source

Kate Trollope, "In Moscow, Business Begins with Basic Training," *Hotels* (May, 1992), 63-64.

Case Study Questions

1. Why did Russian staff find it hard to understand when Western customers complained about their food in hotel restaurants?
2. How was employee training conducted at the Metropol in Moscow and how did the management motivate local employees to take initiatives?
3. Are most of the new employees qualified for the service jobs at Western hotels?
4. How was employee training conducted in the Grand Hotel Europe in St. Petersburg?

5. How did the management of the Western hotels motivate their employees to work hard?
6. Why did Paul Dalrymple, assistant executive manager of the Penta Hotel in Moscow, question the effectiveness of productivity bonuses?
7. Explain the practice of productivity bonuses as an incentive scheme for the Western hotels in Moscow by applying Maslow's hierarchy of needs model.

Chapter 12

International Hospitality Marketing

You want the country to have an emerging middle class. You want
those customers to have a propensity for consuming your product. In
Portugal, they don't even have a word for popcorn, so we're not
likely to open a KarmelKorn outlet there.[1]

Ed Watson
Executive Vice President, International Dairy Queen

LEARNING OBJECTIVES

In this chapter, you will study:

1. Strategic marketing planning for long-term international hospitality
   development
2. Management of information systems and the research process
3. Hospitality marketing mix
4. Consumer behavior and brand decision
5. Distribution strategy
6. Communication strategy
7. Price elasticity of demand and pricing strategy

INTRODUCTION

Unlike marketing in home countries, international hospitality marketing
faces a different environment in foreign countries. The differences and challenges are reflected in the different political, legal, economic, and cultural
systems of the host countries. International hospitality firms have to learn the

different cultures of the consumers in each host market, and adjust or modify its products and services to meet the needs of the local markets. Furthermore, as international hospitality expansion increases, market competition will intensify and companies will compete vigorously for international travelers and the local customers. Business success thus will be largely determined by the effective marketing of each hospitality company.

This chapter focuses on international marketing of hospitality products and services. It describes the strategic marketing planning for long-term international hospitality development and discusses the marketing information system and marketing research process. Consumer behaviors as influenced by host cultures are analyzed, and brand decisions of hospitality products and services are discussed. It describes the pricing strategies and promotion of hospitality products and services. It also devotes a section to discussions on the increasingly popular use of the Internet for global hospitality marketing. This chapter presents a comprehensive and up-to-date introduction to international hospitality marketing.

STRATEGIC MARKETING PLANNING

International hospitality corporations develop strategic marketing planning to guide their market expansions in foreign countries. Strategic marketing takes a global and long-term view in setting objectives for overseas operations. The strategic marketing planning starts with the company's mission statement, which defines the purpose and scope of the company's business: why it exists, what markets it serves, and how it serves the markets. As hospitality companies view the whole world as their market, their global development activities must be defined in the mission statement. The following mission statement of Marriott International clearly emphasizes the global perspective and defines the objectives for global development:

> We are committed to being the best lodging and management services company in the world by treating employees in ways that create extraordinary customer service and sharehold value.[2]

Once the mission of global development is determined, hospitality companies scan the international environment to identify desirable markets by using environmental forces to eliminate the less attractive markets. Known as environmental scanning, this method has been effectively used by hospitality firms to seek information about world threats and opportunities.[3] Since a critical aspect of the marketing function is to identify gaps in the global market, environmental scanning can assist international companies to monitor both the changing global market conditions and the domestic companies that are considering expanding operations into the overseas markets to fill the market gap. As discussed in Chapter 6, international hospitality companies have identified that the market gap in many regions of the world is now in the midscale hotel segment. Therefore, development in midscale hotels has been increased in many parts of the world.[4]

INTERNATIONAL MANAGEMENT INFORMATION SYSTEM

To conduct an effective environmental scanning to identify market gaps and opportunities, international hospitality firms use International Management Information System (IMIS), an organized process of gathering, storing, processing, and disseminating information to global managers to assist them in making management decisions. Automated IMIS can enable large international hospitality firms to process and store large quantities of data, which allows marketing managers to use all the sources of information at their disposal.

Information sources for decision making are generally gathered from two major sources: internal and external. Internal sources encompass data from company sales, financial, and accounting records as reported by overseas properties and foreign franchisees. Market analysis and special research reports can be used as internal sources. Survey of sales representatives, in-house guests, and members in the channel of distribution can generate valuable market information for managers.

External sources include government reports, market research studies conducted by trade associations, hospitality consulting and accounting firms, and universities. The survey of customers who have not used the hospitality facility and service previously can give insight to the perceptions of potential customers. External sources also include various databases focusing on international hospitality operations.

Both types of sources provide data on the changes and trends in the uncontrollable environmental variables as well as feedback on the performance of the firm's controllable variables. In today's electronic age, hospitality managers can receive specific answers not only from the firm's database, but also from external online databases as well.

THE HOSPITALITY MARKETING MIX

The traditional marketing mix consists of a set of strategic decisions made in the areas of product and service, promotion, pricing, and distribution for the purpose of satisfying the customers in a target market. Since the hospitality business deals with both tangible products and intangible services, hospitality firms have to provide quality products and excellent services to the customers. The hospitality marketing mix thus focuses on product-service attributes, distribution strategy, communication strategy, and pricing strategy.[5]

Before global expansion and development, many hospitality firms have already established a successful domestic marketing mix. There has been a strong temptation to follow the same marketing procedures overseas. However, important differences between the home and foreign environments can make direct transplanting of marketing procedures impossible. Marketing managers often have to adjust strategy in overseas operations. The following sections will analyze the four major elements of the hospitality marketing mix, and discuss how they can be more effectively used in different countries.

Product-Service Attributes

The hospitality business involves both tangible product and intangible services. Both product and service have many attributes. For instance, the attributes of a hamburger product include size, taste, and texture. The attributes of service rendered in a hamburger restaurant encompass speed, cleanliness, and friendly employees. The attributes of a hotel include a comfortable bed, a clean room, courteous employees, a nice atmosphere, and so on. Hospitality business sells well when the product-service attributes match customer needs and when the prices are appropriate. If hospitality consumers throughout the world have the same needs, a company can simply sell the same product and service worldwide. However, consumer needs vary from country to country due to cultural differences and different levels of economic development. Hospitality marketing managers need to identify the differences and modify the products to suit the cultural needs of different customers.

Cultural differences have therefore important implications for marketing products and services globally. The food service business generally requires greater modification to meet local market requirements. In Saudi Arabia, as discussed in Chapter 2, the scarcity of local suppliers prompted the operators to utilize an enterprising team of global suppliers. As a result, the Saudi Big Mac represents a truly worldwide effort, including sesame seeds and onions from Mexico, buns made of Saudi wheat and Brazilian soybean oil and sugar, beef patties and lettuce from Spain, pickles and special sauce from the United States, cheese from New Zealand, and packaging from Germany.[6]

Hotel products and services are often modified to the local target markets. Hotel architecture and interior decoration of the public areas and guest rooms are designed to represent local cultural trends. International hotels provide amenities that are customary in the local market. For instance, tea and boiling water are offered in countries where tea is a preferred beverage. Disposable slippers are provided in guest rooms in many East and Southeast Asian countries.

DISTRIBUTION STRATEGY

Distribution systems are a critical element of the hospitality marketing mix. This refers to the channels hospitality firms choose for making products and services available for purchase and consumption. Most hotels and restaurants attempt to sell products and services directly to the end user, the consumer. However, hospitality firms need assistance in distributing products and services to consumers. Many customers rely on the distribution channels to find the right product and service. In today's highly competitive international hospitality markets, utilizing channels of distribution effectively will have a major impact on sales.

The development of effective distribution strategies is a difficult task in the home country, but it is even more so internationally where marketing managers face a new market environment. In the United States, hotel companies tend to sell their products and services directly to the consumer by offering central reservation systems (CRS) with toll-free telephone numbers, or by hotel sales representatives contacting business clients directly. Hotels sales through travel retail channels, such as travel agencies, are the least utilized compared to other travel product and service providers in the United States. However, hospitality products and services are distributed differently in many other countries. A recent study found that 35.5 percent of travel agents in the United States recommend hotels to their clients, while 49 percent of travel agents in Europe do so.[7] Tourists tend to consult travel agents more for choosing destinations and lodging accommodations in other countries. Travel agents can shape to some extent the perceptions of tourists and influence their buying decisions. Therefore, establishing an effective channel of distribution through the travel retail network is crucial to hotel sales in other regions. A successful partnership between hoteliers and travel agents can be a partnership in profits.

Another common strategy for product and service distribution is to develop loyalty marketing by forming alliances with many other travel and hospitality providers. Hotel and restaurant chains join telephone companies, rental car companies, major airlines, and other hospitality providers to jointly promote their products and services. Once a consumer has reached a certain mileage with a particular airline, she or he is eligible for a discount room rate in a hotel, or discounted meals at a restaurant. Therefore, hospitality products and services are distributed through such loyalty marketing programs.

Hospitality products and services can also be distributed through travel service providers, such as American Automobile Association (AAA) in the United States. These organizations have large memberships and offer travel advice to the members. Similar organizations can be identified in different countries and utilized as potential distributors of hospitality products and services.

Global Distribution System

Used for marketing hotels internationally, the Global Distribution System (GDS) is the central reservation system used by travel agents to book airline seats, rental cars, hotel rooms, and other travel reservations and services. In the past, travel agencies used the major central reservation systems for booking airline and car rental reservations electronically. Now they are increasingly dependent on GDS computers to display hotel selections and reserve rooms instantly in any geographic location worldwide. The net volume of hotel reservations booked through GDSs grew 18.1 percent in 1997 and has more than doubled since 1993.[8]

GDS allows each hotel to list all of its different room types, descriptions, rate categories, policies, and special packages. The information is then available to hundreds of thousands of travel agents worldwide. Different GDSs compete for their own network of travel-agency subscribers to gain a greater market share. Most of the major GDSs include hotel reservation information and introduce the ability to carry negotiated rates, limitless rate categories, and multiple room types.[9] Its ability to give travel agents direct access to hotels' inventories has enabled agents to provide their clients with instant confirmation numbers.

Exhibit 12.1 illustrates the link of hotel reservations to the global distribution network. For a hotel to be available to all travel agents, it must be linked to every GDS. To simplify and speed the process, automatic switching methods such as WizCom's ResAccess and THISCO's (The Hotel Industry Switching Company) Ultraswitch were developed to connect hotels' central reservation offices directly to the GDSs. Travel agents benefit greatly from these switches because they give the agent access to updated availability information and instant confirmation numbers.

EXHIBIT 12.1. Global Distribution Systems

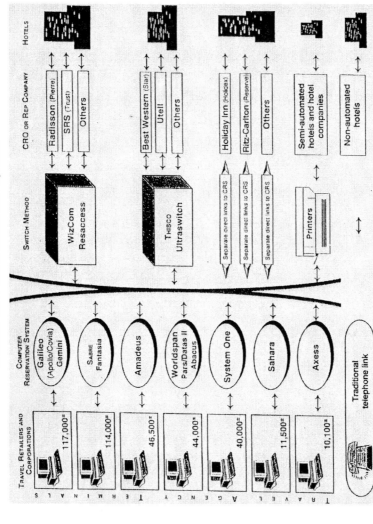

Source: Rita M. Emmer, Chuck Tauck, Richard G. Moore, and Scott Wilkinson, "Marketing Hotels: Using Global Distribution Systems," *Cornell HRA Quarterly* (December, 1993), 84. Adapted from the *Cornell HRA Quarterly*, copyright 1993 Cornell University. Used by permission.

To use GDS as an effective "electronic brochure" for hotels, hotel marketing personnel need to consider: (1) display availability, (2) hotel description, (3) rate descriptions, and (4) the room sale.[10] Display availability refers to the complete display of a hotel's location, rates, services, and room types. When a travel agent searches a particular hotel based on the request of a client, the travel agent may use additional qualifiers such as landmarks, nearby attractions, different rates, or services and facilities to find hotels that meet the guest's needs. The use of qualifiers limits the number of hotels that appear on the travel agent's screen, making it extremely important for hotels to be as accurate and detailed in their indexing as possible.

When a travel agent decides to look further into detailed hotel description, the second screen shows exact rates, room types, facilities available, services offered, and reservation policies. The GDS allows the travel agent to choose other hotels if the detailed description does not meet the client's needs. The quality of information provided by the hotel will determine how well the hotel is presented to the agent and the client. Like a paid advertisement or a listing in a published guidebook, this electronic brochure should be as clear and pleasing as possible to the travel agent.

Due to various requests from clients, travel agents like to have the most up-to-date and detailed room rate descriptions, such as rack rate, corporate rate, weekend rate, convention rate, government rate, package rate, and so on. Hotels that provide accurate and detailed rate descriptions can assist travel agents to determine any amenities that may be included in the rate as well as any special requirements.

Room sale refers to the booking of the room and the confirmation number given by the hotel's central reservation office. Travel agents like to receive an immediate confirmation number after the room has been booked. The direct link between the hotel's central reservation office and the GDS can provide an immediate confirmation number to the travel agent.[11]

As one of the major GDSs, THISCO recently connected Shangri-La's thirty-five hotels and resorts in Southeast Asia and China to all of the global distribution systems, enabling electronic reservations by travel agents worldwide. It currently connects about 27,000 hotels with every major GDS.[12]

Pegasus Commission Processing (formerly the Hotel Clearing Corporation)

As travel agents worldwide make hotel reservations for their clients, commission payments from hotels to travel agents become complicated because of geographic distance and foreign exchanges. This has created a business opportunity for providing commission collection and processing among hotels, travel agents, and GDSs worldwide. Pegasus Commission Processing, a leading provider of global hotel distribution technology solutions based in Dallas, Texas, serves more than 78,000 travel agencies in 206 countries (including over 65 of the top 100 U.S. travel agencies) for collection, processing, and consolidation of commission payments due them from hotels. More than 60 hotel companies participate in this commission payment program, representing more than 23,500 contracted properties in over 60 countries.[13] By using Pegasus Commission Processing's service, hotel companies can pay commissions to travel agents worldwide promptly.

COMMUNICATION STRATEGY

Communication secures understanding between a hospitality company and prospective customers to bring about a favorable buying action, and achieve a long-lasting confidence in the company and the product and service it provides. To communicate effectively to potential customers, a hospitality company can use various communications channels, such as personal selling, sales promotions, advertising, attending trade shows, and the increased use of online promotion. However, marketing hospitality products and services globally faces many barriers. This section will identify the barriers to international marketing communication, and analyze the different forms of communication strategies for eliminating the barriers.

Barriers to International Communications

International communication occurs whenever a hospitality company uses a marketing message to sell its products and services in a foreign country. The effectiveness of international communication is greatly influenced by three major barriers: cultural barriers, source effects, and noise levels.[14]

Cultural Barriers

As emphasized in Chapter 3, culture shapes individuals' value systems and influences their behaviors. The needs and wants of individual consumers are often culturally determined. A major challenge hospitality marketers face is the cultural barriers that make it difficult to communicate messages across cultures. Due to cultural differences, people in different countries may interpret the same message very differently. The same word may be perfectly apt in one country while meaning something significantly different or even vulgar in another. For example, the word hamburger should be avoided in advertising in France. Instead, steak haché should be used. This is because the French government bans by law over 300 anglicisms in order to keep the French language "pure." A U.S. quick-service restaurant was fined $300 in France for advertising hamburger instead of steak haché.[15]

Cultural awareness is very important in overcoming cultural barriers in international communications. Local managers and employees must be consulted in developing any marketing messages. A local advertising agency should be used to develop culturally appropriate strategies for major advertising campaigns. Thus, hospitality firms can avoid cultural blunders in international communication.

Source Effects

In certain countries, people prefer certain products from particular other countries because of former colonial influence, close cultural ties (using the same language), or the quality of the products and services. When a potential consumer evaluates the marketing message based on his or her own feeling about the message sender, it is known as a source effect. Source effects can be detrimental to an international company when potential consumers in a target country have a bias against a certain country or a certain company. Source effects can also be positive if the potential consumers in the host country have a favorable image of the foreign company or country. Consumers in some countries tend to favor European companies over U.S. companies or vice versa. Sometimes, international companies operating in a foreign country with a strong bias have to overcome the source effects by down-playing their national origin in their marketing strategy.

Noise Levels

Noise refers to the volume of marketing messages sent to potential consumers for attention in a particular market. In highly commercialized Western countries, individuals are bombarded with marketing messages daily, and the noise level is very high. The probability of effective communication is reduced substantially. Hospitality marketers have to find creative ways of communicating with potential consumers. However, in most developing countries, the noise level tends to be low since local consumption of hotel products and services is limited. Most of the business for international hotels derives from international visitors. Hospitality marketers therefore need to examine closely the noise levels of the target market and develop effective marketing messages for prospective consumers.

Communication Channels

There are many ways to gain the attention of potential consumers. The tools for communicating marketing messages include advertising, online promotion, personal selling, sales promotion, and public relations. Selection of these tools is normally determined by the type of product and service, the environmental forces, the amount of market penetration desired, and marketing budget.

Advertising

Advertising is paid, nonpersonal presentation of ideas, goods, or services by an identified sponsor. Commercial advertisements are primarily seen in media, such as print advertisement and broadcast commercials.[16] This is one of the most expensive forms of marketing communication. Hospitality companies in Western developed countries spend millions of dollars annually to reach out to consumers. Media are readily available for advertising in the United States, Japan, Canada, and Western Europe in the forms of print media (newspapers and magazines) and electronic media (television, radio, and Internet). However, the level of media sophistication varies greatly from country to country. Even many developed nations have fewer electronic media available for advertising than the United States. In many countries, all electronic media are state-owned and carry no commercials. In Great Britain, BBC television and radio services are state-owned and do not carry commercials.[17] There are also restrictions on media advertising. Germany bans advertising on Sundays and public holidays. Many developing countries have a scarcity of electronic media, particularly in Africa. Advertisers have to compete for available space in the newspapers. But there are too many newspapers and magazines in Latin America and the Middle East. The challenge facing the hospitality marketers is to sort through hundreds of newspapers and select the right ones for the company's target markets.

Cinema advertising is popular in many developing countries, since going to movies is still the major form of entertainment. In the Middle East, where media options are limited, videotape ads are becoming an important part of media advertising. Advertisers penetrate this lucrative market by buying spots on popular videotapes. Three or four breaks with six or seven spots each are created at the beginning, middle, and end of the film. This strategy has been effective since a newly released film can be viewed by about 1 million people in the first three months in Saudi Arabia.[18]

Each country has some kind of media available for commercial advertising. Hospitality marketers need to examine the availability of media and the level of media sophistication in the host country, and determine the advantages of each kind. With cultural sensitivity, proper translation of the language, and appropriate selection of media form, hospitality advertisers can develop effective advertisements that capture prospective consumers in many different countries (see Exhibit 12.2).

Online Promotion

In the past few years, many hotel and restaurant companies have been experimenting with a potentially revolutionary marketing tool—the World Wide Web. As more people have access to the Internet in the United States, online sales of general goods and services increased 271 percent, from $700 million in 1996 to $2.6 billion in 1997.[19] The Internet is thus perceived as a potential electronic channel to influence prospective consumers. At present, most international hotel and restaurant chains, and some independent businesses maintain World Wide Web sites (see Exhibit 12.3). Information provided at these hospitality Web sites varies from establishment to establishment. The many functions of these Web sites primarily include promotion, service, feedback surveys, and reservations.[20] They are described as a

EXHIBIT 12.2. McDonald's Advertisement for Filet-O-Fish in German (Photo used by permission of McDonald's Corporation.)

communication tool that offers an "enabling, engaging, facilitating, sustaining, and rewarding interaction between the consumer and the hotelier."[21]

Although use of the Internet by the hospitality industry is still in the experimental stage, many hotel and restaurant users find it useful as a new promotion tool. Some cyber-hoteliers reported thirty to sixty e-mail messages a month. Monthly online reservations varied from none up to about 200. Respondents to a hotel survey reported that they received from less than 100 to about 100,000 monthly "hits," and monthly e-mail messages received ranged from one to about 400.[22] Many hoteliers indicated their satisfaction with the use of online promotion because it gave favorable publicity in targeted market segments and enhanced exposure to international travelers and travel agents.

EXHIBIT 12.3. Accor's Web Site Home Page

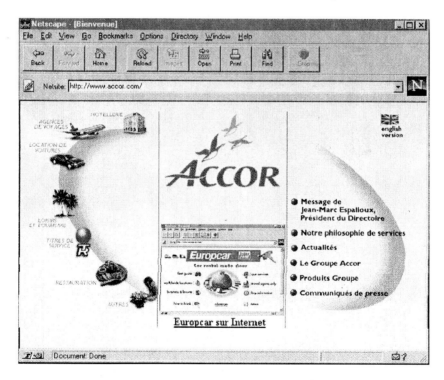

In 1997, Nikko Hotels International launched a new Internet Web site for global hotel reservations and information. Customers who made reservations online for any of Nikko's forty-four hotels around the world were given a discounted room rate in a specified three-month period. Nikko's online promotion was considered a creative strategy for launching a Web site and increasing sales.

Personal Selling

Personal selling constitutes a principal component of the hospitality promotional mix. It is particularly important in hotel sales to group business, such as corporate and association meetings and leisure package groups. Groups attending meetings and conventions are a large source of business for the hotel industry. Group sizes vary from an executive committee meeting of ten to the World Bank annual meeting of several thousands. Meeting and convention groups generally stay longer in the hotels, with an average of three nights. Leisure package groups are a popular form of international travel because most details are prearranged by travel agents, such as transportation, lodging, meals, sightseeing, and entertainment. Normally, such a group is led by a professional tour guide from the tour company to provide personal service. Therefore, foreign tourists, who do not speak the language of the host country and know little about the host country's culture, will feel comfortable to travel with a professional guide and enjoy hassle-free travel arrangements. These types of group business are the major revenue sources for international hotels.

Hotel sales managers make sales calls to solicit group business from various sponsoring companies and organizations. They prospect and qualify potential clients, and then approach the potential clients to present them with the hotel's product, service, and benefit, and ask for business. Sales managers travel frequently to solicit new business and visit regular clients in foreign countries. Once a corporate or association meeting planner or a travel agent agrees to book the business with the hotel, the sales manager needs to close the sale by signing the sales contract which specifies contract period, group rate, and other service and policy items.

Personal selling can be cost-effective if group business is brought in. The success of personal selling depends largely on the personality, industry knowledge, and cultural awareness of the sales manager and staff. In many cultures where trust is valued before doing business, the sales manager and staff need to cultivate the trust first. Established business ties need to be continuously strengthened. Hiring competent local sales staff and managers is a common practice of most international hotels because they are more culturally acceptable to customers and channel members.

Sales Promotion

Sales promotion provides the selling aids for the marketing function and includes many activities such as point-of-purchase displays, contests, trade show exhibits, coupons, and so on. These tactics are all routinely employed by hospitality companies, and some are quite creative and entertaining. For example, Forte Plc's U.S. Travelodge division once had a promotion program called "Passport to Summer Entertainment" with Paramount Studios. Guests staying three consecutive nights at a participating Travelodge received four movie passes, and $15 off if they charged the stay on the American Express card.[23] In the summer of 1996, Ramada teamed with Republic Pictures to offer guests in the United States and Canada a free video for staying at least four nights at participating Ramada hotels.

It is beneficial for hospitality firms to attend international travel, hotel, and restaurant trade shows, which provide an important venue for buyers and sellers to meet and discuss potential business. For international hotels, the three major world travel trade shows offer a great opportunity to seek potential customers from many different countries. The trade shows in Tokyo, London, and Frankfurt attract representatives from all aspects of the world travel and hospitality industry: airlines, travel agencies, hotels, cruises, theme parks, entertainment, food service, car rental companies, and so on. Hotel and restaurant sales managers and representatives can meet travel agents from many different countries to explore future business cooperation.

Hospitality companies that use sales promotions need to be aware of some cultural and legal restrictions in different countries. Some countries have laws that are more restrictive for sales promotions. For instance, "two-for-one" offers are prohibited in Sweden and Norway, and Mexico requires special offers and cents-off deals to be approved by a government agency before they can be used.[24] Local managers or legal advisors should be consulted before the use of any sales promotion activities in a foreign country.

Public Relations

Public relations as a promotional tool refers to various methods of communicating with the firm's publics to secure a favorable impression.

The publics include the local community, existing and potential customers, employees, industry partners, the host government, investors, and the press. Most hotel and restaurant chains are actively involved in various causes of the local community: art, health, education, sports, and the environment. As discussed in Chapter 7, Sheraton's "Going Green" program in Africa seeks to benefit conservation and environmental education by promoting the "Optional Dollar" program in Sheraton hotels in the region. Donations from guests are used for wildlife protection and supporting antipoaching efforts. McDonald's sponsors goodwill sporting events to promote friendship around the world. Examples of social responsibility abound in the international hospitality industry. Community involvement at different levels greatly enhances the company's favorable image in the host country. It is essential to maintain a positive relationship with host governments at all levels, particularly governments with great control over commercial business. A strained relationship can cost the operations in terms of delayed material supply, employee recruits, tax breaks, and even decreased room bookings from the local government.

Positive media relations have a ripple effect and can affect all of a hotel or restaurant's public relations.[25] News is generally presented to the media with a press release that offers genuinely newsworthy information, such as top management appointments, renovations, change of direction in price structure or cuisine, major conferences, and events held in the hotel or major functions catered in the restaurant. The news release needs to be written in the host language and effort must be made to ensure the accuracy of the translation. Most hospitality corporations now announce news releases on the Internet.

Projecting a positive image in the host community and country will enhance business for hotel and restaurant operations. Many hotels and restaurants employ a full-time public relations manager; others engage a local public relations firm or use a combination of in-house and outside resources. It is also highly recommended that local managers and staff be consulted since they know the cultural environment well and can identify the most effective ways of promoting public relations.

PRICING STRATEGY

International pricing for hospitality products and services is an important and complex component of formulating the marketing strategy. Pricing decisions affect consumers' buying decisions, affect the operation's gross revenue, and are a major determinant of profits. International hospitality operations also face government regulations on prices in some countries.

This section discusses several pricing theories and practices employed as international pricing strategy.

Price Elasticity of Demand

The price elasticity of demand is a measure of the responsiveness of demand for a product to changes in price. Demand is said to be elastic when a small change in price produces a large change in demand; it is said to be inelastic when a large change in price produces only a small change in demand.[26] The elasticity of demand for a product in a particular country is influenced by many factors. But the three most important factors are income level, target market, and competition. Generally speaking, price elasticity tends to be greater in countries with low income levels. This is logical since consumers with limited incomes tend to be very price sensitive. They have less to spend, so they look more closely at price.

Target market refers to the primary market the hotel wishes to entice. Many hotel companies expand operations into foreign countries with the purpose of serving visitors from their own countries, such as American hotels in India serving American tourists visiting India. If the overseas visitors from the United States or other developed countries can generate enough volume to support the hotel's business, the hotel can maintain the price level charged in the home country. But, if the hotel cannot attract enough visitors from the home country, other developed European countries, or the local wealthy market, the hotel may have to increase the number of local patrons or international leisure tourists who are sensitive to prices. Therefore, the hotel may have to lower its prices to attract these guests.

The more competitors there are, the greater consumers' bargaining power will be, and the more likely it is that consumers will buy from the firm that charges the lowest price. Thus more competitors cause high elasticity of demand. In such a competitive environment, if a company raises its prices above those of its competitors, consumers will switch to the competitors' properties or restaurants. The common strategy used by new entrants into the market is to lower prices in the hope of intersecting customers from existing businesses. The opposite is true when a firm faces few competitors. When competitors are limited, consumers' bargaining power is weaker and price is less important as a competitive weapon. Thus a firm may charge a higher price for its product and service in a country where competition is limited than in a country where competition is intense.

A good example to illustrate the impact of these factors on hospitality operations is the resort destination of Cancun in Mexico. Cancun was originally developed as a small and exclusive resort destination. However, hotel supply has outpaced demand in the past. As a result, competition intensified and prices were cut substantially. Consequently, wealthy visitors did not return, and Cancun now attracts mostly middle-class tourists with less disposable income, which means less revenue for the resorts. Many hotels want to raise prices so they may have the necessary resources to upgrade facilities and attract higher paying guests. However, it is extremely difficult for hotels to raise prices in such a competitive market where hotels continually undercut each other. Cancun's image as a popular mass tourist destination restricts the hotels from raising rates without losing significant occupancy.[27] Hotel room rates are directly related to market demand, guests' income levels, and competition.

Therefore, the hospitality establishment needs to examine closely the price elasticity of demand in the host country, the demand from overseas target markets, and competitors' pricing practices. A thorough analysis of these major factors can enable hospitality managers to set competitive prices for products and services.

Two other factors that have an impact on pricing in some countries need to be pointed out: high inflation and drastic devaluation of local currencies. As discussed in Chapters 5 and 9, inflation and currency fluctuation can both influence the upward movement of price. In a highly inflationary economy, hospitality management has to pay higher prices for labor and supplies. Therefore, room rates and meal prices have to be raised to cover the increased operation costs. When operating in countries whose currencies depreciate drastically against the hospitality firm's home currency, the management has to adjust its prices regularly if sales are conducted by local currency denomination. As suggested in Chapter 9, hospitality companies operating in countries with continuous devaluation of local currencies should conduct sales in dollar-denominated transactions. For example, during the Mexican peso crisis in late 1994 and early 1995, Posada de Mexico, a leading luxury hotel chain in Mexico, sold rooms to foreign travel agencies in dollar-denominated amounts. Then, the company paid the expenses in pesos. The difference between the dollars that bought tourism and the pesos that covered the costs of operations has benefited Posada financially in a big way.[28]

Finally, hospitality management needs to be aware of the host government's influence on price decisions. In most Western market economy countries, governments have formulated regulations to promote competition and restrict monopoly practices. But in some developing countries and in communist countries, the host governments exert great influence in regulating prices. Hospitality operations have to comply with the host government regulations.

SUMMARY

- Strategic marketing planning starts with a firm's mission statement. The mission statement defines the purpose and scope of a business. As hospitality firms view the whole world as their market, global expansion activities are clearly defined in the mission statement.
- International environmental scanning identifies desirable markets by using environmental forces to eliminate the less attractive markets. It can be used effectively to seek information about threats and opportunities in the global markets.
- The International Management Information System (IMIS) is an organized process of gathering, storing, processing, and disseminating information to global managers for making management decisions. Information is gathered internally and externally.
- The traditional marketing mix of strategic decisions are made in the areas of product and service, distribution, promotion, and pricing.
- Hospitality products and services have many attributes. Hospitality business sells well when the product and service attributes match customer needs.
- The distribution system refers to the channels hospitality firms choose for making products and services available for purchase and consumption. These channels include the travel retailing network (travel agents), travel service providers (American Automobile Association), and loyalty marketing programs.
- The Global Distribution System (GDS) is the central reservation system that travel agents use to book airline seats, rental cars, hotel rooms, and other travel reservations and services. GDS allows each hotel to list all of its different room types, descriptions, rate categories, policies, and special packages.
- Pegasus Commission Processing provides services for commission collection, processing, and consolidation. Hotels and travel agents worldwide use this service to ensure prompt commission payments and build better working relations.
- International marketing communication is influenced by three major barriers: cultural barriers, source effects, and noise levels.
- Media advertising is readily available in some countries, but not in others. The level of media sophistication varies from country to country. Media selection for advertisement needs to be determined by media availability, level of sophistication, and host cultural preference.
- Online marketing has been increasingly used by hospitality firms for marketing communications. The Internet is considered a potential

electronic channel to influence prospective consumers seeking hospitality products and services.

- Personal selling targets group business. It can be cost-effective if group business is brought in. The success of personal selling depends largely on the personality, industry knowledge, and cultural awareness of the sales manager and staff.
- Sales promotions aim to generate sales on a short-term basis. Sales promotions encompass many promotional tactics. Sales manager and staff need to be aware of the cultural and legal constraints when promoting sales in a foreign country.
- Public relations refers to various methods of communicating with the firm's publics to secure a favorable impression. Maintaining a positive relationship with the host government and community is essential to successful hospitality operations.
- The elasticity of demand for a product in a particular country is influenced by three important factors: income level, target market, and market competition.
- Pricing in international hospitality operations is also influenced by inflation, currency fluctuation, and host government control on price.

STUDY QUESTIONS

1. Why is the mission statement so important to international strategic marketing planning?
2. What methods can hospitality firms use to seek information on global development opportunities and threats?
3. What is the market gap? How is the gap identified?
4. Discuss the various market information sources for decision-making considerations.
5. What are the four elements in the traditional hospitality marketing mix?
6. How can you match hospitality product and service attributes to the needs of international travelers and local customers?
7. Discuss the ingredients that make up the Big Mac in Saudi Arabia.
8. What are the distribution channels that hotels tend to rely on for making products and services available to consumers?
9. What can you recommend for improving the working relations between hotels and travel agencies in the United States?
10. Why is it important for international hotels to consider linking their central reservation systems to the Global Distribution System?

11. Describe the Global Distribution System as an "electronic brochure."
12. What are the functions of Pegasus Commission Processing? If you are a hotelier, do you want to use their services?
13. Discuss how the three barriers to international marketing communications can be reduced.
14. What factors does an international hotel or restaurant have to consider to develop effective media advertising in a foreign market?
15. Categorize the many functions of the Web site posted by a hotel. How can the effectiveness of online marketing be measured and evaluated?
16. What is the primary objective of personal selling? What are the major characteristics of a successful sales representative in international hospitality marketing?
17. What should managers consider when pushing sales promotions in foreign countries?
18. How can international hospitality firms develop a positive public image in the host community?
19. How is "price elasticity of demand" defined?
20. What factors can influence the elasticity of demand for hospitality products and services?
21. What other economic, financial, and political factors can influence the pricing of hospitality products and services?

CASE STUDY: MARKETING PLAN FOR DEVELOPING COURTYARD BY MARRIOTT IN CHINA

In early 1998, Marriott International was considering development of several moderate-tier hotels in China and decided to develop its Courtyard brand through cobranding with Hong Kong-based New World Hotels. This case study examines the risk associated with hotel development and operations in China as well as marketing strategies for the Courtyard brand.

Investment Climate

The Chinese economy has benefited from consistent growth over the past eighteen years and has an enormous amount of foreign investment. China has the potential to produce enormous rewards for investors who are willing to take the risk. This is reflected in the relatively high discount rate applied by investors in China at a mean of 20 percent. However, there are also potential risks for international investors. One factor that contributes greatly is political risk. While the political situation has improved in the past ten years, there is still a high degree of government control. Another element of the relatively high rating is economic risk. There is a high degree of government control of the economy motivated by the desire to keep inflation below the real rate of economic growth. This has become a major problem in light of the Asian crisis since other competing Asian countries can provide goods and services at lower prices. If China continues to enforce its policy of price stability, its economy may suffer from the intense competition from neighboring countries. Recently, after the weakening of the Japanese yen, China's projected growth fell to roughly eight percent from its steady growth rate of 10 percent. While this is disturbing, this event should not entirely discourage investment in China.

Despite these risks the investment climate has improved over the past two decades. As the economy has improved, China has become the second largest recipient of foreign direct investment. To continue growth the government constructed a five-year plan to improve the economy. This plan is based on both economic reform and attraction of foreign investment. The increasing upper middle class in China combined with the increase of travel and tourism has created a virtually untapped market for the midscale hotel market to cater to the upper-middle-class domestic and intraregional travelers. These improvements and opportunities outweigh the potential risks associated with political and economic factors including the Asian crisis.

Marriott International

Currently, Marriott International is one of the world's leading hospitality companies, with more than 1,600 units and operations in all fifty U.S. states and fifty-four countries. Major businesses include hotels operated and franchised under the Marriott, Ritz-Carlton, Renaissance, Courtyard, Residence Inn, Executive Residence, Fairfield, New World, Ramada International, and Towne Place Suites brands; vacation club (timeshare) resorts; senior living communities and service; and food service distribution. Across these different brands, Marriott International operates or franchises 235 international hotels. In the next five years, Marriott International plans to add 140,000 hotel rooms, 25 percent of which will be international properties. The company has approximately 129,000 employees and reported total sales of $9 billion for the 1997 fiscal year.

Courtyard by Marriott is the moderate-tier brand that has recently begun to expand globally. Currently, Courtyard hotels are found in the

United States, Britain, Germany, and Australia. Originally, this brand was developed to serve business travelers after extensive research on their needs for lodging accommodations. Features business travelers found important are included in the design of Courtyard: oversized rooms with a comfortable sitting area, large work desks with reach-anywhere phones, cable TV, and in-room coffee. In addition, Courtyard offers a reasonably priced breakfast buffet and often pools or whirlpools and exercise rooms. In the United States, Courtyard has been positioned as the best moderately priced hotel chain for individual business and leisure travelers. Its international positioning is as a superior chain of hotels appealing to individual business and leisure travelers competing in the moderate segment.

Marriott Current Operations in China

Prior to its acquisition of Renaissance Hotels and Resorts in March 1997, Marriott International had no properties in mainland China. One of the motivations behind the purchase of Renaissance was to diversify its international development. The acquisition of Renaissance for $1 billion added 150 hotels to Marriott International's portfolio, several of which are international properties in locations where Marriott has not yet developed. An exciting part of the Renaissance package is a strategic alliance with New World Development Company Ltd., who owns many of the Renaissance hotels. This is a Hong Kong-based hotel company with a strong reputation in China. New World Hotels appeal to business travelers in the Asia/Pacific region by offering business centers, recreational facilities, meeting, and banquet space. This strategic alliance is beneficial to Marriott International because New World is already familiar with development in China where there are currently five New World hotels. The two companies have agreed to jointly develop new hotels to be operated or franchised by Marriott International. Based on Marriott International's expansion goals and its alliance with New World Hotels, Marriott International is ready to expand Courtyard in China. This brand primarily caters to domestic and regional business and leisure travelers who need quality accommodations at a reasonable rate. Five Chinese cities are identified for Courtyard expansion: Beijing, Wuhan, Shunde, Wuxi, and Qingdao.

Marketing Plan

An important element to consider in the development of Courtyard is the best method of marketing that will enable the success of each property. This section discusses the overall international marketing plan for Courtyard including mission and strategic direction, positioning, consumer marketing, and marketing strategies. In each of these categories, recommendations on how each relates to or should be implemented in China are highlighted.

Mission and Strategic Direction

"Keep 'em in our dust" is the slogan associated with Courtyard's international mission. This mission is to retain Courtyard's market leadership by increasing customer and owner preference while maintaining its dominance over new competitive entities. Courtyard will initiate international expansion by opportunistically following Marriott hotels in key markets. To fulfill this mission, a strategic direction has been formulated comprising four elements:

1. To maintain brand positioning and integrity while increasing guest preference and loyalty
2. To pursue operational excellence
3. To meet long-term profit objectives through aggressive and responsible growth
4. To develop an associate (employee) base that delivers high levels of guest satisfaction

The markets that have been targeted for Courtyard international expansion include the United Kingdom, Germany, Eastern Europe, Southeast Asia, Australia, China, and India. Clearly, China is a market that has the ability to achieve dominance over new competitive entities. The Courtyard hotels in the five Chinese cities will complement the other full-service Marriott hotels and enable the development of future properties in prime locations.

Positioning

The positioning of international Courtyard will be similar to U.S. positioning with a few adjustments. Courtyard hotels will be a complement to Marriott hotels globally and provide operational excellence with great service. The main differences in the domestic and international positioning are that it will be seen as a superior chain of hotels in the moderate tier, the amenities and product features will be appropriate to the guest needs of the host country, the food and beverage will be more extensive with multiple restaurants if the area does not provide much selection, and the meeting space will be minimized to maximize profitability and maintain a simplistic approach to service delivery. It is recommended in China that hotels have extensive food and beverage operations including lounges, bars, and Chinese restaurants, since food and beverage sales make up a significant portion of hotel revenues. The modifications are made to cater to Chinese and regional business travelers and the resources they need to conduct business.

Consumer Marketing

The marketing strategies were developed with several objectives in mind. The first is to promote the brand promise of a place to rest, relax, and retool to get ready for the next day. The second is to increase awareness that Courtyard is a "smart choice" in the moderate tier. The third is to grow Courtyard's business share from frequent international business travelers through the Marriott Reward database, and the leisure share by positioning Courtyard for leisure vacations and short breaks. In China, Marriott International decided to cobrand Courtyard with New World Hotels for a period of time as a marketing technique. The goal is to attract clients familiar with New World hotels. The hotels will be named New World Courtyard by Marriott. Eventually, once Marriott is a more established brand in China, the hotels will be renamed Courtyard by Marriott.

Marketing Strategies

The objectives have framed a few different marketing strategies for the international Courtyard hotels, including an announcement of the Courtyard global expansion over a worldwide public relations network. Regionally, the hotels will be promoted one month prior to their openings. The media used will be print ads in business publications, airport/train signage, and outdoor advertisements. Other marketing channels include travel agents, Web sites offering worldwide reservations, and worldwide as well as regional directories. Travel agents are a very effective channel of distribution because of the large scope within which they operate. Specific agencies targeted include American Express, BTI, Maritz, and Carlson. Marriott International will offer seasonal promotions and online bulletins on the travel agent's systems corresponding with each opening.

Because there are a large number of multinationals in China, media advertising is expensive. Consequently the media advertising will be limited. Rather, marketing will focus on sales promotions, cross-referrals, and online advertising through travel agents. Cross-referrals will occur when a guest calls for reservations at a larger property and there is no availability or the guest seems to be price sensitive. Marriott International will also advertise on travel agents' individual reservation systems. The company will cultivate relationships with local travel agents through contacts in its Hong Kong office. Hotel information will also be published on the Internet in English and Chinese, and in worldwide and Asian regional directories. In addition, the cobranding with New World will attract many of their initial guests.

The investment climate coupled with market opportunities and a strategic alliance with an experienced hotelier in Asia has provided Marriott International with the opportunity to become a market leader in the moderate tier in China. With effective marketing, Courtyard hotels will be successfully developed and operated in China.

Case Study Source

This case study was written by Bridget Durbin, Marriott International, 1998.

Case Study Questions

1. Discuss the potential risks for hotel investment in China.
2. Identify investment opportunities for developing moderate-tier hotels in China.
3. Discuss the scope of Marriott International's operations and describe Courtyard by Marriott.
4. What market entry choice did Marriott International use for the Chinese lodging market?
5. What is Courtyard's international development mission and strategic direction?
6. How will Courtyard position itself in China?
7. Why does Courtyard cobrand itself with New World Hotels for the initial period of operations in China?
8. How will the new Courtyard hotels be promoted for the targeted markets? Do you have any suggestions for effectively marketing Courtyard in China to domestic and regional travelers?

Chapter 13

Religion and Food Service Management

Avoid embarrassing missteps by being careful and sensitive to other cultures. Create a locally driven concept. It's important to be perceived as a local business.[1]

Merritt Croker
Vice President of International Business, T.G.I. Friday's, Inc.

LEARNING OBJECTIVES

In this chapter, you will study:

1. Religious influence on dietary preferences and restrictions
2. Regional cuisine and food service management
3. Different food service styles
4. Sourcing of food products
5. Menu modification to reflect cultural preference
6. Service delivery and dining etiquette

INTRODUCTION

Food service operations are a growing component of the international hospitality industry. Serving food in other cultures requires a sound understanding of the local peoples' dietary preferences and restrictions. Diet reflects the lifestyles of cultural groups inhabiting different parts of the world. As the popular saying goes: "One man's meat is another man's poison." Different cultural groups enjoy certain cuisines, but avoid other food items. Such differences are, to a great extent, influenced by peoples' religious beliefs, an essential element of the cultural system.

This chapter begins with a brief discussion of major world religions and their influence on the dietary habits of different cultural groups. Knowledge of religious influence can enable hospitality managers to better understand local consumers' needs and modify certain menus if necessary. It then describes food service management operations, such as food service styles, product sourcing, menu modification, and other pertinent topics on real estate and labor cost. Service delivery and dining etiquette are emphasized in this chapter.

RELIGIOUS INFLUENCE ON DIET

As discussed in Chapter 3, cultural values and norms influence individuals' behaviors in lifestyles and in conducting business. As an important aspect of cultural values, religion influences individuals' behavior in their everyday life, including dietary habits. At this point, a brief overview of the major world religions is necessary to reveal different religious beliefs and practices influencing peoples' dietary preferences and restrictions.

Religion is defined as belief in and reverence for a supernatural power or powers regarded as the creator of the universe. It is the worship of God or dieties and the obedience of followers. There are two major categories of religion in the world: universalizing religion and ethnic religion.[2] Universalizing religion refers to the major religions that actively recruit new members, and have as a goal to convert all of humankind. Three dominant universalizing religions are found in the world: Christianity, Islam, and Buddhism. Ethnic religion, on the other hand, is generally identified with some particular ethnic or tribal groups and does not seek global converts. Some influential ethnic religions in the world include: Judaism, Hinduism, and Shintoism. Following is a discussion of these major universalizing and ethnic religions in the world, and their influence on dietary practice is specifically highlighted.

Christianity

Christianity is the the largest universalizing religion in the world, with about one-third of the world population (approximately 1.9 billion people). However, this religion has long been divided into Western and Eastern Christianity with many national sects and separate churches, such as Greek, Russian, and Serbian Orthodox churches in the East, and Catholic, Baptist, Lutheran, Methodist, Mennonite, Latter-Day Saints, Seventh-Day Adventists, and so on in the West. The main dietary rules observed by some Christian groups are described in this section.

Roman Catholics

Before 1966, Catholics were compelled to abstain from eating red meat on Friday as an act of penance. That rule was later made optional and now applies only to Ash Wednesday and Fridays during the six-week period of Lent (beginning with Ash Wednesday and ending on Easter). Fasting, which means to have only one full meal a day, is recommended on Good Friday and Ash Wednesday.[3] Even though the year-round prohibition on red meat or poultry products on any Friday is no longer obligatory, many restaurants and cafeterias still serve fish on Friday every week of the year. Serving a fish or vegetarian meal on Friday is recommended during Lent.

Eastern Orthodox Church

The Eastern Orthodox Church follows the Julian calendar, thus the Orthodox Christmas falls on January 7. Easter, however, is always celebrated on the Sunday following Passover, which sometimes occurs several weeks after the traditional Christian Easter. The Church restricts the consumption of red meat on Wednesdays and Fridays during the liturgical year, and the very observant will also refrain from eating fish, poultry, and dairy products on these days. Red meat, poultry, dairy products, and fish are not allowed at any time during the six-week Easter Lent. Only small meals and water are allowed from Good Friday until Easter Sunday.[4] There are several other less strict lents during the year, including a six-week lent before Christmas.

Seventh-Day Adventists

Alcohol is strongly discouraged because the Adventists believe nutrition is an important part of their religious experience. Adventists avoid caffeine, aged cheeses, and hot spices such as peppers. A lacto-ovo-vegetarian diet and kosher meat are strongly encouraged by this Christian denomination. Soy-based products and granola are highly favored.[5]

Mormon

Mormons are the members of the Church of Jesus Christ of Latter-Day Saints. This denomination actively seeks new members worldwide by requiring its young members to perform missionary duties overseas for a certain period. Mormons believe that in 1833, founder Joseph Smith received a revelation from God that forbade the consumption of alcohol, coffee, tea, and tobacco. These substances are considered injurious to the body.[6] Mormon teachings encourage eating grains, vegetables, and fruits. They also call for the sparing use of meat and moderation of all things. Substances that contain caffeine, such as chocolate and cola, are not specifically forbidden, and it is up to the individual's discretion whether or not to consume them. Milk and juice are recommended for serving the Mormons. The first Sunday of each month is a voluntary fast day.

Islam

Islam, the second largest universalizing religion, has about 1 billion followers worldwide. Followers of Islam are called Muslims. Islam centers mainly in the great desert belt of Asia and Northern Africa, but extends as far east as Indonesia and the Philippines. This faith accepts as God's eternal word the Koran, a collection of Allah's (God's) revelations to Muhammad, the founder of Islam.

The basic spiritual duties of all Muslims consist of the five pillars of faith:

1. Declaring one's complete faith that Allah is the only supreme being and Muhammad is the messenger of Allah
2. Performing five prayers a day, at dawn, noon, midafternoon, sunset, and before going to bed
3. Donating 2.5 percent of annual income through *Zakat,* a charity tax to help the needy
4. Fasting during the daytime in Ramadan, a 29- or 30-day month in Islamic lunar calendar, normally beginning in January or February of the Christian calendar
5. Making a pilgrimage to Mecca (Muhammad's birthplace) at least once in a lifetime, if financially and physically capable[7]

Of the five basic spiritual duties, the practice of abstaining from food and drink in daylight hours during the month of Ramadan has a direct impact on food service operations in Islamic countries. This religious practice must be respected in the host culture. In addition, Islamic teachings forbid the consumption of alcohol and pork, and prohibit gambling. Alcoholic beverages, like any intoxicant or narcotic, are believed to be harmful to the health. They take away an individual's productivity, and cause much harm to society. Alcohol is also prohibited as a cooking ingredient even though some may think that alcohol can evaporate during cooking.

Pork is avoided by Muslims, and they also restrict the consumption of by-products made with gelatin from pigs, such as marshmallows and gelatin products. Eating flesh and other products from carnivorous animals or from those that eat carrion is strictly prohibited in Islam. Zabihah meat, which is slaughtered according to special rules, is preferred by some Muslims. Very strict Muslims may also object to eating at a banquet where pork as well as nonpork dishes are served, because utensils used in preparing or serving the pork may have touched their food. Fish is an especially appropriate choice for Muslims because the restaurant operators or hotel food and beverage directors do not have to worry about buying zabihah meat. Muslims' main meats are beef and mutton. Islamic countries have very strict regulations on labeling food contents. In Saudi Arabia, government regulations require that food products must list in Arabic all ingredients and dates of production and expiration.[8]

Buddhism

Buddhism is the most widespread religion of the Orient, dominating a region stretching from Sri Lanka to Japan and from Mongolia to Vietnam. It began in India as a reform movement within Hinduism, and was based on the teachings of Prince Gautama Siddhartha, the Buddha (the Enlightened One). In the process of its spread, particularly in China and Japan, Buddhism fused with native ethnic religions such as Confucianism, Taoism, and Shintoism to form composite faiths. Along with Christianity and Islam, Buddhism remains one of the three great universalizing religions in the world.

Gautama Siddhartha preached the Four Noble Truths:

1. Life is permeated with suffering or dissatisfaction.
2. The origin of suffering lies in craving or grasping.
3. The cessation of suffering is possible through removal of craving.
4. The way to this cessation is the Eightfold Path.

The Eightfold Path is a path of life that has eight phases. It involves right views and aspiration; right speech, conduct, and livelihood; right effort, mindfulness, and contemplation. The Buddhist ethic of right conduct and livelihood dictates that the adherent must refrain from the taking of life, including animal life, and refrain from drugs and liquor. Moderate austerity is promoted among Buddhists.

The diets of Buddhists tend to vary from country to country. Chinese, Myanmar, and Thai Buddhists are likely to be vegetarians, while Japanese and Tibetans usually eat meat. Buddhists who keep a vegetarian diet usually eat milk, eggs, and honey, but not fish. Soybeans and products derived from them are therefore a major source of protein for Buddhists.

Buddhism also forbids five "pungent" foods—onions, leeks, garlics, scallions, and chives—as well as other members of the onion family.

Judaism

Judaism is the parent of Christianity, and closely related to Islam as well. The Hebrew prophets and leaders, such as Moses, are recognized in all three religions. Judaism has remained an ethnic religion for most of its existence because it does not seek new converts from other races. Judaism has about 13 million adherents throughout the world. At present, almost half of the world's Jewish population lives in the United States, another 30 percent in Europe, and 20 percent in Asia and Latin America.

In Judaism, a human is conceived of as a psychophysical entity, whose body and spirit are indivisible. In general, it is life in this world, rather than in the next, that forms the focus of Hebrew concerns. Serving God is an activity enjoined here and now in the ongoing vicissitudes of ordinary life. The most profound part of the faith is that: (1) God is good and so is his creation; an omnipotent creator would not have brought into being a world that was essentially corrupt, however much its beauties may here and there be overlaid by the evils that humans may perform; and (2) the God of Moses has shown himself to be for goodness and social justice; his religion must have an ethical dimension that calls us to action in the vicissitudes of history.

Judaism has some very strict rules for eating. By following a spiritual regimen of choosing and restricting food, Jews remind themselves that God took them out of Egypt to be holy in order to witness to the world. Sanctification—the process of becoming holy—involves infusing reverence into all areas of life. When it comes to eating, food is either kosher (ritually fit) or nonkosher. The laws concerning kosher food are complicated, but three basic rules apply. First, pork, shellfish, and their by-products are not kosher. Meat products must come from animals that have cloven hoofs and chew their cud. Therefore, beef can be kosher if butchered properly, while pork can never be kosher. Second, meat and poultry must be slaughtered and processed in a special way. According to Jewish law, the animal must be killed in a humane manner by a butcher recognized by the Jewish community and according to a set process with specified equipment. After the slaughter, the animal must be examined to determine that it was healthy and that the slaughter was conducted correctly. Then the blood is drained, and the cuts are salted to remove all traces of blood.[9] Third, dairy products may not be served at the same meal with meat. For example, serving broiled chicken with a glass of milk would violate the rules. Dishes used to prepare or serve meat may never be used for dairy products and vice versa. After meat is eaten, there must be a waiting period of seventy-two minutes to six hours before dairy food is served. Eating meat is restricted to emphasize the hierarchical value of life itself. In the Jewish diet, all vegetables are kosher.

The popularity of fish as a Jewish food goes back to the sojourn in Egypt before the Exodus. There is a tradition that the Leviathan (a gigantic fish) will be served at the ultimate messianic feast in Paradise. Fish dishes therefore become de rigueur during Shabbat since it is a foretaste of the age of redemption. But fish must have fins and scales. Any leavened grain products must be rejected during Passover. This is because the Bible mentions that in the Exodus the Hebrews had to prepare food hastily at the last moment. The bread was therefore unleavened. Jews now eat unleavened bread (matzo) to identify with liberation. Turning one's back on all forms of leaven (Chametz) became a central metaphor for escaping slavery. In everyday life, methods of food preparation are regulated. Ritual hand washing and blessing precede eating. The use of utensils, particularly during holiday festivals, is strictly prescribed.

In an effort to cater to São Paulo's Jewish community, the 229-room Hotel Inter-Continental introduced the region's first hotel kosher kitchen in May 1997.[10] This service was well received by the local residents and international visitors, and the hotel management expected the new facility to increase annual food and beverage revenues by as much as 20 percent.

Hinduism

Hinduism, a religion closely tied to India and its ancient culture, is an ethnic religion practiced by more than 80 percent of India's population. Hinduism is also a polytheistic religion, which involves the worship of many deities without a single founder or a central authority. The faith takes many local forms and no standard set of beliefs prevail.

Most Hindus believe that everything in the world is subject to an eternal process of death and rebirth and that individual souls migrate from one body to another. They believe one can be liberated from the cycle of death and rebirth and achieve a state of eternal bliss by purification of mind and body, devout worship of the gods, and good works and obedience to the laws and customs of one's caste.

Hinduism is linked to the caste system, a rigid segregation of people according to ancestry and occupation. The highest caste, the Brahmins or priesthood, is followed by the warriors (politicians, landowners), the merchants, the peasants, and the untouchables. An individual's position in a caste is inherited, as is that person's occupation. Movement to a higher caste can be made only in subsequent lives. If the gods choose to punish a person, his or her next life will be at a lower caste level.

Such discrimination based on the caste system is now prohibited by the Indian government. Efforts have been made to improve the social and economic conditions of those in the lower castes. But it is very difficult to eradicate a religious tradition overnight. In December 1997, sixty-one low-caste Hindus in a small village 928 km (580 miles) south of New Delhi were slaughtered by upper-caste landowners, because the low-caste farmers questioned the supremacy of the landowners.[11] Hospitality managers must be aware of the influence of caste systems in seating arrangement in the dining room: seating people from different castes in the same section may offend people from the higher castes. This is also important to human resource management if managers have to work with employees from different castes.

The veneration of all forms of life, involving noninjury to all sentient creatures, keeps Hindus from eating certain animal meat. The consumption of beef is strictly prohibited by Hindu law since the cow is considered a sacred animal. Orthodox Hindus abstain from consuming all animal products. Foods such as milk or butter are considered pure by nature because they are connected to the cow. The avoidance of meat and eggs is tied to the Hindu doctrine of nonviolence. No meat, fish, eggs, mushrooms, or root vegetables that resemble a head are allowed. Alcohol use is strongly discouraged. Before eating, Hindus make themselves ritually clean by taking baths. Hands, feet, and mouth are washed before and after eating. All eating is done with the fingers of the right hand, and no utensils are used. Serving bite-sized food is recommended for Hindu guests.

McDonald's studied the Indian market for a considerable period of time to develop a menu that can serve the Hindu population. The global quick-service giant learned menu modification from an Indian restaurant chain, Nirula's, which operates sixteen restaurants in the New Delhi area, five in Nepal, and one in Muscat, Oman. Nirula's menu includes burgers with lamb or mixed vegetable patties.[12] On October 13, 1996, McDonald's opened its first restaurant in an upscale New Delhi neighborhood. The hamburger, called Maharaja Mac, contains mutton, which is consumed by both Hindus and Muslims. McDonald's thus adopted a menu that keeps with Hindu religious practice (see Exhibit 13.1).

When Domino's Pizza opened its first store in India in 1996 through a master franchise arrangement with the Bhartia family, Domino's respected Hindu reverence for the cow by omitting pepperoni, the beef-based topping popular with Americans. In keeping with Indian custom, vegetarian offerings replaced nonvegetarian ones. Some toppings, such as lamb and

EXHIBIT 13.1. McDonald's Advertisement for Maharaja Mac in India. Used with permission of McDonald's Corporation.

chicken sausage, were introduced to satisfy Indians' taste. The menu also offers "Peppy Paneer," with red peppers and traditional Indian cheese.[13]

Shintoism

Shintoism is an ethnic religion in Japan with no founder or bible. Shinto legends define the founding of the Japanese empire as a cosmic act, and the emperor was believed to have divine status. Therefore it is also known as emperor worship. As a part of the World War II settlement, the Japanese emperor was forced to renounce such a claim.

A strong feature of Shinto is the insistence on purity, which is obtained by ritual washing and bathing. This ideal of purity is symbolized by the mirror found in Shinto shrines. The mirror reflects clearly, and so stands for honesty and sincerity. Shintoism displays a powerful sense of the presence of gods and spirits in nature, such as the sun goddess, storm god, and so on. Shinto is thus closely bound up with the natural world. Shrines typically are located in sacred groves, which express something of the mystery and peace pervading a beautiful and formidable countryside.

Such beliefs directly influence Japanese business operations. For instance, a Shinto priest is always invited to conduct a ceremony for the opening of a new restaurant. At the ceremony, the Shinto priest presents several offerings to the gods by using something from the land (rice and fruit) and something from the sea (dried squid). The purpose of the religious ceremony is to pray for the Shinto gods' blessing for a prosperous business. Many international firms in Japan, particularly the joint ventures, follow the host religious practice in business grand openings. No specific dietary restrictions are emphasized in Shinto. The only aspect that deserves attention is that eating meat is considered to render a person unclean for several days and thus makes the person ineligible to enter a shrine.

REGIONAL CUISINE AT HOTEL RESTAURANTS

One of the travel motivations for international tourists is to sample the local cuisine in different countries. They expect authentic local cuisine offered by the hotels where they are staying. Palatable local cuisine provided by a hotel's restaurants always enriches tourists' travel experience in a foreign country. International hotels normally offer several food service outlets to provide specialties of local cuisine. Many international hotels are known for their exquisite cuisine and first-class service (see Exhibit 13.2).

This tradition can be traced back to the late nineteenth century in Europe and North America when railroad development greatly increased leisure travel. The great hotels were then built to cater to well-to-do travelers. The great chef Georges-Auguste Escoffier (1846-1935) played a significant role in the development of the fashionable hotels, such as Ritz, Savoy, and Carlton. Escoffier thus became one of the central figures in a network of influence connecting the kitchens of leading hotels and restaurants in all the major cities of the Western world. Today, international tourists associate great food with many international hotels, such as French cuisine at Meridien hotels and Japanese cuisine at Nikko hotels.

Hotels magazine conducts a regular survey to select the world's greatest hotel restaurants, which are chosen by an international selection committee. Each of the selected restaurants receives a Great Hotel Restaurants Trophy in recognition of its magnificent food service performance. These great hotel restaurants give travelers culinary adventures to match the excitement of the hotels themselves. Interested readers are referred to this journal for periodic selections.

EXHIBIT 13.2. Guests Dining at Radisson Aruba Caribbean Resort (Photo courtesy of Radisson Aruba Caribbean Resort.)

TYPES OF FOOD SERVICE

Food can be served to customers in different ways. Food service style reflects the level of service in a particular restaurant, and cultural influence in different countries. Each service style is performed to satisfy customers' dining needs. This section describes the six food serving styles commonly found in different countries.

Cart Service

Also known as Russian service, cart service provides a high degree of personalized dining service. To perform cart service, a chef loads raw and semiraw food items on a cart and places it by the table. Food preparation is done on the cart, and guests can observe how the food is cooked. The demonstration adds to the excitement of the dining experience. However, cart service is highly labor intensive and expensive. This food service style is performed in luxury and upscale restaurants.

Platter Service

For platter service, the chef places the food on a big platter, and the server puts the platter in the center of the table. Each guest is given a clean plate and the server serves the food from the platter to each individual guest's plate by using a serving spoon. If the meal has multiple courses, the server will change each guest's plate for a clean one at the end of each course. This style provides personal service to the guests, and is rendered in upscale restaurants.

Plate Service

This style is also known as American service since it is commonly used in the United States. Food is placed on each plate in the kitchen, and the server brings the plate to each individual guest. Each guest eats from his or her own plate. Compared to platter service, personal service is reduced, but labor cost is correspondingly reduced, too.

Family-Style Service

Food is placed on a big platter in the kitchen and the platter is brought to the center of the table by the server. Each guest gets the food from the platter directly, or by passing the platter around. A "lazy Susan" (dining table with revolving top) is often used in family-style service in Chinese restaurants to accommodate large groups. Each platter is placed on the revolving tabletop and guests can reach the food by spinning the tabletop.[14] This style resembles the way people eat at home; hence the name.

Banquet Service

Banquet service requires a manager's efficient planning and coordination. Normally, plate service is used for banquet dining. However, if banquets are hosted for important events, such as a state dinner, platter service is often used to demonstrate a higher level of personalized service. Platter service for banquet functions is quite common in Asian countries.

Buffet Service

Buffet service allows guests to help themselves. Personal contact between the servers and guests is reduced to a minimum. However, the display of food gives guests a range of choices to select what they like or try a little bit of everything. Thus buffet service offers the guests variety and flexibility. This type of service is now used widely in both hotel restaurants and commercial restaurants throughout the world.

Food service can be performed with various service styles. Food service managers need to understand the prevailing local practice and adopt the most effective service style to satisfy guests' needs and generate profit.

PRODUCT SOURCING

One of the main challenges facing food service development in foreign countries is the sourcing of food products, since host distribution and supply issues have been identified as major elements in international restaurant operations. Retention of reliable distributors and suppliers is crucial to operation success. Many restaurants have to import food products from their home countries or from other countries to continue normal operations. Restaurant managers should be familiar with the host government policy on the importation of certain food products from foreign countries. When Minneapolis-based International Dairy Queen prepared to set up operations in South Korea, the host government provided the company with a list of products that could be imported to supply the operations. But when the operations were set to go and Dairy Queen tried to import toppings for its sundaes, the company found it was not allowed to import anything with preservatives. So the company had to scramble to create an importable product for the scheduled grand opening.[15] As already discussed in the previous chapter on marketing, the Big Mac in Saudi Arabia is made from products of many countries.

To minimize the sourcing problems, food service companies attempt to source the majority of their products inside the host country, and enter into partnerships with local companies. McDonald's in Russia has proven the success of such partnerships. When McDonald's opened its first joint-venture store in Pushkin Square in Moscow, the store had to import potatoes, beef, and lettuce from other European countries. From the beginning, McDonald's and the joint-venture partner had worked persistently with local suppliers to develop reliable, high-quality sources of raw materials for processing meat patties, producing fresh fries, preparing dairy products, and baking buns and apple pies in the joint-venture's state-of-the-art food processing plant and distribution facility. Now all food products are obtained locally.[16] McDonald's also had to import packaging materials for its Moscow operations at the outset. Efforts to obtain local packaging products were made and local supplies are now used.[17] By sourcing locally through the joint development of food processing plants in Russia, McDonald's can ensure that products conform to McDonald's internationally uniform standards. It has also, through processing, enabled the use of local raw materials, thereby reducing the enormous hard-currency burden the operation would otherwise confront if it imported such items from abroad.

MENU MODIFICATION

Respecting local cultural customs, particularly dietary practices as influenced by religion, is crucial to the success of overseas food service operations. In addition to religious influence, people in different cultures simply differ in taste: some like a particular food and some do not. However, the challenge is to know which areas can be altered without losing the attributes that have been most essential to the company's domestic success. Normally, food is the most likely component to be modified. Therefore, overseas food service operations must be flexible in menu planning, adjust the menu to the local peoples' taste, and therefore increase sales potential.

When KFC first began operations in Japan in the early 1970s, the managers soon found out that the Japanese customers complained about the cole slaw being too sweet. KFC quickly downplayed cole slaw on the menu.[18] In another example, having been a pizza and Coke restaurant in the United States for about forty years, Domino's let its overseas franchisees tailor their menus to the local markets. As a result of international franchisees' success with flexible menus, Domino's management has also learned the benefits of adaptation. The inclusion of chicken wings on Domino's national menu was largely determined by their success in overseas operations.

An international food service operation survey conducted by the National Restaurant Association in the United States revealed that 79 percent of respondents had modified their menus at non-U.S. food service locations, reflecting the willingness of American food service companies to alter their menus to suit global and regional differences. Exhibit 13.3 illustrates the reasons given by the respondents for menu modification in foreign markets.

The main reason for modifying a menu in a foreign market is the different local tastes. Differences in taste are clearly influenced by culture and religion. Unavailability of certain food products in the local markets is identified as another important reason for menu modification. For example, wheat products might be somewhat more difficult to obtain in Southeast Asia because rice is the primary staple grain in the region. Some food service companies have to change menus due to high prices for food products charged by vendors. Religious considerations and government restrictions are cited by some companies as reasons for menu alteration.[19]

EXHIBIT 13.3. Reasons for Modifying Menus in Foreign Markets

Reasons	Percentage of Respondents
Local tastes differ	90%
Food products unavailable	51%
High vendor prices	26%
Religious considerations	10%
Government restrictions	10%

Source: National Restaurant Association, "International Food-Service Survey" (Washington, DC, 1995).

However, many offerings on the menus of lower-price restaurant companies tend to be relatively standardized because food is normally processed in a central facility and shipped to remote units in shelf-stable or frozen form. Conversely, food offerings at higher-price restaurants tend to be less standardized and rely more heavily on procuring unprocessed foodstuffs to prepare menu items. This might cause supply problems in certain regions.

Many food service companies offer new menu items at non-U.S. locations by replacing deleted items with local foods or augmenting core menu offerings with popular local items. Some companies also change the portion size of menu items to suit the local taste. Changing the portion size is often determined by the availability and price of certain food items in local markets as well as established cultural eating patterns and dietary guidelines.[20]

OTHER DEVELOPMENT AND OPERATIONAL ASPECTS

In addition to product sourcing and menu modification, food service companies may encounter some other obstacles when expanding operations into foreign countries. The high cost of real estate in Japan, Hong Kong, Taiwan, and Singapore has forced U.S. companies to reevaluate the functional designs of their stores. Companies have to redesign the back of the house for better flow and optimal use of space. Most companies cannot afford free-standing restaurants and the extra space for a drive-through. The size of KFC stores in the densely populated Japanese cities was reduced from the prototype of 132 m^2 (about 4,400 sq. ft.) to 66 m^2 (about 2,100 sq. ft.).

Labor cost can be very high in some countries, and labor shortages make it very hard to find good employees. Food service companies have to rely on technology to reduce high labor costs, and use incentives to find and keep good employees. In Australia, restaurant servers are paid $10 to $12 an hour. Chili's invested in technology to increase labor productivity, such as using hand-held beepers and kitchen monitors. Chili's was able to find a way to provide the same level of service without paying a large waitstaff. Now Chili's is considering bringing some of that experience and know-how back to its U.S. system.[21] In London, where labor costs are among the highest in the world, The May Fair Inter-Continental Hotel encountered the labor shortage problem from the start when it opened its new restaurant, Opus 70, in early 1997. In addition to paying a competitive salary, the hotel offers an attractive benefits package, such as free uniforms, free uniform cleaning, free lunch and dinner, free taxis home in the evening, an annual Christmas bonus after one year of employment, and free accommodation at other Inter-Continental hotels.[22] Obviously, such an extensive benefit package can properly be offered only by hotel giants such as Inter-Continental. Independent restaurants will find it difficult to offer these incentives.

Host government restrictions are always the main obstacles for international food service operations. When Church's went to register the Church's brand as a trademark in China, the Chinese government thought the name confused the concepts of food and religion, so in China the brand name is known as Texas Chicken.[23] Another incident in China involved a U.S. food service company. Six months after International Dairy Queen launched a successful unit in Beijing, the government notified the company that the department store building in which it and other stores were housed would be torn down to accommodate road expansion. There were no explanations, no discussion, and no government compensation. Dairy Queen's partner lost $2 million on that site.[24]

The success of international food service operations is determined by many factors. Most companies found that hiring and retaining good managers is the most important factor for successful overseas operations. Other important factors include finding and retaining good hourly staff, menu modification, and retention of reliable local distributors and suppliers.[25] New entrants for global food service expansion should heed these factors to be successful in overseas markets.

SERVICE AND DINING ETIQUETTE

Restaurant service requires courteous and prompt personal attention to each guest's needs and wants. Managers and service employees in international operations should be familiar with local service and dining etiquette.

When customers are treated with courtesy, they like to return to your restaurant. Courteous service etiquette can leave a lasting impression.

Rules of etiquette are not set in stone. What works in one country may not work in another. Managers and service employees need to be familiar with local cultural customs as well as the multicultural demands of the customers. For instance, there are two ways to hold flatware in dining: the American style (zig-zag) and the continental style. In the American style, the guest holds the fork in the left hand, tines down, and the knife in the right. The guest uses the fork to hold food while cutting a bite-sized piece with the knife. After cutting one piece of food, the guest lays the knife across the top of the plate with the serrated edge toward himself, transfers the fork to the opposite hand, and inserts the food into his mouth.

In the continental style, a guest holds the knife in the right hand and the fork in the left with tines down. To cut bite-sized pieces, the guest holds the food with the fork and cuts with the knife. He then spears the food with the fork—which is still in the left hand—and puts it in his mouth. As he eats, he uses the knife as a backstop to assist in spearing the food with the fork.

Because of the different eating styles, it is important for service employees to how how to handle silverware correctly, especially in the resting and finished positions. Thus, service employees know when to remove the plate and silverware. In the American style, when resting, the knife stays in the upper-right quarter or one o'clock position of the plate, with the blade turned inward and the fork in the four o'clock position with tines up. When finished, the guest places utensils together on the plate with fork tines up and the knife turned inward in the lower-right portion of the plate between the four and six o'clock positions.

When resting between bites in the Continental style, the guest places the knife and fork on the plate with the fork over the knife and tines pointed down in an inverted V. When finished, the guest places utensils together on the plate with fork tines down and the knife turned inward between the four and six o'clock positions.[26]

In some Asian countries such as Japan and China, chopsticks are used for eating. Each culture adheres to a code of etiquette for using chopsticks. In Japan, a guest should never leave the chopsticks up in the rice bowl, which is the way of offering rice to the dead. A guest never takes something off a serving dish with his or her own chopsticks unless the guest turns them around and uses the large, dull ends. This is done for the sake of hygiene. For platter service, serving chopsticks are always provided, and each guest should use them. A guest should never dally over dishes and try to figure out what is in them. This can be an insult to the host who prepares or orders the dish.[27]

Seating arrangements in different cultures may follow established rules that should be observed to demonstrate proper respect for the local guests. For instance, family dining areas in Saudi Arabia must be separated from dining areas for single men. In many Asian countries, older people are seated at the power seat, which is the head of the table or the seat with the best view. In Japan, red and white are usually used during celebrations. White rice is sometimes mixed with a special type of red bean to make *sekihan*, served during happy occasions such as holidays and weddings. During unhappy times, such as when the Emperor is ill, *sekihan* is not served. Attention to such service details demonstrates a restaurant's understanding of the local culture and can win local customers' trust and business.

SUMMARY

- Religion is an integral part of the cultural system. Serving food in other cultures requires a thorough knowledge of the host religious influence on dietary preference and restrictions.
- Universalizing religion refers to the main religions that actively recruit new members and have a goal of converting all of humankind, such as Christianity, Islam, and Buddhism. Ethnic religion is identified with a particular ethnic group and does not seek global converts, such as Judaism, Hinduism, and Shintoism.
- Christianity is the largest universalizing religion in the world, with many national sects and separate churches. Dietary preferences and restrictions vary to some extent from church to church.
- Muslims, members of Islam, follow the five basic spiritual duties. Pork and alcohol are strictly avoided by Muslims.
- Buddhism is the most widespread religion of East and Southeast Asia. Buddhists believe the Four Noble Truths and the Eightfold Path, and follow an austere lifestyle. They are primarily vegetarians.
- Judaism is the parent of Christianity and closely related to Islam as well. Judaism has remained an ethnic religion throughout its existence and has very strict rules for food preparation and diet.
- Hinduism is an ethnic religion in India. It is a polytheistic religion because it includes many deities. Hinduism is linked to the caste system, and the cow is considered a sacred animal.
- Shintoism is an ethnic religion in Japan. It is closely tied to the natural world. Purity is a strong feature of Shintoism.
- Many international hotels are known for their exquisite cuisine and world-class service. Different service styles are performed to meet the dining needs of international travelers.

- Sourcing of food products can be a challenge for international food service operations. Managers need to know host government policy on the importation of certain food products and the availability of food products in the host country. Good relationships must be built with local food distributors and suppliers.
- Most U.S. food service companies modify their menus in non-U.S. locations to meet customer demands. Appropriate menu modification caters to the local consumers' taste, demonstrates respect for local religious belief, and adjusts to unit cost.
- International food service firms confront many other operational issues: pricey real estate, rising labor costs, shrinking labor pools, and tough host government regulations. Creative solutions to these issues need to be identified and implemented.
- Factors for successful overseas restaurant operations include: finding and retaining good managers and hourly workers, creative marketing, and retention of reliable local food distributors and suppliers.
- Knowledge of service and dining etiquette is important to courteous service delivery in the host country. It is also beneficial to the expatriate managers when they interact with local business partners. The do's and don'ts of dining etiquette will help expatriate managers avoid cultural blunders.

STUDY QUESTIONS

1. Define the concept of religion and discuss the relationship between religion and diet.
2. What is the main difference between universalizing religion and ethnic religion? List some of the religions in each category.
3. What are the similarities and differences in dietary preferences and restrictions observed by Christian churches?
4. What are the five pillars of the Islamic faith?
5. Why do Muslims avoid pork and alcohol? Can you use alcohol as a cooking ingredient in Islamic countries?
6. What are Buddhism's Four Noble Truths? What influence do the Four Noble Truths have on Buddhists' way of life, particularly their eating habits?
7. What are the rules for food preparation and consumption in Judaism?
8. What is a polytheistic religion? Which major religion is polytheistic?

9. Discuss the influence of the caste system on hospitality business operations in India, such as in the areas of food service and human resource management.
10. Why is the consumption of beef strictly prohibited by Hindu law? How did McDonald's and Domino's adapt to the local religious practice for new operations in India?
11. What are the main characteristics of Shintoism? What should we know about Shintoism's influence on food service operations in Japan?
12. How are the world's best hotel restaurants identified? Consult the most current issue of *Hotels* in your library and see which hotel restaurants have been voted for recently as the greatest. Examine why and how these hotel restaurants are selected as the best.
13. Discuss the functions and service levels of the six commonly used service styles.
14. What does a manager need to know about food product sourcing in the host country?
15. How did McDonald's handle product sourcing issues in Russia?
16. Why is menu modification crucial to the success of overseas food service operations?
17. What are the main factors a manager has to consider for menu modification in the host country?
18. What other operational issues does a manager often encounter in overseas operations?
19. What are the main successful factors for overseas restaurant operations?
20. Why is service etiquette so important to food service operations in a foreign country?
21. What are the do's and don'ts in food service in your culture that you would like to share with the class?

CASE STUDY:
U.S. FOOD SERVICE COMPANIES IN CANADA

You would think U.S. food service operators could find plenty of room for expansion right in their own backyard. Think again. Increasingly, U.S. operators are eyeing Canada's wide open spaces, and they are planning to arrive soon on a corner near you. Of course, many concepts that dot the Canadian landscape—McDonald's, KFC, Pizza Hut, and Baskin-Robbins—are the products of American ingenuity. So what's bringing a new generation to Canada? Some operators covet a less saturated market. Others relish the opportunities in a nearby country less dissimilar in culture and business practices than Mexico, Southeast Asia, or Eastern Europe. Those who operate and advertise near the border, including Seattle-based Starbucks Coffee and Cinnabon, which have ventured into Canada, are capitalizing on Canadians' familiarity with their concepts.

Companies such as Ben & Jerry's, The Italian Oven Inc., and Boston Market include Canada on a "one-day" list of expansion sites; others, including Livonia, Michigan-based Hungary Howie's Pizza & Subs; Melville, New York-based Captain Cottage and Bellevue; and Washington-based Country Harvest Buffet Restaurants, have expanded operations there. When they do, they know it takes more than simply rolling across the Rainbow Bridge or past the Peace Arch and hanging out a shingle. Just ask Red Lobster, the Olive Garden, Taco Bell, or Chi-Chi's, who have been unable to duplicate their U.S. success north of the forty-ninth parallel.

"What strikes me is the lack of understanding of the significant differences between the Canadian and U.S. markets," says Richard Hunter, president of Richmond Hill, Ontario-based consultants, Richard A. Hunter & Associates.

Entering any foreign market has its challenges: costly prime real estate; sourcing products and, in Canada, grappling with a supply-management system for chicken, eggs, and dairy products; and understanding local dining preferences. For many growth-oriented companies, the market saturation that initially propels them abroad soon perpetuates the hunt for further-flung locations. These days, U.S. companies approach expansion cautiously—even to "familiar" countries such as Canada. Due diligence makes sense to Hunter who, as president and CEO of Scott's Hospitality, has businesses on both sides of the border. "What separates the winners from the losers is taking the time to understand the differences."

In the early 1990s, Hunter studied those differences for Atlanta-based Chick-fil-A Inc., a U.S. $400-million chargrilled-chicken specialist. Overall, he concluded, Canadian wholesale food costs were 25 to 30 percent higher than in the United States. Supply-managed chicken was 92 percent more expensive; dairy products, 30 to 40 percent. But pork cost about the same in each country, and pasta cost about 40 percent less in Canada. Says Hunter: "Even with marketing boards being replaced by high tariffs, operators will skew their menus to emphasize non-supply-managed products."

Meanwhile, with payroll taxes and minimum hourly rates factored in, Canadian wages were about 35 percent higher than those in the United States. Prime real estate was equally pricey across North America. But equipment and facilities? After reckoning in an exchange rate of 30 to 40 percent on imported goods (which Hunter estimates at about 30 percent of a typical restaurant) and higher construction-industry wages and taxes, the Canadian tally was 40 to 55 percent higher than in the United States. Chick-fil-A stayed home until August 1994, when it licensed Versa Food Services to operate a food court unit at Edmonton's University of Alberta.

For his part, Boyd Simpson views Canada as a "level playing field" for North American operators. Says the chairman of North York, Ontario-based International Hospitality Inc., which opened nineteen Kenny Rogers Roasters units in Canada and the United States in the past sixteen months: "You compete locally. If you've got a good product properly valued, it works on both sides of the border. But when you go into a new market, do your homework. Employ people who won't assume 'If it works in Market A, it'll work here, too.'"

In 1995, Golden Corral, the U.S. $515-million company ranked third behind Sizzler and Ponderosa in the steakhouse segment, opened a 450-seat, 11,000-square-foot restaurant appointed in yellows and browns in suburban Toronto. The company also plans to examine franchise opportunities in Ontario's Oshawa-Pickering, Brampton, and Cambridge areas and British Columbia. Hunter says: "Golden Corral can make it because it's fundamentally self-serve; its labor cost is much lower. And most of today's concepts are casual, upscale hangouts for younger people, like Alice Fazooli's in Toronto. Nobody's zeroing in on older, 'middle Canadians'—where all the dough is." In part, Golden Corral will vie with operators such as Swiss Chalet, Golden Griddle, and fourteen-unit, Ontario-based Mandarin Restaurants. Its all-you-can-eat lunch buffet is expected to be $5.49; its dinner buffet, $6.95. In the United States, Hunter notes, the chain's average check is U.S. $7.45; by comparison, Mandarin's average check is $16 to $24.

Even the bagel market is heating up. Two years ago, Westmont, Illinois-based Great American Bagel exported its concept to Toronto. Now, there are five Great Canadian Bagel stores in Regina and Ontario, says marketing manager Terry Banike. Franchise agreements are being negotiated across North America, including British Columbia. Based in suburban Chicago, the company looked north because president Wayne Flateley is Canadian. (Flateley's brother Pat, a company investor, plays hockey for the New York Islanders.) In Canada, day-to-day operations are handled by Shoopsy's deli scion Neil Shopsowitz.

Meanwhile, three top-ten U.S. dinner-house concepts are or soon will be in Canada. For example, second-ranked T.G.I. Friday's Inc. launched fifty-four units in 1994, including thirty-five international franchises. According to Chris Rich, Friday's director of international development, the 325-unit chain expected to add seventy-five units, including thirty units in ten countries in 1995. By 1995, Dallas-based Friday's expected to have fifteen international franchise agreements. In Canada, it has agreements for the four Western provinces and for the Toronto and Ottawa areas and seeks a partner in Montreal. "We like partners with experience in hospitality, but not necessarily restaurants," says Rich, noting that Friday's partners include a former multiunit restaurateur in Western Canada and a real estate developer. "They need experience in development, because Friday's requires prime locations; design and construction, because we build lasting quality; and financial resources, because it's not inexpensive."

Friday's locations were slated to open in downtown and suburban Vancouver in May and November, 1995. A Toronto location was also planned for May 1995, and an Ottawa location in early 1996. In each case, Friday's hired and trained Canadian managers and staff; and U.S.-based trainers assisted through a unit's "soft opening." Typical units range from 6,000 to 12,000 square feet. Suburban units are free standing or located in shopping centers or office complexes with daytime traffic; downtown units are usually in office towers. In Vancouver, Friday's built a unit with a 5,500 square foot patio; in downtown Toronto, its unit comprises 10,000 square feet on two floors of an Adelaide Street tower. "Friday's has a four-sided, central raised bar and a full-service kitchen serving up to 100 lunch and dinner items seven days a week," Rich says. "Our menu is typical American—everything from burgers, sandwiches, and salads to specialty fajitas and baby back ribs."

Targeting affluent twenty-five- to thirty-nine-year-olds, the U.S. $775-million company opens 200- to 300-seat restaurants in lively "lived-in" downtowns, such as Boston and San Francisco. In the U.S. Southeast and Southwest, it usually opens free-standing units in suburban "dining hubs." A typical Friday's generates annual sales of U.S. $3.4 million; internationally, U.S. $4.5 million. Its leading unit—across from Planet Hollywood in London, where sales jumped 15 percent and stayed up from the day Planet Hollywood opened—generates U.S. $10 million. The average check is U.S. $11.

Like most operators, Friday's prefers to buy locally. In the United Kingdom, it imports only one percent of supplies; in Singapore, 90 percent. Adds Rich: "We hope customs won't be like our southern neighbors. NAFTA has created a regulatory labyrinth, with paperwork changing every week. Of the fifteen countries we operate in, Mexico has been the most difficult country to ship to." Although Friday's moved first into lower-cost European and Asian markets, Canadian expansion is "very important," Rich insists. "Canada has been more difficult to enter, perhaps as a by-product of investment conservatism and the political and economic environment over the past five years. But we intend to be the premium, full-service restaurant worldwide; from a marketing viewpoint, we need to be in Toronto, Montreal, and Vancouver."

Overland Park, Kansas-based Applebee's is also going global. The third-ranked U.S. dinner-house chain opened its first international unit on Winnipeg's Pembina Highway in July, followed by units in Curaçao and Amsterdam. Next summer, Applebee's Winnipeg franchisee, which owns and operates Pizza Huts and Arby's throughout Manitoba, plans to open another Applebee's in Northern Ontario. A franchisee also plans a unit for Thunder Bay.

"Central Canada is a preconditioned market, with spillover from our TV signals and visits to our restaurants in border cities," says Gil Simon, executive director of international franchise development. "People from Thunder Bay and Winnipeg go shopping in Minot, North Dakota, and Duluth, Minnesota. We realized Canadians liked our business, but we had no place in Canada to serve them." Seventy or 80 percent of Applebee's 505 units are free-standing with parking, adds Larry Bader, director of domestic franchise development. Located in neighborhoods rather than tourist areas, the 5,700-square-foot units seat 198 (196 in Winnipeg, due to local liquor laws) and serve "eclectic American" burgers, salads, quesadillas, and tenderloin riblets. "We're not a meet-market; we're family dining with a strong appeal to mature couples and families." In the United States, annual unit sales average U.S. $2.1 million. The average check is U.S. $8.25.

For Applebee's, Winnipeg is a "pure" test market. Says Simon: "If we tried to piggyback on our Michigan success in, say, Windsor, Ontario, I'm not sure it would tell us anything about how we're being received." Operationally, Canada also presented a test. "Our idea was to import everything until we were of sufficient critical mass to fabricate in Canada," Simon says. "But Ottawa didn't see it that way. We were at a disadvantage in that we had to find local sources in a hurry. In the end, it wasn't that difficult, because we're used to dealing with fifty sets of laws in the United States."

This foray provided other eye-openers. "Your employees' tenure is a lot longer, and the minimum wage is usually higher. But labor is about the same percentage of gross volume," Bader says. On the lighter side: "The plane ticket is really expensive from Kansas City to Canada. And there isn't any 'Canadian bacon'—that's what happens to pea-meal bacon when it gets to the States."

Operating in Canada since 1981, U.S. $235-million Red Robin has expanded aggressively since 1990. In four years, its B.C.-based franchisee and operating partner has increased the unit tally to sixteen in British

Columbia and Alberta, including a Vancouver unit opened in December. "Western Canada's economy and growth provided good opportunities," says Madison Jobe, Irvine, California-based vice president of franchising. "So far, Canada is the only other country we're operating in, and we aren't actively looking at other countries."

Ranked seventh in a segment led by Chili's, Red Robin operates 105 upscale, casual-dining restaurants in eighteen U.S. states. The 6,000- to 7,000-square-foot, mostly suburban units feature a full-service bar serving specialty drinks and "mocktails" and a seventy-five-item menu of gourmet sandwiches, salads, and pastas. Recently, top sellers included a grilled focaccia clubhouse and a citrus-marinated tuna melt on focaccia with chipotle mayonnaise (both U.S. $5.99). "The biggest evolution is the level of competition from Canadian and U.S. companies in Canada," says Jobe. "There was a slow start, particularly in Western Canada, but now there's East Side Mario's, Friday's, the Olive Garden and, of course, Earl's Tin Palace."

Inevitably, U.S. companies will lick their lips as they consider the Canadian market, and many will take a bite. But they won't gobble up the pie without interference: increasingly, U.S. companies say, their biggest challenge stems from concepts bred in Canada.

Case Study Source

Marianne Tefft, "Northern Exposure," *Foodservice and Hospitality* (January, 1995), 22-27.

Case Study Questions

1. Explain why market entry to Canada has been so challenging for U.S. food service companies.
2. Compare food service operations in Canada and the United States.
3. What segments of Canadian food service markets are attracting U.S. firms' attention?
4. Discuss Friday's strategic planning for its expansion development in Canada.
5. How did Applebee's test its concept and manage operations in Canada?
6. What will you predict for the future of Canadian food service markets for U.S. companies' expansion?

PART V:
FUTURE DEVELOPMENT
AND CAREER OPPORTUNITIES

Part V has one concluding chapter, Chapter 14, which focuses on future international hospitality development and potential career opportunities for hospitality management students. It discusses the prospects of the world travel and tourism industry in the twenty-first century, and examines the economic impact of the international hospitality industry. It identifies and analyzes the forces that will shape the future of the hospitality industry in the new millennium. Hands-on experience in international travel, overseas study, and work programs are discussed as practical learning resources. Influential hospitality professional associations are identified for student participation and as research resources. A discussion on the tripartite model for educating future global hospitality managers closes this text.

Chapter 14

Prospects and Opportunities

As we approach the twenty-first century, multinational American food service companies have ventured into each corner of the globe, and the roughly 160 companies that collectively operate units on every continent on earth have become important "unofficial" ambassadors for international exchange.[1]

Ralph O. Brennan
President, National Restaurant Association/USA, 1995-1996

LEARNING OBJECTIVES

In this chapter, you will study:

1. World tourism growth trends in the next century
2. Forces shaping the future of the international hospitality industry
3. Food service global expansion trends
4. The tripartite model for educating competent global managers
5. The importance of overseas living, working, and traveling experience
6. Internship opportunities and resources for research

INTRODUCTION

This concluding chapter examines future prospects of the international hospitality industry. International travel and tourism has become one of the largest industries in the world. As an integral part of this industry, the hospitality industry will respond to the rapid growth of international travel by expanding operations globally. This chapter analyzes the changes that will likely affect the industry over the next decade. It will focus on five major forces: (1) capacity control, (2) safety and security, (3) assets and capital, (4) technology, and (5) new management.[2] Understanding these five

353

forces will enable global hospitality managers to anticipate the likely changes within the international hospitality industry in the next decade.

Potential career opportunities in the global hospitality industry are outlined in this chapter. These opportunities can be found in overseas hotel management, overseas restaurant development and operations, and domestic operations focusing on international guests. It identifies educational and professional development opportunities in international hospitality management. Educational trade journals and research periodicals are introduced as research resources. A tripartite model is recommended for educating future global hospitality managers.

WORLD TOURISM IN THE TWENTY-FIRST CENTURY

Travel and tourism will become the world's largest industry in the twenty-first century. As political barriers to international travel are eliminated and economies of the developing countries are improving, global travel will continue to grow at a steady pace. Global travel patterns will also change and outbound tours from the emerging market countries will increase substantially. In the Western technologically advanced countries, tourism will continue to be the top leisure activity for escaping from the high-tech living and work environment. Global tourism growth will generate great economic impact worldwide.

According to a World Tourism Organization report, 1.6 billion tourists will be visiting foreign countries annually by the year 2020, spending more than $2 trillion per year.[3] These predictions represent nearly three times more international tourists than the 613 million recorded in 1997 and nearly five times more tourism spending, which reached $444 billion in 1997. Tourist arrivals are estimated to grow by an average of 4.3 percent per year in the next two decades, and receipts from international tourism will increase by 6.7 percent per year. Exhibit 14.1 shows the world's ten top tourism destinations predicted by the World Tourism Organization by the year 2020. It is interesting to note the emergence of new tourism destinations in the next century: China, Mexico, Russia, and the Czech Republic. These emerging destinations deserve international hospitality companies' close attention as potential new markets.

Another influential international tourism organization, the World Travel and Tourism Council, estimated that the economic impact created by the international tourism industry will be phenomenal in the next decade.[4] As Exhibit 14.2 shows, the world travel and tourism industry is expected to add 130 million jobs by 2006, and the industry will create one new job across the global economy every 2.4 seconds. The spending on investment

EXHIBIT 14.1. World Top Ten Destinations by 2020

Rank	Country	Tourist Arrivals (millions)	World Market Share (%)
1	China	137.2	8.6
2	United States	102.4	6.4
3	France	93.3	5.8
4	Spain	71.0	4.4
5	Hong Kong (SAR)	59.3	3.7
6	Italy	52.9	3.3
7	United Kingdom	52.8	3.3
8	Mexico	48.9	3.1
9	Russian Federation	47.1	2.9
10	Czech Republic	44.0	2.7
Total		708.8	44.2

Source: Adapted from World Tourism Organization, "Tourism 2020 Vision," *WTO Assembly Daily* (October 23, 1997), 1.

EXHIBIT 14.2. Estimates of Travel and Tourism's Economic Impact on World Development by 2006

Economic Activities	Estimates by 2006
Jobs	385 million
Jobs (% of world total)	11.1%
Economic Output	$7.1 trillion
Gross Domestic Product	11.5%
Investment	$1.6 trillion
Service Exports	$1.5 trillion
Total Government Taxes	$1.3 trillion

Source: World Travel and Tourism Council, "Travel and Tourism Economic Impact: 1996-2006," *WTTC Special Report* (March, 1996), 1.

by the world travel and tourism industry is estimated to be more than doubled from $766 billion in 1996 to $1.6 trillion in 2006. A substantial part of the investment increase will be attributed to the rapid expansion of the global hospitality industry in the areas of building new hotels and restaurants in foreign countries. Responding to the rapid growth of international travel, the global hospitality industry will accelerate development to meet travel demands. Strategic development is being carried out by international hotel corporations in Latin America, the Middle East, Southeast Asia, and Eastern Europe. Global development of the hotel industry will continue to have significant impact on the world economy.[5]

FORCES SHAPING THE HOTEL INDUSTRY'S FUTURE

Growth is inevitable in the global hospitality industry. However, the industry is subject to changes in the international environment. Political, economic, and technological changes can have a great impact on the development and management of global hospitality operations, and these forces will shape the future of the industry. Understanding these forces will enable global hospitality managers to anticipate changes in the twenty-first century.

A study conducted by Michael Olsen, a leading scholar on international hospitality strategic development, and released by the International Hotel & Restaurant Association, identified five major forces that are driving changes in the hospitality industry well into the next decade. These five forces are: capacity control, safety and security, assets and capital, technology, and new management.[6] Based on this report, these five forces are discussed in the following section.

Capacity Control

Capacity refers to the inventory of hotel products, that is, the supply of products and services. Traditionally, the sale of room inventories is controlled by hospitality operators through taking reservations or receiving guests who walk into the hotel for lodging accommodations. Therefore, hoteliers have direct control over the sales and distribution of hotel rooms.

However, as discussed in Chapter 12, the emergence of electronic information technology exerts great influence on who will control inventory. The development of electronic reservation systems enables individual travelers to directly reserve hotel rooms from anyplace in the world at any time. Such access to capacity can be provided either by hotel central reservation systems or third parties such as the major Internet access providers. The competition for controlling hospitality product inventories has been intensified by such technological development. Some hospitality and travel companies have identified the trend and have begun to develop cooperation with the major companies that organize information flow on the Internet. For instance, American Express Travel Services formed a strategic alliance with America Online to allow travelers to make reservations anywhere in the world from their personal computers.[7] Another example is the growing popularity of TravelWeb, the electronic booking of hotel rooms worldwide on the Internet. TravelWeb, created by Pegasus Systems Inc., which also operates THISCO and Pegasus Commission Processing as discussed in Chapter 12, has established its niche as one of the largest interactive sites in which consumers can freely research and reserve hotel rooms around the world. As a "one-stop" travel site for both the leisure and business traveler, it connects to approximately 25,000 hotels in 165 countries via the THISCO service, and enables travelers to directly access hotel central reservation systems to check room rates, features and availability, and to make reservations (see Exhibit 14.3).

Another major factor that influences hospitality firms' decisions to seek alliances with information providers is increasing labor costs in North America and Western Europe. Low-cost labor has been shrinking in most industrialized nations. Per-unit cost for hospitality employee has thus been rising. As guests' demands for higher levels of service increase on a global basis, hospitality firms have to balance the two aspects: cost cutting and guest satisfaction. Many hospitality corporations have gone through considerable restructuring in recent years, and one of the strategies is to outsource tasks that have previously been performed in-house. Therefore, many companies have evaluated their central reservation systems and analyzed the cost/benefit objectives as they seek to reduce cost. Hospitality companies have to be more skillful in evaluating the cost/benefit relationship of their reservation systems, and balance that against the economies to be gained by outsourcing this service to a third party. This issue will be a very important decision area regarding the control of hospitality product inventory.

Safety and Security

As discussed in Chapter 4, travelers' choice of destinations is greatly influenced by safety and security issues. Travel safety and security issues can be analyzed from both a macro and micro perspective. At the macro level, the most significant concern is the impact of terrorism on international travel and tourism. A random act of violence can severely curtail tourism and hospitality operations for a short term in the targeted properties or destinations. Hospitality operators must constantly monitor

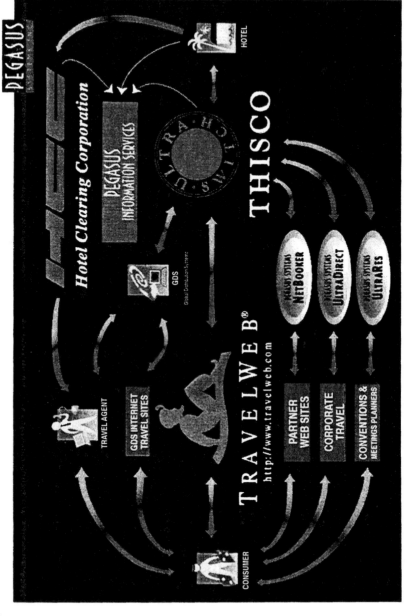

the situation to protect guests and employees. As more hotel companies expand into emerging market countries and developing countries, they have to consider providing safety and security to the guests as a high priority in hotels located in regions where terrorist groups are active. Hotels must be considered a safe haven and the management is responsible for creating such an environment.

Another major safety issue is health concerns. Potential tourists are increasingly concerned with the spread of AIDS and Hepatitis B in many parts of the world. There is also the growing concern over environmental problems, such as air and water pollution. While many global organizations are working hard to meet the challenges of these health issues, it can be expected that hospitality operators will be required to do the same.

The last macro concern is the stability of the host government. As analyzed in Chapter 4, the ability of government to maintain internal peace and protection of foreign business interests is based on the stability of the host governments over time. Instability is often caused by internal conflict, sovereignty disputes, or economic crises. These political events can devastate travel and hospitality operations. The stability of the host governments must always be carefully evaluated as hospitality firms consider expansion into certain countries for development and operations.

At the micro level, guests' concerns must be handled by individual hotels. Safety and health issues directly affect tourists' perceptions of destinations and their selection of travel destinations and properties. The safety concerns must be addressed by improving room and property security. The increasing concern over environmental pollution and degradation is now addressed by hospitality firms' commitment to ecologically sound lodging development, such as the examples illustrated in Chapter 7. As for health concerns, hotel management must take effective measures in food and water handling, employee hygiene, keeping the grounds clean, and properly handling waste disposal. Guest safety must always be the priority of hotel management operations.

Assets and Capital

The explosive economic development in the emerging market countries has generated tremendous demand for capital funds. International companies compete aggressively for whatever capital is available. This competition will result in new higher level demands on business to obtain the most productive use of their assets. Therefore, hospitality companies have to compete not only with direct competitors for capital, but also with other businesses, such as real estate development, office rentals, and so on.

This phenomenon of too many firms chasing limited capital is called the rationing of private capital. Whether in developed countries or in emerging market countries, this rationing will result in investment funds being attracted to the most productive assets. As Nitz Ward, vice president of international development for Marriott International, explained at the 1996 World Bank Annual Meeting, the typical payback period for hotel investment is around fifteen years, but the payback period for office building development is much shorter. Therefore, commercial banks prefer lending money to office building developers. Hotel developers often find it very difficult to raise capital in the international financial markets. That's why Hilton Hotel in Hong Kong was converted to a commercial office building before the management lease was over.[8] The rationing of private capital clearly puts great pressure on a firm's asset performance. Capital funds are normally given to those who can generate higher returns.

In the public sector, governments and other public funding agencies adopt a similar approach to rationing funds. Limited funds are often deployed to develop basic infrastructure needs in developing countries and to upgrade aging infrastructure in developed countries. Hospitality firms now must be creative in planning projects to obtain possible funding from public sources. Development projects need to be integrated with the overall infrastructure and sustainable development.

Hospitality managers are therefore pressured to cut costs, increase sales, and generate higher returns. Particularly if the hospitality firm is publicly held, both individual and institutional investors do not tolerate management that is incompetent to achieve the maximum value for the investors. Global hospitality managers must have the competencies to use the assets most productively.

Technology

Technology is the driving force that shapes the way firms conduct business globally. It will give hospitality firms significant competitive advantage in information management, customer services, hotel designs, creating alternatives to present products and services, and marketing promotions. As discussed earlier, capacity control through the Internet can be accessed by individual travelers around the world. Skillful use of technology can significantly reduce higher labor costs, since the hospitality industry is highly labor and capital intensive.

Technology is now widely used in hospitality management. Computer-based technology is applied in management information and decision support systems, such as property management, yield management, database marketing, and management accounting systems. These applications of computer technology improve management decisions that lead to increased efficiency and effectiveness.

Technology is also applied to the area of guest service support. Automated registration and checkout devices are now commonly used in commercial hotels catering to business travelers. Room and hallway safety, room climate, and communication devices are all in various stages of development and utilization. Another major area of application is the development of an electronic concierge to provide current and accurate travel information to the guests. Such information can be displayed on the TV screen and the guests can select from the menu to check the local weather, find restaurants, choose attractions, and even print out a tour map. The utilization of technology in guest service support can enhance service efficiency and provide considerable competitive advantage.

Technology is now widely used in designing and creating the so-called smart hotel room, which is designed to satisfy every need of the guest. Systems are designed to control temperature, air purity, lights, and sound. These functions are controlled by computer sensors that provide maximum guest comfort at minimum cost. Communication ports in guest rooms are essential now for connecting international business travelers to the outside world. Hotel companies that offer such amenities and provide room design adjustments for the business information needs of the guest will have significant competitive advantage in attracting international business travelers.

Future global hospitality managers must be competent in handling hotel technology. As technology is shaping the daily lives of all individuals, they will expect their new lifestyle patterns to be complemented wherever they may travel. Therefore, hospitality firms need to enhance tourists' travel experience by investing in technology development, both in hardware and software—and managers who are technologically competent.

New Management

As rapid economic and technological changes continue to evolve, future global managers must be able to understand and handle the speed of change. To accomplish this very important task, managers must become boundary spanners who are competent in scanning the business environment to assess patterns of change that will create threats and opportunities. Managers thus have to balance their time between daily operations and scanning the business environment in order to incorporate important trends into daily operating decisions. This scanning role requires managers to think analytically to identify events likely to affect the company, assess the quality of information, and estimate the likelihood of their occurrence and impact upon business. Thus, managers can synthesize a large amount of information from different sources through critical analysis.

To develop these thinking skills, managers need to comprehend and integrate knowledge regarding the standard functional areas of hospitality management, such as finance, human resources, marketing, and food and beverage operations. Changes in the external environment that affect each functional area need to be diligently observed. Thus, managers can effectively address their competencies in each area. "In short, the manager of tomorrow will be expected to be a more competent professional who can balance craft skills necessary to deliver outstanding service with conceptual skills that will ensure a strong strategic position in the competitive marketplace for years to come. More forward thinking, human sensitive abilities will be required in order to obtain more productivity from each employee as a growing worldwide labor shortage appears on the horizon for this industry. The challenge for multinationals will be to move on from giving lip service to these needs to actually incorporating them into their competitive methods of the future."[9]

FOOD SERVICE EXPANSION

The above-mentioned forces of change also influence to varying degrees the global expansion and operation of the food service industry. U.S. food service firms will continue to take advantage of business opportunities around the world. The 1996 Survey of International Restaurant Operations conducted by the National Restaurant Association found that most U.S. food service companies have operations in Central America and the Caribbean region, followed by Japan, South Korea, other Asian countries, North Africa, the Middle East, and Western Europe.[10] The 1995 survey of U.S.-based food service companies revealed that 45 percent of the respondents agreed that the Pacific Rim and Southeast Asia are potentially lucrative regions for foreign expansion (see Exhibit 14.4). Favorable macroeconomic conditions in most of the countries in the region, such as high growth in gross domestic product, contribute to the excitement.

Sixteen percent of respondents identified Europe as the next major international market for expansion. Stable political systems and moderately good economic conditions are the main reasons for this choice. Mexico and the Middle East each captured 10 percent of all respondents' choices. Mexico remains a popular market for U.S. multinational firms' expansion, not just because of its current economic condition but because of its close proximity to the United States and because of Mexican consumers' familiarity with American food. The Middle East is attractive because of its relatively high standards of living and relatively high disposable personal income.

EXHIBIT 14.4. Regions for Potential Global Food Service Expansion by U.S.-Based Firms

Regions	Percentage of Respondents
Central America/Caribbean	2
South America	8
Canada	9
Middle East	10
Mexico	10
Europe	16
Asia/Pacific Rim	45

Source: National Restaurant Association, "International Food-Service Survey" (Washington, DC, 1995).

The survey showed that 9 percent of the food service firms chose Canada, with 8 percent for South America and 2 percent for Central America and the Caribbean region. The food service industry is relatively highly developed in Canada (see the case study in Chapter 13). U.S. companies face stiff competition from Canadian firms and American firms already operating there. Expansion in South America, Central America, and the Caribbean region is still hindered by concerns over high inflation, high real estate prices, and political instability.

Many foreign food service firms are also aggressively expanding in the United States. Due to cultural diversity, Americans enjoy a wide variety of ethnic cuisine and dining out is perceived as a cultural experience. Chi-Chi's Mexican restaurants are a well-known operation in the United States. Many Japanese restaurants entered the U.S. market during the 1980s and the early 1990s. Dosanko, a Chinese noodle shop operator, opened in New York in the early 1980s. Yoshinoya, originally offering a low-price rice menu, now has more than 100 stores in the United States.[11] Japanese food service firms have also entered the Asian market, particularly the Southeast Asia market.

Regional cuisine is also introduced in hotel restaurants operated by international hospitality companies. For instance, authentic Japanese cuisine is offered at Nikko Hotels. It is a strategic consideration to expand food service operations through global hotel development. Banquet and group business constitute a major portion of hotel revenues in many countries, such as in Japan.[12] Clearly, the global marketplace is creating demand for food service development. Products and tastes are now freely exchanged between countries and continents. Such exchanges not only generate business opportunities, but also introduce new cultural elements into the host society.

THE GLOBAL HOSPITALITY MANAGER

Global expansion of hospitality operations has increasingly become a strategic development for many firms. The rapid global development has created a demand from the hospitality industry for competent and qualified global managers. How can one become a competent global manager? One needs to be proficient in management skills and an effective leader in managing cultural diversity. The technical management skills and the people-oriented skills are equally important qualifications one must demonstrate for overseas operations. In essence, the education of future global managers requires a transdisciplinary approach.

One study on global hospitality management education has suggested a tripartite approach for educating global hospitality managers. The tripartite approach consists of three complex components: geographic, sociocultural, and business dimensions of international hospitality markets.[13] These three components are not mutually exclusive because they are not isolated variables in the international hospitality network. They are intermeshed aspects of internationalization and represent the intricacy of the international business environment. Knowledge and understanding of one component will help enhance understanding of other components.

The organization of this textbook attempts to follow this transdisciplinary pedagogical framework and offer a broad-context education for future global hospitality managers. Students who are interested in pursuing a career in global hospitality management also need to learn the three components of knowledge through hands-on working, traveling, or living experience in foreign countries. Many international hospitality firms will recruit candidates who have extensive overseas working or traveling experience, in addition to excellent academic performance and work experience at home. That is why many international hospitality firms like to recruit foreign students and send them back to their home countries to work after graduation.

Today, it is not difficult to obtain hands-on experience through travel and study-abroad programs. But overseas work experience may be difficult to gain due to foreign governments' restrictions on working visa applications. However, some international hotel firms such as Club Med and Pacific Resort Club offer internships to hospitality management students. These internship opportunities give students insight into international hotel operations and help students decide if this is the right career choice for them.

Many hospitality management programs offer study-abroad programs to enhance students' international travel and living experience. Some schools have also developed joint bachelor's and master's degrees in international hospitality management, such as the joint program between the University of Massachusetts and Hotel Consult SHCC College in Brig, Switzerland, and the master's degree program between Cornell University and the Institute de Management Hotelier International/École Supérieure des Sciences Economiques et Commercials (IMHI/ESSEC) in Paris.[14]

Many international, regional, and national hospitality professional associations provide information on international education, training, research, internship, and career opportunities for the members. The global hotel and food service industry is represented by the International Hotel and Restaurant Association (IHRA). Based in Paris, the IHRA has a global role in representing, protecting, promoting, and informing the industry. It represents over 300,000 establishments in 147 countries, including independent hotels, international chains, national associations, and more than 130 educational institutions around the world. The official international journal published by the IHRA, *Hotels,* is the most influential trade publication on international hotel development and management. The IHRA publishes an annual *International Hotel Guide* that lists all members around the world. The three periodic newsletters published by the IHRA, *Action, Impact,* and *The InnDEPENDENT,* provide updates on global development trends and issues concerning both international chains and independent hoteliers.

At the regional and national levels, the Caribbean Hotel Association promotes the entire region as a major international tourism destination and recruits hospitality management graduates from the United States, Canada, and Europe. In the United States, the well-established American Hotel and Motel Association provides students with the most current information on international hospitality development through its several management journals.

The food service professional associations also provide education, research, and career opportunities to their members and the public through membership affiliations and various association publications. Students can follow international hospitality development trends closely by reading these trade journals and various reports on international food service operations. The National Restaurant Association in the United States is a very influential trade association that represents the entire food service industry. It closely monitors current international expansions and identifies new development trends through the survey of international restaurant operations. It offers timely research results for food service companies that are considering entering a foreign market. Similar food service professional associations can be found in many other countries and regions.

Hotels has organized a prestigious club for global hotel managers: the Global Hotelier Club. One of the qualifications for joining this club is that you must have served in hotel management on three different continents. This club provides a forum for global hotel management professionals to share their work and living experience and exchange management experience in different countries. Their perspectives and experience are periodically published in *Hotels,* and Exhibit 14.5 presents comments on operational challenges by two global hotel managers. The challenges they presented are all covered in the text. It would be practical for global food service managers also to form a club and share their perspectives and experience on international operations.

GOING INTERNATIONAL

This textbook has led you through the complicated aspects of hospitality development and operations in an international context. As the global tourism industry continues to grow in the twenty-first century, the hospitality industry will follow international tourists wherever they travel to serve their needs and wants. Therefore, the hospitality industry will speed up its global expansion to meet travel demand in the next century. This increased global expansion of the hospitality industry creates a demand for competent global managers to manage overseas operations. Opportunities abound for those who are interested in international operations. There is great potential for career development, advancement, and personal growth in international hospitality management. This textbook serves as a useful academic guide that leads you into the challenging and exciting field of international hospitality management.

SUMMARY

- The growth of the world travel and tourism industry will be phenomenal in the next century. Substantial spending on investment by the world travel and tourism industry will be in the areas of building new hotels and restaurants.
- The driving forces that shape the future of the international hotel industry include: capacity control, safety and security, assets and capital, technology, and new management.

EXHIBIT 14.5. Comments on Operational Challenges by Two Managers

---

Carlos Franca, General Manager, The Royal Palm Plaza Hotel and Racquet Club, Campinas, Brazil

"Our greatest operational challenge is dealing with taxes. This is a matter we cannot control—we just have to pay the bills. Solutions are not really creative, and sometimes awkward. One way to go is to delay tax payments, then wait for a partial exemption or negotiate the fines or interest rates. You might end up paying 20 percent to 30 percent less than if the tax was paid when due.

"Brazil also will hold federal elections in 1998, with a national vote for the presidency and state votes for governors and senators. If President Cardoso is reelected, this will assure economic stability and, subsequently, additional investment from both foreign and local sources. Our industry will be positively affected, as tourism and hotels have been a great investment target of pension funds and private enterprise.

"Near Campinas, expansion of the international airport at Viracopos and construction of Great Adventure, a theme park, also should bring more visitors to the region, increasing business at our hotel."

Philippe Attia, Director of Activities, Wyndham Sugar Bay Beach Club and Resort, St. Thomas, U.S. Virgin Islands

"Our greatest operational challenges are hiring qualified employees and managers and reducing labor costs, particularly the high hourly rate for front-line employees. The creation of a hospitality or tourism school in the area, perhaps in Puerto Rico, could be a solution.

"Legislation under consideration that positively impacts the hotel industry here is the legislation of hotel casino gaming. A decision is expected within two years.

"As for infrastructure, an increase in the number of direct flights from the northeast United States to St. Thomas would help. For example, add a charter from New York's JFK or La Guardia airports during the high seasons."

Source: Steven Shundich, "Politics, Labor Concern Hoteliers," *Hotels* (October, 1997), 52. Reprinted by permission of *Hotels* magazine, a publication of Cahners Business Information.

- The development of information technology exerts great influence upon who will control hotel product inventories. Many hospitality firms seek alliances with information providers to provide greater access to international consumers.
- Safety and security issues can be analyzed at both macro and micro levels. Terrorism, health, and the stability of the host government are macro safety and security issues. At the micro level, travelers' safety and security concerns must be handled at each individual hotel.
- The phenomenon of too many hospitality firms chasing limited capital is known as the rationing of private capital. This rationing of private capital exerts great pressure on global managers to manage assets most productively.
- Technology will give hospitality firms significant competitive advantage in information management, customer service, hotel design, creating alternatives to present products and services, and marketing promotions.
- Future global managers must be able to understand and handle the speed of change. They must become boundary spanners who are competent in scanning the business environment to assess patterns of change.
- Future global managers have to balance the time between daily operations and scanning the business environment in order to incorporate important trends into daily operating decisions.
- U.S. food service companies will continue to take advantage of business opportunities in Asia, Europe, and the Middle East. The Pacific Rim and Southeast Asia are identified as lucrative regions for rapid expansion.
- The education of future global managers requires a transdisciplinary approach. The tripartite model emphasizes the geographic, sociocultural, and business dimensions of international hospitality markets.
- International working, living, and traveling experience can be gained through internships with international hospitality companies, study-abroad programs offered by many hospitality management schools, or joint degree programs.
- Hospitality professional associations provide useful information on current development trends, management issues, internship and scholarship opportunities, and research resources.
- Global hotel managers who have served in hotel management on three continents can join the Global Hotelier Club, in which they share management experience.

• Career opportunities abound for students who are interested in international hospitality management.

STUDY QUESTIONS

1. What are the predictions of the World Tourism Organization for international travel in the next century?
2. What are the top ten tourism destinations by 2020? What opportunities can these destinations present to international hospitality firms?
3. According to World Travel and Tourism Council estimates, what economic impact will the international travel and tourism industry have on the world economy?
4. Discuss the impact of the international hotel industry on the world economy.
5. Identify and discuss the five factors that will shape the international industry in the twenty-first century.
6. In what ways can electronic information technology influence the capacity control of hotel products?
7. Why do some hospitality firms seek alliances with information providers?
8. What safety and security issues can you identify at both macro and micro levels?
9. What is the rationing of private capital?
10. Why do global managers feel pressure to use assets most productively?
11. How is technology used in hotel operations?
12. Define the concept of a boundary spanner.
13. What regions have been identified by U.S. food service companies as potential markets for future expansions?
14. Do you know any foreign food service companies developing restaurant businesses in the United States?
15. Explain the tripartite approach for educating competent global hospitality managers.
16. How can you gain hands-on experience in international hospitality operations?
17. What functions does the International Hotel & Restaurant Association serve?
18. Who can join the Global Hotelier Club and what is the function of this professional club?

CASE STUDY: MIDDLE EAST MOMENTUM

Despite headline-grabbing news and surprises—such as recent peace talks between Israel and Palestine and periodic terrorist incidents—progress should continue for hotel development along with the general economic growth in much of the Middle East. "The occasional ghastly thing—whether it's suicide bombs in Israel or the machine-gunning of a busload of tourists in Cairo—ultimately doesn't affect the long-term picture," said Laurence Geller, chairman of the international hospitality consulting firm Geller & Co., Chicago. "Economics plays a much more important role."

Eric Pfeffer, chairman and CEO of Cendant Hotels Division, Parsippany, NJ, noted that deals usually move forward despite changes that may occur in government. "With Benjamin Netanyahu now Israel's prime minister, the peace process may take a different path at a slower pace. But it won't retreat," Pfeffer said. "Everyone can see Israel's strong economy as evidence of what peace can do."

In fact, Geller said, there are a number of hotel-building issues in Israel that have almost nothing to do with the peace process. For instance, Eilat, located at Israel's southernmost tip, continues to be extremely popular among Europeans no matter what the political climate in Israel happens to be. "Nothing stops Germans who suffer from sciatica from traveling to Eilat to let the desert sun bring them relief," Geller said. "One key reason is that government insurance pays for this therapy."

Geller said the Israeli government is concerned about the cash outflow from citizens who take junkets to Turkey to gamble because they can't gamble at home. He said he expects that at some point the government will lift the gaming ban in order to keep those revenues in-country. And Eilat could be where casinos appear.

Geller said that the Israeli government has a very aggressive hotel development program. Depending on the geographic region, benefits range from low interest rates to outright subsidies. He also said there is a significant undersupply at the budget and motel end. "To date, there hasn't been a real effort to develop limited-service properties in Israel," Geller said.

Pfeffer said Cendant is trying to remedy that situation. His firm entered into an agreement to place Howard Johnson properties in such cities as Tiberias, Eilat, and Jerusalem. The same cities also will be home to three- and four-star Days Inns.

Geller said he feels Jordan is also very receptive to hotel construction. "They are aggressively soliciting deals for properties in Amman, Aqaba, and Petra," he said. Along with five-star properties, Geller said he sees the development of "tourist hotels along the lines of a Hampton Inn or Marriott Courtyard" in Aqaba and Petra.

Geller said he expects Beirut, Lebanon, to be another market that will see ongoing development. Despite the U.S. government's advisory to U.S. travelers to avoid Lebanon, Geller said, "There's a Marriott being built there, and a large number of proposed mixed-use projects, each of which includes a hotel." Geller predicted that some growth will occur in Egypt. But, he added, investors have become worried about the possibility of Muslim fundamentalists taking over the government.

Should this happen, he said, casinos could be forced to close and tight liquor-law restrictions would likely occur. Ultimately, a fundamentalist-led state would mean the end of what has been an oasis for residents of stricter Muslim countries. And all of this could crush, or at least severely hamper, regional as well as international tourism.

Unlike the caution and concern looming over Egypt's future, Dubai, in the United Arab Emirates, is one Middle East market where there appears to be little standing in the way of massive development. The most liberal and open of the seven United Arab Emirates, Dubai has long been a major commercial, distribution, and transportation hub—and in 1998, it became home to the world's tallest hotel building.

The futuristic Chicago Beach Resort includes three components: a 600-room, five-star resort hotel; a water theme park (reputedly the first in the Middle East) and adjoining villas; and the 1,000-plus-foot-high Chicago Beach Tower featuring 200 suites. The tower sits offshore, accessible by bridge, boat, and helicopter.

Other Dubai projects included the opening of Sheraton's 245-room Four Points Dubai (the first Four Points Hotel to open outside the Americas); the opening of a 257-room SAS Radisson hotel on the beachfront; the 350-room Mercure; the 154-room Holiday Inn; and the 110-room Howard Johnson Hotel in the past five years.

A second venture, a Howard Johnson Plaza Hotel, opened at the end of 1996. Pfeffer said he expects this to spark further development of other UAE properties and that he expects real growth to emerge once potential investors visit and experience functioning properties. "Once you penetrate a market, the phones start to ring," he said. "Once an international flag is in place, competing independent properties immediately appreciate the need to also have an international tie."

Pfeffer said the time is right for developing midmarket properties throughout the Middle East. "Right now, the social middle class is emerging like never before," he said. "The demand is particularly there from travelers who can't afford five-star [hotels], but who require comfortable accommodations. I see a real growing market that meets the needs of technicians and regional managers, not just company presidents."

Pfeffer said he expects more properties to arise outside of expensive Middle East downtowns. Lower land costs make lower rates possible. Particularly in a location such as Dubai, with its excellent roads and other infrastructure, moderately priced hotels beyond the city center make sense.

"The Middle East has much to offer," Raymond Chigot, vice president for corporate development, Hilton International, said, "particularly when you realize that five to ten years ago there was very little tourism in much of this part of the world." Chigot said he feels strongly that today's barriers are tomorrow's opportunities.

Major growth areas he mentioned are Dubai City and Abu Dhabi. Hilton currently has two hotels in both locations and is building third properties in each. Also, even though terrorist incidents and political strife are always possible in Egypt, Chigot is certain it still has plenty of profit-making potential. "We have nine hotels there at present with more than 7,000 bedrooms. And yet Cairo has one of the highest hotel occupancies," he said. One factor he emphasized is the country's extraordinary ability to absorb seemingly unabsorbable events, and move on at its own pace.

"It seems that every five years there is a coup, and then, three weeks later, everyone has forgotten about it. Politics comes and goes, but Egypt's incredible attractions remain," he said. Hilton International recently opened an 800-room hotel in Mecca, 440 rooms in Jeddah, and a 450-room hotel in Medina. Other Hilton projects are underway in Amman, Jordan (260 rooms), Cairo (150 rooms), Aswan (350 rooms), Hurghada (180 rooms), Beirut (430 rooms), Jerusalem (340 rooms), and Haifa (380 rooms).

Holiday Inn reported that it had ten hotels on site by the end of 1997. It is now the largest international chain represented in Israel. Current projects include a 250-room property in Eilat, the Holiday Inn Crowne Plaza Dead Sea, Holiday Inn Haifa, and a 100-room Holiday Inn in Nahariya.

Hyatt International completed its 578-room Hyatt Regency Dead Sea Resort & Spa in September 1996. Other projects include a 425-room hotel in Sharm El Sheikh, Egypt, the 400-room Grand Hyatt Tel Aviv, and the 311-room Grand Hyatt Amman.

Inter-Continental developed several hotels in the region in the past few years, including the 700-room Hurghada Forum Resort, the 94-room Le Vendome Inter-Continental Beirut, the 272-room Sharm El Sheikh Inter-Continental Resort & Casino, the 320-room Hotel Inter-Continental Luxor, 600-room Phoenicia Inter-Continental Beirut, and 200-room Forum Hotel Beirut.

Marriott opened two new properties in the region in the spring of 1996—the 212-room Sharm El Sheikh Marriott Resort in Egypt and the 174-room Beirut Marriott.

Case Study Source

Adapted and updated from Robert Selwitz, "Middle East Momentum," *Hotel & Motel Management* (July 3, 1996), 20-21, 25.

Case Study Questions

1. How did the industry experts view the future prospects of hospitality development in the Middle East region?
2. Why is Eilat in Israel such a popular destination for European tourists?
3. What segment of the hotel market is at present underdeveloped in Israel?
4. What is the Jordanian government's attitude toward hotel construction in their country?
5. What is the major political concern for hotel development in Egypt?
6. Why were international hospitality firms attracted to Dubai in the United Arab Emirates for hotel development?
7. Explain the statement made by Eric Pfeffer: "Once an international flag is in place, competing independent properties immediately appreciate the need to also have an international tie."
8. Describe the current development race among the major international hotel chains in the Middle East.

Notes

Chapter 1

1. Peter F. Drucker, *Managing in a Time of Great Change* (New York: Truman Talley Books/Dutton, 1995), p. 144.

2. John D. Daniels and Lee H. Radebaugh, *International Business: Environments and Operations*, Updated Sixth Edition (Reading, MA: Addison-Wesley Publishing Company, 1994), pp. 10-12.

3. John H. Dunning and Sumit K. Kundu, "The Internationalization of the Hotel Industry—Some New Findings from a Field Study," *Management International Review* (Number 2, 1995):101-133.

4. J.J. Boddewyn, M.B. Halbrich, and A.C. Perry, "Service Multinationals: Conceptualization, Measurements and Theory," *Journal of International Business Studies* (Number 3, 1986):41-57.

5. Bertil Ohlin, *Interregional and International Trade* (Cambridge, MA: Harvard University Press, 1935), pp. 12-20.

6. World Tourism Organization, *Technical Handbook on the Collection and Presentation of Domestic and International Tourism Statistics* (Madrid: World Tourism Organization, 1981).

7. Donald Lungberg, *The Hotel and Restaurant Business* (New York: Van Nostrand Reinhold, 1989), pp. 24-25.

8. David Mondey, "Aviation," in *Transportation Through the Ages*, ed. G.N. Georgano (New York: McGraw-Hill Book Company, 1972), p. 225.

9. Ibid., p. 232.

10. Ibid., p. 250.

11. J.B. Snell, "Land Transportation," in *Transportation Through the Ages*, ed. G.N. Georgano (New York: McGraw-Hill Book Company, 1972), p. 79.

12. Donald Macintyre, "Ships," in *Transportation Through the Ages*, ed. G.N. Georgano (New York: McGraw-Hill Book Company, 1972), p. 163.

13. Ibid., p. 166.

14. Somerset R. Waters, *Travel Industry World Yearbook: The Big Picture* (Rye, NY: Child and Waters, Inc., 1997), pp. 162-165.

15. John H. Dunning and Matthew McQueen, "The Eclectic Theory of International Production: A Case Study of the Hotel Industry," *Management and Decision Economics* (Number 4, 1981):197-210.

16. Frank M. Go, Philip Goulding, and David Litteljohn, "The International Hospitality Industry and Public Policy," in *International Hospitality Manage-*

ment: Corporate Strategy in Practice, eds. Richard Teare and Michael Olsen (New York: John Wiley and Sons, 1992), pp. 36-66.

17. Ibid., p. 67.

18. M. Chase Burritt, "Japanese Investment in U.S. Hotels and Resorts," *The Cornell Hotel and Restaurant Administration Quarterly* (October, 1991):60-66.

19. *World Trade,* "1993 International Franchise Directory," (Number 7, 1993): 58-66.

20. Eliza Tse and Joseph J. West, "Development Strategies for International Hospitality Markets," in *International Hospitality Management: Corporate Strategy in Practice*, eds. Richard Teare and Michael Olsen (New York: John Wiley and Sons, 1992), pp. 118-134.

Chapter 2

1. "Carlson Hospitality Worldwide Expands Aggressively," *Hotels* (November, 1995):59-60.

2. Arthur N. Strahler and Alan H. Strahler, *Elements of Physical Geography,* Second Edition (New York: John Wiley and Sons, 1979), p. 13.

3. Ibid., p. 13.

4. Arnie Weissmann, *Travel Geography and Destinations*, Fourth Edition (Austin, TX: Weissmann Travel Reports, 1993), p. 6.

5. Ibid., p. 6.

6. Koichi Satow, "Hotel Okura," Special Japan Advertising Supplement, *Forbes* (March 27, 1995):S-52.

7. Lloyd E. Hudman and Richard H. Jackson, *Geography of Travel and Tourism* (Albany, NY: Delmar Publishers Inc., 1990), p. 5.

8. Ibid., p. 7.

9. Terry G. Jordan and Lester Rowntree, *The Human Mosaic: A Thematic Introduction to Cultural Geography*, Fifth Edition (New York: Harper and Row Publishers, 1990), p. 7.

10. Donald A. Ball and Wendell H. McCulloch, Jr., *International Business: Introduction and Essentials*, Fifth Edition (Burr Ridge, IL: Irwin, 1993), pp. 142-145.

11. Mark V. Lomanno, "Examining Worldwide Trends," *Hotel and Motel Management* (December 11, 1995):15.

12. Tony Dela Cruz, "Global Optimism Tempered by Regional Crises," *Hotels* (January, 1998):48-52.

13. Jeff Weinstein, "Inter-Continental Sells Muscle," *Hotels* (August, 1995):18.

14. Frances Martin, "Hotels Giants: Corporate 20," *Hotels* (July, 1995):35-36.

15. Allen F. Richardson, "Marriott Eyes Global Growth Options," *USA Today* (March 11, 1996):8B.

16. "Court OKs Use of 'Conrad' Name," *Hotel and Motel Management* (November 20, 1995):1, 54.

17. David Belman, "International Expansion: Exporting the American Experience," *Restaurant USA* (Number 10, 1995):26-31.

18. "Friday's Turns 30 and Reaches $1 Billion Mark," *Hotels* (November, 1995):66-67.

19. John Rossant, Douglas Harbrecht, and Ronald Grover, "How Disney Snared a Princely Sum," *Business Week* (June 20, 1994):61-62.

20. Edward Watkins, "The Hotelier as Revolutionary," *Lodging Hospitality* (May, 1995):18-21.

Chapter 3

1. James Harper, "What Struck My Fancy," *Hotels* (January, 1993):11.

2. I. Brady and B. Isaac, *A Reader in Cultural Change*, Vol. 1 (Cambridge, MA: Schenkman Publishing, 1975), p. x.

3. Edward T. Hall, *Beyond Culture* (Garden City, NY: Doubleday, 1977), p. 16.

4. Charles W.L. Hill, *International Business: Competing in the Global Marketplace* (Burr Ridge, IL: Irwin, 1994), pp. 71-72.

5. John D. Daniels and Lee H. Radebaugh, *International Business: Environments and Operations*, Sixth Edition (Reading, MA: Addison-Wesley Publishing Company, 1994), p. 91.

6. Philip R. Harris and Robert T. Moran, *Managing Cultural Differences*, Third Edition (Houston: Gulf Publishing Company, 1991), pp. 399, 517.

7. Ibid., p. 506.

8. Helen Deresky, *Managing Across Borders and Cultures* (New York: Harper-Collins College Publishers, 1994), p. 80.

9. Donald A. Ball and Wendell H. McCulloch, *International Business: Introduction and Essentials,* Fifth Edition (Burr Ridge, IL: Irwin, 1993), p. 325.

10. Harry C. Triandis, "Dimensions of Cultural Variation as Parameters of Organizational Theories," *International Studies of Management and Organization* (Winter, 1982-1983):143-144.

11. Charles W.L. Hill, *International Business: Competing in the Global Marketplace* (Burr Ridge, IL: Irwin, 1994), pp. 74-75.

12. Geert Hofstede, "The Cultural Relativity of Organizational Practices and Theories," *Journal of International Business Studies* (Fall, 1983):75-89.

13. Fons Trompenaars, *Riding the Waves of Culture: Understanding Diversity in Global Business (*Burr Ridge, IL: Irwin, 1994), pp. 57-59.

14. Roland Leiser, "Ritz Reduces Turnover with Self-Directed Work Teams," *Hotel and Motel Management* (211:4, 1996):27.

15. Charles W.L. Hill, *International Business: Competing in the Global Marketplace* (Burr Ridge, IL: Irwin, 1994), p. 78.

16. Philip R. Harris and Robert T. Moran, *Managing Cultural Differences*, Third Edition (Houston: Gulf Publishing Company, 1991), p. 210.

17. Vern Terpstra, *The Cultural Environment of International Business* (Cincinnati: South-Western Publishing Co., 1978), p. 2.

18. Lawrence Yu and Goh Siong Huat, "Perceptions of Management Difficulty Factors by Expatriate Hotel Professionals in China," *International Journal of Hospitality Management* (3/4, 1995):375-388.

19. Edward T. Hall, *The Silent Language* (New York: Doubleday, 1973).

20. Edward T. Hall and Mildred Reed Hall, *Understanding Cultural Differences* (Yarmouth, ME: International Press, 1990), pp. 36-39.

21. Ibid., p. 47.

22. Philip R. Harris and Robert T. Moran, *Managing Cultural Differences*, Third Edition (Houston: Gulf Publishing Company, 1991), pp. 42-43.

23. Emmanuelle Ferrieux, "Hidden Message," *World Press Review* (July, 1989):39.

24. Philip R. Harris and Robert T. Moran, *Managing Cultural Differences*, Third Edition (Houston: Gulf Publishing Company, 1991), pp. 42-43.

25. Edward T. Hall and Mildred Reed Hall, *Understanding Cultural Differences* (Yarmouth, ME: Intercultural Press, 1990), p. 52.

26. Ibid., p. 69.

27. John D. Daniels and Lee H. Radebaugh, *International Business: Environments and Operations*, Sixth Edition (Reading, MA: Addison-Wesley Publishing Company, 1992), p. 101.

28. Edward T. Hall, *Beyond Culture* (New York: Doubleday, 1976).

Chapter 4

1. Frank H. Andorka, Jr., "Hot Global Market," *Hotel and Motel Management* (August 11, 1997):87.

2. David Easton, "An Approach to the Analysis of Political Systems," *World Politics* (Number 9, 1957):379-389.

3. Charles F. Andrain, *Comparative Political Systems: Policy, Performance and Social Changes* (Armonk, NY: M.E. Sharpe, 1994), p. 7.

4. James MacGregor Burns, J.W. Peltason, Thomas E. Cronin, and David B. Magleby, *Government by the People* (Englewood Cliffs, NJ: Prentice Hall, 1993), p. 2.

5. Robert L. Lineberry, George C. Edwards, and Martin P. Wattenberg, *Government in America: People, Politics, and Policy,* Sixth Edition (New York: Harper-Collins College Publishers, 1994), p. 9.

6. Arend Lijphart, "Democratic Political Systems," in *Contemporary Political Systems: Classifications and Typologies,* eds. Anton Bebler and Jim Seroka (Boulder, CO: Lynne Rienner Publishers, 1990), p. 72.

7. Ibid., p. 73.

8. Leonardo Morlino, "Authoritarianism," in *Contemporary Political Systems: Classifications and Typologies,* eds. Anton Bebler and Jim Seroka (Boulder, CO: Lynne Rienner Publishers, 1990), p. 91; Mattei Dogan, "Use and Misuse of Statistics in Comparative Research," in *Comparing Nations: Concepts, Strategies, Substance,* eds. Mattei Dogan and Ali Kazancigil (Oxford, UK: Blackwell, 1994), p. 91.

9. Ibid., Morlino, pp. 91-92.

10. Bernard Chavance, *The Transformation of Communist Systems: Economic Reform Since the 1950s* (Boulder, CO: Westview Press, 1994), pp. 9-21.

11. Bahgat Korany, "Arab Political Systems," in *Contemporary Political Systems: Classifications and Typologies,* eds. Anton Bebler and Jim Seroka (Boulder, CO: Lynne Rienner Publishers, 1990), pp. 322-325.

12. Anton Bebler, "Typologies Based on Civilian-Dominated Versus Military-Dominated Political System," in *Contemporary Political Systems: Classifications*

and Typologies, eds. Anton Bebler and Jim Seroka (Boulder, CO: Lynne Rienner Publishers, 1990), pp. 261-274.

13. Charles W.L. Hill, *International Business: Competing in the Global Marketplace* (Burr Ridge, IL: Irwin, 1994), p. 39.

14. Scott Mainwaring and Timothy R. Scully, eds., *Building Democratic Institutions: Party Systems in Latin America* (Stanford, CA: Stanford University Press, 1995), p. vii.

15. Mary Scoviak-Lerner, "Hotel Chains See a Future in South America," *Hotels* (May, 1992):71-72; Steven Shundich, "Bright Skies on the Horizon," *Hotels* (October, 1997):44-50.

16. *The Economist,* "The Struggle for Vietnam's Soul" (June 24th, 1995): 33-34.

17. *Hotels,* "World Watch: Cuba" (August, 1995):20; Amanda A. Austin, "Cuban Market Provides Healthy Competition," *Hotel and Motel Management* (March 17, 1997):4.

18. Ibid., *Hotels,* p. 20.

19. Marianne Tefft, "Going Global," *Hotelier* (January/February, 1995):8-10.

20. Y.K. Kim and J.L. Crompton, "Role of Tourism in Unifying the Two Koreas," *Annals of Tourism Research* (Number 3, 1990):352-366.

21. Lawrence Yu, "Travel Between Politically Divided China and Taiwan," *Journal of Pacific Asia Tourism Research* (Issue 2, 1997/98):19-30.

22. Lawrence Yu, "Tourism in the Egyptian Red Sea Area: A Responsible Development Approach," *FIU Hospitality Review* (Number 2, 1994):37-44.

23. Carla Hunt, "Hilton International Slates Three Red Sea Resorts," *Travel Weekly* (April, 1992):33.

24. *Flight to Changes,* a videotape produced by Common Destiny series, 1986.

25. David L. Edgell, *International Tourism Policy* (New York: Van Nostrand Reinhold, 1990), p. 43.

26. Charles W.L. Hill, *International Business: Competing in the Global Marketplace* (Burr Ridge, IL: Irwin, 1994), p. 62.

27. Steven Strasser, Tom Post, and B.J. Lee, "Roh's Spreading Shame," *Newsweek* (November 27, 1995):43; *The Economist,* "Catching South Korea's Tigers" (December 2, 1995):29-30.

28. Stephen J. Kobrin, "The Political Environment," in *The Cultural Environment of International Business* by Vern Terpstra (Cincinnati: South-Western Publishing Co., 1978), pp. 225-226.

29. *The Economist,* "Meltdown at the Cultural Chernobyl" (February 5, 1994):65-66.

30. Felix Kessler, "France's Erratic Policies on Investment by Foreigners Confuse Many U.S. Firms," *The Wall Street Journal* (April 7, 1980):24.

31. *The Economist,* "Japan: The New Nationalist" (January 14, 1995):19-21.

32. Donald A. Ball and Wendell H. McCulloch, *International Business: Introduction and Essentials* (Burr Ridge, IL: Irwin, 1993), p. 352.

33. Michael M. Lefever and Cathleen D. Huck, "The Expropriation of the Habana Hilton: A Timely Reminder," *International Journal of Hospitality Management* (Number 1, 1990):14-20.

34. Ann Hadedorn Auerbach, "When Travelers Are Targets: The Growing Threat of Kidnapping Abroad," *The Washington Post* (July 12, 1998):C1-C2.

35. John Lancaster, "Killers Hunted Down Tourists in Egyptian Temple's Recesses," *The Washington Post* (November 17, 1997):A1, A27.

36. Chris Ryan, "Tourism, Terrorism and Violence: The Risks of Wider World Travel," *The Study of Conflict and Terrorism* (September, 1991):1-30.

37. Ibid., p. 8.

38. Ibid., p. 9.

39. Donald Masur, "Going Global," *Restaurant USA* (January, 1997).

40. Helen Deresky, *International Management: Managing Across Borders and Cultures* (New York: HarperCollins College Publishers, 1994), pp. 50-51.

Chapter 5

1. Aristotle, *Politics*, 2.3 (Cambridge, MA: Harvard University Press, 1977), p. 1261 B 34.

2. Morris Bornstein, "The Comparison of Economic Systems," in *Comparative Economic Systems: Models and Cases,* ed. Morris Bornstein (Homewood, IL: Irwin, 1989), p. 4.

3. Nicholas V. Gianaris, *Contemporary Economic Systems: A Regional and Country Approach* (Westport, CT: Praeger, 1993), pp. 12-25.

4. Andrew Zimbalist, Howard J. Sherman, and Stuart Brown, *Comparing Economic Systems: A Political-Economic Approach*, Second Edition (San Diego: Harcourt Brace Jovanovich Publishers, 1989), p. 8.

5. *Far Eastern Economic Review*, "Vietnam: Investment" (Number 36, 1991):62; Turgut Var, "Tourism Industry in Vietnam," *Annals of Tourism Research* (Number 2, 1994):420-438; J.S. Perry Hobson, Vincent C.S. Heung, and Kaye-Sung Chon, "Vietnam's Tourism Industry: Can It Be Kept Afloat?" *The Cornell Hotel and Restaurant Administration Quarterly* (Number 4, 1994):42-49.

6. The World Bank, *World Development Report 1997: The State in a Changing World* (Washington, DC: The World Bank, 1997).

7. E.K. Hunt and Howard J. Sherman, *Economics: An Introduction to Traditional and Radical Views*, Sixth Edition (Harper-Collins Publishers, 1990), pp. 554-555.

8. John D. Daniels and Lee H. Radebaugh, *International Business: Environments and Operations*, Sixth Edition (Reading, MA: Addison-Wesley Publishing Company, 1992), p. 70.

9. Keith B. Richburg and Steven Mufson, "In Hindsight, Signs of Asian Crisis Appear Clear," *The Washington Post* (January 4, 1998):A1, A20.

10. John F. Mathis, "International Risk Analysis," in *Global Business Management in the 1990s*, ed. R.T. Moran (Washington, DC: Beacham, 1990), pp. 33-44.

11. Andreas F. Lorenz and Thomas P. Cullen, "Hotel Investment Opportunities in Hungary," *The Cornell Hotel and Restaurant Administration Quarterly* (Num-

ber 6, 1994):18-32; Jeffrey F. Scott and Leo M. Renaghan, "Hotel Development in East Germany: Opportunities and Obstacles," *The Cornell Hotel and Restaurant Administration Quarterly* (Number 4, 1991):44-51.

12. Adrian Bull, *The Economics of Travel and Tourism* (Melbourne, Australia: Pitman, 1991), p. 7.

Chapter 6

1. Juergen Bartels, CEO of the Hotels Group, Starwood Hotels and Resorts Worldwide. This quote is about the continued branding and consolidation of the hotel industry, published in *Hotels* (July, 1996):18.

2. M. Krisshna Erramilli, "Influence of Some External and Internal Environmental Factors on Foreign Market Entry Mode Choice in Service Firms," *Journal of Business Research* (Number 4, 1992):263-276.

3. Frances Martin, "Partnerships, Mergers Dominate in a Competitive Year," *Hotels* (July, 1992):56-59.

4. Andrew C. Inkpen, *The Management of International Joint Ventures: An Organizational Learning Perspective* (London: Routledge, 1995), p. 1.

5. John D. Daniels and Lee H. Radebaugh, "Disneyland Abroad: A Case Study," *International Business: Environments and Operations* (Reading, MA: Addison-Wesley Publishing Company, 1992), p. 32.

6. Ray Pine, "Technology Transfer in the Hotel Industry," in *The International Hospitality Industry: Organizational and Operational Issues*, eds. Peter Jones and Abraham Pizam (New York: John Wiley and Sons, 1993), pp. 226-240.

7. C. Liu, "China's Joint Venture Policy," in *Business in China: An International Reassessment*, ed. N.T. Wong (New York: Pergamon, 1980), pp. 73-77.

8. Lawrence Yu, "Hotel Development and Structures in China," *International Journal of Hospitality Management* (Number 2, 1992):99-110.

9. Jian Zhao, "Overprovision in Chinese Hotels," *Tourism Management* (Number 1, 1989):63-66.

10. Mahmood Khan, "International Restaurant Franchises," in *The International Hospitality Industry: Organizational and Operational Issues*, eds. Peter Jones and Abraham Pizam (New York: John Wiley and Sons, 1993), pp. 104-116; James R. Brown and Ckekitem S. Dev, "The Franchisor-Franchisee Relationship: A Key to Franchise Performance," *Cornell Hotel and Restaurant Administration Quarterly* (Number 6, 1997):30-38.

11. Tim McIntyre, "Domino's Pizza Establishing an International Presence," Domino's Pizza International, 1995.

12. Peter Barge, "International Management Contract," in *The International Hospitality Industry: Organizational and Operational Issues,* eds. Peter Jones and Abraham Pizam (New York: John Wiley and Sons, 1993), pp. 117-125.

13. Rocco M. Angelo and Andrew N. Vladimir, *Hospitality Today: An Introduction* (East Lansing, MI: Educational Institute of the American Hotel and Motel Association, 1994), p. 388.

14. Ibid., pp. 387-388.

15. Chris Baum, "Management Companies Face Tough Times," *Hotels* (April, 1993):50-51.

16. Ibid., p. 51.

17. Frances Martin, "The Management Triangle," *Hotels* (September, 1995): 35-38.

18. *Hotels,* "4 Management Companies to Watch," *Special Report* (September, 1995):43-44.

19. Frances Martin, "Partners, Mergers Dominate in a Competitive Year," *Hotels* (July, 1995):56-59.

20. Frances Martin, "*Hotels* Giants: Corporate 200," *Hotels* (July, 1995): 35-36.

21. Ibid., p. 35.

22. *Hotel and Motel Management*, "Strategic Alliances Aid in Globalization," (November 6, 1995):76.

23. Frances Martin, "Partners, Mergers Dominate in a Competitive Year," *Hotels* (July, 1995):56-59.

24. Scandic Hotel, "The Scandic and Holiday Inn Worldwide Partnership," *Scandic Hotels Corporate News Release* (Stockholm, Sweden, 1995).

25. Frances Martin, "Hotels Giants: Voluntary 25," *Hotels* (July, 1995):62.

26. Ibid., p. 62.

27. Charles W.L. Hill, Peter Hwang, and W. Chan Kim, "An Eclectic Theory of the Choice of International Entry Mode," *Strategic Management Journal* (Number 11, 1990):117-128.

28. Michael D. Olsen and Katherine M. Merna, "The Changing Character of the Multinational Hospitality Firm," in *The International Hospitality Industry: Organizational and Operational Issues,* eds. Peter Jones and Abraham Pizam (New York: John Wiley and Sons, 1993), pp. 89-103.

29. Ibid., p. 96.

30. Ibid., p. 97.

31. Bonnie Farber and Preston D. Probasco, "Comparative Corporate Structures and Design," in *International Hospitality Management: Corporate Strategy in Practice*, eds. Richard Teare and Michael Olsen (New York: John Wiley and Sons, 1992), pp. 171-198.

32. Ibid., p. 190.

33. Ibid., p. 191.

Chapter 7

1. Jonathan Porritt, "The Prince and the Hoteliers," *Lodging* (October, 1995):46.

2. Somerset R. Waters, *Travel Industry World Yearbook: The Big Picture*, Vol. 38 (Rye, NY: Child and Waters, 1994), p. 132.

3. *Hotels,* "Dealmakers Plot to Franchise the World," *Special Report* (February, 1996):31-32, 34, 36.

4. Ibid., p. 31.

5. Margaret Huffadine, *Project Management in Hotel and Resort Development* (New York: McGraw-Hill, 1993), p. 31.

6. Stanley Turkel, "Little Reality in Typical Feasibility Study," *Hotel and Motel Management* (November 6, 1995):56, 70.

7. *Hotels,* "Dealmakers Plot to Franchise the World," *Special Report* (February, 1996):32.

8. Margaret Huffadine, *Project Management in Hotel and Resort Development* (New York: McGraw-Hill, 1993), p. 29.

9. Edward Inskeep and Mark Kallenberger, *An Integrated Approach to Resort Development* (Madrid: World Tourism Organization, 1992), p. 70.

10. Fred Lawson, *Hotels and Resorts: Planning, Design and Refurbishment* (Oxford, UK: Butterworth-Architecture, 1995), p. 293.

11. Ibid., p. 294.

12. Ibid., p. 297; Julia Miller, "Enhanced Illumination," *Hotel and Motel Management* (May 4, 1998):54-55.

13. Edward Inskeep and Mark Kallenberger, *An Integrated Approach to Resort Development* (Madrid: World Tourism Organization, 1992), p. 72.

14. *The Economist,* "Still Trying to Connect You" (April 2, 1994):47.

15. Fred Lawson, *Hotels and Resorts: Planning, Design and Refurbishment* (Oxford, UK: Butterworth-Architecture, 1995), p. 309.

16. Ibid., p. 295.

17. Ibid., p. 69.

18. Mary Scoviak-Lerner, "Making a Mark in Europe," *Hotels* (January, 1996):40-42.

19. Fred Lawson, *Hotels and Resorts: Planning, Design and Refurbishment* (Oxford, UK: Butterworth-Architecture, 1995), p. 139.

20. Ibid., p. 139.

21. *The Economist,* "A Matter of Title" (December 9, 1995):47.

22. John Harrison and Rory Frampton, "Tourism," in *How to Assess Environmental Impacts on Tropical Islands and Coastal Areas*, eds. Richard A. Carpenter and James E. Maragos (Honolulu: Environment and Policy Institute, East-West Center, 1989), pp. 148-160.

23. William Steif, "St. Thomas Rebounds from Hurricane," *Hotel and Motel Management* (November 6, 1995):6, 52.

24. Edward Inskeep, *Tourism Planning: An Integrated and Sustainable Development Approach* (New York: Van Nostrand Reinhold, 1991), p. 305.

25. William Steif, "Earthquake Results Still Hurt Occupancy," *Hotel and Motel Management* (November 6, 1995):31, 36.

26. *The Economist,* "Doing Their Own Thing" (July 29, 1995):8.

27. *The Economist,* "Plaza of Death" (August 21, 1993):30.

28. Jonathan Porritt, "The Prince and the Hoteliers," *Lodging* (October, 1995): 44-48, 50-51.

29. Hana Ayala, "Ecoresort: A 'Green' Masterplan for the International Resort Industry," *International Journal of Hospitality Management* (Number 3/4, 1995): 351-374.

30. Jonathan Porritt, "The Prince and the Hoteliers," *Lodging* (October, 1995):46.

31. Hana Ayala, "Ecoresort: A 'Green' Masterplan for the International Resort Industry," *International Journal of Hospitality Management* (Number 3/4, 1995): 351-374.

32. Ibid., p. 353.

33. Ibid., p. 354.

34. Elizabeth Boo, "Ecotourism Planning for Protected Areas," in *Ecotourism: A Guide for Planners and Managers,* eds. Kreg Lindberg and Donald Hawkins (North Bennington, VT: The Ecotourism Society, 1993), pp. 15-31.

Chapter 8

1. Comments made by an Austrian expatriate hotel manager on a survey questionnaire for research conducted by the author to study expatriate managers in China in 1995.

2. Dennis Campbell, *International Handbook on Comparative Business Law* (Boston: Kluwer Law and Taxation Publishers, 1979), p. 4.

3. Carolyn Hotchkiss, *International Law for Business* (New York: McGraw-Hill, 1994), p. 49.

4. Alan Evans, *The Legal Environment of International Business: A Guide for United States Firms* (Jefferson, NC: McFarland and Company, 1990), p. 28.

5. Ibid., p. 28.

6. William F. Fox, *International Commercial Agreements: A Primer on Drafting, Negotiating and Resolving Disputes*, Second Edition (Boston: Kluwer Law and Taxation Publishers, 1992), p. 32.

7. Alan Evans, *The Legal Environment of International Business: A Guide for United States Firms* (Jefferson, NC: McFarland and Company, 1990), p. 37.

8. Erin Arvedlund, "Murder in Moscow," *Fortune* (March 3, 1997): 129-134.

9. *The Economist*, "Russian Law: Groping Ahead" (September 2, 1995): 42-43, 48.

10. Bruce Urdang, "Investing in Hospitality Operations in the People's Republic of China: The Legal Framework," *FIU Hospitality Review* (Fall, 1996):7-12.

11. Joyce Barnathan, "The Gloves Are Coming Off in China," *Business Week* (May 15, 1995):60-61.

12. Carolyn Hotchkiss, *International Law for Business* (New York: McGraw-Hill, 1994):78.

13. *The Economist*, "Big Mac's Folly" (July 1, 1995):5; Fred Barbash, "Big Mac v. Small Fries," *The Washington Post* (June 20, 1997):A1, A16.

14. Norman G. Cournoyer and Anthony Marshall, *Hotel, Restaurant, and Travel Law* (Albany, NY: Delmer Publishers Inc., 1988).

15. Michael West, "British Beef Exports Banned," *Arizona Daily Sun* (March 27, 1996):3; John Burgess, "Britain to Ban Some Beef in 'Mad Cow' Scare," *The Washington Post* (December 5, 1997):A51.

Chapter 9

1. Isaac A. Levi, "Peso Crisis Haunts Mexico," *USA Today* (December 20, 1995):4B.

2. Michael Melvin, *International Money and Finance,* Third Edition (New York: Harper Collins Publishers, 1992), p. 1.

3. Orlin J. Grabbe, *International Financial Markets* (New York: Elsevier, 1986), p. 64.

4. Philippe Jorion and Sarkis Joseph Khoury, *Financial Risk Management: Domestic and International Dimensions* (Cambridge, MA: Blackwell Publishers, 1996), p. 144.

5. Jeff Madura, *International Financial Management* (St. Paul, MN: West Publishing Company, 1995):89.

6. John D. Daniels and Lee H. Radebaugh, *International Business: Environments and Operations,* Updated Third Edition (Reading, MA: Addison-Wesley Publishing Company, 1994), p. 240.

7. Charles W.L. Hill, *International Business: Competing in the Global Marketplace* (Burr Ridge, IL: Irwin, 1994), p. 256.

8. Philippe Jorion and Sarkis Joseph Khoury, *Financial Risk Management: Domestic and International Dimensions* (Cambridge, MA: Blackwell Publishers, 1996), p. 78.

9. Nick Douch, *The Economics of Foreign Exchange: A Practical Market Approach* (New York: Quorum Books, 1989), p. 98.

10. Ibid., p. 99.

11. Ibid., pp. 94-95.

12. Julian Walmsley, *The Foreign Exchange and Money Market Guide* (New York: John Wiley and Sons, 1992), pp. 299-301.

13. Donald A. Ball and Wendell H. McCulloch, *International Business: Introduction and Essentials*, Fifth Edition (Burr Ridge, IL: Irwin, 1993), p. 675.

14. Jeffrey Hertzfeld, "Joint Ventures: Saving the Soviets from Perestroika," *Harvard Business Review* (September, 1991):69-80.

15. Steven Shundich, "Art of the Deal," *Hotels* (September, 1997):42-54.

16. *Cooper and Lybrand,"*Decline in Break-Even Occupancy: Follows Improved Industry Efficiency," *Hospitality Directions: Forecast and Analysis for the Hospitality Industry* (November, 1997):11-16.

17. Steven Shundich, "Art of the Deal," *Hotels* (September, 1997):42-54.

18. Cooper & Lybrand, "Decline in Break-Even Occupancy: Follow Improved Industry Efficiency," *Hospitality Directions: Forecast and Analysis for the Hospitality Industry* (November, 1997):13.

19. Steven Shundich, "Art of the Deal," *Hotels* (September, 1997):42-54.

20. Zheng Gu, "Raising Tourism Funds on International Capital Markets: Benefits, Problems and Strategies for China," *Tourism and Recreation Research* (Spring, 1996):29-34.

21. Stuart Auerbach, "Marriott's Polish Pursuit," *Washington Business* (January 8, 1990):1, 30.

22. Ibid., p. 30.

23. Paul Einzig and Brian Scott Quinn, *The Euro-Dollar System* (New York: St. Martin's Press, 1977), p. 2.

24. Ibid., p. 3.

25. Ian M. Kerr, *A History of the Eurobond Market: The First Twenty-One Years* (London: Euromoney Publications, 1984), pp. 17-28.

26. Ibid., p. 19.

27. Jeff Madura, *International Financial Management* (St. Paul, MN: West Publishing Company, 1995).

28. Isaac A. Levi, "Peso Crisis Haunts Mexico," *USA Today* (December 20, 1995):4B.

29. Philippe Jorion and Sarkis Joseph Khoury, *Financial Risk Management: Domestic and International Dimensions* (Cambridge, MA: Blackwell Publishers, 1996), p. 87.

30. Jeff Madura, *International Financial Management* (St. Paul, MN: West Publishing Company, 1995).

31. Charles W.L. Hill, *International Business: Competing in the Global Marketplace* (Burr Ridge, IL, Irwin, 1994), p. 335.

32. Bill Montague, "Japan Pulling Out of U.S. Real Estate" *USA Today* (April 10, 1996):1B.

Chapter 10

1. Donald E. Kieso and Jerry J. Weygandt, *Intermediate Accounting*, Seventh Edition (New York: John Wiley and Sons, 1992), pp. xxvi-2.

2. Mahmound Qureshi, "Pragmatic and Academic Bases of International Accounting," *Management International Review* (Volume 2, 1979):61.

3. Ahmed Belkaoui, *International Accounting: Issues and Solutions* (Westport, CT: Quorum Books, 1985), p. 4.

4. Gerhard G. Mueller, Helen Gernon, and Gary Meek, *Accounting: An International Perspective* (Burr Ridge, IL: Irwin, 1994), p. 1.

5. G. Chevalier, "Should Accounting Practices Be Universal?" *CA Magazine* (July 5, 1977):47-50.

6. Ahmed Belkaoui, *International Accounting: Issues and Solutions* (Westport, CT: Quorum Books, 1985):41-42.

7. Gerhard G. Mueller, Helen Gernon, and Gary Meek, *Accounting: An International Perspective* (Burr Ridge, IL: Irwin, 1994):6.

8. Ibid., p. 6.

9. Ibid., p. 6.

10. Ibid., pp. 8-13.

11. Ahmed Belkaoui, *Multinational Financial Accounting* (Westport, CT: Quorum Books, 1994), p. 94.

12. Ibid., p. 125.

13. Jerry Morrison, "Uniform Systems Publication Makes Changes," *Hotel and Motel Management* (August 11, 1997):19.

14. John D. Daniels and Lee H. Radebaugh, *International Business: Environments and Operations,* Updated Sixth Edition (Reading, MA: Addison-Wesley Publishing Company, 1994):709-710.

15. Frederick D.S. Choi and Ashwinpaul Sondhi, "SFAS No. 52 and the Funds Statement," in *Frontiers of International Accounting: An Anthology,* eds. Frederick D.S. Choi and Gerhard G. Mueller (Burr Ridge, IL: Irwin, 1985), pp. 53-69.

16. Gerhard G. Mueller, Helen Gernon, and Gary Meek, *Accounting: An International Perspective (*Burr Ridge, IL: Irwin, 1994):12.

17. T.W. McRae, *International Business Finance: A Concise Introduction* (New York: John Wiley and Sons, 1996), pp. 170-171.

18. Ibid., p. 166.

19. Gabriel D. Donleavy, *Cash Flow Accounting: International Uses and Abuses (*London: Routledge, 1994), p. 84; Gerhard G. Mueller, Helen Gernon, and Gary Meek, *Accounting: An International Perspective (*Burr Ridge, IL: Irwin, 1994), pp. 60-166.

20. Jeff Madura, *International Financial Management,* Fourth Edition (St. Paul, MN: West Publishing Company, 1995), pp. 624-625.

21. *Hotel and Motel Management,* "Report Urges Governments to Revamp Tourism Taxes" (June 15, 1998):6.

22. Michael Melvin, *International Money and Finance (*New York: Harper-Collins Publishers, 1992), pp. 201-218.

23. Eugene Willis, William H. Hoffman, David M. Maloney, and William Raabe, eds., *West's Federal Taxation: Comprehensive Volume* (Minneapolis/St. Paul, MN: West Publishing Company, 1994), pp. 24-26.

Chapter 11

1. Frank H. Andorka, Jr., "Hot Global Markets," *Hotel and Motel Management* (August 11, 1997):87.

2. Sandra Watson and David Litteljohn, "Multi- and Transnational Firms: The Impact of Expansion on Corporate Structures," in *International Hospitality Management: Corporate Strategy in Practice*, eds. Richard Teare and Michael Olsen (New York: John Wiley and Sons, 1992), pp. 135-159.

3. Lawrence Yu and Siong Huat Goh, "Perceptions of Management Difficulty Factors by Expatriate Hotel Professionals in China," *International Journal of Hospitality Management* (Number 3/4, 1995):379-380.

4. R.W.Y. Yu and Ray Pine, "Attitudes of Hong Kong Hotel Managers Towards the Use of Expatriates," *International Journal of Hospitality Management* (Number 2, 1994):183-187.

5. Jeffrey Shay and J. Bruce Tracey, "Expatriate Managers: Reasons for Failure and Implications for Training," *Cornell Hotel and Restaurant Administration Quarterly* (February, 1997):30-35.

6. Elizabeth Sheridan, "Labor Shortage Could Cripple South Africa," *Hotel and Motel Management* (July 7, 1997):8, 37.

7. Rosemary Lucas, *Managing Employee Relations in the Hotel and Catering Industry* (London: Cassell, 1995), pp. 85-89.

8. Kathy Seal, "Recruiters Find Labor Worldwide," *Hotel and Motel Management* (March 2, 1998):8, 13.

9. Tom Baum, *Managing Human Resources in the European Tourism and Hospitality Industry: A Strategic Approach* (London: Chapman and Hall, 1995), pp. 74-75.

10. Jeffrey Shay and J. Bruce Tracey, "Expatriate Managers: Reasons for Failure," *The Cornell H.R.A. Quarterly* (Number 1, 1997):30-35.

11. Charles W.L. Hill, *International Business: Competing in the Global Marketplace* (Burr Ridge, IL: Irwin, 1994), p. 511.

12. Paul Sherer, "Values of Asian, North American Executive Differ," *The Wall Street Journal* (March 8, 1996): A5F; R.L. Tung, "Patterns of Motivation in Chinese Industrial Enterprises," *Academy of Management Review* (1981): 481-489.

13. R.L. Tung and E.L. Miller, "Managing in the Twenty-First Century: The Need for Global Orientation," *Management International Review* (Number 1, 1990):5-18.

14. P.J. Dowling and R.S. Schuler, *International Dimensions of Human Resource Management* (Boston: PSW-Kent, 1990), p. 124.

15. Renaldo Flores, "Labor Relations, Culture and Service," in *World-Class Service*, eds. Germaine W. Shames and W. Gerald Glover (Yarmouth, Maine: Intercultural Press, 1989), pp. 138-144.

16. Germaine W. Shames, "Service Quality and the Multicultural Manager," in *World-Class Service*, eds. Germaine W. Shames and W. Gerald Glover (Yarmouth, Maine: Intercultural Press, 1989), pp. 129-130.

17. Dianne H.B. Welsh and Skip Swerdlow, "Hospitality Russian Style: Nine Communication Challenges," *The Cornell H.R.A. Quarterly* (December, 1992): 64-72; Dianne H.B. Welsh and Skip Swerdlow, "The Hospitality Gap: Bridging Russia into the 21st Century," *FIU Hospitality Review* (Fall, 1995):67-76.

18. Yasuyuki Miura, "Success Strategy: Nikko Hotels International Smiles a Hearty Smile," in *World-Class Service*, eds. Germaine W. Shames and W. Gerald Glover (Yarmouth, Maine: Intercultural Press, 1989), p. 39.

19. Rosemary E. Lucas, *Managing Employee Relations in the Hotel and Catering Industry* (London: Cassell, 1995), p. 57.

20. Ibid., p. 57.

21. Vickie Siu, Nelson Tsang, and Simon Wong, "What Motivates Hong Kong's Hotel Employees?" *The Cornell H.R.A. Quarterly* (Number 5, 1997): 44-49.

22. Lina Anastassova and Kate Purcell, "Human Resource Management in the Bulgarian Hotel Industry: From Command to Empowerment?" *International Journal of Hospitality Management* (Number 2, 1995):171-185.

23. Alan R. Nankervis and Debrah Yaw, "Human Resource Management in Hotels: A Comparative Study," *Tourism Management* (Number 7, 1995): 507-513.

24. Charles W.L. Hill, *International Business: Competing in the Global Marketplace* (Burr Ridge, IL: Irwin, 1994), pp. 518-522.

25. Jeff Weinstein, "1997 Salary Review," *Hotels* (October, 1997):62-68.

26. *USA Today,* "Senate OKs 90¢ Wage Increase" (July 10, 1996):B1.

27. Tom Baum, *Managing Human Resources in the European Tourism and Hospitality Industry: A Strategic Approach* (London: Chapman and Hall, 1995), p. 80.

28. Eun Young Kim, *A Cross-Cultural Reference of Business Practices in a New Korea* (Westport, CT: Quorum Books, 1996), p. 107.

29. Ibid., p. 108.

Chapter 12

1. *Restaurant USA*, "Before You Pack Your Bags . . . ," (November, 1995):31.

2. Marriott International, "The Spirit to Serve," *Marriott International Annual Report* (Bethesda, Maryland, 1998).

3. Jin-Lin Zhao and Katherine M. Merna, "Impact Analysis and the International Environment," in *International Hospitality Management: Corporate Strategy in Practice*, eds. Richard Teare and Michael Olsen (New York: John Wiley and Sons, 1992), pp. 3-30.

4. Robert Selwitz, "Malta Calls for Midpriced Chains," *Hotel and Motel Management* (October 8, 1997):6, 67.

5. Robert C. Lewis, Richard E. Chambers, and Harsha E. Chacko, *Marketing Leadership in Hospitality: Foundations and Practices* (New York: Van Nostrand, 1995).

6. *The Annual: McDonald's Corporation 1994 Annual Report* (Oak Brook, IL: McDonald's Corporation, 1995): p. 2.

7. Fletch Waller, "Agents Not Just Dumb Channels," *Hotels* (February, 1998):96.

8. *Lodging*, "GDS Reservations Volume Climbs" (June, 1998):14.

9. Rita Marie Emmer, Chuck Tauck, Scott Wilkinson, and Richard G. Moore, "Marketing Hotels: Using Global Distribution Systems," *The Cornell H.R.A. Quarterly* (December, 1993):80-89.

10. Ibid., pp. 85-86.

11. Ibid., p. 86.

12. Pegasus Systems, "THISCO," *Corporate Fact Sheet* (October, 1997):1.

13. Pegasus Systems, "Hotel Clearing Corporation," *HCC Corporate Fact Sheet* (October, 1997):1-2.

14. Charles W.L. Hill, *International Business: Competing in the Global Marketplace* (Burr Ridge, IL: Richard D. Irwin, 1994), p. 487.

15. Donald A. Ball and Wendell H. McCulloch, Jr., *International Business: Introduction and Essentials*, Fifth Edition (Burr Ridge, IL: Richard D. Irwin, 1993), p. 320.

16. Jessica Miller, "Marketing Communications," *The Cornell H.R.A. Quarterly* (October, 1993):48-53.

17. Charles W.L. Hill, *International Business: Competing in the Global Marketplace* (Burr Ridge, IL: Richard D. Irwin, 1994), p. 489.

18. *International Advertiser*, "Videotapes Are Common Throughout Middle East" (February, 1986):31.

19. Rajiv Chandrasekaran and Margaret Webb Pressler, "More Shoppers Are Shopping Online," *The Washington Post* (December 24, 1997):C1, C3.

20. Jamie Murphy, Edward J. Forrest, C. Edward Wotring, and Robert A. Brymer, "Hotel Management and Marketing on the Internet," *The Cornell H.R.A. Quarterly* (Number 3, 1996):70-82.

21. Ibid., p. 29.

22. Ibid., p. 77.

23. Chris Baum, "In the USA, Managers Try Anything to Fill Rooms," *Hotels* (September, 1992):57.

24. Donald A. Ball and Wendell H. McCulloch, Jr., *International Business: Introduction and Essentials*, Fifth Edition (Burr Ridge, IL: Richard D. Irwin, 1993), p. 539.

25. Jessica Miller, "Marketing Communications," *The Cornell H.R.A. Quarterly* (October, 1993):49.

26. Roger N. Waud, *Micro-Economics*, Fifth Edition (New York: HarperCollins Publishers, 1992), pp. 106-116.

27. Steven Shundich, "Politics, Labor Concern Hoteliers," *Hotels* (October, 1997):52.

28. Carlo Wolff, "Such a Deal: Resolution of Mexico's Economic Crisis," *Hotels* (September, 1995):43-44.

Chapter 13

1. Merritt Croker, "Before You Pack Your Bags," *Restaurants USA* (November, 1995):31.

2. Terry G. Jordan and Lester Rowntree, *The Human Mosaic: A Thematic Introduction to Cultural Geography*, Fifth Edition (New York: Harper and Row, Publishers, 1990), p. 190.

3. Rebecca Reisner, "Multi-Cultural Menu Planning," *Meeting News* (January, 1993):15, 17.

4. Beth Dugan, "Religion and Food Service," *The Cornell H.R.A. Quarterly* (December, 1994):85.

5. Ibid., p. 85.

6. Rebecca Reisner, "Multi-Cultural Menu Planning," *Meeting News* (January, 1993):15.

7. Akbar S. Ahmed, *Living Islam* (New York: Facts on File, Inc., 1994), pp. 39-45.

8. Donna Fenn, "Saudi Arabia: Veiled Opportunities," *Inc.* (January, 1994): 66-67.

9. Beth Gugan, "Religion and Food Service," *The Cornell H.R.A. Quarterly* (December, 1994):83.

10. Cherie Hensdill, "Zen and the Art of Foodservice Management," *Hotels* (November, 1997):88.

11. *The Washington Post*, "Caste-Related Massacre Claims 61 Lives in India," (December 3, 1997):A38.

12. *Fortune*, "Where's the Beef?" (January, 1994):16.

13. Kenneth J. Cooper, "In India's Pizza, the Crust's the Thing," *The Washington Post* (March 11, 1996):A21.

14. Liping Cai and Jack D. Ninemeier, "Food Service Styles in Chinese Hotels: Tradition and Tourism Pressures Merge," *FIU Hospitality Review* (Fall, 1994):33-40.

15. David Belman, "International Expansion: Exporting the American Experience," *Restaurant USA* (Number 10, 1995):26-31.

16. Jeffrey Hertzfeld, "Joint Ventures: Saving the Soviets from Perestroika," *Harvard Business Review* (September, 1991):69-80.

17. Ibid., pp. 76-78.

18. Warren J. Keegan, *Global Marketing Management*, Fourth Edition (Englewood Cliffs, NJ: Prentice Hall, 1989):178-191.

19. Stephen Chapdelaine and Allison Kindelan, "Foodservice Expansion Heads East," *Restaurant USA* (Number 10, 1995):40-42.

20. Ibid., p. 41.

21. David Belman, "International Expansion: Exporting the American Experience," *Restaurant USA* (Number 10, 1995):30.

22. Cherie Hensdill, "Zen and the Art of Foodservice Management," *Hotels* (November, 1997):87-88.

23. David Belman, "International Expansion: Exporting the American Experience," *Restaurant USA* (Number 10, 1995):30.

24. Ibid., p. 30.

25. National Restaurant Association, *NRA 1996 Survey of International Restaurant Operations* (Washington, DC: National Restaurant Association, 1997).

26. Angie Michael, "Charming the Bottom Line," *Lodging* (November, 1995): 70-72, 74, 76.

27. Diana Rowland, *Japanese Business Etiquette: A Practical Guide to Success with Japanese*, Updated and Revised Second Edition (New York: Warner Books, 1993), pp. 134-135.

Chapter 14

1. Ralph O. Brennan, statement quoted in *Restaurants USA* (November, 1995):4.

2. Michael D. Olsen, *Events Shaping the Future of the Lodging Industry* (Paris: International Hotel Association, 1995).

3. The World Tourism Organization, "Travel to Surge in the Twenty-First Century," *TWO News* (November, 1997):1-2.

4. World Travel and Tourism Council, *Travel and Tourism's Economic Impact 1996/2006* (London: WTTC, 1996).

5. Glenn Hasek, "New Study Captures Industry's Scope," *Hotel and Motel Management* (February, 1996):1, 33.

6. Michael D. Olsen, *Events Shaping the Future of the Lodging Industry* (Paris: International Hotel and Restaurant Association, 1995).

7. Ibid., p. 38.

8. William Hsu and Robert O'Halloran, "The Hong Kong Hilton: The Case of the Disappearing Hotel," *Cornell H.R.A. Quarterly* (August, 1997):46-55.

9. Michael D. Olsen, *Events Shaping the Future of the Lodging Industry (*Paris: International Hotel and Restaurant Association, 1995):45.

10. National Restaurant Association, *NRA 1996 Survey of International Restaurant Operations* (Washington, DC: National Restaurant Association, 1997).

11. Toshio Doi, "An Inside Look at Japanese Food Service," *The Cornell Hotel and Restaurant Administration Quarterly* (December, 1992):73-83.

12. Robert Selwitz, "Japan's Adverse Exchange Rates Chase Away Meeting Planner," *Hotel and Motel Management* (November 20, 1995):4, 31.

13. Lawrence Yu, "Teaching International Hospitality Management: A Tripartite Approach," *Hospitality and Tourism Educator* (Number 1, 1992):7-10.

14. Jack J. Clark and Avner Arbel, "Producing Global Managers: The Need for a New Academic Paradigm," *The Cornell Hotel and Restaurant Administration Quarterly* (August, 1993):83-89.

Index

Page numbers followed by the letter "e" indicate exhibits.

HAWORTH HOSPITALITY PRESS
Hospitality, Travel, and Tourism
K. S. Chon, PhD, Executive Editor

THE PRACTICE OF GRADUATE RESEARCH IN HOSPITALITY AND TOURISM edited by K. S. Chon.

THE INTERNATIONAL HOSPITALITY BUSINESS: MANAGEMENT AND OPERATIONS by Larry Yu. "The abundant real-world examples and cases provided in the text enable readers to understand the most up-to-date developments in international hospitality business." *Zheng Gu, PhD, Associate Professor, College of Hotel Administration, University of Nevada, Las Vegas, CA*

CONSUMER BEHAVIOR IN TRAVEL AND TOURISM by Abraham Pizam and Yoel Mansfeld. "A must for anyone who wants to take advantage of new global opportunities in this growing industry." *Bonnie J. Knutson, PhD, School of Hospitality Business, Michigan State University*

LEGALIZED CASINO GAMING IN THE UNITED STATES: THE ECONOMIC AND SOCIAL IMPACT edited by Cathy H. C. Hsu. "Offers a fresh new look at one of the areas in tourism that has not yet received careful and serious consideration in the past." *Muzaffer Uysal, PhD, Professor of Tourism Research, Virginia Polytechnic Institute and State University, Blacksburg*

HOSPITALITY MANAGEMENT EDUCATION edited by Clayton W. Barrows and Robert H. Bosselman. "Takes the mystery out of how hospitality management education programs function and serves as an excellent resource for individuals interested in pursuing the field." *Joe Perdue, CCM, CHE, Director, Executive Masters Program, College of Hotel Administration, University of Nevada, Las Vegas*

MARKETING YOUR CITY, U.S.A.: A GUIDE TO DEVELOPING A STRATEGIC TOURISM MARKETING PLAN by Ronald A. Nykiel and Elizabeth Jascolt. "An excellent guide for anyone involved in the planning and marketing of cities and regions. . . . A terrific job of synthesizing an otherwise complex procedure." *James C. Maken, PhD, Associate Professor, Babcock Graduate School of Management, Wake Forest University, Winston-Salem, North Carolina*

Order Your Own Copy of
This Important Book for Your Personal Library!

THE INTERNATIONAL HOSPITALITY BUSINESS
Management and Operations

_____ in hardbound at $79.95 (ISBN: 0-7890-0559-X)

COST OF BOOKS _____

OUTSIDE USA/CANADA/
MEXICO: ADD 20% _____

POSTAGE & HANDLING _____
*(US: $3.00 for first book & $1.25
for each additional book)
Outside US: $4.75 for first book
& $1.75 for each additional book)*

SUBTOTAL _____

IN CANADA: ADD 7% GST _____

STATE TAX _____
*(NY, OH & MN residents, please
add appropriate local sales tax)*

FINAL TOTAL _____
*(If paying in Canadian funds,
convert using the current
exchange rate. UNESCO
coupons welcome.)*

☐ **BILL ME LATER:** ($5 service charge will be added)
(Bill-me option is good on US/Canada/Mexico orders only;
not good to jobbers, wholesalers, or subscription agencies.)

☐ Check here if billing address is different from
shipping address and attach purchase order and
billing address information.

Signature _____

☐ **PAYMENT ENCLOSED:** $ _____

☐ **PLEASE CHARGE TO MY CREDIT CARD.**

☐ Visa   ☐ MasterCard   ☐ AmEx   ☐ Discover
☐ Diner's Club

Account # _____

Exp. Date _____

Signature _____

Prices in US dollars and subject to change without notice.

NAME _____

INSTITUTION _____

ADDRESS _____

CITY _____

STATE/ZIP _____

COUNTRY _____ COUNTY (NY residents only) _____

TEL _____ FAX _____

E-MAIL _____

May we use your e-mail address for confirmations and other types of information? ☐ Yes   ☐ No

Order From Your Local Bookstore or Directly From
The Haworth Press, Inc.
10 Alice Street, Binghamton, New York 13904-1580 • USA
TELEPHONE: 1-800-HAWORTH (1-800-429-6784) / Outside US/Canada: (607) 722-5857
FAX: 1-800-895-0582 / Outside US/Canada: (607) 772-6362
E-mail: getinfo@haworthpressinc.com
PLEASE PHOTOCOPY THIS FORM FOR YOUR PERSONAL USE.

BOF96